Hidden Multilingualism in 19th-Century European Literature

Hidden Multilingualism in 19th-Century European Literature

Traditions, Texts, Theories

Edited by
Jana-Katharina Mende

DE GRUYTER

Free access to the e-book version of this publication was made possible by the 40 academic libraries and initiatives that supported the open access transformation project in German Linguistics.

ISBN 978-3-11-221408-4
e-ISBN (PDF) 978-3-11-077865-6
e-ISBN (EPUB) 978-3-11-077871-7
DOI https://doi.org/10.1515/9783110778656

This work is licensed under the Creative Commons Attribution 4.0 International License. For details go to https://creativecommons.org/licenses/by/4.0/.

Creative Commons license terms for re-use do not apply to any content (such as graphs, figures, photos, excerpts, etc.) not original to the Open Access publication and further permission may be required from the rights holder. The obligation to research and clear permission lies solely with the party re-using the material.

Library of Congress Control Number: 2023940505

Bibliographic information published by the Deutsche Nationalbibliothek
The Deutsche Nationalbibliothek lists this publication in the Deutsche Nationalbibliografie; detailed bibliographic data are available on the internet at http://dnb.dnb.de.

© 2025 with the author(s), editing © 2025 Jana-Katharina Mende, published by Walter de Gruyter GmbH, Berlin/Boston. This book is published with open access at www.degruyter.com.
This volume is text- and page-identical with the hardback published in 2023.

Cover image: KrimKate / iStock / Getty Images Plus
Printing and binding: CPI books GmbH, Leck

www.degruyter.com

Open-Access-Transformation in Linguistics

Open Access for excellent academic publications in the field of German Linguistics: Thanks to the support of 40 academic libraries and initiatives, 9 frontlist publications from 2023 can be published as gold open access, without any costs to the authors.

The following institutions and initiatives have contributed to the funding and thus promote the open access transformation in German linguistics and ensure free availability for everyone:

Dachinitiative „Hochschule.digital Niedersachsen" des Landes Niedersachsen
Universitätsbibliothek Augsburg
Freie Universität Berlin
Staatsbibliothek zu Berlin – Preußischer Kulturbesitz
Technische Universität Berlin / Universitätsbibliothek
Universitätsbibliothek der Humboldt-Universität zu Berlin
Universität Bern
Universitätsbibliothek Bielefeld
Universitätsbibliothek Bochum
Universitäts- und Landesbibliothek Bonn
Staats- und Universitätsbibliothek Bremen
Universitäts- und Landesbibliothek Darmstadt
Sächsische Landesbibliothek – Staats- und Universitätsbibliothek Dresden
Universitätsbibliothek Duisburg-Essen
Universitäts- und Landesbibliothek Düsseldorf
Universitätsbibliothek Eichstätt-Ingolstadt
Universitätsbibliothek Johann Christian Senckenberg, Frankfurt a. M.
Albert-Ludwigs-Universität Freiburg – Universitätsbibliothek
Niedersächsische Staats- und Universitätsbibliothek Göttingen
Fernuniversität Hagen, Universitätsbibliothek
Gottfried Wilhelm Leibniz Bibliothek – Niedersächsische Landesbibliothek, Hannover
Technische Informationsbibliothek (TIB) Hannover
Universitätsbibliothek Hildesheim
Universitätsbibliothek Kassel – Landesbibliothek und Murhardsche Bibliothek der Stadt Kassel
Universitäts- und Stadtbibliothek Köln
Université de Lausanne
Zentral- und Hochschulbibliothek Luzern
Bibliothek des Leibniz-Instituts für Deutsche Sprache, Mannheim
Universitätsbibliothek Marburg
Universitätsbibliothek der Ludwig-Maximilians-Universität München
Universitäts- und Landesbibliothek Münster
Bibliotheks- und Informationssystem (BIS) der Carl von Ossietzky Universität Oldenburg
Universitätsbibliothek Osnabrück
Universität Potsdam
Universitätsbibliothek Trier
Universitätsbibliothek Vechta
Herzog August Bibliothek Wolfenbüttel
Universitätsbibliothek Wuppertal
ZHAW Zürcher Hochschule für Angewandte Wissenschaften, Hochschulbibliothek
Zentralbibliothek Zürich

Contents

Jana-Katharina Mende
Introduction: Hidden and Invisible Multilingualism in 19th-Century European Literature: Theory and Practices —— 1

Part 1: Multilingual Histories of National Literatures

Mariyana Tsibranska-Kostova, Irena Kristeva
Traces of Hidden Multilingualism in 19th-Century Bulgarian Literature and Culture —— 25

Iulia Dondorici
Plurilingualism in 19th-Century Romanian Literatures —— 47

Charlotte van Hooijdonk
Uncovering Multilingual Strategies —— 69

Joanna Pietrzak-Thébault
The "French" History of Polish Literature or Two Languages — One "Oeuvre" —— 95

Part 2: National Authors as Covert Multilinguals

Gábor Gángó
Proofreaders, Translators – Co-authors? József Eötvös's Concealed Bilingualism —— 119

Katrin Gunkel
Multilingualism and Nationality in Theodor Fontane's *Kriegsgefangen. Erlebtes 1870* —— 143

Orlando Grossegesse
The Hidden Greek Odes in "Um poeta lírico" (1880) —— 169

Sabira Ståhlberg
Meine lieben fellow-pupils: Edith Södergran's Hidden Multilingualism —— 185

Part 3: Hidden Multilingualism: Typologies and Theoretical Approaches

Sandra Vlasta
Multilingualism in 19th-Century Travel Writing —— 219

Marília Jöhnk
Literary Multilingualism and Women's Writing in 19th Century Europe —— 241

Jochen A. Bär
18th and 19th Century Linguistic and Literary Criticism as a Source of Multilingual Research —— 265

Jana-Katharina Mende
Zooming In and Out of Historical Multilingual Literature —— 295

Index —— 323

Acknowledgments

I would like to sincerely thank the following individuals and organizations for their contributions to this book:
I am deeply grateful to the participants of the online conference that sparked the idea for this book during the early days of the Covid-19 pandemic in 2020. Their lively discussions and valuable insights were instrumental in its development.

My heartfelt thanks to my former colleagues at CIRTI, Centre Interdisciplinaire de Recherche en Traduction et en Interprétation, University of Liège, for their support in organizing the online conference, especially to the co-organizers, Valérie Bada and Myriam Walburg.

Special appreciation goes to De Gruyter, particularly Svetoslava Antonova Baumann, Albina Töws, and Gabriela Rus for their invaluable assistance in publishing this book. I am also grateful to the anonymous reviewers for their constructive feedback. I would like to acknowledge de Gruyter's Open Access Transformation Packages for supporting the publication of this book as an open access resource.

I would like to thank Natalie Sauer for her meticulous correcting of the texts and for making my English less 'nouny'.

I am fortunate to have received guidance and advice from Dr. Claudia Hein, my colleague at the University of Halle (Germany), whose expertise and attention to detail greatly contributed to the editing process.

Lastly, I want to express my deepest appreciation to my husband, Gábor, for his diligent proofreading and cheerful support throughout.

Jana-Katharina Mende

Introduction: Hidden and Invisible Multilingualism in 19th-Century European Literature: Theory and Practices

1 The myth of monolingual national literature and 19th-Century Europe

Literature in 19th-century Europe is conceptually national and monolingual. Through the combined efforts of existing and developing language institutions, emerging philological disciplines, the literacy of the general population, and a strong ideological connection between emerging nation states and linguistic homogeneity, the nationalization and standardization of one language in many European states seemed complete by the end of the 19th century (cf. Mattheier 2000: 1097).

The relationship between nation and multilingualism however appears equally straightforward: given the demand for national unity and linguistic homogeneity multilingualism is most often characterized as a disturbance or cause of conflict within nation states (excepting deliberately multilingual nation states within Europe like Switzerland or Belgium). In theories of nation-building, a common language is one of the most prominent factors: Anderson quotes Johann Gottfried Herder's demand that each people has its own national education and language and characterizes this as a specifically European construct (Anderson 2006: 67–68). As Habermas puts it concisely for the conceptualization of the German nation in the 19th century: "The linguistic community had to coincide with the legal community within one nation-state." (Habermas and Pensky 2001: 9). However, below those "national print-languages" (Anderson 2006: 67) linguistic variety and multilingual activity in day-to-day life as well as in culture and literature still existed and even flourished. Thus, the perception that multilingualism is not a feature of the 19th century, but a phenomenon that only became relevant during the 20th century, is, as Gogolin pointed out for the history of education in Europe, a myth (Gogolin 2021: 298).

Jana-Katharina Mende, Martin-Luther-University Halle-Wittenberg, e-mail: jana-katharina.mende@germanistik.uni-halle.de

The myth of a common and national language and literature, as told from the 18th and 19th centuries onward, is designed to create unity and exclusivity within national communities. Multilingualism plays a role in creating, maintaining, and deconstructing this myth. To question the creation of this myth and the roles of multilingualism in it, the contributors had to do necessary "spadework in the archives" (Brown 2018: 42).

The scope of the volume ranges from Belgian, Romanian, Bulgarian and Polish "national" literatures to case studies on German, Swedish, Portuguese, and Hungarian "national" authors. Theoretical contributions focus on particular social groups and genres and offer new approaches to multilingual women's writing, travelogues, multilingual theories *avant la lettre*, and quantitative approaches to multilingual literary history.

Because of its broad scope the volume offers heuristic explorations in the field along three lines: hidden multilingualism of so-called national authors, hidden multilingualism within national literatures, as well as typological and theoretical approaches of hidden multilingualism.

2 Constructions of monolingualism in 19th-Century language and literature histories in Europe

Two mutually influential tendencies were at work at the end of the 18th and beginning of the 19th century. The democratization of language during the French Revolution was an important factor against multilingualism. The nationalization of language and literature aimed not only at general understanding but also at linguistic and cultural homogeneity.

The nationalization of language originated in Germany with the monolingual interpretation of Herder's diction of unity between nation and language. Together, both tendencies helped to bring forward a new paradigm of language – the monolingual paradigm: "For the monolingual paradigm, the mother tongue is the site of nativity and pure origin" (Yildiz 2012: 67).

However, the difference between the effort to democratize through the means of a common language and to nationalize through the means of one particular language should be considered as Fishman points out (cf. 1968: 44–45). As he explains "[n]ot all language differences that exist are noted, let alone ideologized" (Fishman 1968: 44).

The ideologic meaning can also be connected to multilingualism. National monolingualism might accept particular linguistic combinations in diglossic use and reject others (Fishman 1968: 45) whereas democratic monolingualism rejects multilingualism, as it must always exclude some groups.

However, the early beginnings of the monolingualization of Europe did not have an immediate impact on the general population who as of that moment did not know that they were supposed to limit themselves to one language and continued to use several languages, according to the region, different domains, or speakers in their lives. Literacy and monolingualism emerged at the same time and people went from illiterate multilingualism to literate monolingualism within a century. This led to a historically new (self-)perception as monolingual nations and individuals (Gogolin 2021: 298). The success, Gogolin argues further, of this perception was so strong that until today the 19th century appears firmly monolingual and knowledge of its construction and constructedness is lost outside of expert circles:

> The extent to which this implementation process was successful can be demonstrated by the fact that the knowledge of this history *as history* has largely disappeared from memory (apart from the memory of specialists). It belongs to the lost memory, that many aspects of what counts as self-evident today constitute the reified, de-historicized version of propositions of a not too-distant past (Gogolin 2021: 300).

The hidden, lost, and ignored information about multilingualism in the history of and during the 19th century culminates in Gogolin's monolingual habitus: "This is what I called a 'monolingual habitus' [...]: the forgetting of history, or in other words, the transfer of a man-made concept into the idea that it represents the nature of the things" (Gogolin 2021: 300).[1] Uncovering hidden multilingualism, therefore, is the only strategy to counter this.

Methodological monolingualism (Leperlier 2020: 3) and the monolingual paradigm dominate 19th-century literary history writing as has been pointed out most succinctly by Casanova:

> As a result of the appropriation of literatures and literary histories by political nations during the nineteenth century, although we do not always realize it, our literary unconscious is largely national. Our instruments of analysis and evaluation are national. Indeed the

---

[1] Gogolin's monolingual habitus is responsible for the creation of the monolingual paradigm: "For the monolingual paradigm, the mother tongue is the site of nativity and pure origin" Yildiz (2012: 67) Leperlier identifies this unconscious standard of one language as the basis of philological research methodological monolingualism Leperlier (2020: 3).

study of literature almost everywhere in the world is organized along national lines (Casanova 2004: XI).

The responsibility for this lies, according to Biti, clearly with German Romanticism and the unity of nation, language and literature propagated by Herder, Fichte, Goethe, the Schlegel brothers, and others:

> As a matter of fact, German Romanticists promoted German language as the platform of unification and consolidation of the homeless, 'humiliated and insulted' individuals and nations at the beginning of the nineteenth century, trusting that it would become universal currency for all foreign spiritual wares and that Germans would concomitantly take over the command of the world partition of symbolic values (Biti 2013: 2).

Nevertheless, 19th-century European ideas of nationhood and national culture still referred to a multitude of nations as Hárs emphasizes in his analysis of the reception of Herder's notion of *Kulturnation* and *Nationalkultur* (cultural nation and national culture) (Hárs 2008: 12).

Recent research has provided a more nuanced understanding of the works by the aforementioned authors. August Wilhelm Schlegel, the older Schlegel brother, is the most openly multilingual among them, and his oeuvre can only be comprehended from a transcultural and European perspective (Mix/Strobel 2010: 1). Friedrich Schlegel's translations, lectures on European literature, and works on Sanskrit language and literature oscillate between transculturalism and national appropriation. A study by Weissmann (2021) examines Goethe's multilingual competencies. Herder's work as a translator has been interpreted as a form of intercultural transfer (Maurer 2012), and his notion of culture has been re-examined as a form of intercultural transfer (Adler 2012). Hence, even the staunchest advocates of 19th-century monolingualism only appear so at first glance. A closer examination often reveals an at least ambivalent position concerning the diversity of languages and nations, ranging from what Herder succinctly termed "unentbehrliches Übel" [indispensable evil] to "beinahe ein wirkliches Glück" [almost a true bliss] (Herder 1985: 24).

Undoubtedly, Romantic theory also exhibits monolingual preferences. This is also represented in writings on polyglottism – celebrated in Renaissance and Baroque times – from the time of Romanticism as we can see in Schleiermacher's reflections on translation:

> Denn so wahr das auch bleibt in mancher Hinsicht, daß erst durch das Verständniß mehrerer Sprachen der Mensch in gewissem Sinne gebildet wird, und ein Weltbürger: so müssen wir doch gestehen, so wie wir die Weltbürgerschaft nicht für die ächte halten, die in wichtigen Momenten die Vaterlandsliebe unterdrückt, so ist auch in Bezug auf die Sprachen eine cloche allgemeine Liebe nicht die rechte und wahrhaft bildende, welchen

für den lebendigen und höheren Gebrauch irgend eine Sprache, gleichviel ob alte oder neue, der vaterländischen gleich stellen will. Wie Einem Lande, so auch Einer Sprache oder der andern, muß der Mensch sich entschließen anzugehören, oder er schwebt haltlos in unerfreulicher Mitte
[However true this may hold in some respects, that it is only through the understanding of several languages that man is educated in a certain sense, and becomes a citizen of the world, we must admit that, just as we do not consider world citizenship to be genuine, which in important moments suppresses the love of the fatherland, so also with regard to languages such a general love is not the right and truly educating one, which for the vivid and elevated use of any language, whether old or new, wants to put it on an equal footing with the native tongue. As to one country, so also to one language or the other, man must decide to belong, or he floats unstable in unpleasant midst] (Schleiermacher 2002 [1813]: 87).

The relation between nation and language, nation, linguistic choice and individuum in Schleiermacher's reflections seem entirely clear. As nobody wants to float helplessly in unpleasant middle ground, everyone must choose one language.

This overview makes it clear that the monolingual paradigm is rooted in 18th and 19th century European thought and brought forward an ideal of monolingual national literature which in turn had a huge effect on the perception of literature and nation in colonial and postcolonial settings. But even from within Europe, the formula of one nation, one literature, and one language was by no means representative of the linguistic, literary, and social reality. Literary reality, as this volume will show, demanded several language choices from its authors but also allowed for middle ground and linguistic diversity.

3 Framing (hidden) multilingualism in 19th-century theory and now

Contemporary theories on multilingual literature frame multilingualism most often in the context of migration and globalization and link it to multiculturism (Olsson and Englund 2013, vol. 13; Schmitz 2009; Vorderobermeier and Wolf 2008, 3; Kriegleder et al. 2014; Siller and Vlasta 2020; Schmeling and Schmitz-Emans 2002). Multilingualism, in that sense, becomes a visual signal for texts that are interpreted as simultaneously multilingual, multicultural, and transnational. Unlike linguistic research (Blommaert 2012), literary analysis of multilingual texts often implicitly favors multilingualism as a sign for a more open worldview. World literature and the study of global literary connections are linked to this view on multilingual and transnational literature, the analysis of which is characterized by "the importance of non-translation, mistranslation, incomparability and untranslatability." (Apter 2013: 4). In Apter's view multilingual writers belong to this "new" world literature in a modern sense which includes power dimensions and political stances through language choices in a global postcolonial world and are directed against a monolingual (English) literature of translations.

Structurally, the phenomenon of multilingualism can refer to authors or texts. By now, the designation of translingual or exophonic writers has been established for those writing in a language different from their first language (Kellman 2020) while multilingual writers are those whose language biography includes the simultaneous learning of more than one language which is then found in their works.

The terminology used in this book relies on several decades of research on modern multilingual literature. Until today, no consistent terminology has been agreed upon, instead several 'quasi-synonyms' are being used to describe various types and forms of language contact in literature: Knauth lists *multilingualism, bilingualism, colingualism, plurilingualism, polyglossy, interlingualism* and mixed language (2004: 266). Grutman had already coined the term *heterolinguism* and added it to the list, referring to the linguistic situation of Quebecoise literature (Grutman 1997: 9). The general 'foreignness' of poetic language is one of the meanings of term *exophony* which simultaneously refers to writing in a language that is a writer's first or native tongue and deconstructs Eurocentric monolingual norms (Stockhammer, Arndt, and Naguschewski 2007: 21). Exophony recalls notions of intertextuality and limitless poeticity which marks poetical language: "How can the quantity of conventions, formulas, and commonplaces that make up the language of literature be limited, even for a single era? We would never be able to reach the end – 'es würde ins Grenzenlose gehen' – to quote Goethe's words again." (Guillén 1993, 42: 260). This "flou terminologique et conceptual" [terminological and conceptual flow] (Anokhina and Sciarrino 2018: 13) leads from Grutman's *heterolingualism* to Kellman's *translingualism* and the distinction of *multi-* and *plurilingualism* designating the difference between the use of several languages by a group of people vs. the linguistic versatility of an individual (Anokhina and Sciarrino 2018: 14).

Likewise, the spatial metaphor "between languages" (*Zwischen den Sprachen, entre les langues, między językami*) is often used to denote ambiguous language use and linguistic contacts in literature (Zanetti, Marchi, and Baschera 2019).

The latest in this long list of terminological attempts to grasp the complex intersections of different languages, literatures, and cultures is Gramling's notion of *supralingualism* and *ordolingualism* to refer to the global and technological use of language diversity to profit from it on a global and interconnected market (Gramling 2021: 13).

Despite the terminological flow and development, the terms belong to certain areas that overlap. Whereas some refer to social or collective forms of language contact like polylingualism, plurilingualism, supralingualism and ordolingualism, others refer to both that and textual phenomena like heterolingualism, translingualism, and exophony. Multilingualism functions like an umbrella term to include all those different aspects.

We do not want to add to this already impressive list and have opted instead for the common denominator multilingualism, adding different definitions or classifiers when necessary.

Furthermore, as Guillén declares for comparative literature and its relation to multilingual literature, multilingual literary studies also need a historical perspective (Guillén 1993: 42–16; Lennon 2015). This has already been outlined in a pioneering volume on 19th-century multilingual literature aiming to "close the gap" (Anokhina, Dembeck, and Weissmann 2019: 2) between plurilingual Renaissance and multilingual avantgarde.

The specific linguistic, literary, and cultural constellations of 19th-century literature have to be considered when analyzing its multilingualism. While forms of written multilingualism appear similar in today's multilingual literature and literary texts from the 19th century, functions might differ widely. The use of multilingualism and language in 19th-century literature changed significantly compared to today's literature or even 20th century experimental actions in different languages. Now, multilingualism is strongly connected to translingual, liminal, hybrid transfers between languages and literatures, often questioning hegemonic and (post-)colonial power structures and leading to multilingual ethics (see Kilchmann 2019: 79, Alexandrova 2020: 219). What might be a transcultural function in a text today could help to create a unique national identity in the 19th century as we can see in the cases of Bulgarian (Kristeva and Tsibranska-Kostova), Romanian (Dondorici) and Hungarian (Gángó) literature. The English language – as sign of hegemony, global communication, or postcolonial situation today – played a much lesser role in 19th-century literature. Recognizing the cultural values and reconstructing the usage of different languages leads to the discovery of historical functions of multilingualism. Linguistic differences in historical texts demand even greater attention than today's multilingual literature, as the historical difference goes together with other linguistic varieties making it hard for today's readers to identify historically meaningful differences.

The question of how to investigate multilingual historical literature also raises issues of how to interpret linguistic variation. The ethical background of linguistic choices and of multilingualism in general are completely different for the 19th century – instead of writing against nation states and national literature, multilingual authors more often than not helped to create national literature and strengthen nation states and nationalism through multilingualism while simultaneously and actively contributing to knowledge transfer and literary exchange.

The central aspect of multilingualism in the 19th century is that it is perceived as an exception by today's research and that it often occurs in hidden and invisible forms. Hidden multilingualism describes the strategic efforts to make multilingual literature in the 19th century invisible to create a homogenous monolingual picture of national literature and national authors. Theoretical approaches to hidden multilingualism as well as case studies show how – despite the thick blanket of monolingual research and material, archives, and texts – researching hidden multilingualism is possible and leads to new findings on 19th-century literary history.

Hidden multilingualism shares traits with Radaelli's concept of latent multilingualism, which is used to describe forms of multilingualism within a literary text which are not apparent on the surface of the text (Radaelli 2011: 61).[2] However, hidden multilingualism is not only limited to those forms which, according to Radaelli, appear intratextually as loan translations, mirror translation or below the lexical level of language as morphemes or phonemes creating a "strange" foreignized word. Similarly, Dembeck and Parr define latent multilingualism as mere mentions of other languages in the text which indicate its fictive otherness (Dembeck and Parr 2017: 10).

Hidden multilingualism also entails what is called false monolingualism by Anokhina and Sciarrino (2018: 20):

> Enfin, une autre de ces situations est le faux monolinguisme ou monolinguisme apparent. Celle-ci concerne les auteurs que l'on considère traditionnellement comme monolingues,

---

2 Radaelli defines latent multilingualism opposite to manifest multilingualism in literary texts as follows: "Latente Mehrsprachigkeit dürfte die häufigste Form von literarischer Mehrsprachigkeit überhaupt sein. Ein Text ist immer dann latent mehrsprachig, wenn andere Sprachen nur unterschwellig vorhanden und nicht unmittelbar wahrnehmbar sind; er weist also auf den ersten Blick eine einsprachige Oberfläche auf" [Latent multilingualism is probably the most common form of literary multilingualism of all. A text is always latently multilingual when other languages are only present indirectly and are not immediately perceptible; thus, at first glance, it has a monolingual surface] Radaelli (2011: 61).

mais dont le processus d'écriture a en fait mobilisé plusieurs langues. Pour ne citer qu'un exemple, le roman *I Promessi Sposi* d'Alessandro Manzoni, considéré comme le texte fondateur de la langue moderne italienne, a connu plusieurs phases de rédaction où le dialecte milanais était mélangé à du français, avant de connaître une nouvelle version normalisée selon la norme toscane

[Finally, another of these situations is false monolingualism or apparent monolingualism. This one concerns authors who are traditionally considered monolingual, but whose writing process actually involved several languages. To give just one example, the novel *I Promessi Sposi* by Alessandro Manzoni, considered the founding text of the modern Italian language, went through several phases of writing in which the Milanese dialect was mixed with French, before a new version was standardized according to the Tuscan standard].

Multilingualism appears during the production of texts and can be found in manuscripts, letters, on the margins but not in the final publication. Different, but similar aspects of this type of hidden multilingualism are receptive or passive multilingual forms which become apparent in intertextual references,[3] through research on readings and translations, published and unpublished, of seemingly monolingual authors.

Yet another facet of hidden multilingualism concerns forms of multiple and hybrid multilingual authorship and the involvement of translators, correctors, and publishers in the creation and production of literary texts. This aspect refers to multilingualism of marginalized groups in literary history which were structurally underrepresented: female writers, writers writing in minority languages, or members of socially disadvantaged groups. According to Kilchmann, multilingualism itself could also be a disadvantage that led to an exclusion from the canon (Kilchmann 2019: 82). Elitist and non-elitist forms of multilingualism are thus equally investigated, resulting in new findings beyond the canon.

Whereas hiddenness describes the strategies of making multilingualism invisible, invisibility is an established concept in translation studies and research on female writing to describe the lack of attention and visibility this kind of writing has gained so far (Venuti 1995; Sanmann, La Hennard Dutheil de Rochère, and Cossy 2018). Especially Venuti's invisible translator[4] has brought this metaphor to the forefront of discourses on language and literary transfer, multilingual authors are, however, even more in the shadow of monolingual national literature. This volume offers several examples and approaches to un-

---

3 Receptive and intertextual multilingualism is described as covert and translated multilingualism by Hitzke (2019, Band 6: 29), referring to Walkowitz's concept of literature that is "born translated" (2015).
4 On the connection and conflicts between the study of plurilingualism and translation see Lennon (2010: 55–56).

derstanding the linguistic and literary functions at play, referring both to current theoretical concepts as well as offering new ways to grasp hidden multilingualism.

4 Multilingual reflections: what to expect in this volume

Working on multilingual literatures from different European regions and languages meant that we had to include examples and quotes from more than 15 languages, and even more linguistic combinations in the form of translations, code-switching or language mixing. Making all this available to an equally heterogenous multilingual audience from different philologies, countries and linguistic backgrounds was a challenge. This challenge was solved by going (partly) monolingual: through translations and by choosing English as the language of publication, we have created a book which contains the original quotes in different languages and multilingual combinations as well as English translations.

In our decisions regarding the language of publication we, all contributors, tried to include questions raised by Dembeck and Mein about postmonolingual scholarly writing (Dembeck and Mein 2013: 134). The tension between linguistic precision and interlingual transfer – unavoidable when writing about multilingualism (Dembeck and Mein 2013: 139) – is reflected in the many translations of original quotes, which all contributors included in their analysis. Thus, this volume makes hitherto lesser-known texts, which have mostly not been translated, at least partly accessible in English. Using English as the language of publication and not one of the other languages of the authors (German and French were also candidates as the working languages of several of the contributors) was mainly an editorial decision which allows for the distribution of the text to a wider audience. As much as we are happy to be read, we also regret the necessity to publish a volume on multilingualism not multilingually but in a hegemonic language of an academia of the Global North. Multilingualism appears however in other forms in the text. Sometimes, the need for translation has led to extensive back-and-forth translations to render different versions of a text in English. We hope for multilingual and postmonolingual readers who will accept quattrolingual tables as well as skipping those parts of the text which feel redundant for our multilingual readership.

The volume is structured in three parts: Part 1 investigates the multilingual backdrop of national literatures and literary history of Bulgarian, Belgian, Romanian, and Polish literature. Part 2 presents interpretations of works of national authors, their literary production and their reception as monolingual authors through the lenses of hidden multilingualism with examples from German, Portuguese, Swedish, and Hungarian literature. Part 3 offers typological and theoretical approaches for a systematic study of 19th-century hidden multilingualism in literature.

4.1 Part 1: National literatures and their forgotten multilingual history

The first part of the book examines the multilingual foundations of national literature in the center and periphery of Europe. Strategies of covert linguistic and literary transfers through cultural mediators, translations, relay-translation published as books, essays, articles, and journals were fundamental in creating a picture of a homogenous monolingual closed national literature. Rewriting the histories of national literatures from a multilingual angle these articles shine a light on the covered up and forgotten layers of literary history and create a heuristic typology of hidden multilingualism within national literature.

Kristeva and Tsibranska-Kostova retrace the creation of Bulgarian national literature in the time of the Bulgarian National Revival (1762–1878) through translations and relay-translations of English literature into Bulgarian. By analyzing the various multilingual actors and actions responsible for "transcreating" Benjamin Franklin's essay *The Way to Wealth* (1758) into Bulgarian via French, the authors uncover the hidden multilingual history of the translator, Gavril Krŭstevich, as well as the multilingual foundations of Bulgarian literature itself. The intensive translatory work of the time transferred texts from Greek, Russian, French, and German into Bulgarian, thus modeling it after existing literatures as well as creating new and hybrid forms for a Bulgarian audience as the detailed analysis of the relay-translation of Franklin's essay via the French version shows. At the same time, the tensions between building the foundation of a monolingual national literature in Bulgarian and the multilingual way it is done are brought to light through the comparison of different linguistic versions of the texts.

Nation-building is also a factor in van Hooijdonk's chapter in which the author uncovers multilingual genres and strategies to show how the field of Flemish literature emerged between French and Dutch literature. Literary and linguistic politics were negotiated in literary and cultural journals like *Le

Spectateur Belge, ouvrage historique, littéraire, critique et moral [The Belgian Spectator, Historical, Literary, Critical, and Moral Work] edited by the Flemish abbot Leo De Foere and the *Letter- en Staatkundig Dagblad* [Literary and Political Daily] (1 February 1820–29 August 1820), published in Ghent by the brothers Pierre and Johan Hendrik Lebrocquy. These journalists, translators, and editors were cultural mediators: "Polyglots themselves, they can highlight but also strategically hide the multilingual reality of the Southern Netherlands" (van Hooijdonk in this volume, p. 73). Van Hooijdonk analyzes how literature is portrayed in those journals to demonstrate the liminal position of Flemish literature in French and Dutch in the 19th century. Discursively, the editors strive to create a unique Flemish literature while at the same time using their multilingual language skills to portray Flemish literature as a monolingual and national unity in their journals. Hidden multilingualism appears on many levels: within the work of the cultural mediators, in texts and articles in those journals, sometimes mocking mixed-language use, sometimes engaging in translatory practices. Lastly, the article investigates the medium of literary journals as a tool in building a national literature as well as a place of multilingual and translatory exchange.

Dondorici examines and evaluates the multilingual foundations of Romanian literary history in the 19th century. The Romanian literary field experienced an influence from "Western" culture at the end of the 18th and first half of the 19th centuries, the impact of Greek literature and language giving way to French. Education in different European capitals made most Romanian writers multilingual. Society was equally if not more multilingual than their authors. Most Romanian writers in the 19th century were multilingual, using different languages for correspondence and Romanian for immediate publication. Dondorici analyzes the complex multilingual societal situation and how it overlaps with literature in the 19th century. Detailing the cases of Mihail Kogălniceanu and Alecu Russo, both highly multilingual writers, she shows how they were instrumental in creating the emerging Romanian literature through translation. After analyzing the intense bilingual exchange with French literature on a linguistic, textual, and thematic level, Dondorici researches the reception of multilingualism as hidden multilingualism in Romanian literary historiography and concludes that multilingualism thus far has mainly been seen as a betrayal or deviation from an implied monolingual norm.

The chapter on French-Polish literature and the oeuvre of Zygmunt Krasiński begins with a general introduction on the position of French literature and language in Polish (Romantic) literature and then considers the specific bi- and trilingualism in the works of one of its most important representatives,

Zygmunt Krasiński. Pietrzak-Thébault questions the role of passive multilingualism and argues that reading in foreign languages was a common practice not only among Polish, but also among European writers during the Romantic period. Next to hidden passive multilingual practices, she also investigates how scholars have neglected plurilingual sources and their history. Using the example of the most well-known Romantic author, Adam Mickiewicz, she illustrates how scholars have systematically overlooked multilingual writings by the Polish author and how this has influenced the view of his works. Finally, an analysis of Zygmunt Krasiński's writings during his stay in the bilingual surroundings of Geneva (1829–1832) shows the intricate linguistic, social, and poetical developments of his multilingual writing practices. He was influenced not only by his French linguistic environment, but also by his correspondence with the British journalist Henry Reeve, which had a major impact on the development of Krasinski's French texts. His reception of Byron's works in English was the source of intertextual multilingual experiments in his works and also shows the significance of passive multilingualism. The foundations of his poetical multilingual education influenced his entire work as a poet in Polish and French. The article shows how important it is to analyze multilingual poetical works in the context of European Romanticism and how multilingual this epoch of Polish Romanticism has been.

4.2 Part 2: Multilingual re-lectures of national authors

The second part of the book investigates what hiding and forgetting an author's multilingualism implies for the (later) reception and understanding of their works. The image of the national author as a literary and cultural authority of the 19th century always refers to a monolingual writer who might know foreign languages but is not classified as a multilingual writer. Thus, literary history positions national authors as pillars of national literature whereas openly multilingual authors like Heinrich Heine or Adelbert von Chamisso are positioned at the periphery or in the 'in-between' of Schleiermacher's middle ground. Re-reading the works, investigating the creative linguistic production and analyzing the text from a multilingual perspective in this part questions assumptions about those national authors and the role of multilingualism in their own writing. Chronologically and geographically crossing 19th century Europe, this part covers articles on the Hungarian author József Eötvös (1813–1871), the works of the German realist author Theodor Fontane (1819–1898), the Portuguese author José Maria de Eça de Queiroz (1845–1900), and the Swedish poet Edith Södergran (1892–1923). Thus, the development of hidden multilingualism in the perception of multilingualism of authors and the national context can be traced through time and different linguistic and literary constellations.

The case of the bilingual writer József Eötvös perfectly illustrates 19th-century hidden multilingualism as the article by Gábor Gángó argues. Gángó analyzes the language shift of the Hungarian writer who grew up in a German family speaking and writing in German. Gángó reveals not only the already known facts of Eötvös's bilingualism between German and Hungarian but equally includes a thorough analysis of his works in Hungarian which were written with the help of several correctors and even translators. This hybrid multilingual authorship is a central aspect in Eötvös's appearance as a Hungarian language author. Analyzing Eötvös's correspondence with those translators and correctors, often friends, Gángó shows that hiding his faulty Hungarian was an intentional decision meant to strengthen the national role of those works and Eötvös's own position within Hungarian national literature. Also, pseudo-translations of Eötvös's German texts are investigated for the role they play in creating a monolingual image. The research tendencies to stick to the picture of the competent Hungarian writer instead of a bilingual cultural mediator are revealed in the investigation of today's reception of Eötvös's works, thus offering a new reading and rethinking his standing within Hungarian "national" literature.

Gunkel's chapter investigates conflicts of national monolingualism and European multilingualism in the German realist author Theodor Fontane's autobiographical text *Kriegsgefangen. Erlebtes 1870* (1871). The article describes Fontane's language biography and his status as a canonical German author, which developed significantly during his lifetime and makes him an atypical example of multilingual literature. The historical context of the linguistic conflict between German and French is the Franco-Prussian war of 1870, in which the author himself was a prisoner of war. The status of French as a language of prestige and education in Europe is contrasted in the work with French as the language of the enemy. As Gunkel demonstrates linguistic ambiguity through multilingual code-switching enables the narrator to tell the story from a specific Franco-German perspective, as much playing with stereotypes as reaffirming them. Latent and hidden multilingualism often represents national characteristics in the protagonists of the text. Further, the translation of *Kriegsgefangen. Erlebtes 1870* into French by the multilingual Polish-French author and translator Téodor de Wyzewa, *Souvenirs d'un prisonnier de guerre allemand en 1870*, transformed the hidden multilingualism into real monolingualism by undoing French-German code-switching entirely. Gunkel compares the two versions and draws the conclusion that the different forms of hidden multilingualism in the text are essential for its perspective beyond nationalism while the translation as a typical example of 19th century reception of Fontane makes the text less ambiguous and more national by deleting its multilingual elements.

A contemporary of Fontane, the Portuguese author Eça de Queiroz also stood between national realistic and naturalist writing and a polyglot European education in an upper-class living environment. Orlando Grossegesse's article investigates the textual finesse of hiding multilingualism within a highly poetic and ambiguous short story by Eça de Queiroz. The author spent a long time in consular service in Newcastle, Bristol, and eventually as a consul-general in Paris. The national author turned privileged migrant equally reflects on liminal and poetic migratory experiences through latent multilingual elements in his Portuguese short story *Um poeta lírico* (1880). The story of a Greek poet in exile who now earns his living as a waiter allows for multiple allusions to other languages and the condition of multilingualism itself. The short narrative achieves a lot in little space as the analysis of Grossegesse shows. Through hidden intertextual multilingualism via the language of the place of action, English, Greek, and the language of the narrative, Portuguese, several linguistic and social conflicts arise between the elitist polyglot first-person-narrator. Here, the story of a poet turned waiter after migrating can be read as a transcreative play with the liminal position of the author himself. Intertextual forms of a multilingual and cosmopolitan elite are confronted with the worries of an unprivileged migrant working class. Grossegesse also shows how realist literature moves towards multilingual fin-de-siècle literature.

Ståhlberg's study of the avant-gardist poet Edith Södergran investigates the multilingual education and oeuvre of the Swedish author at the beginning of the 20th century and shows how monolingualism has established itself to a degree that it becomes invisible even in blatantly obvious examples. Here, unlike the other examples, multilingualism is not actively hidden by authors to appear more national or to create poetic tension but is simply overlooked by a monolingually trained discipline.

Retracing Södergran's multilingual childhood in Raivola, Karelia and at a German school in St. Petersburg leads to a detailed language biography, investigating the linguistic competences and their use for poetic creation of the poet.

A careful analysis of several poems shows how invisible traces of several languages can be found on the phonetical, morphological, lexical, and cultural level of most of her poems. Ståhlberg concludes that the specific poetic style of Södergran has its roots in her multilingual competences which fueled and enabled her creative literary expression. A multilingual re-evaluation of her works is necessary to find other parts of this hidden multilingualism. Eventually, this article also pleads for a postmonolingual attitude to replace the monolingual habitus in research.

Through individual case studies the shifting attitudes towards multi- and monolingualism in different European regions as well as during the course of the 19th century show different types of false monolinguals and hidden multilingual authors. Eötvös represents the early attempt to transform bi- and multilingual authors into monolingual national authors as part of national reforms,

Fontane embodies the already established monolingual national author whose multilingualism takes on a utilitarian form in his literary writing which is not even classified as multilingualism. Eça de Queiroz represents another variation of this type as the migrant national authors whose migratory identity remains hidden by his national status.

Finally, the established monolingual paradigm even confuses the multilingual traces in the poetic oeuvre of Edith Södergran as avantgarde literature as Ståhlberg demonstrates in her study on Södergran's plurilingual poetic work.

4.3 Part 3: Theoretical contributions on hidden multilingualism

The third part of the volume contains theoretical frames and typologies to analyze, explore and categorize 19th-century multilingualism in literature in a systematic way.

Vlasta proposes a first typology of multilingual travelogues, a genre that links the crossings of geographical and linguistic borders. A popular genre in the 18th and 19th centuries, it held nevertheless a peripheral position within the canon, and its multilingual dimension has not yet been studied systematically. Vlasta investigates three types from more open forms to hidden multilingualism in travel writing as well as the multilingual biographies that are the result of the authors' travels. She shows and explains instances and functions of code-switching and code-mixing in Charles Dickens' *Pictures from Italy* (1846) and George Sand's *Un hiver à Majorque* (1842) [Winter in Majorca]. Intertextuality features strongly in 19th-century travel writing and also causes multilingual transfers which might or might not be visible on the surface of the text. Mary Shelley's travelogue *Rambles in Germany and Italy in 1840, 1842, and 1843* (1844) and Karl Philipp Moritz' travelogue *Reisen eines Deutschen in England im Jahre 1782* (1783) [Journeys of a German in England. A Walking Tour of England in 1782] are used as examples to illustrate the many forms and functions of intertextual multilingualism in travel writing. Latent multilingualism – referencing Radaelli's term for multilingual text elements which are only visible if one understands the source language – plays an important role in many travelogues at the time, among them Goethe's *Italienische Reise* [Italian Journey], Johann Gottfried Seume's *Spaziergang nach Syrakus im Jahre 1802* (1803) [Walk to Syracuse in 1802], and Fanny Lewald's *Italienisches Bilderbuch* (1847) [Italian Picturebook]. Through those three types of open, semi-open, and hidden multilingualism, the article concludes with a first and tentative typology of multilingualism in historical travelogues.

Jöhnk's chapter on female writing and multilingualism gives a systematic approach to (in)visibility of gender and multilingualism in 19th-century female writing. Translingual literature from the 19th century is presented and analyzed as gendered writing, hidden because of the gender of the writer and the multilingual form. Jöhnk adapts theories on gender and multilingualism by Hélène Cixous (*1937) as well as poetical contributions by Gloria Anzaldúa and Yoko Tawada to include historical texts and multilingualism into the analysis. Referring to the works of the sociologist Joanne Nagel, Jöhnk strengthens the link between nationalism and masculinity which in turn paves the way for an intrinsic link between transnational and translingual female writing outside the nation.

The historical analysis of hidden multilingual writing of female writers presents Germaine de Staël's little-known work as a translator from German into French. The study of Staël's translation of Goethe's poem *Der Fischer* [The Fisherman] reveals a creative play with the female voices in the poem which are made more audible in the French translation. Linguistic and literary imperfection characterize Leonor de Almeida's, the 'Portuguese Stael', translations which are part of the correspondence between the author and her friend, Teresa de Mello Breyner. Through careful and detailed close-reading of those texts, Jöhnk concludes that hidden multilingualism is an important feature not only of current female writing but allowed female writers to create translingual and inclusive creative spaces in the 19th century too.

A general theoretical conceptualization of how multilingual writing in 19th century literature can be found and included in linguistic and literary historical studies form the aim of the last two contributions.

Bär's chapter on linguistic and literary criticism as a source of multilingual research gives instructions on how to systematically search for hidden or hard to find multilingual instances in large corpora of 18th and 19th centuries' German and English literature. In two parts, Bär introduces historical language theory in contemporary texts on multilingualism, problematizes variation and 'natural languages', and introduces a corpus-based method to find hidden instances of multilingual language use. He situates multilingualism within historical language theory as part of individual historical language use (called *usage* in Bär's terminology). He investigates multilingualism as a subject in historical texts. Using Goethe's works as a case study he applies a corpus-based methodological search to investigate Goethe's use of multilingualism. Finally, he proposes a database modelled to generate data on forms and functions of (hidden) multilingual historical texts.

Mende's chapter models a mixed-method approach to historical multilingual literature. Based on a corpus of historical biographical literary dictionaries Mende proposes a systematic investigation of traces of hidden multilingualism in monolingual sources like literary histories and biographical literary dictionaries. The dictionaries from the end of the 19th century, Brümmer's *Lexikon der deutschen Dichter und Prosaisten* (1876/1877) [Dictionary of German poets and prose writers] and Pataky's *Lexikon der Frauen deutscher Feder* (1898) [Dictionary of women of the German pen] contain biographical and bibliographical details of 19th-century writers who published in German. The aim of those dictionaries was to include as many authors as possible, without differentiating between genres, influence, success or literary merits. The first part of the article investigates explicit mentions of language skills, multilingual publications and linguistic information about authors in those dictionaries. The second part shows how a semi-automatic analysis of geographical and biographical data can map places of residence of authors. This is based on the hypothesis that multilingual surroundings also lead to multilingual writing activities. The literary scene of Bratislava (Preßburg) in the 19th century serves as a case study to explore the hypothesis. The analysis exposes a large multilingual network of writers, using both regional, interregional, and transnational forms of multilingual exchange. The study recommends a mixed-methods approach, using both quantitative and traditional qualitative methods to study historical multilingual literature.

4.4 Hidden multilingualism continued or "demythologizing" 19th century monolingualism

This volume is indebted to multiple works on literary history of minority literatures, regional multilingualism, and case studies of different types of European multilingualism in 19th century literature. It gives a heuristic approach to one specific phenomenon – hidden multilingualism – which it exposes, analyzes, and makes visible on a transnational, transregional, and translingual level. However, this volume also has a hidden list of themes, examples, approaches that were not or could not be included. Hopefully, the heuristic exploration of the phenomenon leads to further research on other covertly multilingual literary histories and the case studies and proposed approaches may prove useful for enabling and analyzing future sightings of hidden multilingualism. Thus, this volume contributes to demythologizing the myth of one unified monolingual 19th century literature.

5 References

Adler, Hans. 2012. Übersetzen als Kulturtransfer. In Clémence Couturier-Heinrich (ed.), *Übersetzen bei Johann Gottfried Herder: Theorie und Praxis*, 45–61. Heidelberg: Synchron, Wiss.-Verl. der Autoren.

Alexandrova, Boriana. 2020. *Joyce, Multilingualism and the Ethics of Reading*. Basingstoke: Palgrave Macmillan.

Anderson, Benedict R. 2006. *Imagined Communities: Reflections on the Origin and Spread of Nationalism*. London, New York: Verso.

Anokhina, Olga, Till Dembeck & Dirk Weissmann. 2019. Close the Gap! Literary Multilingualism Studies and the 19th Century. In Olga D. Anokhina, Till Dembeck & Dirk Weissmann (eds.), *Mapping Multilingualism in 19th Century European Literatures*: Le plurilinguisme dans les littératures européennes du XIXe siècle, 1–5. Vienna: Lit.

Anokhina, Olga & Emilio Sciarrino. 2018. Plurilinguisme littéraire: de la théorie à la genèse. *Genesis* 46, http:// journals.openedition.org/genesis/2554. (6 November 2019.)

Apter, Emily. 2013. *Against World Literature: On the Politics of Untranslatability*. London, New York: Verso.

Biti, Vladimir. 2013. The Fissured Identity of Literature: The Birth of National Literary History out of International Cultural Transfers. *Journal of Literary Theory* 7(1–2). 1–30.

Blommaert, Jan (ed.). 2012. *Dangerous Multilingualism: Northern Perspectives on Order, Purity and Normality*. Basingstoke: Palgrave Macmillan.

Brown, Hilary. 2018. Women Translators in History: Towards a 'woman-interrogated' approach. In Angela Sanmann, Martine La Hennard Dutheil de Rochère & Valérie Cossy (eds.), *Femin|in|visible: Women authors of the enlightenment: übersetzen, schreiben, vermitteln*, 27–51. Lausanne: Centre de Traduction Littéraire de Lausanne.

Casanova, Pascale. 2004. *The World Republic of Letters*. Cambridge, Mass., London: Harvard University Press.

Dembeck, Till & Georg Mein. 2013. Postmonolingual schreiben: Zum Jargon der Philosophie. *Zeitschrift für interkulturelle Germanistik* (3). 133–147.

Dembeck, Till & Rolf Parr. 2017. Mehrsprachige Literatur. Zur Einleitung. In Till Dembeck & Rolf Parr (eds.), *Literatur und Mehrsprachigkeit: Ein Handbuch*, 9–14. Tübingen: Narr Francke Attempto.

Fishman, Joshua A. 1968. Nationality-Nationalism and Nation-Nationism. In Joshua A. Fishman, Charles A. Ferguson & Jyotirindra Das Gupta (eds.), *Language Problems of Developing Nations*, 39–51, New York: John Wiley & Sons.

Gogolin, Ingrid. 2021. Multilingualism: A threat to public education or a resource in public education? – European histories and realities. *European Educational Research Journal* 20(3). 297–310.
Gramling, David. 2021. *The Invention of Multilingualism* (Key topics in applied linguistics). Cambridge UK, New York: Cambridge University Press.
Grutman, Rainier. 1997. *Des langues qui résonnent: L'hétérolinguisme au XIXe siècle québécois*. Montréal: Fides-CÉTUQ.
Guillén, Claudio. 1993. *The Challenge of Comparative Literature* (Harvard studies in comparative literature 42). Cambridge: Harvard Univ. Press.
Habermas, Jürgen & Max Pensky. 2001. *The Postnational Constellation: Political Essays* (Studies in contemporary German social thought). Cambridge, Mass., London: MIT Press.
Hárs, Endre. 2008. Herder oder die Erfindung des Nationalen. *kakanien revisited* 12(3). 1–13.
Herder, Johann G. 1985. Über den Fleiss in mehreren gelehrten Sprachen. In Herder, Johann G., Ulrich Gaier (ed.), *Frühe Schriften: 1764 – 1772* (Bibliothek deutscher Klassiker 1), 22–29. Frankfurt am Main: Dt. Klassiker-Verl.
Hitzke, Diana. 2019. *Nach der Einsprachigkeit: Slavisch-deutsche Texte transkulturell* (Postcolonial perspectives on Eastern Europe Band 6). Berlin, Bern, Bruxelles, New York, Oxford, Warszawa, Wien: Peter Lang.
Kellman, Steven G. 2020. *Nimble Tongues: Studies in Literary Translingualism* (Comparative Cultural Studies). Ashland: Purdue University Press.
Kilchmann, Esther. 2019. II.3. Mehrsprachige Literatur und Transnationalität. In Doerte Bischoff & Susanne Komfort-Hein (eds.), *Handbuch Literatur & Transnationalität*, 79–89. Berlin, Boston: De Gruyter.
Knauth, K. A. 2004. Multilinguale Literatur. In Monika Schmitz-Emans (ed.), *Literatur und Vielsprachigkeit* (7), 265–289. Heidelberg: Synchron Wiss.-Verl. der Autoren.
Kriegleder, Wynfrid, Manjiri Paranjape, Franz Patocka, Andrea Seidler & Sandra Vlasta (eds.). 2014. *Mehrsprachigkeit und multikulturelle Literatur* Wien: Praesens-Verl.
Lennon, Brian. 2010. *In Babel's Shadow: Multilingual Literatures, Monolingual States*. Minneapolis: University of Minnesota Press.
Lennon, Brian. 2015. 6. Challenges to monolingual national literatures. In Ulrike Jessner-Schmid & Claire J. Kramsch (eds.), *The Multilingual Challenge*, 143–160. De Gruyter.
Leperlier, Tristan. 2020. La langue des champs. *COnTEXTES. Revue de sociologie de la littérature*, https://journals.openedition.org/contextes/9297.
Mattheier, Klaus J. 2000. Die Herausbildung neuzeitlicher Schriftsprachen. In Werner Besch, Anne Betten, Oskar Reichmann & Stefan Sonderegger (eds.), *Sprachgeschichte: Ein Handbuch zur Geschichte der deutschen Sprache und ihrer Erforschung*, 2nd edn. 1085–1107. Berlin: De Gruyter.
Maurer, Michael. 2012. Herder als Theoretiker der interkulturellen Beziehungen. In Clémence Couturier-Heinrich (ed.), *Übersetzen bei Johann Gottfried Herder: Theorie und Praxis*, 29–44. Heidelberg: Synchron, Wiss.-Verl. der Autoren.
Mix, York-Gothart & Jochen Strobel. 2010. Der Europäer August Wilhelm Schlegel: Romantischer Kulturtransfer – romantische Wissenswelten. In York-Gothart Mix & Jochen Strobel (eds.), *Der Europäer August Wilhelm Schlegel: Romantischer Kulturtransfer – romantische Wissenswelten*, 1–10. Berlin, Boston: De Gruyter.
Olsson, Anders & Axel Englund (eds.). 2013. *Languages of Exile: Migration and Multilingualism in Twentieth-Century Literature*. Bern, Switzerland: Peter Lang.

Radaelli, Giulia. 2011. *Literarische Mehrsprachigkeit: Sprachwechsel bei Elias Canetti und Ingeborg Bachmann*. Berlin: Oldenbourg Wissenschaftsverlag GmbH.
Sanmann, Angela, Martine La Hennard Dutheil de Rochère & Valérie Cossy (eds.). 2018. *Fémin|in|visible: Women authors of the enlightenment: übersetzen, schreiben, vermitteln*. Lausanne: Centre de Traduction Littéraire de Lausanne.
Schleiermacher, Friedrich. 2002 [1813]. Über die verschiedenen Methoden des Übersetzens. In Martin Rößler (ed.), *Akademievorträge. Kritische Gesamtausgabe.: 1. Abt. Band 11.*, 65–93. Berlin u.a.: De Gruyter.
Schmeling, Manfred & Monika Schmitz-Emans (eds.). 2002. *Multilinguale Literatur im 20. Jahrhundert*. Würzburg: Königshausen & Neumann.
Schmitz, H. 2009. *Von der nationalen zur internationalen Literatur: Transkulturelle deutschsprachige Literatur und Kultur im Zeitalter globaler Migration*. Brill.
Siller, Barbara & Sandra Vlasta. 2020. *Literarische (Mehr)Sprachreflexionen*. Wien: Edition Praesens.
Stockhammer, Robert, Susan Arndt & Dirk Naguschewski. 2007. Einleitung: Die Unselbstverständlichkeit der Sprache. In Susan Arndt, Dirk Naguschewski & Robert Stockhammer (eds.), *Exophonie: Anders-Sprachigkeit (in) der Literatur*, 7–27. Berlin: Kulturverl. Kadmos.
Venuti, Lawrence. 1995. *The Translator's Invisibility: A History of Translation*. London, New York: Routledge.
Vorderobermeier, Gisella M. & Michaela Wolf (eds.). 2008. *„Meine Sprache grenzt mich ab …": Transkulturalität und kulturelle Übersetzung im Kontext von Migration*. Wien: Lit-Verl.
Walkowitz, Rebecca L. 2015. *Born translated: The Contemporary Novel in an Age of World Literature* (Literature now). New York: Columbia Univ. Press.
Weissmann, Dirk. 2021. *Les langues de Goethe: Essai sur l'imaginaire plurilingue d'un poète national*. Paris: Éditions Kimé.
Yildiz, Yasemin. 2012. *Beyond the Mother Tongue: The Postmonolingual Condition*. New York: Fordham University Press.
Zanetti, Sandro, Pietro de Marchi & Marco Baschera (eds.). 2019. *Zwischen den Sprachen: Mehrsprachigkeit, Übersetzung, Öffnung der Sprachen / Entre les langues: plurilinguisme, traduction, ouverture des langues*. Bielefeld: Aisthesis Verlag.

Part 1: Multilingual Histories of National Literatures

Mariyana Tsibranska-Kostova, Irena Kristeva

Traces of Hidden Multilingualism in 19th-Century Bulgarian Literature and Culture

The Role of the Relay Translation

Abstract: The study problematizes the connection between relay translation and hidden multilingualism in the context of the Bulgarian National Revival (1762–1878). It explores the translation challenges and strategies during this historical period by examining the first translation from English. In 1837, Gavril Krŭstevich translated Benjamin Franklin's essay *The Way to Wealth* (1758) from its French version. The translator's choices attest to the complex tasks of prose translated from Western languages at this time. They valorize Western values, aiming to overcome Oriental backwardness. And lastly, they reflect the real multilingualism within the multi-ethnic and multilingual Ottoman Empire. In short, they prove that hidden multilingualism is crucial to the reception of translated prose during the Revival.

Keywords: Benjamin Franklin, Bulgarian National Revival, Gavril Krŭstevich, Relay Translation, *The Way to Wealth*

1 Introduction

The age of the Bulgarian National Revival (1762–1878)[1] broadened the horizon of the readership. The increase in translation activity during this period aimed to compensate for the lack of valuable authorial works, to make up for the scarcity of books, to develop the readers' taste by introducing new spaces and cultures,

---

[1] Bulgaria was under Ottoman domination for five centuries, from 1396 to 1878, namely from the conquest of the Second Bulgarian State until the Tenth Russo-Turkish War (1877–1878). The Ottoman Empire was multi-ethnic and multilingual. Various peoples coexisted there: Turks, Kurds, Armenians, Circassians, Georgians, Romanians, Bulgarians, Greeks, Serbs, etc. Despite the subordinate economic position and the social and religious segregation to which they were subject, the Bulgarians managed to preserve their national identity thanks to the Orthodox faith, the Cyrillic alphabet, their customs, and traditions.

Irena Kristeva, University of Sofia Saint Kliment Ohridski, e-mail: krustevagr@uni-sofia.bg;
Mariyana Tsibranska-Kostova, Bulgarian Academy of Sciences, BAS, e-mail: tzibran@abv.bg

Open Access. © 2023 the author(s), published by De Gruyter. This work is licensed under the Creative Commons Attribution 4.0 International License.
https://doi.org/10.1515/9783110778656-002

and to serve as inspiration for original literary creation. Translators assumed responsibility for the selection of moralizing or didactic works suitable for educating the reading public. Alongside religious works, texts from Antiquity were also translated, mainly from Greek (Aesop, Homer, Plutarch, Sophocles, Theophrastus, Xenophon, etc.), as well as contemporary texts from Russian (Pushkin, Gogol, Karamzin, Lermontov, etc.), from French (Hugo, Lamartine, Dumas, Georges Sand, etc.), and from German (Goethe, Heine, Schiller, Schmid, etc.). Translation acquired three main functions at this time: it compensated for cultural gaps, it shaped the literary taste of readers, and it provided literary paradigms.

Multilingualism is characteristic of the enlightened and economically active part of the Bulgarian population throughout the Revival. However, it is not perceived as such. The peculiarity is that not only the "literary unconscious is large-ly national" (Casanova 2004: XI), but the literary conscious as well, because it is conditioned by the affirmation of the national consciousness. In this sense, we could define the literary conscious of the Bulgarian intellectuals in the 19th Cen-tury as national, and the literary unconscious as multilingual.

To illustrate the translation challenges and strategies during the National Revival, we are going to examine Benjamin Franklin's essay *The Way to Wealth*, the first text translated from English into Bulgarian. Franklin's essay is a compilation of pieces of advice, hints, and tips on business and money that appeared in *Poor Richard's Almanac* published in 1758 under the pseudonym of Richard Saunders. In 1837, encouraged by his teacher Rayno Popovich,[2] Gavril Krŭstevich[3] translated Franklin's essay from its French version, *La science du bon-*

---

[2] Rayno Popovich (1773–1858) was one of the prominent men of letters of the National Revival who actively participated in the educational reform.

[3] Gavril Krŭstevich (1817?–1910) was one of the first Bulgarian writers during the Revival, a high Ottoman official, politician and historian. He was born in the small town of Kotel, located in the eastern part of the Greater Balkan range. In 1837, he graduated from the prestigious Phanar Greek Orthodox College in Istanbul, where he learned, alongside theology, Greek and French, another testimony of multilingualism in the Ottoman Empire. He studied law at the Sorbonne from 1838 to 1844. After his return, he successively held the positions of judge, member of the Supreme Court and professor of law. Author of the Commercial Code of the Ottoman Empire, he was appointed, in 1868, to the Divan-i Ahkam-i Adliye (The Superior Council of Justice of the Ottoman Empire). Alongside his legal duties, he made literature his vocation. He collaborated and wrote articles in the most important Bulgarian newspapers and magazines published in Istanbul: Любословие [Philology], Цариградски вестник [Constantinople Gazette], Български книжици [Bulgarian Booklets], Съветник [Counselor], Право [Law], Век [Century]. In 1869, the first volume of his *Bulgarian history* came out. He subsequently gave up on publishing the second and the third.

homme Richard, ou Moyen facile de payer les impôts (1777). He titled it *Мудростъ добраго Рихарда* [The Wisdom of the Good Richard]. Besides *The Way to Wealth*, this young polyglot, who spoke Bulgarian, Turkish, Greek and French, "translates various works from Slovene, Greek and Hellenic" (Kepov 1929), as well as the first three songs of the *Iliad* from the original.

The source text of *Мудростъ добраго Рихарда* is a relay translation.[4] Usually, relay translations are used when the original texts are lost and the only way for a language community to gain access to them is to use translations in other languages. Such was the case with the "Protestant" translation of the Bible from Greek into Bulgarian, carried out in 1871 by a team of translators in close collaboration with American missionaries. However, Krŭstevich uses relay translation simply because he does not speak English.

Мудростъ добраго Рихарда presents some singularities. The translator had insufficient knowledge of the French language.[5] The translation reflects the state of the Bulgarian language and the Turkish-Bulgarian bilingualism. It is quite faithful to the American original. Gavril Krŭstevich exposes his biases, confessing to having been driven by patriotic duty; to having sought clarity and perfection; to having used the common language, that is to say the women's language; to having had his translation proofread by his teacher, Popovich, who was not a French speaker. Lastly, he admits to being opposed to the excessive Bulgarization of the text which would have made it unrecognizable: an exceptional fact for the time, when Bulgarization embodied the reaction against all foreign influence (Kristeva 2011: 377–378). After all, this was a period in which Ottoman domination was being contested, a nation was being rebuilt, and Bulgarian identity was being reaffirmed. During this time, cultural manifestations necessarily involved political challenges.

Therefore, *Мудростъ добраго Рихарда* establishis the connection between relay translation, Bulgarization and hidden multilingualism (Filipov 2004: 9–21; Aretov 1996: 70–82). Bulgarization apparently conceals multilingualism in Krŭstevich's translation, where words of Greek and Turkish origin are also used. But since the multilingual vocabulary has entered the spoken language, this multilingualism is often not perceived as such. Hidden multilingualism largely determines the reception of prose translated into Bulgarian during the Revival (Trendafilov 1996: 27). Bulgarization becomes concomitantly the basis of the

---

4 Relay translations are "intermediate translations for a readership" (Washbourne 2013: 608). In this case, the translator works from another translation of the original and not from the original itself (Dollerup 2000: 17–26).
5 The translation was done before he began his law studies at the Sorbonne.

dialogue between the national cultural tradition and the foreign one. Translation and Bulgarization are even often considered synonymous during this period (Filipov 2004: 12).

2 The Bulgarian National Revival: educational and cultural context

Translations have always been a cultural engine for the growth of a nation. The most important feature of a translation – its inclusion in the massified Christian-moralistic reading – has its justification in the socio-cultural environment in the in the 1830s and 1840s. The Revival was an age of modernity: for the first time under Ottoman domination new directions were discovered and new spiritual and intellectual energy manifested itself, seeking a new social carrier (Damyanova 2016: 495–499; Damyanova 2004: 308). Translations and authorial literary works in this period satisfied the reader's needs for didactic literature, and enlightened and morally edifying topics. A thematic analogy can be detected in "teacher's poetry", which emerged after 1835, when the foundations of the Bulgarian secular school were laid.

The first secular school in the Bulgarian lands under Ottoman domination was opened in Gabrovo in 1835 by the Russian graduate Vasil Aprilov,[6] and introduced a modern way of teaching with the so-called Bell–Lancaster, or mutual teaching method. Since then, the number of schools increased, and the 1840s marked the beginning of girls' education, something radically new for the Orient (Genchev 1988: 203). A scholastic reading environment was created. The figure of the teacher was transformed into an authorial presence, although the enlightenment romanticism of "teacher's poetry" sometimes appears naïve and comic. Teachers became the new cultural heroes or the privileged voices of the Revival, but also the most numerous professional group among the intelligentsia. "Teacher's poetry" became a natural manifestation of social needs that pointed towards new spiritual horizons. It developed rapidly, reaching its heyday in the 1850s and 1860s, and then declining towards the end of Ottoman rule. "Teacher's poetry" had been a leading phenomenon for about four decades, until the first university in Bulgaria was opened only in 1888, ten years after its independence.

---

[6] Vasil Aprilov (1789–1847) was a Bulgarian enlightened figure, benefactor, and writer.

The social type of the teacher replaced that of the clergyman – a priest or a monk, who was up to that moment the leading figure in the educational and cultural processes. Teachers created a model for modern Bulgarian education: some of them had graduated from foreign universities and upon their return they not only taught, but also wrote manuals and books. The profession of teacher was a sign of prestige and a special privilege in Revival society. Textbooks were created that introduced students to the main categories of mathematics, grammar, and science. The so-called "school period" of literature contributed to the shaping of a secular world view and of new reading tastes. Along with the educational processes in society, new social forms appeared, which provided an abundance of literary and cultural events: such are *Chitalishta*,[7] the specific institutes for the promotion of culture and education.

During the Bulgarian Revival, some essential questions arose for the first time concerning translation activities: *What should be translated? By whom? How?* The first question concerns the choice of texts according to their typology and their subject. The second relates to the choice of translators based on their linguistic knowledge and cultural skills. The third pertains to the problem of the technique of translating: adaptation or faithfulness to the original. These questions sparked the Bulgarian version of the eternal quarrel of the Ancients and the Moderns, namely the Old versus the Young. The camp of the Old brings together Nesho Bonchev,[8] Marin Drinov,[9] Vasil Drumev,[10] followers of the imitation of the great classics in view of the formation of literary taste. The Young, to whom Rayko Žinzifov,[11] Lyuben Karavelov,[12] Hristo Botev[13] belonged, did not

---

7 Читалище [Reading Centre] – from the Bulgarian Slavonic root *chital-* [reading] and the suffix *-ishte* [place].
8 Nesho Bonchev (1839–1878) was the first Bulgarian literary critic and pedagogue.
9 Marin Drinov (1838–1906) was a historian, philologist and statesman, who worked most of his life in Russia. He was one of the founders of Bulgarian historiography, a professor, co-founder and first chairman of the Bulgarian Literary Society, today the Bulgarian Academy of Sciences.
10 Vasil Drumev (1841–1901) was a Bulgarian writer, clergyman and politician. He is the author of the first Bulgarian novel and the first Bulgarian dramatic play with an original plot. After the Independence he was Metropolitan of the Tŭrnovo Diocese of the Bulgarian Exarchate and twice Prime Minister of Bulgaria.
11 Rayko Žinzifov (1839–1877) was a Bulgarian poet, scholar, translator, and Slavophile.
12 Lyuben Karavelov (1834–1879) was a Bulgarian poet, writer, journalist and ethnographer. He contributed significantly to the development of public thought in Bulgaria during the Revival, wrote bibliographic works, articles on Bulgarian literature, culture, lexicography, political history.

consider the diffusion of classical foreign literature as essential to the formation of the taste of Bulgarian readers, but rather encouraged the spreading of contemporary literature that met specific needs.

This historical and cultural context determines the choice of the source texts, based on a privileged objective and a scale of values. The translated prose from Western languages fulfils complex functions that helped to overcome the perceived Oriental backwardness. But in view of the specificity of the Bulgarian Revival, its main goal is utilitarian. That is why translators turn to works that can be useful to society and bring Bulgarian readers in contact with the ideas of the Enlightenment and Romanticism. Translators are not always guided by the importance of the author or the work, but by what kind of entertaining and instructive reading will be offered to the readership. The relay translation becomes a way to achieve this goal, despite the fact that the source data for the books and their originals are so hybrid that a cultural amalgam of languages, publications, authorial and reworked texts derives from it.

Мудрость добраго Рихарда is one of the many target texts using relay translation during the Revival. Similar in time of origin and in purpose is Daniel Defoe's *Robinson Crusoe* (1719). It first became known as *Робинзон* [Robinson] in Rayno Popovich's manuscript translation (1841), which was never published in print (Aretov 1996: 105–119; Filipov 2004: 9). It is noteworthy that this translation was made from Greek, which itself was not based on the original, but on the German-language adaptation for children (1779) by the pedagogue and theologian Joachim Heinrich Campe. Therefore, the literary reception of popular readings in this case goes through four languages from the original, through two relay translations, to Bulgarian as target language. Following is the first printed translation of *Чудесиите на Робенсина Крусо* [Robinson Crusoe's Wonders] by Ivan Bogorov,[14] which was published as a feuilleton in the *Цариградски вестник* [Constantinople Gazette] from 1848 to 1849. In 1849, it appears as a separate edition. *Robinson*'s second printed translation (1858) is by Yoakim Gruev,[15] and it is still debated from which language it was translated, Russian or Serbian. Some recent studies on the reception of this book in Bulgar-

---

13 Hristo Botev (1848–1876) was a Bulgarian revolutionary, poet and publicist. His poetry marks one of the peaks of Bulgarian literature.

14 Ivan Bogorov (1818–1892) was a well-known Bulgarian encyclopaedist. He was one of the most committed Bulgarian purists and fought for decades against the entry of foreignisms into the language, especially the Greekisms and Russianisms in the Bulgarian literary language.

15 Yoakim Gruev (1828–1912) was a Bulgarian enlightenment figure, teacher, pedagogue, translator, publisher and public man.

ia report that as early as 1835 residents of Karlovo asked Neofit Rilski[16] to translate *Robinson* (Pileva 2016a: 16; Pileva 2016b). In 1868, under the pen of Petko Slaveykov,[17] *Robinson*'s last Revival translation from Greek was published, entitled *Робинсон на острова си* [Robinson on His Island]. The translator and the publisher of the book treat it as a children's book as well as a textbook (Benbasat 2019; Zaharieva 2010: 207).

Мудростъ добраго Рихарда marks the beginning of Benjamin Franklin's reception in Bulgaria. Formally, due to the source language of *Мудростъ добраго Рихарда*, the work falls into the category of translated French prose, which accounted for 10% of all translations at this time. Many works were translated from Russian (50% of all translations), and Greek (25%), whereas English translations made up only 3% of all translations (Pileva 2016a: 8). These statistical ratios reflect the dominant Orthodox and cultural attitudes of Bulgarians. At the time of its creation, however, Krŭstevich's translation focused more on the moralizing pathos, on the interesting, entertaining, and instructive reading, on the so-called *fable stories*, and less on what is understood by today's reception of literary works. Neither the author of the original nor the work itself have a high cultural status in the eyes of Bulgarian recipients. When not translated from the original, the direct connection to the author of the source text and, therefore, to the text itself is lost. Thus, the author's authority is transferred to the relay translation: "In literary translation, relay translation (as well as delay) implies that the sender, the original author, recedes into the background" (Dollerup 2000: 23). This also applies to *Мудростъ добраго Рихарда*.

The examination of the interpretation from the point of view of the author, the work and the reader is the basis of the debate about the meaning of the text. The hermetic-symbolic reading is performed through two approaches. The first, *intentio auctoris*, seeks the meanings inserted by the author; the second seeks the meanings unsuspected by the author on the basis of the compositional coherence of the text, *intentio operis*, or on the basis of the signifying systems for the reader, *intentio lectoris* (Eco 1990: 43–50). The intention of the work differs from the intention of the author, as well as from the intention of the language in which it is written, from the intention of the reader who will read it, and even from the intention of the literary genre to which it belongs. It is related to the

---

16 Neofit Rilski (1793–1881) was a Bulgarian monk, teacher, artist. He was one of the leading figures in the Bulgarian enlightenment movement in the first half of the 19th century.
17 Petko Slaveykov (1827–1895) was a Bulgarian poet, publicist, folklorist, and politician. He was among the leaders of the Liberal Party after the Liberation, chairman of the National Assembly (1880), and minister in several cabinets (1880–1881, 1884–1885).

purpose of the work, that is to the question at the beginning of "The Task of the Translator": "Is a translation meant for readers who do not understand the original?" (Benjamin [1923] 2000: 15). Even in *Lector in fabula* (1979), Umberto Eco distinguishes interpretation from use. The first, which is based solely on the text, stands on the side of the intention of the work. The second, which uses the text to draw its own conclusions about the author's personal life, stands on the side of the reader's intention.

With regard to the reception of *Мудрость добраго Рихарда* and the very peculiarities of translation, there is a shift, compared to that of the Middle Ages, in the triad *author – work – reader*. The author and the work do not have authority for the cultural context of the Bulgarian National Revival. Benjamin Franklin is not very well known: the cover of the Bulgarian translation does not include his name or his pseudonym Richard Sanders, but it has the names of the translator and the editor, as well as the fact that it is a translation from French and not from English.

The work is not as sacred as the religious texts translated in the Middle Ages. Krŭstevich's translation is characterized by its utilitarian goal and morality. Emphasis is put on labour as a value in the Christian paradigm: labour and study are values, not money. However, if we consider the work only through the prism of its reception in the target culture, we risk depriving it of its placement in the context of translated prose in the Revival era (Aretov 1990; Aretov 1995; Aretov 2011; Manolakiev 1994; Lekov 1982) and in one of its profiled subdivisions, Protestant English-language literature (Filipov 2004; Pileva 2016a).

Мудрость добраго Рихарда is a forerunner to the stage of the Bulgarization of translated literature, typical for the period from the 1850s to the 1870s. In 1868, Nikola Pŭrvanov published a new translation of *The Way to Wealth*, entitled *Искуството да стане человек богат* [The Art of Becoming Rich], in two consecutive issues of the magazine *Македония* [Makedoniya]. Pŭrvanov used relay translation again, this time in German. In 1869, another version appeared in Constantinople: *Сиромах Богдан или средство за обогатяване, книжка много поучителна за народа* [Poor Bogdan or a means of enrichment, a very instructive booklet for the people]. In this version Richard becomes Bogdan. It is probably the work of Petko Slaveykov, but the source language is unknown. In 1872, a translation from English appeared in the magazine *Читалище* [Reading Centre]; in 1878, another translation from German was published in the magazine *Летоструй* [Flow of the Years]. These are all cases of Bulgarization, adaptation and socio-cultural contextualisation of the original in the Bulgarian setting; most of them are cases of relay translation.

Bulgarization is a typical phenomenon for literary communication during the Revival, directly related to the utilitarianism of translation as well as to the specific forms and methods of translation. It highlights the utilitarian function of the source texts, reworked, and updated to the limit of the possible. It marks the transitional stage between literary translation and literary creation (Kristeva 2008: 396–397). At its base, there is the purposeful adaptation, change or shift in the relation between the translation and the original in terms of cognitive and axiological facts and emphases. These liberties are a signal not only of perception, but paradoxically of differentiation: the identity of the work is taken away and it is credited to the national fund to fill gaps of aesthetic or genre nature (Lekov 1982: 246). The plot and composition can be changed; realia, toponyms, and names can be bulgarized, so that researchers are faced with the difficult questions of determining where it is exactly translated from – from the original or from a relay translation – and of connecting each translation with the exact literary term – *adaptation, processing, Bulgarization*.

Translators who practiced Bulgarization adapted the translated works to the expectations of their potential readers. To this end, they implemented several strategies, such as changing the names of the characters, transposing the action to Bulgaria, removing or adding scenes and cultural references, as well as modifying the language and the style of the source texts. Such processes burden the translation from this era with specific functions. For example, Yoakim Gruev is known for not only changing the name of the main character from Бедная Лиза [Poor Liza] (1792) by Nikolay Karamzin to Сирота Цветана [Poor Tzvetana] (1858), but also for shortening many sentimental passages to give greater naturalness to the plot and to the behavior of the characters. The translator himself called this short story a "fairy tale". Stefan Bobchev, the translator of *Die Wasserflut am Rheine* [Flooding of the Rhine] by the German writer Christoph von Schmid, decides, for his part, to change the title to Наводнение на Дунав [Flooding of the Danube] and to bulgarize the names of the characters. Incidentally, "translated by" does not appear on the cover, but rather "bulgarized by Stefan Bobchev" (Schmid 1871).

Thus, bulgarized works always fulfill specific public functions. Bulgarization is a process of adaptation to the local reality at different literary levels: realia, ideas, messages, and language. It meets the social, psychological, cultural, and spiritual needs of the Bulgarian people. It allows for the assimilation of new genres in Bulgarian literature (Lekov 1982: 246).

3 The translation strategies of *Мудрость добраго Рихарда*

Through *Мудрость добраго Рихарда* Gavril Krŭstevich introduces themes and motifs, which he adapts semantically and linguistically for a Bulgarian audience. In other words, he privileges *intentio lectoris*. His specific translation strategies are implemented by hierarchizing the values that he considers important and that he excerpts from the work itself (Aretov 2011; Damyanova 2016, 495–499). The main value in *Мудрость добраго Рихарда* is the role of labor for personal and social well-being. The text reveals key contrasting concepts, organized mainly around labor – diligence, perseverance, decision and care, study, abstinence, parsimony and frugality, slothfulness, sleep, idleness, wasting time, the vices of gluttony, lust, gambling, prodigality and indebtedness, and the madness of life equivalent to stupidity. It is no coincidence that Krŭstevich uses various translations for the word *laziness*, drawing on both Bulgarian tradition and Turkish-Bulgarian bilingualism. Ancient Bulgarian words such as *нерадение* [inactivity], *леност* [slothfulness], *мързел* [laziness], *праздьньство* [idleness] are used as equivalents to *laziness*, as is the complex word *лениви-тембели* [slothful],[18] which is indicative of Turkish-Bulgarian bilingualism. Carrying particularly strong potential, *праздьньство* [idleness] is preferred by the translator in a number of sententious expressions and aphorisms to emphasize the need for industriousness, self-reliance, and predominance of deeds over words. When choosing one of the many possible equivalents of a word, the translator interprets its meaning based on itself and its context. The criterion of economy leads to the choice of the simplest solution when there are no other selection criteria. Thus, the act of translation becomes a problematic negotiation between the competence required by the text and the actual competence of the translator.

In *La traduction et la lettre ou l'auberge du lointain* (1999: 58–62) Antoine Berman offers a typology of the deformations that potentially threaten the target text. Even when he is aware of their threat, the translator is often unable to prevent them, although he could try to limit them. Qualitative impoverishment, for example, manifests as a replacement or simplification of the terminological and stylistic richness of the original. It is observed in the translation of puns, metaphors, and metonymies. Gavril Krŭstevich replaces *drive the business* with

---

[18] *Лениви–тембели* is composed of the Bulgarian adjective *лениви* [slothful] and the Turkish noun with Persian-Turkish origin *tembel* [slacker].

push your business; *in the grave* with *in the coffin*. As for the destruction of stable word combinations, it affects the specificity of idioms, proverbs, aphorisms, and wise sayings. Since, in these cases, the literal translation is rather exceptional, functional equivalents are systematically used.

Here are some examples of translation of wise sayings in *Мудрость добраго Рихарда*:

	Original (1758)	French translation (1777)	Krŭstevich's translation (1837)	Our reverse translation of Krŭstevich's translation
1	Sloth, like rust	L'oisiveté... ressemble à la rouille	Празностьта е подобна на раждата	Idleness is like rust
2.	there will be sleeping enough in the grave	nous aurons assez de temps à dormir quand nous serons dans le cercueil	Чи имами доволно време да спимъ, кога ни тѫрнатъ в носилото	We will have enough time to sleep when we are put in the coffin
3.	drive the business, let not that drive thee	poussez vos affaires ... que ce ne soit pas elles qui vous poussent	Бутайте дълата си за да не вы бутатъ тïя	Push your business, so it doesn't push you
4.	then help hands, for I have no lands	Il faut me servir de mes mains puisque je n'ai point de terres	Треба да употребѧ рацьть си кога немамъ мюлкове[19]	I must use my hands since I have no estate
5.	many words won't fill a bushel	Ce n'est pas la quantité de mots qui remplit le boisseau	Многото хораты не полнять кри́ната[20]	It's not the many words that fill the bushel
6.	a life of leisure and a life of laziness are two things	La vie tranquille ... & la vie oisive font deux choses fort différentes	Мирныо животъ и неработливыо животъ са две много различни нѣща.	The quiet life and the idle life are two very different things

Krŭstevich manages to avoid the use of functional equivalents. In these six examples, he offers a literal translation of the French translation, but example n. 3 is quite close to the original as well. Although it resorts to relay translation

---

[19] *Мюлкове* – from Arabic-Turkish *mülk* [estate].
[20] *Хоратувам* [to talk, to say, to speak] – a typical vernacular verb of Greek origin; *хоратà* [tales, words, speaking] (Ilchev et al. 1974: 548).

in general, *Мудрость добраго Рихарда* is true to the original. Of course, it is more verbose, but this is largely due to the transition from the French language.

One last wise saying points out slothfulness as the root cause of unhappiness:

> We are taxed twice as much by our idleness, three times as much by our pride, and four times as much by our folly. (Franklin 1758: 1–2)
> Nous sommes cotés pour le double au moins par notre paresse, pour le triple par notre orgueil, pour le quadruple par notre étourderie. (Saunders 1777: 23–24)
> Лѣностьта ни зема два пати повече ѿ Правленїето, гордостьта три пати, и несмѧтанѣто иоще четыре пати повече. (Franklin 1837, 1–2)
> [The slothfulness takes from us two times more than Government, the pride three times, and the thoughtlessness four times more.] (Our reverse translation)

In this sentence lies the opposition between the man as an individual and the citizen as a social agent, obliged to pay taxes. Krŭstevich's version deviates from both the original and the relay translation, as he adds government to the comparison, and thus shifts the focus of the sentence. Referring to the government as a tax collector, he makes explicit what is merely implicit in the original and in the relay translation. What the government can take away from you is nothing compared to what you deprive yourself of, when you fall prey to negative qualities such as laziness, pride, etc.

Мудрость добраго Рихарда emphasizes universal human categories. Pragmatism, practical attitude to life, and money are new values for the Bulgarian Revival man. However, these axiological units have some points of intersection with the medieval value paradigm that stresses the importance of labor, humility, study and moderation in the life of a devout Christian. Thus, the small treatises on the economic history of society, which Franklin bequeathed to his prosperous nation, find their semantic equivalence in Krŭstevich's translation. Money, wealth, and possessions are the main pillars of earthly existence, but they are achieved through labor and perseverance, commercial skills, and human dignity. This semantic dominant is embedded in the original title of Franklin's book, *The Way to Wealth*, and adequately transmitted in modern Bulgarian translations of the book – *Пътят към богатството* [The Way to Wealth] (Shipside 2008) and *Пътят към парите и успеха* [The Way to Money and Success] (Franklin 2011). The Revival title *Мудрость добраго Рихарда* [The Wisdom of the Good Richard] has an adapted moralizing accent: two attributes with high moral status, *good* and *wisdom*, are included. The name of the character, Richard, remains in the title of the relay translation, *La science du bonhomme Richard* [The Knowledge of the Good Richard], so he can set an example to follow.

The second major topic is that of enlightenment as a way to achieve personal and social prosperity. It corresponds even more to the Revival public attitudes. Believing that all suffering and unhappiness come from ignorance and unawareness, the Revival raises Enlightenment thought to a cult. From Paisius of Hilandar[21] and his *History*, this idea is grounded in the cultural stereotype of the Bulgarian people and in their world view. The struggle against the darkness of ignorance begins with study and labor. Moreover, in the Revival axiological paradigm, enlightenment and culture are practically synonymous. The rise of cities and growing crafts and trades predetermined the relevance of good Richard's wise advice for successful financial and economic investments as well as a new way of life.

The third aspect of this translation is the role of the moral judge, the all-seeing eye of God, without whose favor no earthly goal can be accomplished. This tangent achieves the continuum of values much needed on the threshold of the Middle Ages and the New Age. Several scientific publications are dedicated to the relevance of Biblical and Christian themes and motifs in foreign literature translated at the time of the Bulgarian Revival (Pileva 2018). Although the problem of the religious topic as the basis of conceptual thought is very broad, a distinctive leitmotif is strongly emphasized through Krŭstevich's translation: *the blessing of heaven* is above all other reasons and that gives the moral sanction. The call to "Be humble and free" is only at first sight antinomic because of the opposition of personal freedom and the omnipresent will of God. In fact, it is an attempt at a synthesis between the philosophical and cultural heritage of the past and the values of the New Age. In the Christian paradigm since the Middle Ages, compassion to the poor, kindness, and almsgiving are the standards of piety. In this respect, Krŭstevich's translation revives religious motifs (Pileva 2016a: 12). The ending of *Мудрость добраго Рихарда* puts the reader in a paradoxical situation: despite the moral instruction, the result is the same – people remain sinners, do not learn the lesson and embark on a path of reckless spending. The narrator resists the desire to buy a new garment and declares that he will keep the old one. A metaphor for the eternal battle between new and old as well as between righteous and sinful is reinforced even by the narrator's name *Grandpa Abram*. His name combines several biblical beings – the prophet, the elder, the spiritual mentor – and builds a bridge between the eternal values of the Bible and the text.

---

[21] The National Revival was inaugurated in 1762 by the publication of *История славяноболгарская* [A Slavonic-Bulgarian History], written in Church Slavonic by the monk of Mount Athos Paisius of Hilandar (1722–1773).

Regardless of the transformational dependencies between the source and target languages, Krŭstevich's translation adequately conveys the idea of the work. Yet, the text is bulgarized in the sense that the translation is at times free, semantically adapted and based on the spoken language – a complex amalgam of the old Bulgarian literary heritage, colloquial Turkisms and Greekisms, blended with new realia and concepts from the domestic and economic sphere. The hybridity of the language remains typical in Bulgarian literature for many years.

The lack of a linguistic norm contributes to Krŭstevich's violation of the strict relations in the classical triad *source language – translation strategies – target language*. He often uses a double translation in brackets[22]: he puts the Bulgarian equivalent first and the Turkish equivalent in parentheses. The percentage of Turkisms in his translation is relatively high: *прибытоцитѣ* (*кѧровитѣ*) [income], *лавката* (*дюкѧнатъ*) [kiosk], *раскайванѣ* (*пишменликъ*) [repentant], *торговски домъ* (*магаза*) [store with commercial staff], etc. There are two main linguistic principles: 1. the literary tradition, supported by the Old Bulgarian verbal heritage and the related idioms of the Russian and Church Slavonic languages; 2. the words of Turkish and Greek origin, reflecting the real language situation in pre-Independence Bulgaria. Gavril Krŭstevich replaces some foreignisms, modern for the time, such as *автор* [author] and *цитат* [quote], with Bulgarian words: *сочинител* [author], *Календарскитѣ Сочинители* [Authors of Almanacs]; the quotes from wise Richard are *пословици* [proverbs] or *достопамѧтны изречениѧ* [wisdom sentences]. A number of professions, such as *съдебен изпълнител* [bailiff] and *полицай* [policeman], are translated with Turkisms, *бумбашири* [bailiffs] and *чауши* [constables], as well as some denotations for *office* and *estate*, which are translated with Greek or Turkish words: *нито мюлко* [estate], *нито торговскио домъ* (*магазата*) [store with commercial staff] – *neither the estate, nor the office*. Some realia are kept. For example, regarding unreasonable spending, the translator conveys the author's irony that even *малко чаецъ, неколко чашки пончь* [a little tea, a little punch] can weaken one's vigilance and lead a person down the wrong path. He translates *чаецъ* [tea], but keeps *пончь* [punch].

---

[22] The practice of explanations in brackets and the use of words from different layers and origins to name the same designation continues even during the first period after the Independence, when translations became a cultural engine for legitimizing the Bulgarian language at an academic level (Danova 2012: 263).

4 The hidden multilingualism and the translator's choices

Concerned with the purity of the Bulgarian language, Gavril Krŭstevich wants his translation to be built on a solid foundation of a living vernacular language. When Rayno Popovich sends him his translation of *Robinson* for an opinion, he replies to him with the following:

> Не би било излишно да се допитвате и до други, ако и невежи по слога, а най-вече до жените, които еднички говорят по-правилно и на които мнението по тоя въпрос не трябва да презираме. Недейте се никога заблуждава от надути и велеречиви слова на самомнимите млади славонисти. Гледайте да излагате фразите си по такъв начин, че да не остава по между нищо нито съмнително, нито тъмно, та читателят, като чете, да се услажда.
> [It would not be superfluous to consult others, even if they are uneducated in the ways of expression, and especially women, who speak more correctly and whose opinions on this subject we should not despise. Do not ever be deceived by the arrogant and eloquent words of the self-centred young Slavists. Try to present your phrases in such a way that there is nothing doubtful or ambiguous in between, so that the reader can enjoy reading].
> (Kepov 1929, our translation).

Krŭstevich attempts to apply this advice in *Мудрость добраго Рихарда*. He uses the colloquial vernacular to make his translation accessible and the language of women to make his translation correct; he avoids ambiguities, so as not to mislead the reader; he tries to produce a readable and enjoyable text. In this regard, let us consider the relationship between the source text, the relay translation, and the target text in two longer excerpts.[23]

> Courteous Reader,
> I have heard that nothing gives an author so great pleasure, as to find his works respectfully quoted by other learned authors. This pleasure I have seldom enjoyed; for tho' I have been, if I may say it without vanity, an eminent author of almanacs annually now a full quarter of a century, my brother authors in the same way, for what reason I know not, have ever been very sparing in their applauses; and no other author has taken the least notice of me, so that did not my writings produce me some solid pudding, the great deficiency of praise would have quite discouraged me. (Franklin 1758: 1)
> J'ai ouï dire que rien ne fait autant de plaisir à un Auteur, que de voir ses ouvrages cités avec vénération par d'autres savans Écrivains. Il m'est rarement arrivé de jouir de ce plaisir. Car, quoique je puisse dire, sans vanité, que depuis un quart de siècle, je me suis

---

[23] The deviations of the relay translation and the Bulgarian translation from the original are in italic.

fait annuellement un nom distingué parmi les Auteurs d'Almanachs, il ne m'est guère arrivé de voir que les Écrivains, mes confrères dans le même genre daignassent m'honorer de quelques éloges ou qu'aucun autre Auteur fit la moindre mention de moi; de forte que sans le petit profit effectif que j'ai fait sur mes productions la disette d'applaudissement m'aurait totalement découragé. (Saunders 1777: 5–6)

Чюлъ самъ да казватъ, чи нищо дрȣго не докарва толика радость на едного списателѧ, колкото да глѣда своитѣ списаниѧ чи сѧ приносѧтъ въ примѣръ ѿ дрȣгитѣ оучены списатели. Менѣ рѧдкю сѧ е слȣчило да полȣча таѧ радость: защо, макаръ да мога да река, безъ да сѧ хвалѧ, чи ѿ двадесѧть и пѧть годины насамъ ми сѧ е прославило на всѧко лѣто имато междȣ Календарскитѣ Сочинители, не ми сѧ е мнюгю слȣчило да видѧ да мѧ почитатъ съ нѣколкю похвалы моитѣ собратïѧ списатели, или дрȣгъ нѣкой Сочинитель да мѧ помане малю дѣгюди; за това, ако да не бѣше и малката ползица, коѧто самъ придобилъ ѿ моитѣ изданïѧ, похвалната юскȣдность со всѣмъ мѧ бы ѿчаѧла. (Franklin 1837: 1–2)

[The address is missing]

[I have heard say that nothing gives a writer so much pleasure as to see his works given as examples by other learned writers. It has seldom happened to me to have this pleasure: for, although I can say, without vanity, that for twenty-five years I have annually made myself a distinguished name among the Authors of Almanacs, it has hardly happened to me to see that my brother writers deign to honour me with some praise, or some other Author make the slightest mention of me; therefore, without the small effective profit I made on my editions, the applause scarcity would have totally discouraged me.] (Our reverse translation)

Krŭstevich's semantic deviations from the original are minimal and are largely due to his strict adherence to the relay translation: *so much pleasure* instead of *so great pleasure*; *writer(s)* instead of *author(s)*; *a distinguished name* instead of *an eminent author*; *applause scarcity* instead of *the deficiency of praise*; *totally* instead of *quite*. Some grammatical deviations also result from faithfulness to the latter text: *I have heard say*; *to see his works given as examples*; *deign to honour me with some praise*. He skips the address *Courteous Reader* and the inserted remarks *tho' I have been, for what reason I know not*, as they are not present in the French version. He allows himself some liberties only with *for twenty-five years* instead of *a full quarter of a century*. At times he even paradoxically sticks closer to the original than the relay translation as he does with the expression *without vanity*; but unlike this version, he does not allow himself to separate the sentences.

In the second excerpt, similar trends can be observed:

This doctrine, my friends, is reason and wisdom; but after all, do not depend too much upon your own industry, and frugality, and prudence, though excellent things, for they may all be blasted without the blessing of heaven; and therefore ask that blessing humbly, and be not uncharitable to those that at present seem to want it, but comfort and help them. Remember Job suffered, and was afterwards prosperous.

And now to conclude, experience keeps a dear school, but fools will learn in no other, and scarce in that, for it is true, we may give advice, but we cannot give conduct, as Poor Richard says: however, remember this, they that won't be counseled, can't be helped, as Poor Richard says: and farther, that if you will not hear reason, she'll surely rap your knuckles. (Franklin 1758: 6)

Cette doctrine mes amis, et celle *de la raison & de la prudence*. N'allez pas cependant vous confier uniquement à votre *industrie* à votre *vigilance* & à votre *économie*. Ce sont d'excellentes choses à la vérité mais elles vous seront tout-à-fait inutiles si vous n'avez, avant tout les bénédictions du Ciel. Demandez donc humblement ces bénédictions ne soyez point insensibles aux besoins de ceux a qui elles sont refusées mais donnez-leur *des consolations & des secours*. Souvenez-vous que *Job fut pauvre & qu'ensuite il redevint heureux. Je n'en dirai pas davantage.*

L'expérience tient une école où les leçons coûtent cher; mais c'est la seule où les insensés puissent s'instruire encore n'apprennent-ils pas grand' chose: car, comme le dit le bonhomme Richard, "on peut donner un bon avis, mais non pas une bonne conduite. Ressouvenez-vous donc que celui qui ne sait pas recevoir un bon conseil ne peut pas non plus être secouru d'une manière utile; car, comme dit le bonhomme Richard, « Si vous ne voulez pas écouter la raison, elle ne manquera pas de se faire « sentir ». (Saunders 1777: 24–25).

Това, приѧтели мои, ны по8чава правдата и раз8ма: словесностьта и м8дростьта. Не дѣйте пакъ обаче да сѧ надѣйте самѡ на дѣлото си, на прилѣжанïето си и на икономïата си. Тïѧ са изрѧдны вещи воистина, но нищо не ще вы ползоватъ, ако да не имате, прежде всѣхъ, небесното благословенïе, и недѣйте бади ѿнюдъ (хичь) нечувственни камъ онïѧ, които иматъ потрѣба ѿ васъ, ами ги оутѣшавайте и имъ помагайте, знающе, чи и Iωвъ бѧше сиромахъ, но ѿ сетнѣ стана пакъ благопол8ченъ.

Опыто е едно училище, гдѣто маѳимытѣ сѧ продаватъ скапѡ: но той самѡ може да на8чи без8мнытѣ и пакъ не много нѣщо: защо може да даде едно наставленïе, но не и добро поведенïе. Помнете прочие, чи който не знае да прïемне единъ добръ сов8тъ, том8 не може и да сѧ помогне ползователнѡ: защо, както каже добрый Рïхардъ, ты ако не щешь да посл8шашь правдината, тïя сама ще направи да я чувствовашь. (Franklin 1837: 43–44).

[This, my friends, teaches us truth and reason: literature and wisdom. Do not, however, rely solely on your activity, your diligence and your economy. These are excellent things, in truth, but they won't serve you at all if you do not have, above all, the blessing of heaven, and do not be quite insensitive to those who need you, but give them comfort and help, knowing that Job was also poor, but then he became happy again.

[...] Experience is a school where lessons are sold at a high price: but it is the only one that can instruct the foolish, and only a little: for [...] it can give a good education, but not a good conduct. Remember then that he who does not know how to receive good advice, cannot be helped in a useful way either: for, as good Richard says, if you do not want to listen to the truth, the truth will make you hear it.] (Our reverse translation).

Gavril Krŭstevich ignores the sentence added in the relay translation: *Je n'en dirai pas davantage*. He omits the first mention of *as Poor Richard says*. He translates *wisdom* and *reason* correctly, but adds two more words: *truth* and *literature*. He uses double translation in brackets ѿнюдъ *(хичь)*, which means *quite*. He divides the sentences as they are divided in the French version and adheres to the grammatical structures of the latter. Some more serious deviations from the original are also due to his close adherence to the relay translation: *Experience is a school where lessons are sold at a high price* instead of *experience keeps a dear school*; *Job was also poor, but then he became happy again* instead of *Job suffered, and was afterwards prosperous*; *it can give a good education, but not a good conduct* instead of *we may give advice, but we cannot give conduct*; *if you do not want to listen to the truth, the truth will make you hear it* instead of *if you will not hear reason, she'll surely rap your knuckles*.

We can spot in Krŭstevich's translation, which is strongly influenced by the relay translation, a few others of Berman's deforming tendencies (1999: 53–56). Linked to the requirements of fluidity, semantic explanation and sentence structure, rationalization, clarification and expansion seek to elucidate the translated text. The rationalization refers to the syntactic structures and to the punctuation of the original, in other words, to the order of the discourse. The clarification concerns the level of semantic clarity of the text to be translated and tends to define the indefinite. This immanent tendency of translation manifests itself in the explicitation of the implicit, the explanatory periphrases, and the additions. It results in an increased length of the translation compared to that of the original. In this case, the Bulgarian translation is a little longer than the original. That is especially visible in the second excerpt quoted above, which is within the norm.

Despite its imperfections, additions, even the distortions it contains, Krŭstevich's translation testifies to his courage to go against the current of the dominant trend to defend his translation project. The contradiction between this fairly clear and well-defined project and the sometimes altered result is explained by the transition from the relay translation. The chosen title, *Мудрость добраго Рихарда*, already reveals a double deformation compared to the original title and to the French title. After all, his translation is quite close to the American original, despite going through the French version. This oddity could be explained either by an elective affinity or by the similarities presented by two young nations, the Bulgarian and the American one, which had the same economic and educational priorities and an equal value system that placed labor and study at the forefront. *Мудрость добраго Рихарда* is an educational project, since Franklin's life is an example of success through hard work, perseverance, diligence, and discipline.

5 Conclusion

We can apply two general theoretical statements to *Мудрость добраго Рихарда*, which is an eloquent example of real multilingualism within the multi-ethnic and multilingual Ottoman Empire. Firstly, translations were used to compensate for a lack of authorial works during the Revival. Secondly, the translated literature of the Enlightenment is characterized by universality and manages to enter into intercultural communication with different peoples and traditions, some of which, such as the Bulgarian, are too distant in level of development and mentality. Therefore, those books were a real challenge not only, or at least not so much, in terms of the target text itself, but in terms of socio-cultural perception of the source text (Aretov 2011).

Krŭstevich's translation reflects the didactics of the time and the desire of the intelligentsia to foster respect in readers for the Bulgarian language. Its benefits "should be sought in two directions: a general enlightenment benefit from the knowledge of the world around us and a financial benefit from the translated prose publishing" (Aleksandrova 2018: 164–165). In a broader sense, the target text and the relay translation clearly specify the processes and mechanisms that led to the multi-faceted social functions of literature and its dominant importance in the culture of the Bulgarian Revival (Zaharieva 2010: 22, 36). On the one hand, relay translations led to more objective assessments of the translation phenomenon. On the other hand, they stimulated general theoretical reflections on the eternal and universal values contained in and transmitted through books. Reverence for books and for their defining role in the success of specific translations is characteristic of the Bulgarian context.

Мудрость добраго Рихарда is one of the voices of modernity, a new expression of thinking, orientation and choice of cultural values, regardless of the specific ways, techniques and models used to achieve this purpose. Gavril Krŭstevich and other translators from the Revival paved the way for the cultural rise of Bulgaria after the Independence. One of the priorities was the integration of the young country into the European tradition, an integration realized thanks to the efforts of intellectuals who had the insight to look beyond national borders.

Following Bulgaria's Independence, the translator came to be acknowledged as a respectable profession. Translators assumed, however, full responsibility for the selection of the works to be translated, deemed suitable for the education and acculturation of the readers. They were writers, scholars, and even politicians, who were aware of the importance of translation for the inclusion of world literature into the national literary polysystem and for the satisfaction of the needs of the educated people.

6 References

Aleksandrova, Nadezhda. 2018. Osobenosti na balgarskata prevodna knizhnina v osmanskiya kontekst na XIX vek. [Peculiarities of the Literature Translated in Bulgarian in the Ottoman Context of the 19th Century]. *Annual of Sofia University "St Kliment Ohridski"*, Faculty of Slavic studies, 154–203.

Aretov, Nikolay. 1995. *Balgarskoto vazrazhdane i Evropa* [The Bulgarian Revival and Europe]. Sofia: Kralitsa Mab.

Aretov, Nikolay. 2011. *Balgarskite interpretatsii na beletristikata ot epochata na Prosvechtenieto* [The Bulgarian Interpretations of the Belles-lettres from the Enlightenment Period] https://aretov.queenmab.eu/archives/reception/85-types-of-reception-of-translated-european-fiction.html (accessed 10 June 2022).

Benbasad, Albert. 2019. 300 godini s "Robinzon Kruzo". Svetovni i balgarski literaturno-izdatelski proektsii [300 Years with *Robinson Crusoe*. Literary and Publishing Screenings in the World and in Bulgaria]. *Kultura* 10.06.2019, https://kultura.bg/web/300- (accessed 10 June 2022).

Benjamin, Walter. 2000. The Task of the Translator. An introduction to the translation of Baudelaire's *Tableaux Parisiens* [1923]. Translated by Harry Zohn. In Lawrence Venuti (ed.), *The Translation Studies Reader*, 15–23. London: Routledge.

Berman, Antoine. 1999. *La traduction et la lettre ou l'auberge du lointain*. Paris: Le Seuil.

Casanova, Pascale. 2004. *The World Republic of Letters*. Translated by Malcolm DeBevoise. Cambridge, MA, London: Harvard University Press.

Damyanova, Rumyana. 2004. *Otvad tekstovete: kulturni mehanizmi na Vazrazhdaneto* [Beyond the Texts. Cultural Mechanisms of the Revival]. Sofia: Elgateh.

Damyanova, Rumyana. 2016. Tipologiya na priviligirovanite glasove prez Vazrazhdaneto. [Typology of the Privileged Voices in the Revival]. In Anna Aleksieva, Nadya Danova, Nikolay Chernokozhev (eds.), *Kultura, identichnosti, samneniya* [Culture, Identities, Doubts], 495–499. Sofia: Izdatelstvo na BAN "Prof. Marin Drinov".

Danova, Nadya. 2012. Fragmenti ot istoriyata na izgrazhdaneto na pravna kultura pri balgarite [Fragments from the History of the Establishing of Legal Culture among the Bulgarians]. *Kritika i Humanizam*, 37(2), 201–265.

Defo, Daniel. 1849. *Chudesiite na Robensona Kruso* [Robinson Crusoe's Wonders]. Prevod Ivan Bogorov. *Tsarigradski vestnik*, 1848–1849.

Defo, Daniel. 1858. *Robinzon. Sakratena prikazka za detsa* [Robinson. An Abridged Tale for Children]. Prevod ot Ivan Gruev. Belgrad: Pravitelstvenata knigopechyatna.

Defo, Daniel. 1868. *Robinzon na ostrova si. Prikazka tvarde nravouchitelna* [Robinson on His Island. A Quite Moralistic Tale]. Prevedena i izdadena ot Petko R. Slaveykov za upotreblenie v uchilishtata. Sofia: Pechatnitsa na Kushliev.

Dollerup, Cay. 2000. 'Relay' and 'Support' Translation. In Andrew Chesterman, Natividad Gallardo, San Salvador et al. (eds.), *Translation in Context: Selected Contributions from the EST Congress, Granada 1998*, 17–26. Amsterdam, Philadelphia: John Benjamins.

Eco, Umberto. 1979. *Lector in fabula*. Milano: Bompiani.
Eco, Umberto. 1990. *I limiti dell'interpretazione*. Milano: Bompiani.
Filipov, Vladimir. 2004. *Pronikvane na angliyskata i amerikanskata knizhnina v Balgariya prez Vazrazhdaneto*. [Penetration of the English and the American Literature in Bulgaria during the Revival]. Sofia: Universitetsko izdatelstvo "Sv. Kliment Ohridski".
Franklin, Benjamin. 1758. *The Way to Wealth*. In *Poor Richard's Almanack*. https://minio.la.utexas.edu/webeditor-files/coretexts/pdf/175820franklin20wealth.pdf (accessed 10 June 2022).
Franklin, Benjamin. 1837. *Mudrost dobrago Richarda* [The Wisdom of the Good Richard]. Prevod ot frenski ezik Gavril Krŭstevich, redaktsiya Rayno Popovich. V Budime grade: Pismeni Kral vseuchilichta vengersk.
Franklin, Benjamin. 1868. *Iskustvoto da stane chelovek bogat* [The Art of Becoming Rich]. Prevod ot nemski ezik Nikola Pŭrvanov. *Makedoniya*, II(21), 2; II(22), 1–2.
Franklin, Benjamin. 1869. *Siromah Bogdan ili sredstvo za obogatyavane, knizhka mnogo pouchitelna za naroda* [Poor Bogdan or a means of enrichment, a very instructive booklet for the people]. Tsarigrad: Pechatnitsata na v. Makedoniya, 26–30.
Franklin, Benjamin. 2011. *Patyat kam parite i uspeha. Dvuezichno izdanie* [The Way to Money and Success. Bilingual edition]. Prevod Stanimir Yotov. Sofia: Pergament-Press.
Genchev, Nikolay. 1988. *Balgarskata kultura XV–XIX v. Lektsii*. [The Bulgarian Culture 15th–19th Centuries. Lectures]. Sofia: Universitetsko izdatelstvo "Sv. Kliment Ogrdiski".
Ilchev, Stefan, Ana Ivanova, Angelina Dimova, Maria Pavlova. 1974. *Rechnik na redki, ostareli i dialektni dumi v literaturata ni ot XIX i X vek* [Dictionary of Rare, Obsolete and Dialect Words in Our Literature from the 19th and the 20th Century]. Sofia: Izdatelstvo na BAN.
Karamzin, Nikolay. 1858. *Sirota Tsvetana*. Pobalgaril Yoakim Gruev [Poor Tsvetana. Bulgarised by Yoakim Gruev]. Tsarigrad: v knigopechatnitsata na D. Tsankova i B. Mirkova.
Kepov, Ivan. 1929. Gavril Krŭstevich. https://liternet.bg/publish10/ikepov/gkrystevich.htm (accessed 10 June 2022).
Kristeva, Irena. 2008. De la pulsion de traduire aux limites de l'interprétation. In Dina Mantchéva et Raya Kountchéva (eds.), *L'homme dans le texte*, 391–398. Sofia: Universitetsko izdatelstvo "Sv. Kliment Ohridski".
Kristeva, Irène. 2011. Déformations inconscientes en traduction. *Nasledje*, 8(19), 373–382.
Lekov, Docho. 1982. *Literatura, obshtestvo, kultura. Literaturno-sotsiologicheski i literaturno-istoricheski problemi na Balgarskoto vazrazhdane* [Literature, Society, Culture. Literary-Sociological and Literary-Historical Problems of the Bulgarian Revival]. Sofia: Narodna prosveta.
Manolakiev, Hristo. 1994. Nablyudeniya varhu literaturnata retseptsiya prez Vazrazhdaneto [Observations on the Literary Reception during the Revival]. In *Studiorum causa*. 215–233. Sofia: Universitetsko izdatelstvo "Sv. Kliment Ohridski".
Pileva, Maria. 2016a. *Religioznite motivi v balgarskite prevodi na angloezichnata beletristika prez XIX*. [Religious Motifs in the Bulgarian Translations of the English Belles-lettres in the 19th Century]. Sofia University "Sv. Kliment Ohridski". http://digilib.nalis.bg/dspviewerb/srv/image_singpdff/f27f9482-910e-4101-83d3-09c9de39a48c
Pileva, Maria. 2016b. Balgarskite prevodi na Robinzon Crusoe – detstvo, yunoishestvo, zastoy i sryalost [Bulgarian Translations of „Robinson Crusoe" – Childhood, Adolescence, Stagnation and Maturity]. *Literaturata*, 17, 195–244.

Pileva, Maria. 2018. *Bunt. Nadezhda. Izkuplenie. Angloezichnite prevodi ot balgarskiya XIX vek.* [Revolt. Hope. Redemption. Translations from English during the Bulgarian 19th Century]. Sofia: Kralitsa Mab.

Saunders, Richard [Benjamin Franklin]. 1777. *La Science du Bonhomme Richard, ou moyen facile de payer les impôts*. Traduit de l'anglais. Paris: chez Ruaut, Librairie de la Harpe.

Shipside, Steve. 2008. *Patyat kam bogatstvoto* [The Way to Wealth]. Benjamin Franklin. *52 significant ideas and their interpretation*. Sofia: InfoDar.

Schmid, Hristofor. 1971. *Navodnenie na Dunav*. Pobalgaril Stefan Bobchev [Flooding of the Danube. Bulgarised by Stefan Bobchev]. Tsarigrad: Izdanie na Balgarskoto pechatarsko druzhestvo "Promishlenie".

Trendafilov, Vladimir. 1996. *Neizlichimiya obraz v ogledaloto. Aktualnata balgarska retseptsiya na Anglia, anglichanina i angliyskata missal prez 19 i nachaloto na 20 vek* [The Indelible Image in the Mirror. The Current Bulgarian Reception of England, of the Englishman and of English Thought in the 19th and Early 20th Century]. Sofia: Kralitsa Mab.

Washbourne, Kelly. 2013. Nonlinear Narratives: Paths of Indirect and Relay Translation. *Meta*, 58(3), 607–625.

Zaharieva, Yordanka. 2010. *Promeni v (po)znanieto u vazrozhdenskiya balgarin*. [Changes in the Knowledge of the Bulgarian in the Revival]. Sofia: Avangard Prima.

Iulia Dondorici
Plurilingualism in 19th-Century Romanian Literatures

A Case Study of Alecu Russo

Abstract: This article deals with the question of plurilingualism in 19th-century Romanian literatures. Romanian literatures have never been monolingual or monocultural; throughout their history, they have been defined by a plurilingualism which, in its different historical constellations, has often been linked to a whole series of migratory phenomena, as well as to the coexistence of a multitude of languages and idioms in Romanian culture and society. Nevertheless, the importance of plurilingualism in Romanian literatures has been obscured by literary historiography as well as by the majority of critical studies, including the most recent ones. This elision assumes diverse forms, such as marginalization, ignorance, rendering plurilingualism invisible, or denial. Through these biases, historic accounts construct the image of a homogeneous Romanian literature that is fundamentally monolingual. This study is conceived on three axes. First, I define the more general characteristics of literary plurilingualism in the 19th century in its relations to the specific multilingual configurations in Romanian culture and society. Second, I show how this plurilingualism manifests itself in the literary works of one of the most representative writers of 19th-century Romania, Alecu Russo (1819–1859). Finally, I briefly point out how literary history managed to make the fundamental plurilingualism of Romanian literatures in the 19th century invisible by creating the narrative of a monolingual national literature.

Keywords: Plurilingualism, Romanian literature, 19th-Century Literature, Alecu Russo, Literary Field, Translation

1 Introduction

While the majority of studies on literary plurilingualism focus on the premodern period in Europe as well as on literature of the twentieth and twenty-first centu-

Iulia Dondorici, Freie Universität Berlin, e-mail: dondorici@zedat.fu-berlin.de

ries, the phenomenon of plurilingualism is as old as literature itself.[1] The same applies to Romanian literatures.[2] Constituting the very bases of cultural and literary exchange, plurilingualism had a foundational impact on the 16th and 17th centuries; later on, it accelerated literary and cultural development, serving as a catalyst in key moments of literary life. Moreover, a whole series of literary periods, such as the 19th century or literary movements such as the avant-gardes of the twentieth century, only become intelligible when analyzed in the plurilingual, international and transnational configurations in which they were embedded.

To reveal the whole complexity and significance of literary plurilingualism in the 19th century, a combination of two methodological approaches seems appropriate: a sociological approach based on Pierre Bourdieu's field theory and an immanent analysis of representative plurilingual texts of 19th-century Romanian literature. Thus, I will situate the plurilingual works and writers of the 19th century within the emerging Romanian literary field, focusing on the most manifest forms of plurilingualism specific to Romanian literatures, namely polyglot writers and their bilingual works.

In this article, the use of the term "plurilingualism" will be limited to those cases of several idioms at work within a single literary text or within the body of an author's work.[3] Like Elvezio Canonica, I will distinguish between a simulta-

---

[1] "While literary multilingualism has become an important research area during the last two decades, scholarship on multilingual literature from Europe seems to suffer from a historical bias. This 'blind spot' of scholarship becomes evident as a chronological gap: up to now, as a quick survey shows, research has mostly focused either on pre-modern periods (e.g., Medieval and Renaissance multilingualism), or on avant-garde modernism (e.g., Futurism and Dada), and on the present (e.g., postcolonial literature, literature of migration, etc.). The nineteenth century in particular appears to remain a sort of 'dark continent' of literary multilingualism scholarship" (Anokhina, Dembeck, and Weissmann 2019: 1).

[2] The use of the plural to refer to what is usually called "Romanian literature" is not accidental. My aim is to highlight the diversity of Romanian literature, and more specifically the fact that the literature written on the territories of Romania is not and has never been exclusively "Romanian." The term "Romanian" in this article is not meant to suggest that literature belongs to a nation or people, nor to the territory of a country.

[3] Referring to Rainier Grutman's groundbreaking studies, which use the term heterolingualism (*hétérolinguisme*) to refer to "la présence *dans un texte* d'idiomes étrangers, sous quelque forme que ce soit, aussi bien que de variétés (sociales, régionales ou chronologiques) de la langue principale" [the presence in a text of foreign idioms, in whatever form, as well as varieties (social, regional or chronological) of the main language] (Grutman 1997: 37), many authors use the terms "plurilingualism" and "multilingualism" in this specific meaning.

Other researchers attempt to differentiate between multilingualism and plurilingualism. For example, Tristan Leperlier uses "la notion de plurilinguisme, qui invite à observer des relations

neous plurilingualism and an alternating one. If the first supposes "la cohabitation de plusieurs langues [...] à l'intérieur de la même œuvre" [the cohabitation of several idioms [...] within a single work], the second is found "dans le cas où l'auteur change de langue à l'intérieur de son système littéraire pour produire des œuvres monolingues, mais dans une autre langue" [in the case in which an author changes languages within his literary system to produce monolingual works, but in a different language] (Canonica 2015: 64). As we will see, most writers and their literary works intermingle these forms.

2 Plurilingualism in Romanian society and literatures of the 19th century

Within different constellations, plurilingualism constituted the dominant model in Romanian literatures in the 18th and 19th centuries.[4] The most important writers of the 18th century – Ienăchiță Văcărescu (1740–1797), Ion Budai-Deleanu (1760–1820), Dinicu Golescu (1777–1830), Iancu Văcărescu (1786–1863) and Gheorghe Asachi (1788–1869) – are all polyglots educated in the great cities of Poland or Russia, and towards the end of the century, more and more in Central and Western Europe. The end of the 18th century and the first decades of the 19th century (1779–1826) began with a developing "westernization process" within Romanian society.[5] Describing this period, historians highlight

---

actuelles entre langues, de définition réciproques, de rapport de force, et de transferts ; plutôt que celle de multilinguisme qui postule une égalité entre une infinité de langues" [the notion of plurilingualism, which invites the observation of current relations between languages, of reciprocal definitions, of power relations, and of transfers; rather than that of multilingualism, which postulates an equality between an infinite number of languages] (Leperlier 2020). I have chosen this term in order to underline precisely these power relations between different languages, as this aspect plays a key role in the development of Romanian literatures throughout their history.

4 As far as the European literatures of the nineteenth century are concerned, Anokhina, Dembeck, and Weismann. conclude that "the 'monolingual paradigm' does not simply supplant previous multilingual practices. These practices rather enter into a potentially conflicting, but generally creative tension with the now dominant ethnocentric concepts of nation, language, and culture, without disappearing. All over the nineteenth century, multilingual traditions remain largely present in the European literatures." (Anokhina, Dembeck, and Weissmann 2019: 5)

5 See Călinescu (1986: 61). All English translations of Romanian and French texts are mine.

> [...] dubla influență, greacă și franceză, pe care cultura română o suferea, începând chiar de la limbă (cea greacă era ca și oficială, cea franceză o concura deja de la mijlocul secolului XVIII mai ales ca limbă a culturii
> [the double influence, Greek and French, manifest in Romanian culture, starting with the linguistic situation: Greek being the official language, while French competed with it as early as mid-century, notably as a language of culture] (Manolescu 1997: 102).[6]

In his work *Iassy et ses habitants en 1840* [Iassy and its inhabitants in 1840], Alecu Russo gives an overview of the plurilingual configuration specific to the Moldovan capital in the middle of the 19th century. According to Russo, populations of numerous origins (Romanian, Greek, German, Russian, Polish, Armenian, Jewish, etc.) in the lower urban classes spoke in their respective languages, with Romanian being the common language of communication. Greek was no longer spoken except by those who did not understand French or Romanian.[7] The aristocracy used French in salons and in private correspondence and spoke Romanian while performing administrative duties and communicating with domestic servants. Indeed, in this time, in the two Romanian principalities, as well as in Transylvania, "le monolinguisme est surtout un mythe" [monolingualism is essentially a myth], while "la diglossie, voire la polyglossie seraient pluton la règle générale" [bilingualism, even polylingualism was the general rule] (Moura 1999: 73).

We can thus talk about plurilingualism in literature and widespread polyglossia in society, but the two phenomena only partially overlap. Indeed, literary plurilingualism is not an expression of the polyglossia of the Romanian societies of the era; it is merely the linguistic configuration characteristic of the dominant classes, reflected in the literary domain. At the same time, the Romanian language was in the process of becoming the national language. Next to Greek, which became less and less widespread in the second half of the 19th century, only Western languages, which constituted important cultural and literary capital (namely French, Italian, and German) were used in local literary production. Nevertheless, far from being the privilege of writers of aristocratic origins or of the bourgeoisie educated in the West, plurilingualism was as widespread in Moldova as in Wallachia, including among authors from the popular urban classes. Thus, Anton Pann (1790–1854), born of a mixed Roma-Greek family closer to the bottom of the social ladder with whom he experienced a

---

6 On the French influence on Romanian society at the beginning of the nineteenth century, see also Djuvara 1989: 307–312.
7 See Alecu Russo, "Iașii și locuitorii lor în 1840 (Fragmente)." In Alecu Russo (1985: 294).

nomadic childhood, spoke Russian and Romanian, among other languages, all while writing his literary works exclusively in Romanian.

Among all idioms spoken and written in the Romanian principalities, French had a particular status, in society as well as in literature. In his study *Littératures francophones et théorie postcoloniale*, Jean-Marc Moura includes Romania, along with Egypt and Bulgaria, among the "pays non francophones, mais appartenant officiellement aux institutions de la Francophonie, par suite [...] de liens culturels particuliers" [non-French-speaking countries that belonged officially however to the institutions of Francophonie, as a result of [...] particular cultural links] (Moura 1999: 26). Indeed, there are numerous similarities between the Romanian literary field of the 19th century and those of the postcolonial Francophone countries in the second half of the twentieth century.[8] In social terms, both cases denote a "francophonie des élites" [Francophonie of the elite] (Moura 1999: 34). For the Romanian writer as for the postcolonial Francophone writer, both placed in a situation of "dépendance symbolique" [symbolic dependence] upon a Parisian center, French "est moins une langue de communication, un moyen d'échanger des informations, qu'une langue de recours" [is less a language of communication, a way to exchange information, than a language of prestige] (Moura 1999: 62). Consequently, the literary plurilingualism of the Romanian 19th century intersected with relations of power between, on one side, French and Romanian and, on the other side, Romanian and the idioms of minority populations with less cultural capital, such as the Turkish and Tatar idioms, or the Russian, Romani and Armenian idioms. As Tristan Leperlier puts it for Algeria, in the 19th-century Romanian literary space, language, as a "potentiel objet d'identification nationale" [poten-

---

8 See Djuvara (1989: 308): "Le Français d'aujourd'hui n'a plus qu'une vague idée de ce qu'a représenté l'influence française en Europe au XVIIIe et dans la première moitié du XIXe siècle. De Lisbonne à Saint-Petersbourg, de Stockholm à Athènes, les moeurs, les institutions, la pensée, la langue, ont été partout bouleversés par l'intrusion du modèle français. Mais nulle part en Europe, l'influence française n'aura été plus profonde qu'en pays roumain [...] On peut dire sans exagération que pendant plus d'un siècle, du début du XIXe siècle et jusqu'au lendemain de la première guerre mondiale, les Roumains ont été littéralement ‚colonisés' par la France – sans presence du colonisateur." [Today's Frenchman has only a vague idea of what French influence meant in Europe in the 18th and first half of the 19th century. From Lisbon to Saint Petersburg, from Stockholm to Athens, morals, institutions, thought and language were all overturned by the intrusion of the French model. But nowhere in Europe was the French influence more profound than in Romania [...] It is no exaggeration to say that for more than a century, from the beginning of the nineteenth century until the aftermath of the First World War, the Romanians were literally 'colonized' by France – without any presence of the colonizer.]

tial object of national identification] is also, "contre ce que Bourdieu appelle la 'communauté linguistique', un facteur d'inégalités symboliques, socio-politiques, mais aussi spécifiquement littéraires" [contrary to what Bourdieu calls the 'linguistic community,' a factor of symbolic, socio-political, yet also specifically literary inequalities] (Leperlier 2000).

3 Plurilingual writers in the emergent Romanian literary field

The Romanian literatures of the 19th century are eclectic, dominated by pre-Romanticism and Romanticism, but with strong classicist, baroque and Realist tendencies.[9] The most representative writers of this time included Costache Negruzzi (1808–1868), Mihail Kogălniceanu (1817–1891), Alecu Russo (1819–1859), Ion Ghica (1816–1897), Costache Negri (1812–1876), Nicolae Bălcescu (1819–1852), Ion Heliade Rădulescu (1802–1872), Iacob Negruzzi (1842–1932) and B.P. Hașdeu (1838–1907). The majority of them created truly bilingual literary works, in French[10], in German[11] or Italian[12] and in Romanian. These writers chose "foreign" languages to compose their correspondences and their diaries, while reserving Romanian for their literary and journalistic writings destined for immediate publication. The critic Nicolae Manolescu describes this particular linguistic constellation as follows:

> Franceza este o limbă pe care ei o învață de copii și o vorbesc apoi în societate. Este expresia educației pe care o primesc, de multe ori în străinătate. Tuturor intelectualilor pașoptiști și din generația următoare le vine mai la îndemână să se exprime în franceză, în care văd în plus limba par excellence a unor îndeletniciri (cum ar fi jurnalele intime și corespondența) [...] Româna le pretindea un efort pe care-l făceau în operele publice, din patriotism, continuând a prefera, în cele private, înlesnirile francezei, mai cu seamă în condițiile în care nimeni din jur nu se abate de la regulă
> [French is the language that they learned in childhood and then speak in society. It is the expression of the education that is offered to them, often abroad. All intellectuals of 1848, as well as the subsequent generation, feel more at ease in French, which they even perceive as the language *par excellence* for some activities (like private journals or letter exchange) [...] Expressing oneself in Romanian required of them efforts that they made, first

---

9 See Cornea (1972: 77–88).
10 Alecu Russo, Ion Ghica, C. Negri, C.A. Rosetti, Alexandru Odobescu.
11 Titu Maiorescu, Iacob Negruzzi.
12 Ion Heliade Rădulescu.

and foremost out of patriotism, in those works destined for publication, all while continuing to use French in their private writings, especially since no one around is deviating from the rule] (Manolescu 1997: 267).

Such is the case of Ion Ghica's *Scrisori către Vasile Alexandri* [Letters to Vasile Alecsandri] and of most of Costache Negri's correspondence. Similarly, C.A. Rosetti wrote his diary in Romanian, while for the rich correspondence with his wife, the journalist Maria Rosetti, he chose French. Iacob Negruzzi wrote his diary in German while studying in Berlin. Alexandru Odobescu had a very lively correspondence with his family in French. Kogălniceanu's correspondence with his father between 1834 and 1838 was written in Romanian, while that addressed to his sisters in French.[13]

While Manolescu accurately perceives the privileged position of French among the Romanian intellectuals, including in their private lives, the question about the choice of language in their literary writing proves more complex and goes beyond the issue of individual language acquisition. Since the writers referred to by Manolescu show a perfect command of Romanian in their literary and journalistic works, it seems that their choice of language depends not so much on the level of mastery of the languages, but rather involves strategies of legitimation and recognition within the literary field. It is in relation to the writers' position in the Romanian and French literary space of the time that we must (re)consider their choice of language and the plurilingual poetics deployed in their works.

At first glance, the choice of a plurilingual literary writing on the part of so many Romanian writers of this era may seem paradoxical to us, if not even contradictory, since in their programmatic writings (literary programs, manifestos, etc.) these same writers never passed up the opportunity to demand a literature of Romanian expression and local inspiration. In this sense, the program of the review *Dacia literară* [Literary Dacia], formulated by Mihail Kogălniceanu, himself a bilingual writer, is exemplary:

> Mai în toate zilele ies de sub teasc cărți în limba românească. Dar ce folos! că sînt numai traducții din alte limbi și încă și acele de ar fi bune. [...] Istoria noastră are destule fapte eroice, frumoasele noastre țeri sunt destul de mari, obiceiurile noastre sunt destul de pitorești și poetice pentru ca să putem găsi și la noi sujeturi de scris, fără ca să avem pentru aceasta trebuință să ne împrumutăm de la alte nații

---

13 The letters that are mentioned here all have literary value — Manolescu, for example, even considers those of Costache Negri, Iacob Negruzzi and Alexandru Odobescu to be more important than their actual literary writings. See Manolescu (1997: 241, 255, 266).

[More and more books in Romanian come out of the woodwork every day. But what is the use! They are only translations from other languages and if at least they were good. [...] Our history has enough heroic deeds, our beautiful lands are large enough, our customs are picturesque and poetic enough for us to find subjects to write about, without having to borrow from other nations] (Kogălniceanu 1840, cited in Călinescu 1986: 181).

In reality, like all writers occupying dominated positions in "la République mondiale des lettres" [the World Republic of Letters], 19th-century Romanian writers were also divided between the will and the necessity to illustrate, through their creations, the richness of the national language, and the desire to be read in a dominant language, the only possibility for them to gain recognition and be read by an international public (Casanova 2008: 359–365). The hegemonic position of French language and literature in relation to the emerging Romanian language and literature was in this way at the heart of the tensions and hesitations that have marked Romanian writers in their choice of language.

By the end of the 19th century, the Romanian literary field was in an emergent phase, characterized, as many other dominated plurilingual spaces, by the fact that "lutte politique et littéraire se rejoignent dans le nationalisme" [political and literary struggles are joined together in nationalism] (Leperlier 2020). This field arose from the demand to create a literature that is both written in the Romanian language and inspired by local realities. The imperative to write in Romanian is doubled by a process of unification of the language and the spelling, in order to build a national literature adapted to the needs of a local readership. Yet, this national literature, in which bilingual works seem to be the rule, deals with local subject matters informed by models of French and, more generally, Western aesthetics. Thus, the plurilingualism of writers and of the readership, anchored in the process of multiple cultural exchanges, transfers and translation processes, constitutes the foundation for the emergence of a "national" literature of Romanian expression and the development of a local literary field.

In this context, those writers who choose French are explicitly targeting an international Francophone public. It is in this way that, during his studies in France, Mihail Kogălniceanu wrote and published in French on the history and society of Romania.[14] Conversely, after his return to Moldova, he published mostly in Romanian, seizing the opportunity to assert himself in the emerging

---

14 Kogălniceanu published a sketch on Romanian literature in Lehmann's *Magazin für die Literatur des Auslandes*, followed by the brochure *Esquisse sur l'histoire, les moeurs et la langue de Cigains* (Berlin and Behr 1837), as well as, in the same year, the first (and only) volume of a *History of Wallachia, Moldavia, and the Transdanubian Vlachs*.

local literary arena. Indeed, Kogălniceanu is among the writers who participated in the creation of specific instances of production, reception, and recognition in the Romanian literary field. They established literary reviews and publishing houses, wrote literary texts and critical articles, and established the rules of orthography for the Romanian language. Among the numerous revues appearing in this time, *Curierul de ambe sexe* [Courier of Both Sexes] (1837), *Dacia literară* [Literary Dacia] (1840), *Propășirea* [The Progress] (1844), and *România literară* [Literary Romania] (1855) are the most notable. Beginning in 1821, theaters and a Romanian press emerged as well. The position of pioneering writers within the field of Romanian literature grew more and more influential, such that gradually the field itself stabilized and received more recognition. While a public able to consume Romanian literary and language production was emerging, it became more and more attractive for certain writers to write in Romanian, particularly because the French field, from which they were progressively distancing themselves, failed to offer them opportunities for publication and recognition. At this point, we might conclude that the writers engaging in the local literary field and "winning" the battle for "national" recognition were precisely those who had "lost" the game in the (Francophone) transnational literary field (or who even lacked the necessary symbolic and cultural capital to play there). As a matter of fact, Kogălniceanu's political and literary activities go hand in hand, both arising from a project of modernization through the "nationalization" of Romanian political, economic, and cultural life.

Even more complex and ambiguous than the case of Mihail Kogălniceanu is that of Alecu Russo. After having studied in Switzerland and Vienna[15], Russo returned to Iassy in 1837. In the following years, he took several trips to Moldova and Wallachia, which he recounted in French. His life in the Moldovan capital inspired him to write *Iassy et ses habitants en 1840* [Iassy and its inhabitants in 1840], also written in French. In the same period, Russo published a number of essays on linguistic, social and political issues, some of them written in Romanian and others in French.[16] In Romanian, Russo wrote plays, one of which, entitled *Băcălia ambițioasă* [The Ambitious Grocer's Wife] (1846), performed in Iassy the same year, resulted in his forced exile to the Soveja Monastery (February – April 1846). The diary that he kept there, also written in French, ranks among Russo's best works. His second exile came at the end of the Revolution of

---

15 At the age of ten, Russo went to school at the *Institute François Naville* in Vernier, close to Geneva (1829–1835), and later moved to Vienna (1835–1836).
16 These are "*Studie moldovană*", "*Cugetări*", "*Dezrobirea țiganilor*", and "*Studii naționale*", to mention only the most important.

1848.[17] Taking refuge in Paris, Russo wrote his best-known work in French: *Cântarea României* [The Chant of Romania] – an epic poem which became emblematic of the nascent national literature. Translated into Romanian around 1850, probably by Nicolae Bălcescu, another representative writer of this period, the text also circulated in a later translation by Russo, while the French manuscript has not been found. Once again, we see the essential role played by translation (also in the form of auto-translation or co-translation) and by "foreign" languages in the same process of creating Romanian literatures.[18]

Russo's hesitation in choosing between Romanian and French is explained in part by his conviction, largely shared by writers of his generation, that the conditions for the emergence of a Romanian literature had not yet been fully met. The state of the literary field, as well as the double engagement of these writers in the Romanian culture and language as well as in "Western" literatures, summarizes the tensions and contradictions which marked their literary careers. While affirming that translations do not make a literature[19], the majority of them were also and above all translators, both in the broad sense of the term as *passeurs* of culture and literature, but also in the literal one, since they provided Romanian translations of important pieces of "world literature." In this sense, Margareta Gyursik points out that "tous les écrivains roumains importants du XIXe et du XX siècle, à peu d'exception près, ont traduit de la littérature française. Ces traductions ont joué un rôle actif et sont devenues une composante de la vie culturelle, au même titre qu'en Allemagne et en Russie" [all the important Romanian writers of the 19th and 20th centuries, with few exceptions, translated French literature. These translations played an active role and

---

17 The critic Geo Șerban analizes as follows these writings of Alecu Russo: "Aparținând cu toate epocii dinainte de *Cântarea României*, ele se împărtășesc din indistinctul prozei noastre de început, amestec de 'fiziologii', jurnale de călătorie, amintiri, agrementate din destul cu episoade aventuroase trăite de autor sau cu 'istorii' senzaționale auzite, și unele și altele mai mult sau mai puțin (de regulă, mai puțin) iscusit introduse în trama narativă" [Belonging to the era before *Cântarea României*, they share the indistinctness of our early prose, a mixture of 'physiologies', travel diaries, memories, supplemented from time to time with adventurous episodes lived by the author or with sensational 'stories' that he heard, all more or less (usually less) cleverly inserted into the narrative plot] (Geo Șerban 1959, In: Russo 1959: XVII–XVIII).
18 The role played by translation, especially from French and Italian, in the nineteenth century Romanian literatures has not been yet studied in its complexity.
19 See Alecu Russo. Critica criticii. 1846. Reprinted in Russo (1985: 3). Mihail Kogălniceanu defended the same idea, in 1840, in the revue *Dacia literară* [Literary Dacia].

became a component of cultural life, just as in Germany and Russia] (Gyurcsik 1993: 121).[20]

Remaining for the most part in manuscript form, Russo's French writings were translated for publication into Romanian posthumously. As a matter of fact, this was the destiny of all bilingual works by Romanian authors of the 19th and 20th centuries. They are all only published in their Romanian translation, which renders their bilingualism invisible. The fact that the names of the translators are not mentioned in the editions further masks their character as a translation and permits their integration *a posteriori* into the corpus of a so-called monolingual Romanian literature.[21]

While Alecu Russo and Mihail Kogălniceanu belong to Francophone literature by virtue of one of their literary languages, they nevertheless do not belong to the French literary field. However, other Francophone Romanian writers of the time, such as as Anna de Noailles (1876–1933), Marthe Bibesco (1886–1973) or Hélène Văcărescu (1864–1947) provide a counterexample. These authors chose to settle in Paris and, in this way, they participated in literary life there and fully integrated themselves successfully into the French literary field.

4 The bilingual literary work of Alecu Russo – a case study

Russo wrote *Iassy et ses habitants en 1840* [Iassy and its inhabitants in 1840] only three years after his return to Iassy. This text has never been published in the French original, neither in Romania nor in France. It was only published as a Romanian translation done by the well-known writer Mihail Sadoveanu in

---

20 See I. Brăescu. (1980). *Perspective și confluente literare româno-franceze*, 269. Bucharest: Ed. Univers. See also the groundbreaking research by Georgiana Badea, especially the following studies: Badea, Georgiana (ed.). 2006. *Repertoriul traducerilor românești limbile franceză, italiană, spaniolă (secolele al XVII-lea si al XIX-lea). Studii de istorie a traducerii*. Cluj: Editura Universității de Vest; Badea, Georgiana (2016): „Despre traducerea în limba română (secolele al XVIII-lea și al XIX-lea". In Analele Universității de Vest din Timișoara. Seria științe filologice. 2016/12, 37–50.
21 There is hardly any research on the Romanian translations of the nineteenth-century prose in French written by Romanian authors, nor have the original manuscripts in French been published or studied.

1912 in the review *Viața românească* [Romanian Life] and later in different editions of Russo's oeuvre.[22]

Iassy et ses habitants en 1840 is a text narrated from the view of a repatriated migrant writer who sees his country of origin in constant relation to his experiences and the places he has seen abroad. In this sense, the choice to write in French is not only due to the Francophone readership he was addressing, but it is also and foremost an aesthetic strategy to achieve distance to his homeland and show it in a radically different light to his local readership. Thus, Russo often compares Iassy with the foreign cities he knows and, in doing so, forms judgements about the lifestyles of their respective inhabitants: "[…] s'il y avait [à Jassy] un pont de fil de fer par dessus cela, ce serait Fribourg du coté du Mont moins la sauvage et limpide Sarine."[23] [… if there were [in Jassy – my note] a wire bridge over this, it would be Fribourg on the Mont side minus the wild and limpid Sarine]. And: „Mais tous ces alentours [de Jassy] ne présentent aucun de ces jardins riants, de ces pavillons pittoresques, de ces guinguettes […] qui font apprécier aux promeneurs les environs de Vienne, attirant la foule naive des bourgeois, tout y est sauvage, agreste, inculte." [But all these surroundings [of Jassy] do not present any of these delightful gardens, these picturesque pavilions, these guinguettes […] which make the walkers appreciate the surroundings of Vienna, attracting the naive crowd of the bourgeois, everything here is wild, agrarian, uncultivated].

Numerous contradictions inherent to Russo's situation as a Francophone writer in the emergent Romanian field are reflected in this text, not only at the thematic level, but also in its poetics. Thus, the first part of the text is clearly addressed to an international Francophone readership, with the goal of offering a reliable, up-to-date panoramic account of the Moldavian capital. Russo begins his account with a brief critical evaluation of the existing accounts on Moldova, which are all published by foreign travelers or diplomats. This kind of evaluation appears necessary to him, since, as he says, hardly any foreign readers will have the chance to verify the exactness and pertinence of these accounts themselves. Therefore, for the young author, first-hand knowledge through experience and belonging to Romanian society become sources of authority and legitimacy in the writing process.

Yet, while writing, the author begins to take into consideration a possible Romanian readership, so that the last part of the text clearly develops as a dia-

---

[22] *Iașii și locuitorii lui în 1840*, Viața românească, 9/1912, 292–314.
[23] All quotes from Russo's writing *Iassy et ses habitants en 1840* in this section are from the manuscript preserved at the Biblioteca Academiei Române in Bucharest. Ms rom 311, 1–211.

logue with his local readers. Such a gradual change of perspective might be due to Russo imagining a publication of his text in Romanian translation, but it is also linked to the uncertainties and the 'in-between' status inherent to the author's position as a repatriated migrant writer. In this sense, it is interesting to notice that, when addressing his Romanian readers, the author's tone is much less confident; he seems to lack authority, and he therefore carefully presents a whole range of arguments to establish the credibility of his account explicitly and to justify his critical attitude implicitly. From this perspective, we might assume that Russo chose to write his accounts on Moldavia in French because of a certain sense of confidence and familiarity with his (imagined) Francophone readership, with whom he had a whole cultural and literary background in common, whereas the links to a possible Romanian readership were rather weak.

Moreover, we perceive a similar change at the thematic level of the text. If the subject as such remains the same throughout the book – an ethnographic description of Iassy and its inhabitants, enriched with a brief history of the town, landscape descriptions, an analysis of the linguistic situation, of cultural and social life – the author seems less and less interested in a picturesque presentation of local life for a foreign reader and more and more engaged in a critical evaluation of local social and cultural life addressed to a local readership. Russo's goal is not only to observe and describe the places and the society; he gradually wants to participate in what appears to him a necessary process of modernization and progress towards "Western" standards in both private and public life in Iassy. This change in perspective can also be detected in the author's interest in the development of Romanian literature, as local subject matters are no longer seen in their picturesque aspects for foreign French readers, but in their potential for Romanian literature:

> Nos moeurs, nos usages, notre caractère ou celui qui nous donnent les circonstances serait une matière neuve, originale et quoique jusqu'à aujourd'hui il n'ait rien paru, il ne faut pas désespérer qu'il ne vienne un jour un Homer national qui s'en ira par le pays fouillant chaque pierre, chaque monastère, interrogeant les souvenirs enfouis, retournant dans les pas de la redingote et de l'antéréou, le béniche et le gilet, le calcalpae rebondie et la culotte moderne pour leur demander le secret de leur fusion et le sort qui les attend
> [Our customs, our habits, our character or that which gives us the circumstances would be a new, original matter and although up to now nothing has appeared, we must not despair that there will not come one day a national Homer who will go through the country searching every stone, every monastery, interrogating buried memories, returning to the steps of the frock coat and the anteréou, the bonnet and the waistcoat, the rebounded calcalpae and the modern breeches to ask them the secret of their fusion and the fate that awaits them].

And

> Figurez-vous un peu le pêle-mêle de toutes ces races, peuples, castes avec leur couleur locale, leurs costumes bigarrés, leurs moeurs particulières, leurs physionomies tranchantes dans un contact journalier, se rencontrant, se saluant dans la rue [...] castes, peuples, races aux traits distinctifs qui mériteraient chacun un livre à part. Dommage que la littérature indigène n'exploite pas la mine féconde qu'elle a sous les yeux, et s'amuse à tronquer les productions étrangères
> [Imagine the mishmash of all these races, peoples, castes with their local color, their colorful costumes, their particular customs, their sharp physiognomies in daily contact, meeting and greeting each other in the street [...] castes, peoples, races with distinctive features which would each deserve a book of their own. It is a pity that indigenous literature does not exploit the fertile mine it has before its eyes, and amuses itself by truncating foreign productions].

Similarly, the author oscillates between an outer and inner perspective on the town and more generally on Romanian society. Especially in the first part, it is striking that he views his country of origin through the eyes of a foreign observer. Therefore, a whole range of motifs from ethnographic and travel literature on the Romanian principalities is present in Russo's text, such as the picturesque, the extraordinary beauty of the landscape, their savage and/or pastoral character, or the mixture of Orient and Occident. This distant, detached point of view, for example, is evident in the following passage:

> Iassy elle-même est un monstrueux amalgame de constructions massives ou élégantes, de palais et de bicoques entourés d'immenses cours; ses rues fourmillent d'attirails de campagne, de luxe à profusion, d'équipages fringants, de livrées, de toilettes parisiennes ou viennoises, de haillons franco-moldaves, de physionomies, plaisantes, rébarbatives, originales, pittoresquement encostumées comme pour un bal masqué. La population de plus de soixante mille âmes est aussi diverse par ses costumes, et un observateur de moeurs aurait, de sa fenêtre, en une demi-heure assez à observer pour faire connaissance avec dix peuples et voyager en France, en Allemagne, en Orient
> [Iassy itself is a monstrous amalgam of massive or elegant constructions, of palaces and shanties surrounded by immense courtyards; its streets are teeming with country paraphernalia, with luxury in profusion, with dashing crews, liveries, Parisian, or Viennese dresses, with Franco-Moldavian rags, with physiognomies pleasing, off-putting, original, picturesquely dressed up as if for a masked ball. The population of more than sixty thousand souls is also diverse in its costumes, and an observer of manners would have, from his window, enough to observe in half an hour to make acquaintance with ten peoples and travel to France, Germany, and the Orient].

It is precisely the position of the observer "from his window" that the author assumes. Among all of the senses, sight dominates his perception – the gaze presuming a (critical) distance between the seeing subject and his object. Russo lets "le regard plonge[r]" ["the penetrating gaze"] in the places he describes, but he never appears himself in them, he never mingles among the people or in the daily scenes he describes. Another example in this sense: he presents the different populations of Iassy by making them pass in an imaginary cavalcade before the eyes of the reader, with the picturesque aspects being consistently underlined, as in this presentation of the Roma population of Iassy at that time:

> Viennent[24] les fils de Pharaons, les énigmatiques Égyptiens ou Bohémiens en français, Gitanos, Zigani en espagnol, Ziganes en moldave, qui ont essoufflé un jeune lionceau de notre littérature nationale : hâlés, mélangés avec le sang indigène ou d'autres races pures; noirauds parfaits avec leur langage nasillard, leur poitrine découverte, ne portant de vêtement que ce qu'il faut pour ne pas outrager les premiers principes de la décence, avec leurs femmes effrontées et hideuses de saleté, peuple bizarre avec lequel nous vivions depuis des siècles sans le connaître encore, le démêler, misérable et nu, et vivant cependant gaiement et sans souci sous la tente nomade, maraudant, jouant du violon dans les cabarets, connaissant de religion et de patrie la tente et le ciel[25]
> [Then come the sons of Pharaohs, the enigmatic Egyptians or Bohemians in French, Gitanos, Zigani in Spanish, Ziganes in Moldavian, who have breathed out a young cub of our national literature: suntanned, mixed with the native blood or other pure races; perfect blacks with their nasal language, their uncovered breasts, wearing only as much clothing as is necessary not to outrage the first principles of decency, with their shameless and hideously dirty women, a strange people with whom we have been living for centuries without yet knowing or understanding them, wretched and naked, and yet living happily and carefree in the nomadic tent, hustling, playing the violin in the cabarets, knowing the tent and the sky as their religion and their homeland].

Furthermore, Russo often internalizes what can be called a colonial point of view. He speaks of "les habitants demi-civilisés de cette ville" [the half-civilized inhabitants of this city] or makes remarks like the following one: "Généralement les peuples enfants sont peu portés à jouir des beautés de la nature, il en est de même des Iassiens, placés plus près de la nature que de la civilisation" [Generally speaking, childish people are not very inclined to enjoy the beauties of nature; the same is true of the Iassians, who are closer to nature than to civilization].

---

24 Other kinds of populations are introduced in a similar way, by stressing the picturesque aspects, in a dynamic series of street scenes: "Voici plus loin le patient et industrieux Allemand [...]" or: "Par ci par là sont semés des milliers d'individus, Grecs, Serviens, Bulgares, races croisées [...]."
25 See for example Ion Ghica's realistic account of the living conditions of the Roma populations in Moldavia, which is quite opposed to this kind of picturesque presentation. In Ghica (1967) *Scrisori către Vasile Alecsandri* [Letters to Vasile Alecsandri], 12. Bucharest: Editura pentru literatură.

The motif of Iassy, profoundly marked by the contrast between Orient and Occident[26], goes hand in hand with that of a more or less conflicting coexistence of tradition and modernity. Moreover, the conflict between tradition and modernity takes the form of a conflict or even fight between the older and the younger generation. Russo speaks of a "lutte entre le vieux et le jeune" and the last part of his text in particular stresses the difficulties and impediments that the young repatriates face from their elders as soon as they try to introduce cultural and social changes. In these imaginary dialogues with his compatriots, especially with the older ones who mostly resisted changes, the author's tone becomes emotional, involved, oscillating between sadness and hope. For Russo, innovations and change are "preuve de force et de vie" [proof of force and of life], and he stresses once again the "lutte à mort entre le nouveau et l'antique où la victoire laborieuse restera au dernier venu" [a struggle to the death between the new and the old, where the laborious victory will go to the last comer].

This contrast between old and new also manifests itself in the linguistic situation in the Moldavian capital, whose eclecticism Russo presents and analyzes as follows:

> Tout ce mélange de population parle son langue à lui : russe, allemand, grec, polonais, idiomes estropiés et barbares de toutes les langues et de tous les temps, surdominé par le roumain, la langue des langues pour le peuple. Les Seigneurs de la haute volée ont impatronisé le Français dans les salons et les correspondances intimes, le moldave leur sert aux tribunaux, ou avec leurs gens, le grec est réservé pour ceux qui n'entendent ni le français ni le moldave. À l'exemple des dames élégantes et des fashionables la noblesse de seconde classe ne parle que Balzac et [...] Lamartine et Hugo, Koth et Dumas. Paul de Koth surtout ils l'adorent. [...] la troisième, 4e, 5e [noblesse] [...] ne sont encore qu'aux classiques, si bien que vous entendiez à Passy tout le monde parler français sans y comprendre un mot. Les amateurs d'équivoques ont beau jeu à Iassy. Superbe langage pour le grammairien aux inversions poétiques, aux constructions hardies, inouïes, fardées d'allemand, de grec, de russe et de moldave. En général, nous sommes ennemis du purisme. L'accent grotesque et sa défiguration de mots des Allemands et surtout des Zigaines et des Juifs sont mis à contribution journellement [...]
> [All this mixture of population speaks its own language: Russian, German, Greek, Polish, crippled and barbaric idioms of all languages and all times, overpowered by Romanian,

---

26 With regard to the contrast between Orient and Occident, which is a very frequent motif in the literature of the nineteenth century, Nicolae Manolescu remarks that it appears as such only from the point of view of the foreign, mostly Western traveler. For Manolescu, the specificity of the Romanian culture and society of this time lies rather in the complex "mixture" and perfect assimilation of two influences, the Oriental and the Western one. See Manolescu (1997: 102).

the language of languages for the people. The lords of the upper class have incorporated French in the salons and in intimate correspondence, Moldavian serves them in the courts, or with their people, Greek is reserved for those who hear neither French nor Moldavian. Following the example of the elegant ladies and the fashionable, the second-class nobility speaks only Balzac and [...] Lamartine and Hugo, Koth and Dumas. Paul de Koth especially, they adore him. [...] the third, fourth and fifth [nobility] [...] are still only familiar with the classics, so that in Iassy you hear everyone speaking French without understanding a word. Those who like equivocation are at ease in Iassy. It is a superb language for the grammarian with poetic inversions, bold and unheard-of constructions, with German, Greek, Russian and Moldavian flavor. In general, we are enemies of purism. The grotesque accent and its disfiguration of words of the Germans and especially of the Zigaines and the Jews are put to use daily [...]].

Russo didn't seem to have any difficulties in treating these local subject matters in the French language, in which he continued to write a part of his texts until his premature death in 1859. The only constraint or limitation he seemed to feel in writing in French was that the "multitude d'anecdotes locales, expressions" [multitude of local anecdotes, expressions] are "intraduisibles" [untranslatable].

The influential critic George Călinescu notes that, by adding Romanian words to it, Russo transforms the French language that he uses into a "dialect local" [local dialect] (Călinescu 1986: 193). In fact, the non-French words Russo uses with the highest frequency in his French text are of Turkish origin, especially those describing local clothing habits ("*chalvar*," "*antéréou*," and many others). It is as if the battle between old and new, (Oriental) traditions and (Western) modernity is thus made visible in this text on the linguistic level, of a French language disturbed if not dislocated by Turkish words.

5 Plurilingualism in the Romanian literary histories

If, in its different historical constellations, plurilingualism has always been a constitutive dimension of Romanian literatures, literary histories, on the other hand, construct the image of a monolingual Romanian literature. Proof of this is found in the two most important literary histories, which have deeply shaped the Romanian literary canon: George Călinescu's *Istoria literaturii române de la origini până în prezent* [The History of Romanian Literature from Its Origins to the Present] (1941) and Nicolae Manolescu's *Istoria critică a literaturii române* [The Critical History of Romanian Literature] (2008).[27]

An influential critic and historian of the interwar period, George Călinescu, the founder of literary historiography in Romania, claimed his history was entirely based on the principle of aesthetic value. Wanting to compile a literary history and not a cultural one, he tried to exclude religious, scholarly, and historical texts from his account, especially if they were not written in the Romanian language. Despite the apparent neutrality of the principle of aesthetic value, Călinescu considers the national identity of the Romanian people and the way it is reflected in the local literature. The critic asserted an "organic" evolution of Romanian language and literature. At the same time, literatures written in the languages of minority populations, as well as literary works of emigrant or women writers, were marginalized. Similarly, the literature of the avant-gardes, or that of other modern movements, such as symbolism, which were not inspired by local realities, was highly problematic for Călinescu. In fact, one of the most obvious contradictions in Călinescu's historical narrative lies in the tension between the universal vocation of literature and the national imperative, the ethnic specificity, of which literature must be an expression.

While placing literary texts written in Romanian at the center of his historical account, Călinescu nonetheless succeeds in creating a complex picture of 'Romanian' literature, highlighting the close relationships between the different languages, traditions and scholarly cultures that marked its development. The historian often points at the multiple relations that Romanian (plurilingual) writers had with cultural centers throughout Europe as well as with the Ottoman Empire. The plurilingualism of most writers demonstrates their ability to integrate into the European culture of their time. Thus, focusing on both the works and the biographies of the writers, in a monographic approach, Călinescu highlighted, despite himself, the role of migration and of plurilingualism in the lives and works of many writers in this emerging phase of Romanian literatures.

With regard to Romanian literatures of the 18th and 19th centuries, Călinescu tells the story of an organic literary evolution, of a linear progression from French to Romanian, as if the writings in French constituted a preliminary phase of literature in the Romanian language. Instead of the coexistence, at the time, not only of Romanian and French, but also of Greek, Italian and German, and thus the dominance of a plurilingual model, Călinescu's account suggests a

---

27 Space only allows me to dwell in exemplary manner on these two canonical histories of the Romanian literature.

succession of monolingual models that culminate in the definitive establishment of Romanian as the national language at the end of the 19th century.

Even more than for Călinescu, for Nicolae Manolescu, the absolute criterion for defining literature is language. Assuming that Romanian literature can only be written in Romanian, Manolescu excludes any text written in another language from the historical narrative of Romanian literature:

> Poezia românească nu poate să înceapă decât cu texte scrise în limba română. Faptul de a fi scris în Evul Mediu românesc în mai multe limbi nu ne îndreptățește să socotim respectivele texte ca aparținând literaturii romăne. [...] Ele nu sunt românești nici în conținut nici în formă
> [Romanian poetry can only begin with texts written in Romanian. The fact that during the Romanian Middle Ages we wrote in several languages does not give us the right to consider these texts as belonging to Romanian literature. [...] They are Romanian neither in content nor in form] (Manolescu 1997: 27).

For Manolescu, the history of literature "se confundă cu însuși drumul pe care-l străbate limba română, cu transformările, eșecurile și biruințele ei" [merges with the path taken by the Romanian language itself, with its transformations, failures, and victories] (Manolescu 1997: 27). Thus conceived, this literature can only be monolingual. If Manolescu intends to write the first "istorie critică și stilistică" [critical and stylistic history] (Manolescu 1997: 18) of Romanian literature, making aesthetic value the only valid criterion of judgement, in reality his approach is underpinned by the ideology of "national" literature (one nation – one (native) language – one literature) and fits perfectly into what Tristan Leperlier calls "le monolinguisme méthodologique qui fait du national et de la langue le cadre impensé de nombreuses recherches" [the methodological monolingualism that makes the national and the language the unconscious framework of much research] (Leperlier 2020).

Although Manolescu's intentions could not be clearer, he nevertheless had considerable difficulty adhering to them in his analyses of literary works. Thus, he was obliged to include numerous works of medieval 'Romanian' literature in his account that are either self-translations or translations. But, while these texts are important milestones in the development of the Romanian language, Manolescu does not take their status as translations into account, thus obscuring the essential importance of plurilingualism and translation in the emergence of Romanian literary languages. With regard to a part of medieval popular literature, whose multilingual character is too obvious to be left out, Manolescu recognizes its aesthetic value without, however, modifying his theoretical premises of a Romanian literature that is by definition monolingual. Thus, Manolescu's literary history ignores, or willfully sidelines, the significance of plurilingualism. Not being able to conceal them entirely, the historian developed strategies to minimize their role.

As far as the 19th and 20th centuries are concerned, Manolescu's historical account creates an incomplete, truncated picture of the literary production of multilingual writers, since only their writings in Romanian are considered. For example, instead of analyzing Russo's bilingual poetics, Manolescu merely regrets that "Russo nu ne-a oferit el însuși [...] versiunea românească a acestor prime texte și mai ales a *Sovejei*, unul din primele noastre jurnale intime, în care talentul se pune cel mai bine în valoare" [Russo himself did not offer us [...] the Romanian version of these texts, especially his diary in Soveja, one of our earliest diaries, and which best highlights the literary talent of its author] (Manolescu 1997: 207).

As these analyses have shown, Romanian literatures have always been embedded in different plurilingual configurations, partly as a result of the polyglossia of the local societies, but, even more importantly, due to the bi- and multilingual education of the majority of Romanian writers, often pursued in cultural and literary centers of their time. If historical and critical accounts have by now obscured phenomena of literary plurilingualism in the "Romanian" literatures, new literary histories should question these monolingual paradigms, highlighting the diversity and multiplicity of languages and cultural transfers which are constitutive for these literatures.

6 References

Anokhina, Olga, Dembeck, Till & Weissmann, Dirk. 2019. "Close the Gap!" Pour une étude du plurilinguisme littéraire européen au XIXe siècle. In Olga Anokhina, Till Dembeck and Dirk Weissmann (eds.), *Mapping Multilingualism in 19th Century European Literatures. Le plurilinguisme dans les littératures européennes du XIXe siècle*, 5–12. Vienna: LIT.

Badea, Georgiana (ed.). 2006. *Repertoriul traducerilor românești limbile franceză, italiană, spaniolă (secolele al XVII-lea si al XIX-lea). Studii de istorie a traducerii*. Cluj: Editura Universității de Vest.

Badea, Georgiana. 2016. Despre traducerea în limba română (secolele al XVIII-lea și al XIX-lea). In *Analele Universității de Vest din Timișoara. Seria științe filologice*. 54, 37–50.

Canonica, Elvezio. 2015. Panorama et enjeux du plurilinguisme littéraire dans le domaine ibérique, des origines au Siècle d'Or. *Littératures classiques*, 2015/2 (87), 63–78. Available online: https://www.cairn.info/revue-litteratures-classiques-2015-2-page-63.htm.

Casanova, Pascale. 2008 [1999]. *La République mondiale des Lettres*. Paris: Seuil.

Casanova, Pascale. 2011. La guerre de l'ancienneté. In Pascale Casanova (ed.), *Des littératures combatives. L'internationale des nationalismes littéraires*, 9–31. Paris: Raisons d'agir.

Călinescu, George 1986 [1941]. *Istoria literaturii române de la origini până în prezent* [The History of Romanian Literature from Its Origins to the Present]. Bucharest: Minerva.

Ciopraga, Magda. 1993. Paroles d'un croyant, Cântarea României de l'écho de Lammenais à la voix d'Alecu Russo. In Georges Cesbron (ed.), *Voix d'Ouest en Europe. Souffles d'Europe en Ouest. Actes du Colloque International d'Angers, 21–24 mai 1992*. Angers: Presses de l'Université d'Angers.

Cornea, Paul. 1962. Alecu Russo, Nicolae Bălcescu şi Cântarea României [Alecu Russo, Nicolae Bălcescu şi Cântarea României]. In Paul Cornea (ed.), *Studii de literatură română modernă* [Studies on Modern Romanian Literature]. Bucharest: Editura pentru literatură.

Cornea, Paul. 1962. O epocă luminoasă a literaturii romăne: epoca 1848 [A bright epoch of the Romanian Literature: the epoch of 1848]. In Paul Cornea, *Studii de literatură română modernă* [Studies on Modern Romanian Literature]. Bucharest: Editura pentru literatură.

Cornea, Paul. 1972. *Originile romantismului românesc. Spiritul public, mișcarea ideilor și literatura între 1780–1840* [The origins of Romanian Romanticism. Public spirit, movement of ideas and literature between 1780–1840.]. Bucharest: Minerva.

Djuvara, Neagu. 1989. *Le Pays roumain entre Orient et Occident. Les Principautés danubiennes au début du XIXe siècle*. Paris: Publ. Orientalistes de France.

Grutman, Rainier. 1997. *Des langues qui résonnent. L'hétérolinguisme au XIXe siècle québécois*. Montréal: Fides.

Ghica, Ion. 1967. *Scrisori către Vasile Alecsandri* [Letters to Vasile Alecsandri]. Bucharest: Editura pentru literatură.

Gyurcsik, Margareta. 1993. Voix de l'Ouest de la France en Roumanie: Du Bellay, Ronsard. In Georges Cesbron (ed.), *Voix d'Ouest en Europe. Souffles d'Europe en Ouest. Actes du Colloque International d'Angers. 21–24 mai 1992*. Angers: Presses de l'Université d'Angers.

Leperlier, Tristan. 2020. La langue des champs. Aires linguistiques transnationales et Espaces littéraires plurilingues. *COnTEXTES [Online]* 28, https://doi.org/10.4000/contextes.9297 (accessed 11.06.2023).

Manolescu, Nicolae. 1997. *Istoria critică a literaturii romăne. Vol. 1*. Bucharest: Editura Fundației Culturale Romăne.

Manolescu, Nicolae. 2008. *Istoria critică a literaturii romăne. 5 secole de literatură*. Pitești: Paralela 45.

Martin, Mircea. 1981. *George Călinescu și "complexele" literaturii romăne*. Bucharest: Albatros.

Moura, Jean-Marc. 1999. *Littératures francophones et théorie postcoloniale*. Paris: PUF.

Russo, Alecu. 1985. *Cântarea României*. Edited by Geo Șerban. Bucharest: Biblioteca pentru toți.

Sapiro, Gisèle. 2010. De la construction nationale à la mondialisation: les traductions du français en hébreu. In Anna Boschetti (ed.), *L'Espace culturel transnational*, 327–366. Paris: Nouveau Monde éditions.

Suchet, Myriam. 2010. *Outils pour une traduction post-coloniale: littératures hétérolingues*. Paris: Éd. des Archives Contemporaines.

Șerban, Geo. 1959. Introducere. In *Russo 1959: XVII–XVIII*.

Charlotte van Hooijdonk
Uncovering Multilingual Strategies

Literary Periodicals and the Conceptualization of "Flemish" Literature (1815–1825)

Abstract: At the turn of the 19th century, the Southern Netherlands were under French rule: literature, press and society progressively frenchified. During the following "Dutch period" (1814–1830), the French policy of monolingualism was transformed into a political revival of Dutch language, accompanied by efforts to impose a Dutch written standard and to culturally unify the Southern and Northern Netherlands. Above all, Napoleon's rigid system of censorship was turned into a free press, open to debate. Governmental efforts to defend Dutch were criticized by mostly francophone journalists and defended by some of their Flemish colleagues. At the same time, a growing sense of an autonomous Flemish literary field found its place in certain periodicals. After a decade of frenchification of the press and the literary field, one wonders what the discourse on Flemish literature was like, and how it related to journalistic practices of translation, adaptation and transfer. How did these periodicals reflect the multilingual reality of the Southern Netherlands and the superior place of French? By using a cultural transfer approach that highlights the role played by journalists, this article aims to show the paradoxical but rich variety of discursive stances and mono- or multilingual strategies taken in this debate on Flemish literature. It shows that a different method and a less traditional corpus can help overcome the age-old idea that Flemish literature at the start of the 19th century was non-existent.

Keywords: Flemish Literature, Literary Periodicals, Cultural Transfer, Translation, United Kingdom of the Netherlands, Belgian Literature, Cultural Mediators

---

Charlotte van Hooijdonk, KU Leuven, e-mail: charlotte.vanhooijdonk@kuleuven.be

Open Access. © 2023 the author(s), published by De Gruyter. This work is licensed under the Creative Commons Attribution 4.0 International License.
https://doi.org/10.1515/9783110778656-004

1 Introduction

In 1814, the Congress of Vienna decided to unite the Southern Netherlands (roughly present-day Belgium) and the Northern Netherlands (the present-day Netherlands).¹ Commonly referred to as the "Dutch period" of Belgian history (1814–1830), these years of government under the rule of William I, King of the United Kingdom of the Netherlands, followed a "French period" (1794–1814) marked by a "frenchification" of cultural and political life. The Southern Netherlands had just emerged from an era of censorship and almost total monolingualism. King William I, on the other hand, actively promoted a cultural revival of the Dutch language², for instance by acknowledging Dutch as a "national language" for the first time in the Southern Netherlands, by subsidizing Dutch-language periodicals and by founding literary and linguistic societies. These initiatives served to find and promote a common language in which a (Northern and Southern) Dutch literature could be written in response to the frenchification which had reached its culmination during the French occupation. The linguistic and political components of this conflict have already been the subject of research (Vosters 2009; Vosters and Janssens 2014; Vosters and Weijermars 2012), but the question as to how Flemish-language literature was affected by this unification campaign remains a largely unexplored topic. The consensus was that political turbulence dominated the aesthetic component in the literary field of the early 19th century and that a Flemish literature did not exist before the creation of the Belgian state. This view fails to take two things into account: firstly, literature is not restricted to the production of novels and poetry but also appears on stage and in periodicals. Secondly, it overlooks the fact that often decades of struggle take place before the autonomy of a literary field is achieved. The 1820s marked a clear desire amongst literati to rediscover the sources of a Flemish literature – the famous *Verhandeling over de nederduytsche tael- en letterkunde* [Treatise on Dutch Language and Literature]³ (1819–1824) by

---

1 This article has been prepared within the framework of the interdisciplinary project "Shaping 'Belgian' Literature Before 1830. Multilingual Patterns and Cultural Transfer in Flemish and French Periodicals in the Southern Low Countries" led by Prof. Dr. Tom Verschaffel and Prof. Dr. Beatrijs Vanacker and funded by the Flemish FWO, fund for scientific research (reference number G079620N)
2 Beyond the varying linguistic and historical specificities, we use the term "Dutch" in a somewhat anachronistic but pragmatic sense to refer to the Dutch language with all its variants without geographical limitations and "Flemish" to refer to all the variants in the South.
3 All translations from French and Dutch are mine.

J.F. Willems[4] is just one example — and thus to claim an autonomous Flemish literary field. This claim was particularly made in periodicals, which strove to defend as well as to showcase Flemish literature. As so-called "barometers" of culture (Johannes 1993), these periodicals provide insight into the key ideas on literary and cultural identity which circulated at that time. Through their open structure and periodicity, periodicals had the potential to become a "platform voor actuele discussie en hervormende actie [...] [en] maakt een continue wisselwerking tussen auteur en lezer mogelijk of zelfs noodzakelijk" [platform for current debates and for reformative action [...] [and] make interaction between author and reader possible and even necessary] (Johannes 1993: 11). This specificity of the press is crucial since it had been absent in the Southern Netherlands for fifteen years. Under the French regime, the press had been curtailed to the extent that, as from 1811,[5] all periodicals had to appear either in French or in a bilingual version. No new Flemish periodicals were published after 1806. The press was completely frenchified, but also lacked literature. Periodicals were obliged to copy their articles from the official *Moniteur* so as not to run the risk of being banned. Flemish language and literature had no place there. Taking into account that the revolutionary period of 1780–1790 had given a new impulse to Flemish-language periodicals, one wonders how this freedom, which was regained in 1815, took shape in the periodicals of the Southern Netherlands and what the discourse on Flemish literature was like, finally freed from the "French burden".[6] The new geopolitical constellation[7] would favor the language of the people and the fields of literature and the press were ultimately free: the press laws in place since the Directory and brought to a climax by Napoleon

---

[4] Jan Frans Willems (Boechout, 11 March 1793 – Ghent, 24 June 1846) is perhaps the best-known Flemish writer of this period. He was already well known during his lifetime for his plays, historical and philological essays and poems. His bilingual poem "Aen de Belgen – Aux Belges" in 1818 marks his rise in the literary world of the Southern Netherlands (Stynen 2012).

[5] Although the decree on imperative French translation for the press dates from 26 September 1811, in practice, the prefects of the departments – all of them Frenchmen – no longer accepted the creation of Flemish-language periodicals from the beginning of the Empire and forced existing periodicals to publish in French in order to better control them.

[6] In 1815, J.F. Willems published a poem that connected freedom of language to the new government and characterized the French government as a "yoke": "Triumph!'-onz'Nederduytsche Tael/ Is van het Fransche juk onthéven/ En zal, hoe zeer de nyd ook smael'/ Haer'ouden luyster doen herleéven" (*Antwerpschen Almanach van Nut en Vermaek*, 19)

[7] The first article of the Act of the Congress of Vienna of 21 July 1814 stipulated: "La réunion de la Belgique et de la Hollande devra être intime et complète, de façon à ce que les deux pays ne forment qu'un seul et même Etat" [The reunion of Belgium and Holland shall be intimate and complete, so that the two countries shall form a single state] (von Busekist 1998: 41).

were abolished by the decree of 23 September 1814.[8] An interweaving of the press, literature and the Flemish language was in the offing. How could this emergent "Flemish literary field" find its place in these brand new self-proclaimed literary periodicals? How were these periodicals to reflect, in their text and form, the multilingual reality and the important place that French had taken in Flanders over the previous decades?

As such, this article aligns with a rich tradition of research on periodicals, which has been particularly fruitful for France in the 18th century.[9] For the period after 1830, following the pioneering research done by M.-E. Thérenty, several researchers have studied the progressive mediatization of society in and through periodicals. But what happened in between these two milestones remains largely unknown – regardless of the cultural area being studied. In the Southern Netherlands, the 18th century would have remained uncharted territory if not for the pioneering research of J. Smeyers and J. Huyghebaert, among others, who regularly included the study of periodicals in their analyses. Researchers of Belgian literature after 1830 made the study of periodicals one of their research habits. Among nineteenth-century literature scholars, L. D'hulst, K. Vandemeulebroucke, A. de Clercq, A. Deprez, M. Hanot, R. Merecy and R.F. Lissens stand out for their focus on the study of the journalistic field in Belgium. Similarly, J. Weijermars focuses on periodicals in her research on the United Kingdom of the Netherlands. Nevertheless, for the first decades of the 19th century, the field remains rather unexplored, apart from a few synoptic studies, for example in the literary history of the 19th century by W. van den Berg & P. Couttenier (2016) and in *ENT1815*, the encyclopaedia of Dutch-language periodicals until 1815.[10]

Periodical studies are confronted with nationalist structures and methodological monolingualism in literary research. Both the Dutch and the preceding French period, i.e., the first three decades of the nineteenth century, often fall through the cracks of research because of this division along linguistic lines.

---

8 "Les lois et règlements émanés sous le gouvernement français, sur l'imprimerie et la librairie, en y comprenant tout ce qui concerne les journaux, sont abrogés dans le gouvernement de la Belgique" [The laws and regulations issued under the French government, on printing and bookshops, including all that concerns journals, are abrogated in the government of Belgium] (Pasinomie 1860, 275: Arrêté du Prince Souverain, concernant la liberté de la presse, et règlement pour l'imprimerie, la librairie et les journalistes du 23 Septembre 1814).
9 See, in particular, Sgard (1991).
10 van Vliet, R. (ed.) (s.d.). Encyclopedie van Nederlandstalige Tijdschriften (ENT). Nederlandstalige periodieken tot de aanvang van het Koninkrijk der Nederlanden (tot 1815). [Online]. https://www.ent1815.nl/ (13.06.2023).

Thus, no proto-"Belgian" literary history that includes both linguistic groups has yet been produced. Several researchers, however, using the concept of the cultural mediator and proposing case studies from various periods, have in recent decades shown the need to consider the (proto-)Belgian lands as a whole and to study their intranational relations (Verschaffel et al. 2014). With few exceptions (D'hulst 2018), these studies have so far focused on the period after Belgium's independence in 1830. However, this binary division is particularly untenable in a study of the "Dutch" period in Belgium, where French, standardized Dutch and so-called "Flemish" variants coexisted and conflicted with one another. The Southern Netherlands were at that time, as they had been in the past, a transitional zone, "où se croisent en s'articulant avec les productions indigènes les importations originales et traduites venues du Nord et de la France" [where original and translated imports from the North and France intersected and articulated with indigenous productions] (D'hulst 2018: 1315). Besides discursive analysis, which illuminates the positions taken by the different actors of an emerging literary field in this multilingual and multicultural context, the main working tool of such research is that of cultural transfer (Espagne and Werner 1985, Espagne 2013). The study of transfers allows us to consider the discourses, references and appropriations of these periodicals and their journalists without structuring them hierarchically. Rather than studying the discourse on endogenous literature on the one hand and the influences of other cultures – notably French – on the other, the analysis of cultural transfers directs our attention towards different modes of contact with these cultures and their adaptations within the endogenous literary field.

For this purpose and in order to analyze the complex or "diffuse" transfers in periodicals (Brolsma 2008), the analysis of cultural mediators is of paramount importance. Indeed, "mediators are not merely the support teams of the Literary Greats in the established canon, but agents with a very specific function in the diffusion of literature and culture" (Leerssen 2014: 1401) - who often polish their multilingual, translation and transfer practices (Verschaffel et al. 2014). Polyglots themselves, they can highlight but also strategically hide the multilingual reality of the Southern Netherlands. They can overtly translate but also adapt the transferred elements and articles to an (imagined) monolingual readership. To hide multilingualism[11] thus was one of many possible strategies

---

11 Multilingualism, here, is understood as the sociolinguistic reality of the Southern Netherlands. "Hiding" or "showing" this multilingualism is thus regarded as a textual strategy. The individual component, the third of three levels of multilingualism recorded by R. Grutman, is

to conceptualize a fully autonomous Flemish literature, and one that was frequently used in these decades of French hegemony. More attention should therefore be paid to the choices of these mediators. They change not only the meaning of a cultural good but also its function. Periodical editors recorded these transfers between cultures by writing them down, staging or concealing them, and thus played an important role in the formation of public opinion. They can tell us more about the state of literature at a particular moment in history. Noting the existence of a discourse on "Flemish" language and its emerging literature during the first ten years of the Dutch period (1815–1825), we want to study the role of journalists in the development of this discourse, focusing on the intra- and international relations of the mediators and the linguistic strategies and transfers implemented in their periodicals.

2 The "literary" periodical in Flanders, in search of a language and a literary field

Between 1815 and 1825, the journalistic field in Flemish had to be rebuilt almost entirely. Journals that had appeared in bilingual versions could reappear in Dutch, and new Flemish periodicals emerged although they had difficulty surviving. The pre-eminence of French language in periodicals written in Flanders endured throughout the French period. These French-language periodicals clearly showed a literary inclination, while no Flemish periodicals existed exclusively dedicated to criticism or literary production. Nevertheless, in the French-language periodicals specializing in literature, the debate was almost exclusively on French literature; in the *Mercure Belge* and the *Annales Belgiques*, Flemish literature was discussed but was never the central topic. On the Dutch-speaking side, the beginning of the 19th century witnessed a first wave of philological and historical works on Flemish literature in search of the origins of literature in Dutch (van den Berg and Couttenier 2016: 37).[12] The Dutch period

---

addressed through the analysis of the strategies and opinions of the editors of the two journals (Grutman 2009: 182).

12 This desire to write the history of Flemish literature corresponds to J.F. Willems' emancipatory vision of Flemish literature, one of the three visions noted by Weijermars (2011). This vision asserted the existence of a fully-fledged Flemish literature (under whatever name), which should free itself by searching for its roots and seeking its specific character. At the same time, there was a vision of a Flemish literature "in development", which should be modelled on

was thus a transitional period, a breeding ground for research and creation that resulted, as early as 1828, in the creation of the historical novels of Henri Moke in French and Hendrik Conscience in Dutch. For this, a common history had to be created, and this was the task Flemish "literary" periodicals in the years 1815–1830 took upon them.

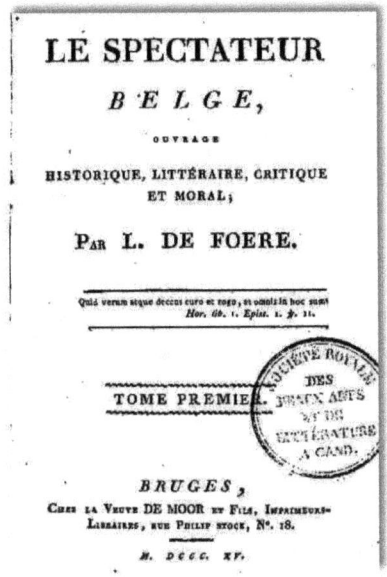

Fig. 1: Le Spectateur Belge, front page

Dutch literature, and an "integral" vision that integrated the two literatures of the North and the South as part of a whole.

Fig. 2: Letter- en Staatkundig Dagblad

Two of these periodicals, which appeared between 1815 and 1825, stand out for the special attention they gave to literature in Flanders and for their unique stance in the linguistic debate. *Le Spectateur Belge, ouvrage historique, littéraire, critique et moral [The Belgian Spectator, Historical, Literary, Critical, and Moral Work]* by the Flemish abbot Leo De Foere[13] was published in Bruges between 1815 and 1823. It was fiercely opposed to the French regime and relied on the new Dutch regime to reestablish the language and culture of the old "Belgians". He pleaded for a *Belgian* national feeling under the protection of William I. However, he became increasingly critical of the king's monocultural policy, leading to a Flemish cultural and linguistic particularism. The *Letter- en Staatkundig Dagblad [Literary and Political Daily]* (1 February 1820–29 August 1820)

---

[13] Leo De Foere (Tielt, 8 February 1787–Bruges, 7 February 1851) was ordained to the priesthood in 1810. He was a teacher at the college in Roeselare until he started writing his *Spectateur Belge* at the end of 1814. After handing over his periodical to Felix De Pachtere in 1823 – who continued it for a year – he disappeared from the public scene, only to return after Belgian independence to play an important role in the constitution of the new state (Simon 1968).

was founded by a community of pro-government Flemings and was approved by the king. It was published in Ghent by the brothers Pierre[14] and Johan Hendrik Lebrocquy[15] with the support of Leo D'hulster,[16] J.M. Schrant[17] and other members of the literary society *Regat Prudentia Vires*.[18] This local anchoring was reflected in its articles, which dealt with Ghent's literary life and the activities of the Chamber of Rhetoric *De Fonteine*.[19]

Today, these journals would be classified under the common denominator of cultural magazines. With a well-defined program (e.g., in flyers, in a preface or discernible in the text itself), they tried to create a (national, local, international) identity to which the reader could relate (Aerts 2002). This was the period preceding the great mediatization of the press that established new genres and assigned specific functions to increasingly specialized periodicals. In 1815,

---

14 Pierre Lebrocquy (Ghent, 1 February 1797–Nivelles, 4 February 1864) had studied law but eventually embarked on a career in journalism. He started out in the *Dagblad* and held various posts and positions in different periodicals in Ghent and Brussels, always with an Orangeist bias. He published poems in French and Dutch and became professor of linguistics at Ghent University (Voordeckers 1964).

15 Johan Hendrik Lebrocquy (Ghent, 1790–Ghent, 2 May 1858) was a teacher at the Ghent and Menin colleges, before briefly becoming a journalist and then a judge at the court of first instance. He also translated Siegenbeek's *Précis de l'histoire littéraire des Pays-Bas* in 1827 and belonged to several literary societies (Van Duyse 1858).

16 Leo D'Hulster (Tielt, 15 January 1784–Ghent, May 1843) was a teacher at various colleges. He was a member of several literary societies and the Orangeist movement. He published collections of poems and essays. Because of his political convictions, he worked for a common Dutch language for the Netherlands and Belgium (Vanacker 1987).

17 The Dutch Catholic priest Johannes Matthias Schrant (Amsterdam, 24 March 1783–Leiden, 5 April 1866) was sent to Ghent in 1817 by William I to become the first professor of Dutch literature at the University. In 1830 he returned to the Netherlands, disillusioned: his courses were hardly attended, which he attributed to the hegemony of the French language and culture in Ghent (Weijermars 2009).

18 The *Maatschappij van Nederlandse Taal- en Letterkunde*, also known by its motto *Regat Prudentia Vires*, was a section of the rhetorical chamber *De Fonteine* in Ghent. Their aim was to promote Dutch language and literature. Founded in 1819, it became autonomous in 1821 and followed the example of northern literary societies in its activities. The society was disbanded with the independence of Belgium in 1830 (De Clercq and Deprez 1996: 59).

19 This chamber was founded in Ghent in the 15th century. It went through many ups and downs in the following centuries, but – unlike other chambers – survived the French period. Between 1800 and 1830 it performed Dutch or Flemish traditional plays and translated plays by Kotzebue, Shakespeare, Schiller and Voltaire (Verschaffel 2017: 71–74; Van den Berg and Couttenier 2016: 180).

the literary press was not exclusively "literary":[20] it dealt with literary, cultural, and social issues. For example, the *Letter- en Staatkundig Dagblad* was advertised as a "literary and political daily". The paper was divided into a political and a literary section with book reviews, poems, and information on cultural life. The title of the *Spectateur Belge* referred to a tradition of satirical literary journals – the English *Spectators*[21] and the French *Spectateurs*: it adopted their polemical and moralistic character and the first- person narration, but not the other formal characteristics of this type of periodical, such as the setting (in an inn, in the streets) of the narrative instance. De Foere used literary forms to convey his message, such as the fictitious letter, the essay and the dialogue (Johannes 1995: 6). These literary journals served the improvement of the Dutch language in the Southern Netherlands. They assigned a dual function to their periodicals: to inform and to educate.

The *Dagblad* wanted to "verspreiden en opbouwen onzer taal" [spread and build up our language], and "derzelver keurigheid, deftigen aard en welluidendheid [aantoonen]" [prove the delicacy, distinction and harmony] of the Dutch language and make it easy to use for the Flemish so as to "de oefening der Nederlandsche Letterkunde bij ons algemeener te doen worden" [generalize our literary practice in Dutch]. They claimed that they had found nothing more suitable to achieve the "[inleiding van] alle taallievende Vaderlanders [...] in het heiligdom der Nederlandsche Spraak en Letteren" [introduction of all patriots who love their language into the temple of Dutch language and literature] than a literary journal (L&SD, 1 February). The *Spectateur* also wanted to achieve this goal by means of discourse and example: "il faut [...] que non-seulement je relève la beauté de la langue flamande par des discussions, mais que par le fait même, je la revête de toute sa dignité et de toute sa grandeur" [I must not only enhance the beauty of the Flemish language by means of discussion, but also by putting it into practice so as to dignify it with all its greatness] (SB 1815: t.1, 91). For example, the *Spectateur* intended to include historical Flemish literary pieces. He hoped that the periodical form would be more suitable for such a task than a book:

---

[20] As early as 1825, literary criticism as we know it today began to emerge in periodicals but really established itself after 1830 (van den Berg and Couttenier 2016: 36).

[21] The first of which, *The Spectator*, was a daily periodical founded in 1711 by J. Addison and R. Steele. This kind of moralising periodical, with a central character who guides the text, was in vogue in the 18th century and was imitated throughout Europe. In the southern Netherlands, the first „spectator", *De Rapsodisten,* was founded in 1784 by a Dutchman. The Ghent press favoured this formula in the early French period (Verschaffel 2017: 114).

> Móoglyks zullen die onbekende waernemingen op onze oudheyd onze landgenooten noyt konnen toevloeyen, 't en zy door de ader van eenige nu en dan utgegeve bladjes, zynde den eenigsten middel, dien ik tans ook verkies, om de zeldzaeme nasporen, op ons vaderland gedaen, tegen eene zekere en betreurlyke vernietiging te verdedigen
> [It is possible that these unknown proofs of our antiquity may never reach our compatriots, if only through the vein of a few pages published from time to time, being the only means, which I now also prefer, of defending the rare traces left on our homeland against certain and regrettable destruction] (SB 1815: t.1, 38)

Thus, the periodical could become a monument for the literature of the Southern Netherlands, since the endogenous literary history had demonstrated an unparalleled richness and should become the source for contemporary authors, rather than foreign literature. Indeed: "waarom onze aandacht uitsluitend aan het vreemde gegeven, en de vruchten van onzen eigen bodem verzuimd?" [why should we pay attention only to foreign things and neglect the fruits of our own soil] (L&SD, 1 February), asked the *Dagblad* rhetorically. The same image is used by the *Spectateur:*

> Que vous vous suffisez à vous-même, pour ne pas ramper servilement aux pieds de vos voisins, qui ne cessent de colporter leurs vaines et frivoles prétentions d'esprit pour la réalité même ! N'allez pas chercher sur le sol de l'étranger, plus ou moins stérile, des productions insipides, tandis que sur votre sol natal, vous pouvez recueillir tant de richesses indigènes
> [May you be self-sufficient, and not grovel slavishly at the feet of your neighbours, who never cease to peddle their vain and frivolous pretensions of spirit for reality itself! Do not go looking for insipid productions on foreign soil, which is more or less barren, while on your native soil you can gather so much indigenous wealth] (SB, 1815, t.1, 29)

Underneath the rejection of this "foreign soil" and these "frivolous pretensions of spirit", an attack on French culture and language can be identified. The *topos* of the French burden was often used during this decade. Commonplaces about the frivolity of the French and the rigorous fixity of French language were contrasted with the flexibility of the Dutch language, which also conveyed moral concepts that the French language supposedly no longer knew. The *Spectateur* even indicated France as the instigator of the decline of Dutch:

> de oudste, de schoonste, de rykste, de uytdrukkenste, de natuerlykste der levende taelen in Europa, het nederduytsch, was [...] uytgeroeyd uyt staetkunde, [...] uytgeroeyd van een rykbestier, 't welk zig, schaemtloos en tot walgens toe, den voorstaener der letterkunde voor geheel Europa uytriep.
> [The oldest, most beautiful, richest, most expressive, most natural of the living languages of Europe, *Dutch*, has been [...] exterminated by politics [...], exterminated by a state which had shamelessly and to the point of disgust elected itself the advocate of literature of the whole of Europe] (SB, 1815, t.1, 43–44)

But the tide had been turning since William I came to power. The *Spectateur* was in favour of the new language law of 15 September 1819: "een lichtje van hóop schemert tusschen véel nevelen" [a light of hope shines in the midst of many fogs] (SB 1815 t.1: 44). The Dutch language was finally being valued and literature could eventually reach the same level as in the Northern Netherlands.

> Sedert dat ons schoon en rijk Belgie aan vreemde heerschappij is ontrukt, ziet men bij ons overal onze schoone en rijke moedertaal geliefkoosd; en wij ook zullen misschien welhaast onze Van der Palms, onze Bilderdyks, onze Feiths, enz. kunnen opnoemen
> [Since our beautiful and rich Belgium has been wrested from foreign domination, our beautiful and rich mother tongue is loved everywhere; and we too may soon be able to name our Van der Palms, our Bilderdyks, our Feiths, etc.] (L&SD, 4 February)

Also, the insistence on language as proof of the existence of a Flemish literary field reveals a sociolinguistic and political issue that played an important role in the Kingdom of the Netherlands.

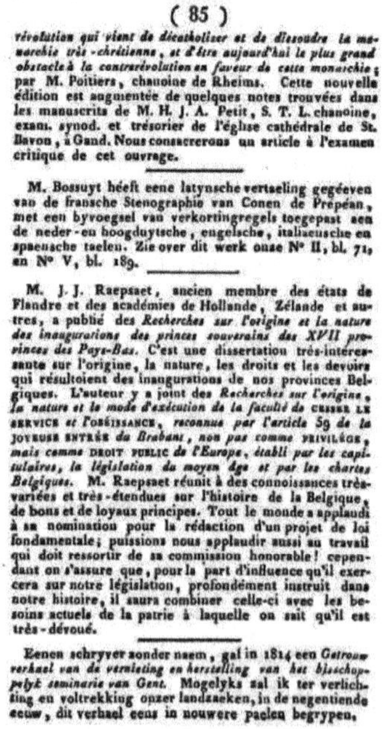

(85)

révolution qui vient de décatholiser et de dissoudre la monarchie très-chrétienne, et d'être aujourd'hui le plus grand obstacle à la contrerévolution en faveur de cette monarchie; par M. Poitiers, chanoine de Rheims. Cette nouvelle édition est augmentée de quelques notes trouvées dans les manuscrits de M. H. J. A. Petit, S. T. L. chanoine, exam. synod. et trésorier de l'église cathédrale de St. Bavon, à Gand. Nous consacrerons un article à l'examen critique de cet ouvrage.

M. Bossuyt héeft eene latynsche vertaeling gegéeven van de fransche Stenographie van Conen de Prépéan, met een byvoegsel van verkortingregels toegepast aen de neder- en hoogduytsche, engelsche, italiaensche en spaensche taelen. Zie over dit werk onze N° II, bl. 71, en N° V, bl. 189.

M. J. J. Raepsaet, ancien membre des états de Flandre et des académies de Hollande, Zélande et autres, a publié des *Recherches sur l'origine et la nature des inaugurations des princes souverains des XVII provinces des Pays-Bas*. C'est une dissertation très-intéressante sur l'origine, la nature, les droits et les devoirs qui résultoient des inaugurations de nos provinces Belgiques. L'auteur y a joint des *Recherches sur l'origine, la nature et le mode d'exécution de la faculté de* CESSER LE SERVICE *et l'*OBÉISSANCE, *reconnue par l'article 59 de la* JOYEUSE ENTRÉE *du Brabant, non pas comme* PRIVILÉGE, *mais comme* DROIT PUBLIC *de l'Europe, établi par les capitulaires, la législation du moyen âge et par les chartes Belgiques*. M. Raepsaet réunit à des connoissances très-variées et très-étendues sur l'histoire de la Belgique, de bons et de loyaux principes. Tout le monde a applaudi à sa nomination pour la rédaction d'un projet de loi fondamentale; puissions nous applaudir aussi au travail qui doit ressortir de sa commission honorable! cependant on s'assure que, pour la part d'influence qu'il exercera sur notre législation, profondément instruit dans notre histoire, il saura combiner celle-ci avec les besoins actuels de la patrie à laquelle on sait qu'il est très-dévoué.

Eenen schryver zonder naem, gaf in 1814 een *Getrouw verhael van de vernieting en herstelling van het bisschoppelyk seminarie van Gent*. Mogelyks zal ik ter verlichting en voltrekking onzer landzaeken, in de negentiende eeuw, dit verhael eens in nouwere paelen begrypen.

Fig. 3: Spectateur Belge, 1815, vol. 2, 85

3 Which national language?

The national language, Dutch, which had been promoted by law, was not able to play a big role in reality. King William I himself, who had supported the creation of a pro-government French-language periodical, the *Journal de Bruxelles* (1820–1827), had realised that in the Southern Netherlands the debate was conducted in French. The *Letter- en Staatkundig Dagblad* had also been supported by the government,[22] but not enough to survive. De Foere initially tried to create a fully bilingual *Spectateur Belge*. A Dutch work was criticized in Dutch; a work in French or another language was reviewed in French (see example opposite). But the latter language became more and more predominant. Already in the second volume, still in 1814, a reader complained that in number 9 he encountered not one Dutch word. In 1816 the first French review of a Dutch work appeared. This review no longer emphasized the usefulness of this type of work in spreading the mother tongue, but rather its formal characteristics and the classic criteria of criticism: "It is a real combination of the useful and the pleasant" (SB 1816 t.4: 186–187). French language and standards prevailed when discussing the political and cultural affairs of the state, both by the king himself and by a large part of the periodicals.

The negative influence of French on Dutch was noted and denounced by several periodicals, which often mocked the hybrid language spoken by the Frenchified bourgeoisie. In a presumably fictitious letter to the editors of the *Dagblad*, the writer prefers the editors to write in a language that is known to everyone, as he himself does. This language turns out to be full of Gallicisms. In the following (Dutch) citation, these Gallicisms for which a Dutch equivalent existed are in italics:

> Ik bemerk dat gij zoodanig hoog reikt om onbekende woorden te *attraperen*, dat men alle momenten in de lectuur *gearreteerd* is [...] Waarom *prefereert* gij zulke woorden niet waar aan ons oor door dagelijksch gebruik *gehabitueerd* is? [...] 'T Zijn *singuliere* geesten die *pretenderen* altijd zulke *pedantische expressien*, die zij zuiver vlaamsch noemen, te *emploijeren*
> [I notice that you reach so high to *catch* unknown words that one is *arrested* at every moment of reading [...] Why do you not *prefer* such words to which our ear is *accustomed* by daily use? [...] It is singular minds that *pretend* always to *employ* such *pedantic expressions*, which they call pure Flemish] (L&SD, 25 February, my emphasis)

---

22 Pierre Lebrocquy stated in his memoirs that his brother's "Dutch periodical" was "favoured" by the government, but he did not specify in what form (Lebrocquy 1842: 2).

In the same issue, another letter took the opposite stance and found, on the contrary, that the *Dagblad* used too many "bastard words". The author of this letter undermined his own argument, however, since even Vondel's language seemed impure to him: "mij [is] laatst Vondel uit de handen [...] gevallen, om dat hij sprak van *trompetten* en *regementen*" [Lately Vondel fell out of my hands, because he spoke of *trumpets* and *regiments*] (L&SD 25 February, my emphasis). In the *Spectateur*, this figure of the French-speaking Flemish parvenu appeared in a dialogue. Here the Gallicisms were pointed out by De Foere himself:

> *Monsieur l'advocat* ik heb d'eer u te *salueeren*, ik heb lang *gedesireerd* u eens over *interessante* zaeken te spréeken, en altyd g'*echouéerd* in die *entreprise* [*Monsieur l'advocat* I have the honour to *salute* you, I have long *desired* to talk to you about *interesting* things, and I have always *failed* in that *enterprise*] (SB t.1: 162).

The *Dagblad* deplores that "in de latere vlaamsche schriften [...] voegt zich de taal naar de woordvoeging *in het fransch*" [in later Flemish writings, language adapts to the *French* word order] (L&SD 18 February). But this French influence on Flemish had not always been the case. Better still, Flemish was already codified long before the French language, said De Foere:

> Van in dat tydvak, wanneer de fransche tael nog ruw en regelloos was, [...] was onze vaderlandsche tael reeds tot zulke beschaefdheyd gevoorderd, dat negentien onzer vlaemsche genootschappen, rederyk-kamers genaemd, in hunne letterkundige betrekkingen een eenstemmige spelling hadden.
> [at that time, when the French language was still crude and without rules, [...] the language of our fathers had already evolved to such a degree of civilization that nineteen of our Flemish societies, called chambers of rhetoric, already had a unified orthography in their literary relations] (SB 1815 t.2: 72)

In the discourse on Flemish language and endogenous literature, the use of the French language was inevitable, even if it was intended to highlight the advantages of the Dutch or Flemish language. In order to build up a barrier against French influence, Dutch language and literature had to be strengthened.

The written form of the newly created "national language" was indeed problematic. There were three competing ways of writing Dutch in the Southern Netherlands: the system developed in the north by Matthijs Siegenbeek and officially recognized in 1804, the Des Roches system dating from 1761, which took into account the spelling habits in the Southern Netherlands, and finally the Behaegel system, published in 1817, which tried to create a synthesis of the Flemish and Dutch ways of writing. This question was on everyone's mind, and the debate took shape in periodicals in particular. The *Spectateur* stuck to the Des Roches spelling in its Flemish articles, while the *Dagblad* adopted the Siegenbeek spelling. In defense of their choice, the Lebrocquy brothers included historical texts to show that the Siegenbeek spelling was already in use in Flanders long before it was officially codified by the Dutch. "Daar zal de lezer zien dat in de XVIe eeuw, gansch Belgie door, eene spelling werd gevolgd, welke [...] even de zelfde is als de hedendaagsche hollandsche spelling." [There the reader will see that in the sixteenth century, everywhere in Belgium, people followed a spelling which [...] was exactly the same as the contemporary Dutch spelling] (L&SD 21 July).

Adopting the already perfected Northern Dutch language would mean a renaissance of literature in the Southern Netherlands. The editors of the *Dagblad* were convinced that J.F. Willems and N. Cornelissen "zullen eerlang de spelling der gezonde reden [...] als de hunne aannemen" [would one day accept the spelling of right reason] (*L&SD* 23 May). The spelling of "bad reason" would, then, be that of P. Behaegel (L&SD 28 March). For the *Spectateur,* on the other hand, Behaegel's system was quite natural: "les principes grammaticaux de Mr Behaegel [ne sont] non-seulement pas nouveaux, mais [ils sont] aussi anciens que la nature elle-même" [Mr Behaegel's grammatical principles [are] not only not new, but [they are] as old as nature itself] (SB 1816 t.4: 255).

When the *Dagblad* disappeared, the *Spectateur* mocked its linguistic and literary stances in allegorical and satirical letters between the cities of Bruges and Ghent:

> Et votre pauvre *Letterkundig Dagblad* qu'est-il devenu? N'avoit-il pas fait, par ses doctes déclamations, assez de prosélytes à la langue hollandaise, la langue nationale [...]? Voyez comme on parle et comme on écrit maintenant le hollandais, et tout cela la patrie le doit à ce grand nombre d'articles dans lesquels il cria si fortement qu'on étoit en conscience littéraire obligé de parler et d'écrire le hollandais, même à l'exclusion du flamand, et sous peine d'être arriéré de trois siècles! Tous ces mémorables exploits, nous les devons à ces littérateurs qui, par des preuves si éclatantes et par des raisonnemens si clairs, démontrèrent évidemment la supériorité de l'orthographe hollandaise sur l'orthographe flamande. [...] Et ce chef-d'œuvre philologique est aussi trépassé!
> [And what has become of your poor *Letterkundig Dagblad*? Had he not, by his learned declamations, made enough proselytes of the Dutch language, the national language [...]? See how Dutch is now spoken and written, and all this the fatherland owes to this great number of articles in which he shouted so strongly that one was in literary conscience obliged to speak and write Dutch, even to the exclusion of Flemish, and on pain of being three centuries behind! We owe all these memorable feats to those writers who, with such striking evidence and clear reasoning, clearly demonstrated the superiority of Dutch spelling over Flemish spelling. [...] And this philological masterpiece has also passed away!] (SB 1820 t.11: 348–349)

The *Spectateur* seemed to claim victory: the language of the Flemish people would be Flemish. All other conceptions, and in particular an adherence to Dutch literature and orthography, did not emanate from the nature of the Flemish people but from a small elitist group of men. Interestingly, the *Spectateur* provided this criticism in French. Indeed, the *Spectateur Belge* appeared only in French after a few months and the *Letter- en Staatkundig Dagblad* disappeared completely – according to P. Lebrocquy because of a general disdain for the Dutch language (Lebrocquy 1842). Several attempts by ambitious journalists to create periodicals in Flemish never came to fruition or were abandoned in favor of a periodical in French. Could we say that this meant the failure of Dutch language in Flanders and the omnipresence of French language and culture?

4 Hiding or playing with the French element: transfer and translation practices

Several studies have demonstrated the existence in the "Belgian" journalistic corps of many liberal French emigrants since the Restoration in France, overlapping with the "Dutch" period for the Southern Netherlands.[23] They joined or founded political periodicals in Brussels, Ghent and Antwerp. In his *Spectateur*, De Foere provided articles on the "good" new periodicals that appeared in the kingdom, explicitly with the aim of serving as a counterweight to these foreign periodicals. He recommended the *Letter- en Staatkundig Dagblad*, whose first issue had not yet been published, but he already praised it: "Tels sont les nobles efforts que d'estimables conpatriotes (sic) se proposent d'opposer aux scandaleux desseins de quelques étrangers qui semblent vouloir établir dans notre patrie [...] des foyers d'impiété et de corruption" [Those are the noble efforts some esteemed compatriots intend to oppose to the scandalous designs of some foreigners who seem to want to establish in our homeland [...] hotbeds of impiety and corruption] (SB 1820 t.9: 130–131).

---

23 See Lemmens (2011). Saint-Jean (2010) has calculated that more or less half of the editors of periodicals in the Belgian regions were French. However, one should not deny the share of Northern Dutch writers, professors and journalists in the Southern Netherlands, especially in the second half of the 1820s. *De Argus* and the *Belgische Muzen-Almanak* were founded by Dutchmen, based on a Dutch model, and their pages were filled with articles communicated from the Northern Netherlands, with the aim of providing an example for southern literati (Weijermars 2011).

The presence of these French emigrants was favored by William I's liberalism and by the governors of the Flemish provinces, who were generally French-speaking. *Den Merkuur van Antwerpen* could not count on the governor's support as long as it did not appear in French; the *Letter- en Staatkundig Dagblad*, supported by the government, was in the paradoxical position that as a semi-official periodical promoting the national language and William I's language policy, it was nevertheless forced to insert official announcements by the governor in French (L&SD 21 March). It turned out that some of these foreign journalists were paid to spread the liberalism dear to William I, indirectly contributing to the hegemony of the French-language press in the Southern Netherlands.[24] These foreign journalists were also involved in the cultural affairs of their host country (Merecy 1945), often taking up peculiar standpoints. In the *Annales belgiques*, a Ghent periodical written by Frenchmen, "Flemish" literature did not seem to be a problem: it was simply part of Dutch literature. The perspective of this periodical was "Belgian", in the broad sense that William I tried to give to this term, encompassing all the inhabitants of the Kingdom.

De Foere and the Lebrocquy brothers wanted to provide a counterweight to this French hegemony and this reading of the literary field by creating periodicals by and for Flemings. This may obscure the fact that they themselves occupied an important position as mediators in the literary field of the Southern Netherlands. In addition to his work as a journalist, De Foere was probably part of a literary circle around Baron d'Eckstein (Charlier 1948) that worked to introduce European Romantic authors in the Southern Netherlands. P. Lebrocquy published and translated several collections of poems into French; J.H. Lebrocquy translated a Dutch literary history for a French-speaking audience. They were therefore immersed in French culture and language and inevitably took a stand towards that culture in their periodicals. France remained in all respects the privileged referent, as it was for most European nations (Thérenty and Vaillant 2010). On the one hand, it was the big sister with whom the Southern Netherlands shared a language. On the other hand, it was the aggressor who had restricted cultural life, press, and the language of the people for twenty years. The two periodicals both claimed they had to position themselves against the influence of this French culture. While the discourse on endogenous literature was therefore full of praise, the reality of the journalistic and literary field –

---

[24] Vermeersch (1992) has shown that this attitude of William I turned against him after 1825: partly due to the liberal teachings of the French emigrants who returned in the 1820s, the new generation of periodicals, even those with a Catholic bias, were more vocal, more political and demanded more self-government for the Southern Netherlands.

which was much more hostile to literature in Dutch – indicates the need to study the relationship that these periodicals had with this French element, which was characterized as foreign but hardly concealable in the cultural life of the Southern Netherlands.

One of the options, taken by some periodicals, was to try to eliminate all French references and turn to the North. The mediation of the Lebrocquy brothers took place from the Northern Netherlands to the Southern Netherlands, all while assimilating this Northern literature. The poems of Flemish and Dutch authors stood side by side and were part of the same literature. Foreign authors and works were mentioned in the "theater" section, since the Ghent theaters mainly put on foreign plays and often hosted French troupes. As far as language was concerned, the *Dagblad* expressed the desire from the outset for a unilingual Dutch text, the only argumentative language used in the journal. However, transfer and translation practices were very present even if they were well hidden under the unilingual text. Many articles were taken in their entirety from French language periodicals, such as the French *Journal des Débats*, the *Mercure Belge* from Brussels, the Parisian *Moniteur*, the *Journal de Paris* and the *Gazette de France*.[25] The Dutch translation was generally faithful to the original but above all very targeted, without making the original language appear. The sources themselves were translated ("Den Belgischen Mercurius" for "Mercure Belge" for example) and the mottos that accompanied certain articles were also translated – the common practice being to leave them in the original language. However, we have found that when the translator was unsure of his translation, he included the original word.[26] This is often the only indication of a multilingual reality and makes us assume that the editors knew their audience to be bilingual. In general, Lebrocquy's journalistic practice tried to hide this actual multilingualism and numerous transfers from French to Dutch, in order to create a monocultural and monolingual illusion. If the other language was present, it was well framed by the *Dagblad* and served as a rhetorical device. For exam-

---

[25] These are the sources for one issue, from 18 February 1820. We also note the presence of an English periodical quoted from time to time (*The Courier*). Dutch sources are quantitatively rather limited. There is the *Algemeen Nederlandsch Nieuws- en Advertentieblad* from 's Gravenhage and the *Letterbode* from Amsterdam.

[26] In the issue of 29 February, when describing a possible Waterloo monument, taken from an article in the *Mercure belge*, the translator spoke of a "verminkte steenen-kegel (un cône tronqué en terre)": this is a way of translating "tronqué", but perhaps not the appropriate meaning in this context. Is this why the translator has left the original term – implying that the necessarily bilingual readership can decide for itself what image this "truncated cone in the ground" provides?

ple, in order to highlight the "national language", it was compared with the French language by placing texts in Dutch and French side by side. The *Dagblad* thus published the poem "De Echtscheiding" by H. Tollens with a translation by a young "Belgian" to show that Dutch productions were on a par with French ones. "echter verhopen wij dat [de Franse vertaling] nog [...] zal kunnen [aantoonen], aan zulke persoonen, wie de taal min bekend is, [...] dat er ook bij ons bewonderingswaardige voortbrengselen gevonden worden" [We hope [...] that [the French translation] will convince those who are less familiar with the [Dutch] language that there are also admirable productions here] (L&SD 4 February)

French translations seemed useful to the editors of the *Dagblad*, "om hen, die nog door vooroordeelen verblind, van onze moedertaal eenen afkeer gevoelen, tot hare kennis en beoefening zachtelijk, en als 't ware ongevoelig, over te brengen" [in order to gently, and as it were imperceptibly, induce those who, blinded by prejudice, still feel an aversion to our mother tongue, to learn and practice it] (L&SD 9 May).

The other option was to include this French reference in a set of other national literatures that could serve "Flemish" literature. The program of the *Spectateur Belge* was to look outwards to "naturaliser dans sa patrie quelques productions des génies [...] de l'Europe" [naturalize in his homeland some productions of the geniuses [...] of Europe] (1823 t.18: 381). Nevertheless, the editor did not go beyond France. His first review was of *De l'Allemagne* by Mme De Staël and he sprinkled his journal with references to Chateaubriand. Still, "Flemish" literature could not be French, since he "déteste *dans ses principes* la Littérature française qui a dominé sur le dix-huitième siècle" [detested *in its principles* French Literature which had dominated the eighteenth century] (SB 1815 t.1: 220). One reader pointed to the overly exaggerated criticism of French literature in the *Spectateur*, and the corresponding lack of Flemish works:

> Vous voulez exalter nos compatriotes en abaissant nos voisins, mais quand l'exagération est aussi palpable, l'effet est manqué [...] Savez-vous, Monsieur, quelle est la meilleure manière de discréditer les Chef-d'œuvres français ? c'est en leur opposant de meilleurs ouvrages nationaux.
> [You want to exalt our compatriots by demeaning our neighbours, but when the exageration is so palpable, the effect is missed [...] Do you know, Sir, what is the best way of discrediting French masterpieces? It is by opposing them with better national works] (1815 t.1: 221–224).

This reader suggests that Flemish writers stop criticizing French literature and concentrate on national literary production. But according to De Foere, Flemish writers had not yet reached a respectable level. Under the guise of cultural and linguistic emancipation, he recommended (good) French works and wrote mainly in French himself: "J'attends avec la plus vive impatience le moment désiré que mes compatriots soient mûrs pour recevoir le *Spectateur Belge* en flamand" [I am looking forward with the greatest impatience to the desired moment when my compatriots are ready to receive the *Spectateur Belge* in Flemish] (1815 t.2: 65). Its purpose was quite unique: although it was written in French, the *Spectateur* is not to be situated in the vein of other French-language periodicals that wrote for the Republic of Letters. The *Spectateur* was initially very "Flemish" in its cultural orientation, with a didactic attitude and explicitly aimed at a local audience. To this end, it produced an assumed multilingualism: according to its program, articles in Dutch and French alternated according to the content. If he reprinted articles from other European periodicals, he reproduced them in their original language without translation. He considered his audience to be (passively) polyglot. However, as the issues progressed, this policy of multilingualism was replaced by a new program since it was the French-speaking public that had to be convinced of the beauty of the Dutch language. The text of the *Spectateur* became more and more unilingual French. The practice of translation became more important than the inclusion of articles in the original language. The *Spectateur* translated articles that were originally in Dutch to enter the debate on national language with the real enemies of Dutch.

> [l'on entend souvent la critique] que c'est *en français même* que sont écrits les ouvrages où l'on représente l'usage de cette langue comme une sorte d'hérésie politique et religieuse , ce qui [...] ne prouve rien contre l'existence positive de la langue nationale des Flamands , attendu que ces ouvrages sont aussi composés pour les Wallons qui ne savent pas le flamand et que d'ailleurs ces ouvrages sont de telle nature qu'ils sont hors du goût ou au-dessus de l'intelligence de ceux qui ne parlent que le flamand
> [we often hear the criticism] that it is *in French* that those works are written, in which the use of French is depicted as being some sort of heresy [...], which proves nothing against the positive existence of the national language of the Flemish, given that these works are also composed for the Walloons who don't know Flemish and that these works are of such a nature that they are beyond the taste or intelligence of those who speak only Flemish]
> (SB 1819 t.7: 174).

After the implementation of the national language laws of William I in 1819, which led to the official valorization of the Dutch language, the defense of the Flemish linguistic and literary identity became more and more linked to political and religious issues. Although De Foere was initially in favor of a national language shared by the Flemish and the Dutch, he became particularistic over the years. As a Catholic priest, he was suspicious of attempts to spread the "national language" through literary societies such as the *Maatschappij tot Nut van 't Algemeen*, which in the north had taken shape in Protestant communities. These societies and their works were, in De Foere's view, intended to spread Protestantism. In the *Letter- en Staatkundig Dagblad*, on the other hand, religion was conspicuously absent, and literature was only linked to its linguistic component. For De Foere, the real battle had become one for the religion of all Belgians, rather than for the Flemish language.[27] The *Spectateur* wanted to engage with the many opinion papers that were being created in Brussels by foreigners; French was thus essential. But beyond that, he wanted his periodical to participate in the international Republic of Letters. In contrast to journalists who intentionally wrote in Dutch in order to reach a local audience and to spread the use of the language – his own initial goal – De Foere was reinserting himself in the old tradition of French-language periodicals produced in the Southern Netherlands but aimed at a European audience (Verschaffel 2017: 109). He could thus state in 1820: "Le *Spectateur* n'est pas un ouvrage de province. Les matières qu'il examine sont d'un intérêt général. Il écrit aussi pour les provinces wallonnes de la Belgique et pour les pays étrangers, où le *Spectateur* est lu, et où la langue flamande n'est pas connue." [The *Spectateur* is not a provincial work. The subjects it examines are of general interest. He also writes for the Walloon provinces of Belgium and for foreign countries, where the *Spectateur* is read, and where the Flemish language is not known] (SB 1820 t.9: 254).

How far we have come from the first issue, where he claimed to be emerging from his "literary solitude" because "Il ne manque à [la] patrie que des mains qui lui rouvrent les sources de son ancienne félicité" [the only thing [the] fatherland lacks is hands that will reopen the springs of its ancient felicity] (SB 1815 t.1: 11). He intended at that time to "réveiller l'esprit national [et] rappeler les mœurs et la religion des Belges" [reawaken the national spirit [and] recall the morals and religion of the Belgians] (SB 1815 t.1: 21) and apologized to his Belgian readership for the few digressions he would make in the Republic of Letters: "que ma chère patrie me permette cette excursion timide dans le monde intellectual" [may my dear fatherland allow me this timid excursion into the intellectual world] (SB 1815 t.1: 9). Now that the Dutch language no longer had to defend itself against French in order to gain the status of national language,

---

27 In a reply to a reader who could no longer find the elements of a "literary journal" in the *Spectateur*, he stated that protecting the religion of the Belgian people had become more urgent than promoting the country's language: "Depuis deux ans, les attaques dirigées contre la religion sont beaucoup plus multipliées. C'est ce qui m'a engagé à donner au *Spectateur* un caractère de religion plus prononcé et plus exclusif" [For the past two years, attacks on religion have been much more numerous. This is what prompted me to give the *Spectateur* a more pronounced and exclusive religious character] (SB 1820 t.9: 79).

French could once again serve as a language of international culture and De Foere's journal became almost unilingual. While De Foere did not include any articles from Dutch periodicals during the first four years of his periodical, as soon as his editorial line changed, he began to include articles from the northern Catholic periodicals *Minerva* (1818–1821) and *De Godsdienstvriend* (1818–1869) – proving that by this time the defense of religion had become more important than the defense of a particular Flemish language and culture.

5 Conclusion

Between 1815 and 1825, the *Mercure belge* was considered by contemporaries to be the best literary journal in the Southern Netherlands. The *Dagblad* quoted an article from the *Mercure* about "het vreemd gelaat van het meeste deel onzer dagbladeren" [the foreign face of most of our periodicals] and the "belagchelijk en zelfs jammerlijk gebruik van het eigene voor het uitheemsche te verwaarloozen" [ridiculous habit of neglecting the endogenous for the foreign] (L&SD 1 February). This habit, "malgré les talens et les efforts redoublés de ses rédacteurs [avait mené vers l'échec du] seul journal littéraire qui existât dans le midi du Royaume" [in spite of the talens and redoubled efforts of its editors [had led to the failure of] the only literary journal that existed in the south of the Kingdom], said De Foere (SB 1821 t.13: 160). However, this *Mercure* was itself a French-language journal, written mostly by French émigrés and including works by foreign authors, such as Byron, Mme de Staël, and Chateaubriand, with only a (small) part of its pages devoted to Dutch literature. Moreover, its aim was to bring people together in the Republic of Letters: Dutch-language literature was taken for granted, and it had no desire to create a Flemish literature and a separate identity. It is revealing for the linguistic and cultural situation in the Southern Netherlands that this European journal, which focused on the French literary field, was revered as the best endogenous literary journal by the *Spectateur Belge*, the *Letter-en Staatkundig Dagblad* and by great figures of Flemish literature such as J.F. Willems. However, this is not an exception in Belgian literary history. Rather, these periodicals continued a "tradition" that already existed in the early days of the first literary periodicals in the Southern Netherlands: a continuous search for an identity of their own in a context of transfers and multilingualism. Discursively, the *Dagblad* and the *Spectateur* were (at least initially) in favor of the new government and the conciliation with the Northern Netherlands, which would push the Dutch language and literature in the Belgian provinces to new heights. Nevertheless, the Northern referent in these periodicals was only historical – contemporary Dutch authors were hardly read at all. The Dutch period, although it enabled new ideas on language and literature and offered the possibility of creating a new discourse on Flemish literature, perpetuated the eternal question of taking a stand for or against French language and culture. Even if the language was abhorred, as in the *Dagblad*, French was still very much present, and the cultural horizon remained French. The Dutch language was hardly ever present, unless, in the case of the *Dagblad*, it was explicitly included in the program and in the text of the periodical. If not through the presence of French journalists in French-language periodicals, French hegemony manifested itself through the content and references of the French-language Belgian periodicals, which were part of a Paris-centered Republic of Letters, and which did not develop any reasoning about Dutch literature in the Southern Netherlands. In the Flemish periodicals, didacticism continued to reign, and here again, it was through comparison with French productions that the reflection on "Flemish" literature was carried out. Openness to other literatures continued to be largely filtered through the French literary field. The *Spectateur Belge* explicitly engaged in this dialogue by commenting in French on works by French authors and by defending Flemish literature in French. But the translation and concealment practices of the *Dagblad* show that even in the context of a periodical with a Dutch cultural and political agenda, the French reference prevailed.

By focusing on the mediators and their mediation and translation strategies, we can better understand how a geopolitical context influenced the positions of journalists and the forms of periodicals. Reading a 19th century periodical dedicated to literature in Flemish gives us an insight into what was happening in this emerging literary field, but more importantly, how this field was constructed through journalistic writing. This construction of a Flemish literature was based on transfers from a wide variety of origins, including French. Whether it was the form of the periodical that praised Flemish literature, the sources used to write the articles, or even the language in which it was praised, this literature, which on the surface looked for its own roots in a medieval past, was undeniably being constructed in a multilingual and increasingly mediatized society. Comparing one editorial program to another and thereby taking into account the numerous ways in which journals attest to the multilingual reality of the Southern Netherlands help us to reveal (un)consciously hidden traditions and trends in journalistic writing in the Southern Netherlands. Periodicals also appear to be a privileged object to grasp not only the similarities, but moreover the nuances different mediators apply to the inevitable intertwinement of language and literature in this beginning of the nationalistic 19th century.

6 References

6.1 Primary Sources

Letter- en Staatkundig Dagblad. 1820. Ghent: G. De Busscher en Zoon.
Le Mercure belge (1817–1820). Brussels: Weissenbruch.
Le Spectateur Belge, ouvrage historique, littéraire, critique et moral (1815–1823). Bruges: La Veuve De Moor et Fils.

6.2 Secondary Sources

Aerts, Rien. 2002. Het algemeen-culturele tijdschrift in het negentiende-eeuwse medialandschap. *Tijdschrift voor tijdschriftstudies*, 11. 34–47.
Berg, Willem van den & Piet Couttenier. 2016. *Alles is taal geworden. Geschiedenis van de Nederlandse literatuur 1800–1900*. Amsterdam: Bert Bakker.
Brolsma, Marjet. 2008. Cultuurtransfer en het tijdschriftenonderzoek. *COnTEXTES*, [Online], http://contextes.revues.org/sommaire2983.html (accessed 1 July 2022).
Charlier, Gustave. 1948. *Le mouvement romantique en Belgique (1815–1850). Partie I: La Bataille romantique*. Brussels: Palais des Académies.
De Clercq, Annemie & Ada Deprez. 1996. De tijdschriften van 1815 tot 1833. *Bibliografie van de Vlaamse tijdschriften in de negentiende eeuw*. Ghent: Cultureel Documentatiecentrum Rijksuniversiteit.
D'hulst, Lieven. 2010. Ecrire dans un 'no man's land' littéraire: les revues 'belges' à l'époque hollandaise (1815–1830). In Susan Bainbrigge, Joy Charnley & Caroline Verdier (eds.). *Francographies – Identité et altérité dans les espaces francophones européens*. 85–97. New York, Bern, Berlin, Bruxelles, Frankfurt am Main, Oxford, Wien: Peter Lang.
D'hulst, Lieven. 2018. Un auteur à la recherche d'une littérature: Clavareau en 'Belgique' pendant la période 'hollandaise'. *Revue belge de philologie et d'histoire*, 96 (4). 1313–1325.
Duyse, Prudens van. 1858. Johan-Hendrik Lebrocquy. *De Eendragt*, 12(5). 97.
Espagne, Michel & Werner, Michael. 1985. Deutsch-französischer Kulturtransfer im 18. und 19. Jahrhundert. Zu einem neuen interdisziplinären Forschungsprogramm des C.N.R.S. *Francia*, 13. 502–510.
Espagne, Michel. 2013. La notion de transfert culturel. *Revue Sciences/Lettres*, 1. https://journals.openedition.org/rsl/219 (accessed 1 July 2022).
Grutman, Rainier, 2009. Multilingualism. In Mona Baker & Gabriela Saldanha (eds.). *Routledge Encyclopedia of Translation Studies*. 182–185. London, New York: Routledge.
Hanot, Michel. 1990. De Brusselse tijdschriften (1815–1846) en de Nederlandse letterkunde. In Deprez, Ana & Walter Gobbers (eds). *Vlaamse literatuur van de negentiende eeuw. Dertien verkenningen*. 84–119. Utrecht: HES.

Johannes, Gert-Jan. 1993. *De barometer van de smaak: tijdschriften in Nederland 1770–1830*. Den Haag: Sdu.

Lemmens, Wim. 2011. Het ontluikend liberalisme: Franse migranten, hun netwerken en journalistieke activiteiten in de Zuidelijke Nederlanden (1815–1820). *Revue belge de philologie et d'histoire*, 89(3–4). 1165–1191.

Lebrocquy, Pierre. 1842. *Souvenirs d'un ex-journaliste (1820–1844)*. Brussels: Géruzet.

Lebrocquy, Johann Hendrik. 1827. *Précis de l'histoire littéraire des Pays-Bas, traduit du hollandais de M. Siegenbeek*. Ghent: Vandekerckhove en Vassas.

Leerssen, Joep. 2014. Networks and Patchworks: Communication, Identities, Mediators. *Revue belge de philologie et d'histoire*, 92(4). 1395–1402.

Lissens, René Felix. 2000. *Een lectuur van 'Le Spectateur Belge' (1815–1823) van Leo de Foere. Traditionalisme in actie*. Ghent: Koninklijke Academie voor Nederlandse Taal- en Letterkunde.

Merecy, R. (1945). De Antwerpsche pers onder het Vereenigd Koninkrijk. *De Gulden Passer*, 23. 81–125.

Pasinomie: *collection complète des lois, arrêtés et règlements généraux qui peuvent être invoqués en Belgique. 1860*. Brussels: Bruylant.

Saint-Jean, Valentin. 2010. Le publiciste de la Belgique hollandaise: entre écrivain et journaliste. *Textyles* 39. 17–26.

Sgard, Jean (ed.). 1991. *Dictionnaire des journaux, 1600–1789*. 2 volumes. Paris: Universitas.

Simon, F. 1968. Leo De Foere, publicist en politicus. *Nationaal Biografisch Woordenboek*, vol. 3. Brussels: Koninklijke Vlaamse Academiën van België. 313–324.

Stynen, Ludo. 2012. *Jan Frans Willems. Vader van de Vlaamse Beweging*. Antwerp: De Bezige Bij.

Thérenty, Marie-Eve & Alain Vaillant (eds.). 2010. *Presse, nations et mondialisation au XIXe siècle*. Paris: Nouveau Monde Editions.

Vanacker, Hans. 1987. Leo d'Hulster. *Nationaal Biografisch Woordenboek*, vol. 12. Brussels: Koninklijke Vlaamse Academiën van België. 391–398.

Vermeersch, A.J. (1992). Willem I en de pers in de Zuidelijke Nederlanden 1814–1830. C.A. Tamse & Els Witte (eds). *Staats- en natievorming in Willem I's koninkrijk (1815–1830)*. 310–322. Brussels: VUBPress.

Verschaffel, Tom, Reine Meylaerts, Tessa Lobbes, Maud Gonne & Lieven D'Hulst. 2014. Towards a Multipolar Model of Cultural Mediators within Multicultural Spaces. Cultural Mediators in Belgium, 1830–1945. *Revue belge de philologie et d'histoire*, 92(4). 1255–1275.

Verschaffel, Tom. 2017. *De weg naar het binnenland. Geschiedenis van de Nederlandse literatuur 1700–1800: de Zuidelijke Nederlanden*. Amsterdam: Bert Bakker.

Vliet, Rietje van (ed.). 2022. *Encyclopedie van Nederlandstalige Tijdschriften (ENT). Nederlandstalige periodieken tot de aanvang van het Koninkrijk der Nederlanden (tot 1815)*. [Online]. https://www.ent1815.nl/ (accessed 1 July 2022).

Voordeckers, E. 1964. Pierre Lebrocquy, journalist en taalkundige. *Nationaal Biografisch Woordenboek, vol. 1*. Brussels: Koninklijke Vlaamse Academiën van België. 665–668.

Vosters, Rik. 2009. Integrationisten en particularisten? Taalstrijd in Vlaanderen tijdens het Verenigd Koninkrijk der Nederlanden (1815–1830). *Handelingen van de Koninklijke Zuidnederlandse maatschappij voor taal- en letterkunde en geschiedenis*, 62. 41–58.

Vosters, Rik & Guy Janssens. 2014. *Sur la langue nationale. Taal en taalpolitiek in het Verenigd Koninkrijk der Nederlanden en het jonge België*. (Noord en Zuid onder Willem I. 200 jaar Verenigd Koninkrijk der Nederlanden 4). The Hague: Algemeen-Nederlands Verbond.

Vosters Rik & Janneke Weijermars (eds.). 2012. *Taal, cultuurbeleid en natievorming onder Willem I*. Brussels: Koninklijke Vlaamse Academie van België voor Wetenschappen en Kunst.

Weijermars, Janneke. 2009. Neerlandistiek als bindmiddel van de natie: hoogleraar Schrant in Gent 1817–1830. *De Negentiende Eeuw*, 1. 4–19.

Weijermars, Janneke. 2012. *Stiefbroeders. Zuid-Nederlandse letteren en natievorming onder Willem I, 1814–1834*. Hilversum: Verloren.

Willems, Jan Frans. 1819–1824. *Verhandeling over de Nederduytsche tael- en letterkunde, opzigtelyk de Zuydelyke Provintien der Nederlanden. 2 volumes*. Antwerp: J.S. Schoesetters.

Joanna Pietrzak-Thébault
The "French" History of Polish Literature or Two Languages — One "Oeuvre"

The Poetic Prose of Young Zygmunt Krasiński in French and Polish (1829–1831)

Abstract: This chapter examines the French history of Polish literature in the first half of the 19th century. During the 18th century the French language was the vehicle of classical culture and literature in Poland. However, only few Polish writers used it in their artistic expression. On the verge between the Classic and Romantic epochs the vivid discussions about a new vision of the literature did not concern the question of the "language". At the same time, the day-to-day knowledge of French was expanding. The most eminent Polish writers of a new Romantic generation were able to use it for evident stylistic purposes or as a hidden bilingual basis – like Adam Mickiewicz. The case of the young Polish Romantic writer, Zygmunt Krasiński, is quite unique. His will to construct his Romantic literary and biographical (pseudo-biographical) myth was based on his bilingual French and Polish oeuvre: poetic prose written in Switzerland, in the short period between the end of 1829 and 1832. The writer, coming from an aristocratic family, used French as a so-called natural language but never came back to it in his literary career again. Still, it could be his early French work that constructed the literary basis of one the most important Polish Romantic authors. This case study concludes the chapter.

Keywords: Polish literature, French language, Romanticism, Classicism, Poetic Prose

1 Introduction: The French language in Poland

In the 1820's and 30's there was no significant French-language literary production in Poland that would be comparable to, for example, that in Russia (cf. Baudin 2013: 81–91; *French and Russian in Imperial Russia* 2015: 228–242).

Joanna Pietrzak-Thébault, Cardinal Stefan Wyszynski University,
e-mail: j.thebault@uksw.edu.pl

ə Open Access. © 2023 the author(s), published by De Gruyter. This work is licensed under the Creative Commons Attribution 4.0 International License.
https://doi.org/10.1515/9783110778656-005

Throughout the entire 18th century and during the transition to Romanticism, numerous Polish authors wrote in French but, above all, they translated foreign-language works into their native language. Initially they translated mostly from French, and as the years passed, also from Italian, German, and English (Bajer 2020: 13, 308–310, 312–314; Jędrzejewski 2016: 19, 34–35).[1] However, few achieved mastery in the field of French-language writing equaling that of King Stanisław August Poniatowski (1732–1798), Jan Potocki (1761–1815),[2] and Wacław Seweryn Rzewuski (1784–1831).[3] But when we pose the question of the actual awareness and popularity of their works among readers, the perspective may change substantially. The history of these texts' reception is not a simple issue, and in the case of the journals written by the last king of Poland it is particularly complex (Casanova 1999: 34, 104, 130).[4]

Somewhat paradoxically, French-language texts were widely circulated: works originally written in French (of purely literary, publicistic, historical and political nature) and translations of classical (mainly dramas) and modern French literature (philosophical treatises, novels, poetry, also including lowbrow works — serving as day-to-day entertainment, such as romances, idylls, song texts, etc.). This must have led to a strong embedding of this literature along the Vistula (Bajer 2020: 299–300, 307–309, 313–314).

Until now, the study of such texts and reading practices has been, if not omitted, then at least neglected by historians and critics of literature wishing to

---

1 See also *Pisarze polskiego Oświecenia* [Writers of the Polish Enlightenment] ed. T. Kostkiewiczowa, Z. Goliński, Wyd. Naukowe PWN, Warszawa 1994–1996, vol. 1–3, passim.
2 He wrote substantially more in French than in Polish. His most original and interesting work, *The Manuscript Found in Saragossa* long remained unknown, until the first edition of Edmund Chojecki's translation (actually, only one of the versions of this work) appeared in 1847, Księgarnia Zagraniczna, Lipsk [Leipzig] (further – ibidem, 1857). French edition: Jan Potocki, *Œuvres*, ed. F. Rosset, D. Triaire, Editions Peeters, Loeuven-Paris, 2004–2006, vol. IV and VI. Pocket edition: Flammarion, Paris 2008. See also *Pisarze polskiego Oświecenia* [Writers of the Polish Enlightenment] op. cit., Warszawa 1994, vol. 2., p. 426–428, 433–437 (Janusz Ryba). About his pluricultural education and practice cf. Ryba 2007: 123–124, 126–127.
3 Wacław Seweryn Rzewuski, Sur les chevaux orientaux et provenant des races orientales / Concerning the Horses of the Orient and those Originating from Oriental Breeds / O koniach wschodnich i wywodzących się z ras orientalnych, ed. Tadeusz Majda, t. I, Rękopis, t. II, Album i Opisy, t. III, Eseje, The National Library of Poland, Warsaw 2017.
4 Was the situation similar with the treatise of another king-author, Friedrich II, who deliberated in French about causes of the development (conceived as the "delay") of German literature? Friedrich II, *De la littérature allemande*, 1780, here after: P. Casanova, *La République mondiale des lettres*, Seuil, Paris 1999, p. 34, 104, 130. Cf. also A. Rivarol, *Discours de l'universalité de la langue française*, published in 1784, after: ibid., p. 104.

ascribe literary works to a strictly defined, narrow and impassable cultural circle (Fumaroli 2001: 463–465).[5]

When critics and historians of literature investigate the transition from the classical to romantic vision of the world and literature, they do not consider a possible different attitude towards native / foreign languages. The question of language remains hidden or neglected – as if writers used to read and create in an abstract manner. The practice of most nowadays editions, even the academic ones, of literary texts, but also of letters, sketches, and writers' notes are usually translated and "clean", deprived of any error or hesitation. They don't give the reader the opportunity to realize how rich and various the linguistic reality of many writers could be. Unfortunately, it does not concern only the Polish field. A single remark about notes in many languages, mixing even some of them in a one single sentence, that Stendhal used to put in margins of his autographs, can help us to look differently at his particularly limpid style in French: was this a kind of game, a way to relax during periods of intensive work – hidden in front of his readers (Martineau 1957: VIII). A more consistent example of the same Romantic period is this of Niccoló Tommaseo, an Italian writer, linguist and critic, provides a more consistent example from the Romantic period. His plurilingual work *Scintille / Iskrice* [The Sparks] (the first edition is from 1841) had to wait until the first years of our century to be edited entirely and appear in a critical version (Bruni 2008: XI, XCIX). Still, today both Croatians and Serbians dispute his paternity for their literary modern tongues (Pietrzak-Thébault 2021: 42, 44). This work, consisting in short fragments in prose and in verse, in Italian, French, Latin, modern Greek and the disputable "*illirico*" has rarely been investigated or appreciated in its integrality – because it has been considered (too?) disparate, odd, and chaotic (Pietrzak-Thébault 2021: 46).[6] Hence, it is clear that this way of composing proceeded from a deliberate romantic vision and a new linguistic attitude – quite different from the common use: not only to

---

5 M. Fumaroli, *Quand l'Europe parlait français*, Ed. de Fallois, Paris, 2001, p. 463–465. Entire edition : Stanislas Auguste, *Mémoires*, ed. A. Grześkowiak-Krwawicz, D. Triaire, Institut d'études slaves, Société historique et littéraire polonaise, Paris, 2012. Cf. also *Writers of the Polish Enlightenment*, op. cit., Warszawa 1992, vol. 1, p. 381–382, and rich bibliography p. 382–385 (Jerzy Michalski). About relations of Poniatowski with French writers see L. Fabre, *Stanisław August i literaci francuscy*, in: idem, *Od oświecenia do romantyzmu. Studia i szkice z literatury i kultury polskiej* [Stanisław August and French writers, in: idem, From enlightenment to romanticism. Studies and sketches from Polish literature and culture], ed. K. Kasprzyk, Tow. Literackie im. A. Mickiewicza, Warszawa 1995, p. 32–79 (French original: *Stanislas-Auguste et les hommes de lettres français*, "Archivum Neophilologicum", Kraków 1936, II, p.1–53)
6 See below about the character of Krasiński's poetic prose in Polish and French.

employ languages already learned to write, but also to learn a new language (on and with an ideological purpose, as Tommaseo did when he had discovered his Slavonic roots) – with the purpose to use it in artistic creation (Bruni 2008: XV–XVII, XIX, XXI; Pietrzak-Thébault 2021: 41–42, 48–49; cf. Maingueneau 1993: 104–106). These examples show how investigating plurilingual works can help us to better understand the oeuvre of poets and writers. Knowing who wrote and in which language can give us insight into the 'main' national, native language of the oeuvre.

If we consider their oeuvre in this way, we see clearly that there are many writers and poets whose works cannot be fully ascribed to one linguistic area, which, at the same time, enriches the heritage of any literature they "belong to".

In practice, at the time, French was treated as a common idiom for literature and as a means of communication for intellectual elites and aristocracy throughout Europe, and it had little in common with the national identity of "Frenchness" as such (Casanova 1999: 99–104). In Poland, in the first half of the 19th century, knowledge of this language was cultivated in aristocratic circles (cf. Czapska 2004: 17–158) and taught to youth (of both sexes), in both home-schooling and institutional educational environments. Over 60 textbooks, grammar books, dictionaries and anthologies ("readers") were used, and in schools, the number of class hours dedicated to teaching the language reached up to 40 per week (Birn 1949: 386–389; Cieśla 1974: 88–109, 142–174, 198; Glixelli 1922: 155–159, 164–165; Zaleska-Stankiewiczowa 1935: 66–67, 105–106, 108–110, 132; Czapska 1958: 26–32; Brunot 1934: 470–471, 483–487). Today, it is difficult to determine the extent to which these efforts in Poland succeeded in making French into more than just a dead language, i. e., a very conventionalized language used exclusively in the context of transferring cultural and literary heritage considered to be universal (Fabre 1980: 305; Beauvois 1991: 358–364).

Such an education certainly contributed to a familiarity with the language, and moreover, a vision as to what function it was to serve, and a desire to use this language in specific social situations. Love correspondence, a genre at the intersection of practical, day-to-day communication (the need to arrange the date and time of a rendez-vous) and quasi-literary ambitions (expression of emotions), provides a meaningful example here: letters written to Adam Mickiewicz by Maryla Wereszczakówna, the love from the poet's youth, from the years 1822–1830, and by Joanna Zaleska, written in Odessa in the spring of 1828 (Kleiner 1848: 517, Pietrzak-Thébault 2011: 213–216).[7]

---

[7] At Musée Mickiewicz, Paris, MAM 640, ff. 1–3, Library of KUL (Catholic University of Lublin), 733, f. 78. French originals have not been published yet. MAM 702, f. 1–2].

In modern Polish literary history, attention has been paid on more than one occasion to the transformations that the poet's literary portrayal of his acquaintance with Maryla during his youth underwent, and the difficulty, or rather the impropriety, of separating reality from literary inspiration, and later – from legend. Wereszczakówna's letters (actually, already Mrs. Puttkamer at the time) demonstrate, however, that a similar desire also existed on her side although her overtures, when viewed as a literary transformation of reality, were comparably more modest (cf. Stefanowska 2007: 7–12). The letters from Joanna Zaleska are, in turn, a testimony to consciously constructed emotional tension. The way in which both ladies used the French language is proof of a familiarity with literature of rather Romantic origin, as well as of a certain fluency in French sentimental rhetoric; however, it also betrays obvious deficiencies in grammar, phraseology and lexis (Pietrzak-Thébault 2011: 213–217).

The examples of modest texts originating from the fringes of literature help to understand the circumstances determining the choice of the given language. On this occasion, one can notice without difficulty the extent to which the language of a literary work is something other than language used by the common user (including a literary author) for communication purposes (cf. Beretta 2013: 9–10; Pirlot 2013: 37–38). This occurs even when a literary work is being written in the native language. This is because the language of literature is a conscious, artistic realization done in the matter of language, whether it be natural or learned (Casanova 1999: 16, 23, 63–64, 68).

2 Was the major Polish poet also a French-language writer?

It is simply impossible, while writing about Polish Romantic literature not to mention Adam Mickiewicz. We focus here briefly only on few, but very significant examples of the strictly literary field, leaving apart the conspicuous lectures on Slave literature from Collège de France (1840–1844), delivered in French, in the obvious Paris context (see Mende 2020: 50, Prussak 2011: 17–20). *Dziady* (1832) [Forefathers' Eve], written around the same time as Krasiński's prose, exemplifies how multilingualism can function within a single literary work. In scene VIII of the third part, the Russians, the Senator (Novosiltzov) and Baïkov as well as the traitor Docteur (Bécu), weave French expressions into their speech, thereby showing their alienness with respect to the Polish heroes of the drama. The French language takes on an unambiguously negative undertone in this context. In conversation, those who are hostile to and have contempt for young Poles and their ambitions of independence use the French language (Stefanowska 1976: 135).

Another very interesting example of hidden bilingual writing can be found in an autograph n° 84 (Musée Mickiewicz, Paris). It was somehow "omitted" ("forgotten"?) by editors of Mickiewicz's writings not only because of its complicated context, related to Towiański's messianic ideology, but also because of a lyric distich in Polish is followed by a piece of French prose, probably being a poet's version of another person's. The text demonstrates an internal tension and reveals intellectual process occurring in two different directions and in two languages letter. (Szczeglacka-Pawłowska 2013: 195). Apparently simpler but surely not better known and still very impressive are cases in which Mickiewicz uses in French in his last years. Who is the intended audience of Conversations des malades, a short prose sketch written in Constantinople where Polish, Hungarian, and French officers are discussing cholera morbus and attempting to find a remedy with the assistance of French cognac? The very illness described with much black humor in his last literary work killed the poet suddenly two weeks later (Pietrzak-Thébault 2013: 491–504; Stefanowska 2005: 75–77). Even more intimate testimony of Mickiewicz's use of the literary French remains hidden in his notes. He copied some fragments of the Lamartine's poem *Quatrième meditation. Le Soir* together with "titles": *L'étoile* and *Inconsolé* by Gérard de Nerval. He put this literary collage on the same blue letter paper he took then to Constantinople. According to the testimony of his daughter, he did it at his wife's deathbed. Visibly, the Polish poet considers French contemporary poetry the most appropriate remedy / way to express and a remedy for his own pain. But, at the same time, he was probably looking for a new literary expression, appealing to French contemporary poetry. Has, in the space of twenty years, the foreign language become so much intimate, so well-known that he could draw from it as from his native tongue (*Katalog...* 1996: 67–70; Pietrzak-Thébault 2018: 19–20; Suchet 2014: 40, 43)?[8] It is not easy to understand the real meaning of these literary and linguistic "games".

---

[8] However, when he started to deliver his lectures in the Collège de France, in December 1840, he said this: "La langue française est pour moi comme une chaîne..."

3 Between two epochs

As already mentioned, reference to the French language did not have clear nationalistic connotations at the turn of the 18th century nor did it. Thus, the choice of the French language did not raise controversy, as it had primacy not only in diplomacy, but also in salon conversation and literature and philosophy. In the new era, in which the thought of Herder and then Schelling was widely propagated and strengthened, in which Byron became an obsessive point of reference for the literature created throughout Europe and in which the Romantic paradigm sought its identity in language and turned towards translations rather than towards universalism, using the French language required courage (Berman 1985: 21–22, 25–42, 101–103; Fabre 1980: 328; Zgorzelski 1961: 8). All the more so since reference to a classical idiom also entailed an attempt to transform it in accordance with the requirements of the aesthetic of new Romantic literature (Prussak 2011b: 423–437).

The French language was also considered a vehicle of literature associated with by a very high level of prestige, the one that transmitted and created classic European heritage (cf. Maingueneau 1993: 107). Thus, it was present in a Polish cultural area, treated not as an "example" but as a "source" (Rejman 2007: 241, 243, 246, 252). Though, the clash between the classics and romantics that occupied very much the literary and cultural life of Poles at the turn of the 18th century did not take up the question of language or languages (Wyka 1989: 169–170; Jędrzejewski 2016: 23–26). These debates concerned much more the nature of poetry in general than the existence of a "national" or "patriotic" element that it should contain (Jędrzejewski 2016: 21, 26–29, 49, 50). So, paradoxically, the multiplicity of inspirations and a new vision of literature could lead writers and poets also to look for new linguistical adventures in the same way they looked for new genres, new rules (or a lack of them…) of composition, and new syntactic or semantic experiments. Thus, a "foreign" learned language could become new artistic raw material, without provoking any ideological assessments or any theorical debates on its existence or role (Suchet 2014: 42).

4 Zygmunt Krasiński as a French-speaking *aristocrate*

The voice of young Zygmunt Krasiński seems to be significant in these struggles (Berlin 1991: 39, 194; Pietrzak-Thébault 2013: 22–23). As an aristocrat and cosmopolitan, for whom the French language was naturally inscribed into the day-to-day practices of his environment, Krasiński did not have to deal with difficulties of a purely linguistic nature. Belonging to the aristocratic class meant (and means) belonging to a thin social layer of similar people, regardless of their country of origin. Therefore, this layer, while few in number, is present practically everywhere and has a distinctly cosmopolitan character (Czapska 2004; Pietrzak-Thébault 2019: 481–483). The very fact of belonging to this privileged group did not necessarily cause the works of a writer among its ranks to be classified as part of the literature of the country of his origin. However, the direct points of reference are changed because of this, as the circle of what is accepted as available, understandable, and finally, "own", is widened (Prussak 2011b, passim). The ease with which the son of the Napoleonic general Wincenty, born in Paris and educated from his youngest years by a French governess, used the French language, puts his literary and language choices in a different light (Janion 1962: 24–25). It is in just such cases, when the boundaries between methods of using two languages are fluid and inconspicuous that the issue of the manner in which the writer creates gets pushed into the background (cf. Maingueneau 1993: 105–111).[9]

Meanwhile, the view of literature that had dominated for many decades until that time, as developing solely within the framework of a single language, made such a perspective practically impossible. Being the inheritor of nationalistic thought, from the mid-19th century and for many decades of the 20th century, this vision saw in literature the sole, justified expression of national belonging. Largely based on the idea of nation-states and criteria of belonging to them on the awareness of language, it remained faithful to this conviction for many long decades (Thiesse 1999: 83–94; Baggioni 1997: 74–77; Casanova 1999: 58–59).

The works of Zygmunt Krasiński, especially from the 1820's and 30's, were exploratory ones (Bagłajewski 2018: 235–236), and as such can be read in context of the many conscious choices made by the author. Among these decisions, the issue of language as creative matter played a significant role. The French language appears next to the Polish language on equal terms (cf. Szczeglacka-Pawłowska 2015: 404–406).[10] The "naturality" with which Krasiński approaches

---

[9] The value of a sculpture does not depend only on the fact if it is of stone or marble, of bronze or alabaster...

[10] The new edition: Zygmunt Krasiński. 2017. demonstrated it very clearly. A chronological order of texts, regardless of the language in which they were written, was adopted. See in particular vol. 6.

and uses the French language arises not only from his cosmopolitan freedom of association with various high circles, but also his freedom of movement, ease of travel, and the possibility of choosing the places where he stays. This arises from a sense of belonging to a European cultural community, to the "common classical capital" (Casanova 1999: 28, 32, 37–38; Larbaud 1936: 11). This underlines the fact that literature, despite rising nationalist tensions, was becoming "pan-European" at the time, that it was at times detached from national or state affiliation to the detriment of no one (cf. Casanova 1999: 60).

The writer ostensibly only took style lessons from his Genevan teacher, François Roget (of whom he wrote in a letter to his father dated June 12th, 1830) and avidly read contemporary French literature (Szczeglacka 2005: 136, 144; Clément 1964: 183–184 and in nota). He is proud of that fact – at the time when the direct relation master / pupil seems to be definitely broken (Wyka 1989: 89–91, 141). Krasiński continues in the "classical" direction, using a "classical" language to create, paradoxically, one of the most romantic collection of texts in the Polish literature.

5 Between the Classical idiom and a Romantic expression

The young writer employs his mastery of the classical idiom and his skill in using this strongest and most far-reaching cultural tool of the time not to strengthen this idiom but rather in an attempt to dismantle it in search of a new language that would be "adequate"[11] for romantic themes, Byronic inspirations, and a new sensitivity expressed in sensations as a subjective experience, in the blurring of the boundaries between description and narration...

The French language is highly intellectualized, rational, and expresses thoughts precisely. Meanwhile, Krasiński, whose native tongue is undoubtedly more pictorial, uses French above all to create images. In crossing the frames and boundaries of his still nascent writing ability, he rejects easy and obvious choices. Yet, he does not always emerge victorious in these endeavors. He often suffers defeat, but has not a similar failure also been the lot of much French Romantic literature? For the new imagery had to yield to pressure from iron logic of French syntax and the centuries-old tradition of the skill and need of

---

11 "Adequacy" – this is one of the key expressions used to denote what is desirable and proper in the French language and literature of bygone centuries.

clear leading of thought, speculative and narrative alike (Krasiński 1963: 159). French literary language faced multiple dilemmas on the threshold of the Romantic era: how to develop an alternative to the "noble" style, how to deal with attempts to renew syntax, to inject romantic grandeur into the traditionally rigid, unchanging metric forms. This was not an unambiguous or easy period for French literary language (François 1959: 169, 175–179). This must be remembered when analyzing the struggles of Polish authors with this language, and of Zygmunt Krasiński in particular. Krasiński bravely "pushes the boundaries" of this language – "breaking" himself in the process.

The fact that the Count turned to the French language did not at all mean that he abandoned writing in the Polish language, and hence can be perceived as a courageous choice, betraying, despite the appearance of "youthful frivolity" a universal, universalist vision of literature, within reach of his quill (Krasiński 2017: vol 6/1 159–178, 187–204, 211–256, 269–409; vol. 6/2 15–96, 109–120, 135–370; vol. 6/3 11–243, 257–272, 498–522).[12] With these French-language works at our disposal, it is time to turn critical attention to these texts and their premises for an in-depth investigation. In doing so, these works, composed on the shores of Lake Léman (a place that has particularly made its mark on the European map of Polish literature)[13] by the young writer, Count Zygmunt, can be restored to their rightful place.

Understanding the role that the French language played in Krasiński's development as a writer does not in any way depreciate his works in his native language. However, it does demand consideration of his works as a whole, and thus seeking their cohesion, with the need of arriving at this vision. So, this is one more piece of evidence indicating how significant this fragment of Krasiński's literary legacy is, both in the context of the entirety of his work (including his way of thinking about literature), and more broadly – in the European space of the new Romantic paradigm. The poet thereby stands in opposition to the general trend of separating "modern" linguistic and literary identity (Casanova 1999: 60–61; Berlin 1991: 307; Berlin 2004: 71–73, 85–107, 140–141, 192–194; Wyka 1989: 40–51, 77, 85), and explores the extent to which universal expression is capable of adapting to new literature. Deliberate contraction of them

---

[12] See the new edition of the writer's works, which, thanks to a chronological arrangement of works of similar genre, makes it possible to perceive the interpenetration of plots and construction of parallel artistic visions in two languages, which is of particular significance precisely in the context of a global assessment of poetic prose.

[13] See the outstanding *Liryki Lozańskie – The Leman Lake Lyrics* by Mickiewicz. Written in 1839–1840, these texts were only recognized as new, original, modern poetry decades later.

forms the basis of writing, in which a fleeting moment is juxtaposed with a description of that which seemed most permanent on Earth to the author (the peaks of the Alps). That the young writer (born only in 1812) immersed himself deeper in the practice of the French language and in the common classical civilizational community than other Polish authors of the time gives proof of his autonomy of thought and artistic courage through his choice of linguistic apparatus, which is only ostensibly obvious. This did not mean in any way that Krasiński wrote French literature from spirit and tradition. Most texts contain an epigram from Byron, to whose poetry Krasiński directly refers. Stories set in the Middle Ages clearly relate to the Walter-Scott narrative, building the Romantic vision of that literary era (Berlin 2004: 194–196).

6 What really happened on the banks of Lake Léman?

The bulk of Zygmunt Krasiński's work in French was written in Geneva, where the poet stayed intermittently between the fall of 1829 and the summer of 1832. He did not arrive there as a renowned author, certainly, but not as a beginner either. In Warsaw he had written and published prose poems, historical short stories and a longer historical novel, as well as a translation of Byron's *Parisina* (Markuszewska 2021: 26). However, he showed no indication of an exceptional talent for writing. The very intense years in Geneva resulted in a set of about fifty texts. The vast majority of them are short texts, which can be defined as poetic prose (Markuszewska 2021: 27). Many texts are, as we have already mentioned, "impressionistic" descriptions, or very brief reports of simple episodes or events which are presented as something experienced by the narrator (or claimed to be so), while the others have a narrative character, revolving around a protagonist, presented in the third person ("he"), who remains anonymous. There is also a collection of texts, all of them of a narrative character, set in a medieval setting and showing Walter Scott's influence on the writer, an influence which was already present in the Polish beginnings of his work, it is evident that this process continues in his French works. Still, other texts are plunged into a frenetic, dark and gloomy atmosphere, in a strongly gothic vein (Pietrzak-Thébault 2020: 343–356). Three texts are longer: two short stories: *Adam le Fou* [Adam the Fool], *Le Cholera*, and the *Journal* (Szczeglacka 2005: 155–159), a report of a long excursion to the Alps in August 1830. *Adam le Fou* is indeed a multilingual creation as it has in fact two versions: neither of them is not the translation (or rather a 'self-translation').

The difficulty in defining these texts stems from the extremely uncertain, not to say vague, character of their genre and of the overall picture they create. Critics and literary historians usually emphasize this fragmentary, uncertain, chaotic character of Krasiński's Genevan legacy (Szczeglacka 2005: 130–133, Szczeglacka-Pawłowska 2015: 409–414). The reading usually gives the impression of something more than just an academic, stylistic, and even rhetorical exercise (Wyka 1989: 89–91, 141, Kowalczykowa 1987: 67–74, 95–97).

The internal world of the many texts is also vague: geographically speaking, space is not defined: it can be a flowery path, the vicinity of a chapel, a cemetery, even "a corner" of the cosmic spheres. Time can be limited to a short moment before sunset, to a brief encounter, or it can extend over tens or even hundreds of years. Sometimes there are, all the same, very concrete references to places, such as the foothills of Mont Blanc, the banks of Lake Geneva, the surroundings of Geneva, the Sallanche pass. In most cases, however, the images are barely specified, leaving room for impressions, feelings, descriptions, maybe memories, full of shadows and colors. Such is the case in the text *Le coucher du soleil sur le Mont-Blanc. Extrait du journal d'un voyageur* [The Sunset on the Mont-Blanc. Extract from the diary of a traveler] (Krasiński 2017: 6/II: 111–120; Krasiński 2021: 167–169)."

> Et je vis lutter le rayon contre l'ombre. Ce fut une agonie lente au commencement, rapide vers la fin. Des flots d'étincelles éblouirent la vue ; elles semblaient s'animer de plus en plus, mais toujours en se retirant vers le sommet ; et quand elles l'atteignirent, elles s'arrêtèrent encore un instant, comme si forcées dans leur dernier poste elles voulaient dignement se défendre. La nuit le poursuivait de l'aile de la destruction ; le combat fut court ; il sembla que tous les rayons, jusqu'au dernier, périssaient. Une contraction de douleur, une teinte blanchâtre et livide se répandit sur tous les cotes de la montagne, et tout était dit ; le jour n'était plus
> [And I saw the ray fighting against the shadow. It was a slow agony at the beginning, rapid towards the end. Streams of sparks dazzled the view; they seemed to become more and more animated, but always retreating towards the summit; and when they reached it, they stopped again for a moment, as if forced into their last position they wanted to worthily defend themselves. The night pursued him with the wing of destruction; the fight was short; it seemed that all the rays, until the last, perished. A contraction of pain, a pale and livid hue spread over all the sides of the mountain, and all was said; the day was no longer] (Krasiński 2017: 6/II 112 ; Krasiński 2021: 168).

Here, as so often, Krasiński resorts to the method of personification – but he does it in his own way, uniting description with the narrative. Nevertheless, either the brief descriptions of the poetic prose, or the much more detailed explanations of the *Journal* about the excursion to the Alps, reveal a great ability to observe, to impart color and movement to scenes, which are vivid still before the eyes of today's readers. However, the reader is often abandoned at the border between what is certain and what appears to be barely sketched out, even provisional.

As for the uncertain indications of time within the literary texts, it is countered by statements indicating the date, and often the exact time of the alleged composition of the text, almost always placed at the beginning of the texts. Is this a true fact or rather a literary game that the young author plays with his reader? Are they paratexts or should the reader see them as an integral part of the work?

> 28 octobre, Genève, 1830
> Farewell – farewell! And it for ever
> Still for ever, fare thee well.
> Byron
>
> L'heure du départ est proche ; les chevaux trépignent d'impatience ; l'air est frai, la route semée de feuilles d'automne ; le voyageur roulera doucement au-dessus. [...] Beau Leman ! [...] J'ai vogue sur tes flots bleus quand le soleil était a son midi ; sur tes flots rougeâtres, quand a son couchant, il s'environnait de gloire ; sur tes flots pales et sombres quand le crépuscule s'étendait au-dessus. [...] La brise est fraiche, elle aura bientôt sèche cette larme qui coule sur ta joue ! Partons ! Les feuilles d'automne couvrent le chemin ; le voyageur roulera doucement au-dessus, et le sommeil endormira ses regrets
>
> [The hour of departure is near; the horses tremble with impatience; the air is fresh, the road is strewn with autumn leaves; the traveler will drive gently over it. [...] Beautiful Leman! [...] I have sailed on your blue waves when the sun was at its noon; on your reddish waves, when at its sunset, it surrounded itself with glory; on your pale and somber waves when the twilight extended above. [...] The breeze is fresh, it will soon dry this tear which runs on your cheek! Let us leave! The autumn leaves cover the path; the traveler will roll gently over it, and slumber will put his regrets to sleep] (Krasiński 2017: 6/II 241–244; Krasiński 2021: 207–210).

The fragmentary character, perceived either at the level of each text – even underlined by the titles *Fragment d'un rêve* [Fragment of a dream], *Fragment d'un journal* [Fragment of a diary], or just *Fragment* – or of the entire corpus is surely deliberate. All this reveals a strong need to search for a new and clean literary expression. Krasiński acts, from the very beginning, as a – modern – Romantic writer in his own right. He finds everything on his own through his readings and quickly understands one of the most important characteristics of Romantic writing and puts it into practice (Zgorzelski 1978: 160–162, 178, Kurska 1989: 16–18).

His world, like his writing, is composed of "fragments", which becomes its true value. Poetic prose – absent so far in Polish literary practice – conveys a well-considered artistic vision in the writing of the young Krasiński. It is perfect in its expression but certainly not in the sense of leading to an artistic masterpiece (Kurska 1989: 33–35, 38, 47–50). What we are talking about is a perfection of artistic creation which pretends, feigns writing a real diary by building a literary creation out of real episodes. Yet the distance between one and the other is maintained, especially when the writer resorts to the character presented in the third person: the anonymous "he" (Szczeglacka 2005: 135–137, 144–145, Szczeglacka-Pawłowska 2015: 35, 407–409; Kurska 1989: 48–49).

7 Writing alone or with / for others?

Rarely does he go on to become the narrator of his own sentimental, aesthetic, and spiritual "adventures". If critics have widely debated the undeniable value and complexity of this literary construction, they have not paid much attention to the fact that most of the "Genevan" texts are written in French. Looking at the context of this creative work perhaps allows us to understand this enigma. Up close, the multilingual context expands even further. For the most part, we can attribute the work to three British people: the poet G.G. Byron (Kurska 1989: 16, 56), Henriette Willan, with whom the author fell passionately and 'emphatically' in love, and, above all, Henry Reeve (1813–1895), a British journalist and translator. Byron appears as the author of several epigrams in Krasiński's texts – he introduces here a real literary and poetic context in which the texts were written (see above).

His friendship with the young Englishman, Henry Reeve, endowed with a deep poetic sensibility who later became an important figure in the intellectual life of England throughout the 19th century (Kallenbach 1902: XVI–XVIII, XXV–XXXVII, Markuszewska 2018: 19–26), gave rise to lively abundant correspondence (about five hundred letters exchanged in the space of two years 1830–1832), in which both young people wrote about their tastes, readings, and feelings, but above all their literary experiences of the time. The letters, written in French, but with important insertions and poetic quotations in English allow us to perceive not only the intensity of the relationship between these two young people, but also that of creation – above all of Krasiński. It would be very careless to neglect the role of this long-lasting friendship and the letters documenting it. Krasiński wrote in French to give his friend a chance to read his own works. Thus, the language of their daily communication, confessions, exchanges of readings also became the language of artistic expression.

L'Étoile [The Star] is among the texts that were sent directly to Henri Reeve, the version in the *editio princeps* (1831) varies slightly from it, and the version published in Paris in a Polish magazine (1834) is yet different. It is also one of those examples in which narrative and description are perfectly united, in which the main literary process consists of personalizing the protagonists who are at the center of the composition. Moreover, it is a good example of Krasiński's French style: somewhat emphatic, accumulating synonyms, ensuring an elegant and complicated syntax, never exceeding the limits of good taste.

> De temps en temps il disparait une étoile des cieux. On la voit briller pendant des siècles ; puis vient un moment ou l'œil ne l'aperçoit plus parmi ses compagnes. [...] Vous avez-vous-même contemple sa course aventureuse, comme elle traversait l'azur, météore d'un instant, faible comme le débris d'un globe puissant disperse autrefois dans l'espace, belle comme un monde nouveau au jour de sa naissance, et pourtant destinée à périr quand ceux qui l'observaient croyaient une aurore. [...] Oui, c'était une jeune comète ; échevelée, flamboyante, indomptable, effrénée, elle s'élança d'un bout du ciel a l'autre, sans compter les années de marche, sans compter les myriades d'obstacles, ne voyant, n'adorant que son but, et poursuivant ses fins
> [From time to time a star of the heavens disappears. One sees it shining for centuries; then comes a moment when the eye no longer sees it among its companions. [...] You yourself have contemplated its adventurous course, as it crossed the azure, meteor of an instant, weak like the debris of a powerful globe once scattered in space, beautiful like a new world on the day of its birth, and yet destined to perish when those who observed it believed it to be an early dawn. [...] Yes, it was a young comet; unbridled, flamboyant, indomitable, unrestrained, it launched itself from one end of the sky to the other, without counting the years of its march, without counting the myriads of obstacles, seeing, adoring only its goal, and pursuing its ends] (Krasiński 2017: 6/III 119–127; Krasiński 2021: 289–291)

Krasiński and Reeve exchanged about five hundred letters between 1830 and 1832. Much less numerous, but also significant, especially for the Polish poet's early stay in Switzerland, are the letters to his Polish friend, Konstanty Gaszyński (Szczeglacka-Pawłowska 2015: 377–393). They are valuable to us because they allow us to see two versions of certain texts: in French and in Polish. Sometimes, as in the case of *Le soleil était derrière moi...* [The sun was behind me...], the Polish text follows the French one. It was sent in a letter to a friend in Poland, and then published in the homeland:

> Le soleil était derrière moi et une des montagnes du Jura, qui couverte de noirs sapins et de neige, semblait un cercueil entoure d'un livide linceul prêt à s'appesantir sur moi ; tandis que devant mes yeux s'élevait le sublime Mont Blanc, dans sa robe d'un éternel hiver, et bravant de ses glaces de diamants tous les rayons d'un ciel de printemps
> [The sun was behind me and one of the mountains of the Jura, which, covered with black fir trees and snow, seemed like a coffin surrounded by a pale shroud ready to cover me; meanwhile before my eyes rose the sublime Mont Blanc, in its eternal winter dress, and braving

with its ice of diamonds all the rays of a spring sky] (Krasiński 2017: 6/I 161 [161–163]; Krasiński 2021: 53 [53–55]).

In the case of the text *L'Exilé* [The Exile] the Polish version came first: it was written in February 1831, whereas the French one came a month later.[14] Krasiński, therefore, is well aware of different needs of different readers and knows how to 'reinvent' himself in another language.

A particular osmosis of literature and correspondence, the constant presence of the epistolary element later became an important feature of Krasiński's entire work (Szczeglacka 2005: 145–148, Szczeglacka-Pawłowska 2015: 371–378). Inserting poems into private letters, writing several letters a day (and in different languages), created at the same time different visions of the events of one's alleged, already interpreted life. Sometimes contradicting each other, they revealed how the poet was taking life for literature and vice versa. This daily practice began in the years in Geneva.

At the same time, he did not write only for his friends. The so-called exercises in style were published extensively in the *Revue Universelle de Genève*. Some of these texts were also sent to Paris or Poland. Krasiński decidedly wanted to become a writer where he was. And where he was, people read in French. Since the autographs of his works are missing, the chronology of publications allows us to judge the intensity and evolution of this very particular way of writing (Szczeglacka-Pawłowska 2015: 414–415). This is a kind of writing, that plays with time, space, reality, friendship (Szczeglacka 2005: 148–154). Playing with languages is just one more element of this work.

Krasiński arrived in Geneva as a 17-year-old student who had previously written a couple of youthful texts. Soon after his departure, he wrote his most important masterpiece: the drama *Nie-Boska Komedia* [The Non-Divine Comedy] (1835). He continued his career as one of the most important authors of the first half of the 19th century. From then on, he wrote only in Polish, reserving French for political, critical and occasional writings and for certain letters. The Geneva "adventure" undoubtedly appears as an essential step on Krasiński's literary path: a unique path of an author and an important link in European Romanticism.

---

14 The Polish version was published in *Listy Zygmunta Krasińskiego do Konstantego Gaszyńskiego* [Letters from Zygmunt Krasiński to Konstanty Gaszyński], Lwów [Lviv], 1882 with a preface by the renowned writer, translator, and editor, Józef Ignacy Kraszewski.

8 References

Bagłajewski, Arkadiusz. 2018. Nowa edycja Krasińskiego [The new edition of Krasiński's œuvre]. *Pamiętnik Literacki* [The Literary Journal] 116(2). 215–240.

Bajer, Michał. 2020. *Klasycyzm Przekład Prestiż Oświeceniowe spolszczenia tragedii Corneille'a i Racine'a (1740–1830) w perspektywie historycznoliterackiej* [Classicism Prestige Translation Enlightenment-era Polish translations of the tragedy of Corneille and Racine (1740–1830) from a historical-literary perspective]. Warszawa: IBL Wydawnictwo.

Baudin, Rodolphe. 2013. Bilinguisme et correspondances d'écrivains en Russie. L'exemple d'Alexandre Radichtev (1749–1802). In Marie-Flore Beretta, Julien Dufour, Isabelle Reck, Edgard Weber (eds.), *Langue(s) d'écrivain*, 81–91. Strasbourg: Presses Universitaires de Strasbourg.

Beauvois, Daniel. 1991. *Szkolnictwo polskie na ziemiach litewsko-ruskich*, [Polish education on Lithuanian and Ruthenian lands], transl. by Ireneusz Kania. Rzym-Lublin: Fundacja Jana Pawła II – Redakcja Wydawnictw KUL. [*Lumières et société en Europe de l'Est : l'université de Vilna et les écoles polonaises de l'Empire Russe (1803-1832)*]. 1977. Vol. I–II. Lille: Atelier des reproductions des thèses, Université Lille III.]

Beretta, Marie-Flore. 2013. Qui suis-je, que dis-je, moi qui parle cette langue ? In Julien Dufour, Isabelle Reck, Edgard Weber (eds.), *Langue(s) d'écrivains*. 9–18. Strasbourg: Presses Universitaires de Strasbourg.

Berlin, Isaac. 1991. Le retour du bâton. Sur la montée du nationalisme. In Gil Delannoi, Pierre-André Taguieff (eds), *Théories du nationalisme*, 301–318. Paris: Editions Kimé.

Berlin, Isaac. 2004. *Korzenie romantyzmu*, transl. by Anna Bartkowicz. Poznań: Zysk i S-ka. [*The Roots of Romanticism*. 1999. Washington D.C.: National Gallery of Art].

Berman, Antoine. 1985. *L'épreuve de l'étranger. Culture et traduction dans l'Allemagne romantique*. Paris: Gallimard.

Birn, Józef. 1949. Język francuski w Polsce w epoce saskiej [French language in Poland in the Saxon era]. In Henryk Barycz, Jan Hulewicz (eds.), *Studia z dziejów kultury polskiej* [Studies of the history of Polish culture], 379–389. Warszawa: Gebethner & Wolff.

Brunot, Ferdinand. 1934. *Histoire de la langue française des origines à 1900. vol. VIII : Le français hors de France au XVIIIe siècle, 1ᵉ partie : Le français dans les divers pays d'Europe*. Paris: Librairie Armand Colin.

Casanova, Pascale. 1999. *La République mondiale des lettres*. Paris: Seuil.

Cieśla, Maria. 1974. *Dzieje nauki języków obcych w zarysie*, [Outline of the history of foreign language education]. Warszawa: Państwowe Wydawnictwo Naukowe.

Clément, Jean-Stanislas. 1964. Krasiński and France. In Wacław Lednicki (ed.), *Zygmunt Krasiński. romantic universalist: an international tribute*. New York: Polish Institute of Arts and Sciences in America.

Correspondance de Sigismond Krasińki et de Henry Reeve. 1902. Joseph Kallenbach (ed. and preface). VI–LI. Paris: Librairie Ch. Delagrave.

Czapska, Maria. 1958. *Ludwika Śniadecka*, Warszawa: Czytelnik.

Czapska Maria. 2004. *Europa w rodzinie* [Europe in the family]. Kraków: Wydawnictwo Znak.

Fabre, Jean. 1980. *Lumière et Romantisme. Énergie et nostalgie de Rousseau à Mickiewicz*. Paris: Librairie C. Klincksieck.

Fabre, Jean. 1995. Stanisław August i literaci francuscy [Stanisław August and French writers]. In Krystyna Kasprzyk (ed.), *Od oświecenia do romantyzmu. Studia i szkice z literatury i kultury polskiej* [From Enlightenment to Romanticism. Studies and sketches from Polish literature and culture]. 32–79. Warszawa: Towarzystwo Literackie im. Adama Mickiewicza. [Stanislas-Auguste et les hommes de lettres français], *Archivum Neophilologicum*, Kraków 1936, II, 1–53.]

François, Alexis. 1959. *Histoire de la langue française cultivée des origines à nos jours*. Vol. 2, Genève: Alexandre Julien.

French and Russian in Imperial Russia: Language Use among the Russian Elite. 2015. Derek Offord, Lara Ryazanova-Clarke, Vladislav Rjéoutski, Gesine Argent (eds.), Edinburgh: Edinburgh University Press.

Friedrich II [king of Prussia]. 1780. *De la littérature allemande*. Berlin: G.J. Decker, Imprimeur du Roi.

Fumaroli, Marc. 2001. *Quand l'Europe parlait français*. Paris: Éd. de Fallois.

Glixelli, Stefan. 1921. O nauce języków romańskich w Wilnie 1781-1832 [On the teaching of Romance languages in Vilnius 1781-1832], *Rocznik Towarzystwa Przyjaciół Nauk w Wilnie* [Annuary of the Society of Friends of Sciences in Vilnius]. 152–166. VII, Wilno [Vilnius].

Janion, Maria. 1962. *Zygmunt Krasiński: debiut i dojrzałość*, [Zygmunt Krasiński: debut and maturity], Warszawa: Wiedza Powszechna.

Jędrzejewski, Tomasz. 2016. Spór klasyków z romantykami. Próba rewizji historycznoliterackiej [Quarell between Classics and Romantics. The attempt of the literary and historical revision]. In Olaf Krysowski (ed.), *Romantyzm warszawski 1815–1864* [Warsaw Romanticism 1815–1864]. 17–56. Warszawa: Wydział Polonistyki Uniwersytetu Warszawskiego.

Katalog rękopisów Muzeum Literatury, t. 1: Literatura polska XIX w. i Mickiewicziana [The Catalogue of manuscripts of the Museum of Literature [in Warsaw]]. Vol. 1: *Polish literaturę of the 18th century and Mickiewicz's papers*. Tadeusz Januszewski (ed.). Warszawa: Muzeum Literatury im Adama Mickiewicza.

Kleiner, Juliusz. 1948. *Mickiewicz*. Vol. I. Lublin: Towarzystwo Naukowe KUL.

Kowalczykowa, Alina. 1987. *Warszawa romantyczna* [The Romantic Warsaw]. Warszawa: Państwowy Instytut Wydawniczy.

Krasiński, Zygmunt. 1963. *Listy do ojca*, [Letters to his father], Stanisław Pigoń (ed.). Warszawa: Państwowy Instytut Wydawniczy.

Krasiński, Zygmunt. 2017. *Dzieła zebrane. Nowe wydanie* [Entire oeuvre. The new edition], Mirosław Strzyżewski et al. (ed.). vol. 1–8. Toruń: Wydawnictwo Naukowe UMK.

Krasiński, Zygmunt. 2021. *Œuvres en français. Prose poétique suivi des Écrits politiques et critiques*. Mirosław Strzyżewski, Joanna Pietrzak-Thébault, Agnieszka Markuszewska (eds.). Paris: Classiques Garnier.

Kurska, Anna. 1989. *Fragment romantyczny* [The Romantic Fragment], Wrocław...: Zakład Narodowy im. Ossolińskich, Wydawnictwo PAN.

Larbaud, Valéry. 1936. *Ce vice impuni, la lecture. Domaine anglais*. Paris: Gallimard.

Maingueneau, Dominique. 1993. *Le contexte de l'œuvre littéraire. Énonciation, écrivain, société*. Paris : Dunod Éditeur.

Markuszewska, Agnieszka. 2021. L'œuvre française de Zygmunt Krasiński — histoire des textes. In Krasiński, Zygmunt. 2021. *Œuvres en français. Prose poétique suivi des Écrits politiques et critiques*. Mirosław Strzyżewski, Joanna Pietrzak-Thébault, Agnieszka Markuszewska (eds.). 26–38. Paris: Classiques Garnier.

Martineau, Henri. 1957. Introduction. In Stendhal, *La chartreuse de Parme*. Paris: Éditions Garnier Frères.

Mende, Jana-Katharina, 2020. *Das Konzept des Messianismus in der polnischen, französischen und deutschen Literatur der Romantik. Eine mehrsprachige Konzeptanalyse.* Heidelberg: Winter.

Pietrzak-Thébault, Joanna. 2011. La langue française est pour moi comme une chaîne ... In Dorota Guzowska, Małgorzata Kamecka (eds.), *Inspirations: English, French and Polish Cultures.* 211–223. Białystok: Wydawnictwo Uniwersytetu w Białymstoku.

Pietrzak-Thébault, Joanna. 2013. Wstęp/Introduction. In Adam Mickiewicz. *Prose artistique. Contes, essais, fragments*, critical edition. 11–50. Warszawa: Instytut Badań Literackich PAN.

Pietrzak-Thébault, Joanna. 2018. Adam Mickiewicz – prozaik francuskojęzyczny: konieczność życiowa czy przejaw wolności twórczej [Adam Mickiewicz – a French prose writer: the vital necessity or the expression of the artistic liberty]. In Ewa Łukaszyk, Krystyna Wierzbicka-Trwoga (eds.), *Niewłasne lektury. Od pisarstwa w języku wyuczonym do wielości kultur czytania* [Not-own lectures. From literary activity in an acquired language towards a multiplicity of cultures of reading]. 13–21. Warszawa: Wydawnictwo DiG.

Pietrzak-Thébault, Joanna. 2019. Hrabia Zygmunt i 'republica litterarum' [The Count Zygmunt and the 'republica litterarum']. In Agnieszka Markszewska (ed.), *Zygmunt Krasiński życie czy literatura?* [Zygmunt Krasiński, life or literature?]. 481–487. Toruń: Wydawnictwo Naukowe UMK.

Pietrzak-Thébault, Joanna. 2020. Groźne przestrzenie, mroczne dusze – gotycyzujące i frenetyczne elementy we francuskojęzycznej prozie Zygmunta Krasińskiego [Dangerous spaces, tenebrous souls – gothic-like and frenetic elements in the French prose by Zygmunt Krasiński]. In Marcin Cieński, Paweł Pluta (eds.), *Gotycyzm w literaturze i kulturze lat 1760-1830* [The Gothicism in literature and culture between 1760 and 1830]. 343–356. Warszawa: Instytut Badań Literackich Wydawnictwo.

Pietrzak-Thébault, Joanna. 2021. Orient na progu domu. Bałkański italianizm czy włoski orientalizm Niccoló Tommasea [The Orient at the door-step. Balcan Italianism or Italian orientalism of Niccoló Tommaseo]. In Michał Fijałkowski, Krystyna Wierzbicka-Trwoga (eds.), *Oblicza orientalizmu* [Faces of the Orientalism]. 41–49. Warszawa: Wydawnictwo DiG.

Pirlot, Gérard. 2013. Le prépuce de la langue maternelle circoncis par l'usage d'une langue seconde. In Julien Dufour, Isabelle Reck, Edgard Weber (eds.). *Langue(s) d'écrivains.* 33–47. Strasbourg : Presses Universitaires de Strasbourg.

Pisarze polskiego Oświecenia [Writers of the Polish Enlightenment]. 1994–1996. Teresa Kostkiewiczowa, Zbigniew Goliński (eds.). vol. I–III. Warszawa: Wydawnictwo Naukowe PWN.

Poniatowski, Stanislas Auguste [king of Poland]. 2012. *Mémoires.* Anna Grześkowiak-Krwawicz, Dominique Triaire (eds.), Paris: Institut d'études slaves, Société historique et littéraire polonaise.

Potocki, Jan. 1847. *Le manuscript trouvé à Saragosse.* Transl. by Edmund Chojecki. Leipzig: Księgarnia Zagraniczna.

Potocki, Jan. 2004–2006. *Œuvres*, François Rosset, Dominique Triaire (ed.). Vol. IV and VI. Loeuven, Paris: Editions Peeters.

Potocki, Jan. 2008. *Le manuscript trouvé à Saragosse.* François Rosset, Dominique Triaire (ed.). Paris: Flammarion.

Prussak, Maria. 2011a. Norma i tożsamość. Starcie romantyków z klasykami — nowe myślenie o filologii [Norm and Identity: The Clash between Romantics and Classics — New Approach to Philology]. In Adam Karpiński (ed.), *Humanizm i filologia*, [Humanism and Philology]. 413–438. Warszawa: Wydawnictwo Neriton.

Prussak, Maria. 2011b. Problemy edytorskie wykładów Adama Mickiewicza w Collège de France [Editorial questions of Adam Mickiewicz's lectures at the Collège de France]. In Maria Kalinowska, Jarosław Ławski, Magdalena Bizior-Dombrowska (eds.), *Prelekcje paryskie Adama Mickiewicza wobec tradycji kultury polskiej i europejskiej. Próba nowego spojrzenia* [Paris lectures of Adam Mickiewicz in relations to the Polish and the European culture. The attempt of a new outlook].17–26. Warszawa: Wydawnictwa Uniwersytetu Warszawskiego.

Rejman, Zofia. 2007. Francja jako antywzór w krytyce literackiej początku XIX wieku [France as an anti-example in [Polish] literary critics of the beginning of the 18th century]. In Elżbieta Z. Wichrowska (ed.) *W stronę Francji... Z problemów literatury i kultury polskiego Oświecenia.* [In the direction of France... Some questions of literature and culture of the Polish Englihtment],. 240–252. Warszawa: Wydział Polonistyki Uniwersytetu Warszawskiego.

Rivarol, de, Antoine. 1784. *Discours de l'universalité de la langue française.* Paris: Bailly, Dessenne.

Romantyczne współpoetyzowanie. Wybór listów Zygmunta Krasińskiego i Henryka Reeve'a [Romantic co-poetization. Selection of letters by Zygmunt Krasiński and Henry Reeve]. 2018. Vol. I–II. Agnieszka Markuszewska (ed, preface). Toruń: Wydawnictwo Naukowe UMK.

Rzewuski, Wacław Seweryn. 2017. *Sur les chevaux orientaux et provenant des races orientales / Concerning the Horses of the Orient and those Originating from Oriental Breeds / O koniach wschodnich i wywodzących się z ras orientalnych*, Tadeusz Majda (ed.). Vol. 1–3. Warsaw: The National Library of Poland.

Ryba, Janusz. 2007. Jan Potocki – "maniak" języka francuskiego [Jan Potocki — the crank of the French language]. In Elżbieta Z. Wichrowska (ed.). *W stronę Francji... Z problemów literatury i kultury polskiego Oświecenia.* [In the direction of France... Some questions of literature and culture of the Polish Enlightenment] 121–127. Warszawa: Wydział Polonistyki Uniwersytetu Warszawskiego.

Stanisz, Marek. 1998. *Wczesnoromantyczne spory o poezję* [Early-romantic disputes about poetry]. Kraków: Universitas.

Stefanowska, Zofia. 2001 [1976]. Croquemitaine w III części Dziadów, [Croquemitaine in the 3. Part of the 'Forefathers' Eve']. In Zofia Stefanowska, *Próba zdrowego rozumu [The Test of Sound Mind].* 141–175. Warszawa: Oficyna Wydawnicza Rytm.

Stefanowska, Zofia. 2005. Duch-powrotnik u Mickiewicza [The ghost that returns all-over at Mickiewicz's writing]. *Pamiętnik Literacki* [The Literary Journal], 96(4). 69–78.

Stefanowska, Zofia. 2007. Rola autobiografii w wierszach miłosnych Mickiewicza [The function of autobiography in erotic lyrics by Mickiewicz]. In Zofia Trojanowiczowa, Jerzy Borowczyk (eds.), *Biografie romantycznych poetów* [The biographies of romantic poets]. 9–15. Poznań: Poznańskie Towarzystwo Przyjaciół Nauk.

Suchet, Myriam. 2014. *L'imaginaire hétérolingue, Ce que nous apprennent les textes à la croisée des langues.* Paris: Classiques Garnier.

Szczeglacka, Ewa. 2005. Ile dzienników pisał Krasiński w Szwajcarii? (Style romantycznej autobiografii) [How many diaires was writing Krasiński in Swiss? (Styles of romantic autobiography)]. In Bernadetta Kuczera-Chachulska, Maria Prussak, Ewa Szczeglacka (eds.).

Zygmunt Krasiński Pytania o twórczość (Zygmunt Krasiński. Questions about his literary production). 129–160. Warszawa: Wydawnictwo UKSW.

Szczeglacka-Pawłowska, Ewa. 2013. „Niewidoczny" autograf Adama Mickiewicza z dwuwierszem „[Jak drzewo przed wydaniem owocu...]" i tzw. „Notą do Francuzów", [An "invisible" autograph of Adam Mickiewicz containing the distich "[Jak drzewo przed wydaniem owocu...]" and an "Adresse to the French"]. *Pamiętnik Literacki* [The Literary Journal], 111(2). 189–198.

Szczeglacka-Pawłowska, Ewa. 2015. *Romantyzm "brulionowy"* [The Romanticism of rough-copies]. Warszawa: Wydawnictwo Naukowe UKSW.

Thiesse, Anne-Marie. 1999. *La création des identités nationales. Europe XVIII–XX siècle*. Paris: Seuil.

Tommaseo, Niccoló. 2008. *Scintille*. Francesco Bruni (ed. and preface) Varese: Fondazione Pietro Bembo/Ugo Guanda Editore.

Wyka, Kazimierz. 1989. *Pokolenia literackie* [The literary generations]. Kraków: Wydawnictwo Literackie.

Zaleska-Stankiewiczowa, Irena. 1935. *Pensje żeńskie w Wilnie (1795–1830)*, [Girls' boarding-schools in Vilnius (1795–1830)], Wilno [Vilnius]: Wydawnictwo Magistratu m. Wilna.

Zgorzelski, Czesław. 1961. *O lirykach Mickiewicza i Słowackiego. Eseje i studia* [About lyrics by Mickiewicz and Słowacki. Essaies and Studies]. Lublin: Towarzystwo Naukowe Katolickiego Uniwersytetu Lubelskiego.

Zgorzelski, Czesław. 1978. *Od Oświecenia ku romantyzmowi i współczesności* [From the Enlightenment towards the Romanticism and the Modern Era]. Kraków: Wydawnictwo Literackie.

Part 2: **National Authors as Covert Multilinguals**

Gábor Gángó
Proofreaders, Translators – Co-authors? József Eötvös's Concealed Bilingualism

Abstract: My study explores the hidden bilingualism of an eminent protagonist of 19th-century nation building in Hungary: József Eötvös (1813–1871), poet, playwright, novelist, and political thinker. To be able to fulfil his life's mission in the interest of Hungarian cultural nationalism, Eötvös, whose native language was German, had to recur to various stratagems during his career to simulate a Hungarian monoliteracy. His efforts encompassed the hired or friendly assistance of a number of fellow intellectuals who corrected Eötvös's Hungarian texts to conceal his insufficient linguistic competence, as well as translated his German writings to make them appear as originals.

Keywords: Hungarian Literature, Bilingualism, József Eötvös, Proofreading, Translation

1 Introduction

My study aims to contribute to the research on literary bilingualism in Europe, especially in the 19th century with a case study regarding Hungary.[*] It explores an era, in which monolingual literacy proved to be a powerful tool in nation building and the formation of modern national identities (Anokhina, Dembeck, and Weissmann 2019b: 1; cf. Blackledge and Creese 2010, ch. 9). However, recent research indicates that the thesis on linguistic homogenization and national monolingualism as phenomena accompanying European nation building

---

[*] This study was supported by the research project "The edition of the correspondence of József Eötvös", funded by the National Research, Development and Innovation Office (NKFIH 131564, principal investigator András Cieger). I am heavily indebted to Orsolya Völgyesi's editing work with the first volume of the new edition of József Eötvös's correspondence (Eötvös Ms.). Transcriptions of Eötvös's letters were established by Orsolya Völgyesi. I thank Jana-Katharina Mende for her help with the secondary literature as well as her remarks and suggestions to the first draft of this paper. I also wish to express my gratitude to Natalie Sauer for the linguistic proofreading of the text.

Gábor Gángó, Research Centre for the Humanities, Budapest, e-mail: gango.gabor@abtk.hu

Open Access. © 2023 the author(s), published by De Gruyter. This work is licensed under the Creative Commons Attribution 4.0 International License.
https://doi.org/10.1515/9783110778656-006

seems to need completion and revision. Elements of bi- and multilingualism, together with their socio-linguistic or socio-literary background, and complex forms of identities can be detected in some authors (Balogh and Leitgeb 2012).

The multi-faceted life's work of a renowned figure in 19th-century nation building in Hungary, József Eötvös (1813–1871), seems particularly suitable for a case study. Born in 1813, Eötvös belonged to the post-1830 generation of the Hungarian reform movement. Before the revolutions in 1848, he contributed with a number of poems, dramatic works, and no less than three novels in Hungarian language to the nation's cultural production. In his political essays, he supported the current projects of European philanthropic liberalism such as the improvement of prison conditions or the social emancipation of the Jews. His pieces of journalism, closely connected to the internal debates of Hungarian liberal opposition against the conservative, Vienna-backed government, advocated the establishment of a centralized government based on the principles of modern constitutionalism. After the collapse of the old regime in 1848, Eötvös was appointed Minister of Religion and Public Education, only to resign from his post amid mounting tensions between the constitutional Hungarian administration and the new Vienna power center, and to leave for Bavaria, where he remained for two years. In his intellectual isolation, he dedicated himself to studying political theory in order to understand the historical-philosophical significance of the 1848 movements in Europe, and especially Hungary. From the late 1850s, he gained increasing authority in the Hungarian cultural establishment and occupied leading positions in important institutions of cultural nation building such as the Hungarian Academy of Sciences. After the Austro-Hungarian political settlement in 1867, Eötvös was appointed Minister of Religion and Education for the second time (for his life and works, see in English Bödy 1985; Vardy 1987; Gángó 2010). With its considerable and complex impact on 19th-century Hungarian national movement, József Eötvös's life's work has long been a subject of scholarly research. Yet, his literary achievement has apparently stood in need of a somewhat charitable interpretation. My study argues that the vulnerability of his literary works has linguistic reasons and reveals the particularity of his literary program in an era in which the creation of national cultural monolingualism was the most important objective.

The particularity of his case consists in the fact that Eötvös, while advocating literary monolingualism, was himself a German-Hungarian bilingual. German was his native language and Hungarian his second language. Despite his bilingual background, he constructed an identity as a monolingual Hungarian writer and intellectual. The pursuit of his greatest ambition required him to conceal his bilingualism. The source data indicating the multi-layered linguistic correction of his works by others are not unknown in Eötvös scholarship. However, no particular study has yet been devoted to this phenomenon on a general level to interpret Eötvös's whole life's work as an outcome of his coping with the consequences of his bilingual socialization in an increasingly monolingual cultural environment (some remarks about Eötvös, as compared with Count István Széchenyi's (1791–1860) German usage in Czinege 2021: 652–654).

The surviving data do not allow a full reconstruction of his childhood transition from monolingualism to bilingualism. Even if his second language, in the strict sense of the term, was Latin, not Hungarian, it seems reasonable to speak about a German-Hungarian bilingualism in Eötvös's case. Latin was considered at that time as a necessary corollary of and instrumental to the education system, rather than a full-fledged language. His first letters from the early 1820s to a relative are in German, and another one to a schoolmate from 1826 was written in Latin. This seems to harmonize with the account of one of his first biographers that Eötvös spoke broken Hungarian at the age of eleven or twelve (Ferenczi 1903: 12). However, this knowledge was enough to classify him, when matriculated, after years of private instruction at home, at the Buda Gymnasium in 1824/25 and 1825/26, in terms of "Linguae" as a "Hungar. German." bilingual. At the gymnasium, Eötvös learned, as a part of the Latin curriculum, Hungarian language and literature. His instruction in Hungarian language and culture continued in the philosophical classes of the Pest University at which he matriculated in the academic years 1826/27 and 1827/28. Eötvös was *eminens primus* in all classes during his years in public education, with the only exception of Hungarian language and literature at the university: in one semester, he was sixth, in another tenth, and in a third semester even thirty-first (Ferenczi 1903: 295). This fact is indicative of the challenge the acquisition of the Hungarian language posed to him. He must have received further motivation to learn Hungarian from his fellow students, László Szalay (1813–1864) among them, as well as from the encounters with leading figures of intellectual circles in Pest, which he frequented with Szalay during their years at the juridical faculty 1828 to 1831 (Devescovi 2007: 298).

József Eötvös began writing in Hungarian around 1830, i.e., at the age of seventeen or eighteen. This transition between primary language acquisition and learned literacy (García, Bertlett, and Kleifgen 2007: 207), in German and Hungarian respectively, provoked a deep and lasting conflict, as the principal goal in Hungarian literature at that time was the emancipation of the Hungarian language. How could someone whose mother tongue was not Hungarian take part in this project? Hungarian aristocracy, to which Eötvös's family belonged, was as a rule multilingual, and Hungarian political identity until the end of the

18th century did not involve personal identification with the cause of the national language. Eötvös's decision was made once for all – later, the successful simulation of Hungarian mono-lingualism required a huge amount of effort not only from him but also from his friends and assistants. My study presents, on the methodological basis of current scholarship on literary bi- and multilingualism (Oksaar 1987a; Ferdman, Weber, and Ramirez 1994; Auer and Wei 2007; Blackledge and Creese 2010; Radaelli 2011; Aronin and Singleton 2012; Willms and Zemanek 2014; Anokhina, Dembeck, and Weissmann 2019a), Eötvös's lifelong efforts to conceal his literary bilingualism. It argues that Eötvös's life's work exemplifies a special case of latent bilingualism: a deliberately concealed bilingualism (Radaelli 2011; cf. Zemanek and Willms 2014).

Thanks to the ongoing edition of his correspondence, the use of Eötvös's written language can be investigated in two aspects: public and private. As his private hand-written letters reveal, his Hungarian orthography is characterized by uncertainty and hesitation, while his German orthography was faultless and consequent. Furthermore, his style in German was more flexible, comfortable, and witty.

The study presents the two basic challenges of his bilingualism in chronological order as well as Eötvös's responses to them. The first is his coping with an insufficient linguistic command for literary creation in Hungarian. The second is the dissimulation of factual German literacy or the reversal of the factual hierarchy of his linguistic competencies. After giving an account of his public debut at the age of seventeen, my paper examines the genesis of his early works from the point of view of his efforts to conceal the traits of his non-native command of Hungarian. Thereafter, it presents the situation in which he found himself in the late 1830s when, as an elected member of the Hungarian Scholarly Society and as such, the guardian of the language, Eötvös himself became the reviewer of the linguistic proficiency of others. At that time, he also embraced the thought of reverting the naturally given order of linguistic proficiencies by an act of voluntarism. As editor and translator of the poems of his late friend Baron Tivadar Palocsay (1810–1836), who wrote in German, Eötvös adopted the bold idea of presenting translations as originals: an idea which he was unable to implement in this project but widely used after 1850 to dissimulate the fact that he composed his political essays in German.

2 Family

Eötvös's family, at least his mother's line, with the members of which correspondence survived, was monolingual German. Accordingly, he corresponded with his family members in German. Words in Trans-Danubian dialect in his early works indicate that he communicated with residents at the Ercsi family estate, South-West from Pest and Buda, in Hungarian. They also indicate, indirectly, that the language demarcation line between German and Hungarian provided Eötvös with a social demarcation line. His bilingualism was neither a "societal bilingualism" nor a "family bilingualism" (Lanza 2007: 46) but the result of his communication with two distinctly monolingual environments. This demarcation corresponds to his subsequent separation of the private (family) use and public use of the language, leading to separate developments of his German and Hungarian through a "sequential or simultaneous biliteracy" process (García, Bertlett, and Kleifgen 2007: 212). This did not exclude some significant, transitory phenomena in the sphere of social connections, as his private correspondence with Hungarian aristocrats, from whom he had nothing to conceal, was mainly in German. In this sense, his early love poetry (Eötvös 2021), inspired by his Ercsi acquaintances of his adolescence, aimed at no less than marking his own social sphere in Hungarian. These poems testify that the young girls, to whom his poems were addressed, must have fulfilled an important role in Eötvös's linguistic socialization.

The same can be said about his written correspondence with his family members in terms of his German literacy. Family correspondence was the exclusive place of German literacy before 1848. Letters to his mother, the Baroness Ignácné Eötvös Jr., née Anna Lilien (1786-1858), his aunt, the Countess Ferencné Teleki, née Leopoldina Szapáry (1794-1866) and others contain elements, which go, in their subject matter and vocabulary, far beyond usual family correspondence. Eötvös riddled his letters with descriptions of his experiences, reflections, and social observations accompanied by commentaries. These letters show that his essays are deeply rooted in his German literacy. As these letters were published in the collection of his correspondence in Hungarian translation (Eötvös 1976: 106-114; 80-82), modern editors of Eötvös's works conspired with him to hide his multilingualism.

Eötvös had two languages for emotions. German remained his language to express emotions in the family circle, while he wanted Hungarian to be elevated, on an individual as well as a collective level, to the language of literature, which expresses the emotions of a nation. When, as a father and husband, he looked at the idyllic picture formed by the members of his own family, he wrote in his diary as late as in 1870, in one of the rare mixed-language annotations, the following German sentence: "Ach, wenn es doch immer so bliebe!" [I wish it could last forever!] (as quoted in Devescovi 2007: 282. Here and in the following, translations are mine. G. G.).

Hence, Eötvös's biliteracy was not a "literacy across languages and cultures" (Ferdman, Weber, and Ramirez 1994: quoted by 209) but two ideally separated, and discretionally functioning literacies. These literacies, however, in spite of Eötvös's intentions, and in harmony with the "objective" rules of language acquisition, necessarily interacted with each other (Wandruszka 1987: 39–41; Mende 2020: 398). This is exactly why he needed acceptance and assistance as soon as his language use went public.

The denial of his mother tongue in his literacy had, of course, nothing to do with his good relationship to his mother and German conversation in the family circle. Quite the opposite: his mother supported his literary ambitions in the Hungarian language. The members of his family were his "litterarius ellenei" [literary adversaries] (Eötvös to Szalay, autumn 1835. Manuscript Collection of the Library of the Hungarian Academy of Sciences – in the following: MTA KIK Kt. –, Ms 1186/4. With standardized orthography (also in the following): Eötvös 1976: 91) in the sense that conversation in general hindered him from devoting more time to literature.

He toyed with the rather vague thought that the country (the Hungarian soil in its concrete reality) might be considered the "mother" of his literary identity: "De én, – mesze, töletek – testemet idegen föld nyelendí el" [But I, far from you, my body will be absorbed by foreign soil]; "'s én [...] kinek minden gondolatja s' szándéka csak a szent hon volt, [...] más föld anya méhében alszom vegsö álmomat [and I, [...] all whose thoughts and intentions were of the holy fatherland, [...] will sleep my final sleep in the womb of another soil] (Eötvös to Szalay, Vienna, 2 August 1831. MTA KIK Kt. Ms 1186/1. Eötvös 1976: 72). He viewed himself as an outcast in Vienna: "Egy éve már, hogy itt Bécsben hontalan tengődöm" [I have been vegetating here as a stateless fugitive in Vienna for a year] (Eötvös to Szalay, Vienna, 24 June 1832; Szalay 1942: 160–162; Eötvös 1976: 79).

Eötvös separated the literary fatherland from the political fatherland. He remained Hungarian in his literacy even in the period when he advocated the idea of a common Austrian Empire *(Gesamtstaat)*. The Hungarian soil as fatherland remained, however, abstract, as Eötvös had little first-hand experience of the landscape. The landscape with which he cultivated an intimate relationship was that of the Austrian provinces. As he writes to László Szalay from Vienna, on 10 September 1831: "az egész tegnapi napot Badenba töltém nagy hegyeken másztam fel 's alá, ruinák közöt andalogtam, ábrándoztam mindaddig, míg lelkem lankadtabb nem volt testemnél" [I spent the whole day of yesterday in Baden: I climbed big mountains, strolled among ruins, and dreamed so long as my soul was more languid than my body] (Szalay 1942: 159–160. Eötvös 1976: 77).

3 Eötvös's Hungarian literacy: written with assistance, received with acceptance

As an adolescent, Eötvös chose a literary identity and, with it, a cultural homeland: the Hungarian language and culture. The beginnings of his bilingualism are rooted in the moment when he stepped out from the German-speaking family circle to the public sphere of Hungarian literature. His commitment was expressed to Ferenc Kazinczy (1759–1831), coryphée of the Hungarian literary movement, who embodied, in Eötvös's eyes, the language-centered Hungarian cultural nationalism: "ki vágyodo szemmel tekintek hazám tündöklö tsilagira" [I look with coveting eyes at the bright stars of my country], he wrote to Kazinczy, to express "hodolatomat mellyel mint magyar tartozom" [my reverence which I owe you as a Hungarian] (Eötvös to Ferenc Kazinczy, Pest, 30 December 1830. MTA KIK Kt. M. Irod. Lev. 4r. 29. Eötvös 1976: 62–63). Eötvös's most profound desire was to belong to those who were put, as he wrote in a letter to Count László Teleki (1811–1861) "a' magyar civilisatio küszöbére" [at the threshold of Hungarian civilisation] (National Archives of Hungary, P 654-III-39. tétel - 59.). This is what ultimately motivated him to write in Hungarian. Literature was, in his opinion, only a means for attaining a higher goal, namely the breakthrough of modern Hungarian civilisation.

This is the reason why he expected, sometimes even demanded, acceptance and help from those with whom he shared this objective. In his letter from 26–27 March 1831 to another senior figure of Hungarian cultural nationalism, Count József Dessewffy (1771–1843), Eötvös gave the first and at the same time the fullest account of his language shift from German to Hungarian, and the two fundamental mainstays of his literary program:

> Ez csekély véleményem a magyar ortographia felöl, ha ez hibás vagy a magyarságomban akár miféle hibákat találsz, kérlek jobbits, és ne tunyaságomnak, csak környülményimnek tulajdonitsd. Idegen hangok érdeklék az alig született [újszülött] füleit, idegen hangokat rebegének elöször megnyilt ajkaim, anyanyelvem német, az örökséget mellyet minden anya legszegényebb gyermekének is hagy önnön fáradságommal kelle szerzenem, a köte-

léket melly legerössebben köt mindenkit hazájához a nyelvet önnön karokkal fonnom, ha csekély is a' mit birok, – mondhatom az én mivem, és bizvást várhatok engedelmet és segédet mindeniktöl kinek alkalma nálaménál boldogabb volt, föképpen töled

[This is my humble opinion about Hungarian orthography. If it is mistaken, or you find any errors in my Hungarian, please correct them, and attribute them not to my torpidity but my circumstances. Foreign voices stimulated the ears of the new-born baby: my lips, when they first opened, uttered foreign voices. My mother tongue is German. I had to construct my heritage, which each mother leaves even to her poorest child, with my own efforts; I had to weave the cord, which binds everyone in the strongest manner to their country, with my own arms. If it is little that I have, I can say though that it is my work. Therefore, I surely can expect acceptance and assistance from everyone, whose opportunities were happier than mine were, and especially from you] (National Széchényi Library, Levelestár, (in the following: OSzK Lt.) Eötvös József ismeretlenhez (a Dessewffy család valamely tagjához), 1. sz. irat. Eötvös 1976: 64–65).

According to this account, Eötvös held his original grasp of reality (Oksaar 1987b: 7; Kühlwein 1987: 1) in the mother tongue to be inadequate, as he had to learn the "Hungarian" world through a foreign language. Eötvös's literary career is nothing less than putting into practice the twofold demand resulting from the inadequacy of his original linguistic appropriation of the world. His literary activity unfolded through his recurring appeals to others for acceptance and assistance. While he found acceptance among many, he received actual help from very few. As a rule, this assistance was justified by reference to the "common cause" promoted by him and his helping friends. Together they formed the collaborating members of his intellectual circle, called the "Centralists", as they propagated the idea of a centralized constitutional government.

Eötvös's adopted artistic-intellectual program claimed that he was an author with an exclusive Hungarian literary identity, writing exclusively in the Hungarian language. Neither the first, nor the second part of this claim was true. To be able to believe in this identity construction, his fellow intellectuals had to accept two assumptions about him as matters of fact, despite contrary evidence. First (in his youth), the paradoxical statement that his mother spoke to him *in a foreign language*. Just because of this underprivileged start, he was entitled, as a Hungarian writer, to acceptance and assistance. His works, once corrected linguistically by others, should be regarded as his own contributions to Hungarian literature. Secondly (in his post-1848 period), the obviously untrue claim that he wrote on politics and social theory, similarly to his literary works, in Hungarian. In fact, native speaker assistants (proof-readers and translators) had to be mobilized to implement this program.

The denial of his native language in the beginning of his career was merely a part of his literary identity. He did not revolt against the use of the "foreign language" in his family circle. What Eötvös achieved through this decision was a Hungarian–German "biliteracy" (García, Bertlett, and Kleifgen 2007: 207), rather than Hungarian monolingualism. To be a Hungarian intellectual, he acquired (as a student and an autodidact) the necessary cultural background knowledge: geographical and historical knowledge of the country, its social stratification, political culture, and literary tradition. On the other hand, he had a solid knowledge of German literary culture, which he acquired at home, during his stays in Vienna or family visits in Bavaria. This familiarity with the works of Goethe, Schiller, Jean Paul, and others remained intact behind the facade of his public Hungarian literacy and resurfaced time and again. As a volunteer émigré, he resumed the use of his native language in his post-1848 literary activity focused on political theory.

Eötvös's bilingualism was not typical insofar as his second language was not the more powerful one, acquired in order to increase his career chances, social standing, or access to cultural resources (as in the case of (former) subjected nations) (Mansour 1993: 101–104). Eötvös switched to a less powerful language – but only with regard to one of its functions, namely the public use of the literary (and later the political) language. In adopting the Hungarian language, he did not devote himself (like many other Eastern European intellectuals) to the project of full emancipation from and future hegemony of a less powerful and culturally-politically weaker language. Eötvös can rather be considered as a partial linguistic renegade. He opted for the Hungarian identity in the context of cultural nation building, while preserving the German language as a mainstay of his social standing and foundation of his political participation. His twofold political identity – in support of Hungarian cultural nationalism within the intact political hegemony of the Austrian Imperial center – is analogous with his linguistic identity.

Within the bilingual option, Eötvös adopted the "demanding" version of bilingualism, measuring his knowledge of Hungarian against his native language competence, while knowing very well that he could (and would) not reach this level. Interestingly, and perhaps as over-compensation, he did not allow himself any "liberal" bilingualism. As a novelist, in contrast to Mór Jókai (1825–1903) for example, he did not use any foreign words for depicting an atmosphere or individuating the language of his protagonists. As a remarkable exception, his socialization as an aristocrat is ironically mirrored by the mixed French-Hungarian language of the protagonists of his dramatic comedy, *A házasulók* [Marriageable Youth] (Eötvös 1833). Even in his texts for private use, there is very little mixed language. His letters, diary entries, sketches (in contrast, say, to Count István Széchenyi's diaries) are as a rule monolingual, written either in German or in Hungarian.

Eötvös's bilingualism was further reinforced by the fact that he did not display knowledge of any other language publicly. In the English and French languages, no full-spectrum (reading, spoken, written) knowledge can be documented, apart from a couple of private letters written in French. Of course, he read in English and French, but there is little evidence of how he acquired and used these languages during his journeys. He wrote to his English and French correspondents in German, however, he showed consideration for the limited competence of the addressees by writing in Latin rather than German letters. He believed that the Latin language had been abolished alongside the late feudal Hungarian administration, which had promoted its use. It only appears in a clearly disapproving context in several scenes of his satirical novel about a Hungarian feudal County, *A falu jegyzője* [The Village Notary] (Eötvös 1845). Hence, the literary co-existence of the Hungarian and German languages was not embedded in multi-sided interferences and tolerant varieties of multilingual mirroring of the world (Aronin and Singleton 2012: 5).

4 Project one: simulating monolingualism and linguistic proficiency

4.1 László Szalay's role as a proofreader and translator

By implementing his literary project, a central role was assigned to his schooltime friend, László Szalay who later became a renowned historian. A number of places in their correspondence indicate that Szalay was the primary linguistic reviewer of Eötvös's texts. "[E]szrevehetted már régen", wrote Eötvös to Szalay on 30 June 1836, "barátimmal majdnem ugy bánok mind az Ur Istennel, minden szó mellyet hozzájok intézek egy egy kérés" [You must have noticed long ago that I treat my friends almost like the Lord God: every word that I address to them is a request] (Eötvös to Szalay, 30 June 1836. MTA KIK Kt. Ms 1186/9. Eötvös 1976: 105). The basic tone of Eötvös's requests to Szalay for linguistic proofreading was one of fear. The fear of criticism, and even more of getting caught and being unmasked. This unmasking would have resulted in shame, i.e., the loss of honor, and, with it, a farewell to his literary ambitions. As he wrote in a letter to Szalay from Bratislava, 1833: "A Mottoval megelégszem, a stylussal és ortographiaval éppen nem, azért kérlek, potoly, törülj, változtas kényed szerént. Legfőkép ami a nyelvet illeti légy szorós 's kegyetlen, mert félek az Akademia parokaitol; ha szeretsz korrigalj" [I am content with the motto [to the comedy

The Marriageable Youth] but not quite with the style and the orthography. Therefore, I beg you to substitute, delete, change as you wish. Above all, what regards the language, be strict and merciless, because I am afraid of the wigs of the Academy. If you like me, do correct] (Szalay 1942: 162–163. Eötvös 1976: 83). The most profound meaning of his friendship with Szalay was that Szalay was in the possession of the ultimate secret of Eötvös's Hungarian literacy. The young baron wanted to hide his non-native competence even from his paternal friend Ferenc Kölcsey (1790–1838) and sent him the already corrected copy of one of his works. So, he requested Szalay's help once again: "arra kérlek edjszersmind, hogy corrigált manusriptumomnak leirását mennél elébb küld el[,] Kölcseinek 's edjebeknek kivánnám mutatni. Ha szeretsz corrigály, minden változással, melyet te csinálsz én megelégszem" [At the same time, I ask you to send me the transcribed copy of my corrected manuscript. I want to show it to Kölcsey and others. If you like me, do correct; I am happy with every change that you make] (Eötvös to Szalay, Bratislava, early 1833. OSzK Lt. Eötvös 1976: 84).

Szalay's commission extended to a thorough proofreading of Eötvös's texts, including grammar, wording, orthography, or rhythm. Eötvös even demanded Szalay to invent new words, by sending him a poem entitled *To L's scrapbook*: "Lnek Stambuchjába – neologizálj!" [To L's Stambuch – forge a neologism!] (Eötvös to Szalay, Bratislava, before 26 February 1833. MTA KIK Kt. Ms 1186/2. Eötvös 1976: 85). The burden and responsibility on Szalay's shoulders became even heavier once Eötvös was elected member of the Hungarian Scholarly Society (later: Hungarian Academy of Sciences) – that is, guardian of the Hungarian language. Eötvös expressed his fears to Szalay in a most open manner, saying, "gyámod nélkül hirem tenkre jút" [without your tutorship, my reputation is ruined] (Eötvös to Szalay, autumn 1835. MTA KIK Kt. Ms 1186/4. Eötvös 1976: 91). That is why he begged Szalay to do the most meticulous proofreading work with his translation of Victor Hugo's *Angelo*, and the translator's foreword, written originally in German, and translated hastily by Eötvös himself. The fact that Eötvös even sends "hasonlo papírt" [similar paper] to his friend indicates the amount of effort and circumspection the convincing dissimulation of his primary German literacy made necessary:

[I]de csatlom [...] [a]z elöszót, mind németül, mind rosz forditásomban. (Azt is kérlek ird le, itt küldok hasonlo papírt.) Itt leginkább kérlek, figyelmezz hogy az istenért szégyenbe ne maradjak; tudom, menyire fekszik becsületem sziveden, és én nem jobbíthatám mert ma éjjel forditottam a legnagyob ínreszgések között. A Forditás egyes részei talán éppen azért jók, mert sebessen iródott, de jobbító kezedre van szüksége, mert ugy tartom, ha igy lépne ki a világ elébe, borzadna az egész Academía új tagján

[I attach here [...] the foreword in German as well as in my bad translation. (Please write down it too, I am sending here similar paper.) Here I beg you most, be careful so that I will not be disgraced. I know how much my honor is at your heart. I could not improve them because I have translated them tonight amid the greatest trembling. Some parts of the translation are perhaps good just because they were written hastily. But they need your correcting hand, as I believe that if they saw the light as they are now, the whole Academy would be appalled at its new member] (Eötvös to Szalay, autumn 1835. MTA KIK Kt. Ms 1186/4. Eötvös 1976: 91–92).

Later, Eötvös also relegated the linguistic supervision of his essays and speeches to Szalay. His requests were becoming more and more routine-like and demanding. He sent a copy of one of his essays (probably on *Szegénység Irlandban* [Poverty in Ireland]) with these words: "Bucsúzolátogatásim végett értekezésemmel elkéstem: a' leirás szép de nem vala idöm azt egészen átnéznem, 's lekötelezné́l ha magad tennéd" [Because of my farewell visits, I am late with my treatise. The description is beautiful, but I did not have time to revise it fully: I would be obliged, if you yourself did it] (Eötvös to Szalay, October 1837. MTA KIK Kt. Ms 1186/10. Eötvös 1976: 116). Or, concerning one of his (not identified) speeches: "Kérlek küld át [...] beszédem [...] másolatát mellyet tegnap felolvasál, hogy a' tisztázott kéziratot átnézhessem" [Please send me the copy of my speech [...] so that I could look into the fair copy] (Eötvös to Szalay, November 1839. MTA KIK Kt. Ms 1186/18. Eötvös 1976: 134). Virtually, every text written by Eötvös underwent Szalay's revision – which must have been a remarkable sacrifice from Szalay for Eötvös's career. Eötvös's gratefulness for this sacrifice seems to have been rather limited. For example, he was worried about Szalay's health only because without him his literary career would possibly be over. He wrote him with a code-switch into Latin: "nyugtass meg egészségedröl is mellyröl soraidban nem szolsz, de csak egy kis szót sem, et quid mei sine te mihi prosunt honores" [please also reassure me about your health, about which you don't write in your lines, not even a small word, et quid mei sine te mihi prosunt honores] (Eötvös to Szalay, 6 June 1841. MTA KIK Kt. Ms 1186/21. 1. Eötvös 1976: 141).

4.2 Ferenc Toldy's criticism of Eötvös's linguistic competence

As mentioned above, Eötvös turned at the beginning of his career to members of the older generation of Hungarian literary intellectuals, who gave him recognition and encouragement. In contrast to this, overt hostility emerged between Eötvös and his circle and the established and authoritative critics of the 1830s, whose main organ was the almanac *Aurora* (1822–1837) and later the review

Athenaeum (1837–1843): Ferenc Toldy (1805–1875), József Bajza (1804–1858), and the renowned poet Mihály Vörösmarty (1800–1855). As a matter of fact, Eötvös attacked them first in his satirical drama *A kritikusok* [The Critics] (now lost), and its prologue entitled *A' kritikus' apotheosisa* [The Critic's Apotheosis] (Eötvös 1831). As a kind of revengeful response, Toldy published a devastating critique of Eötvös's comedy, *Marriageable Youth*. This critique proved to be the most dangerous challenge to Eötvös's literary program as Toldy, as a remarkable exception among Eötvös's fellow intellectuals, was neither accepting of nor helpful in improving Eötvös's linguistic competence. After some introductory criticism of Eötvös's mixed vocabulary in the only work in which he made use of this poetic tool ("hogy mikép lehet a' magyar conversatiót franczia kifejezésekkel annyira tarkázni, mint szerző teszi?" ["how can Hungarian conversation so dotted with French expressions, like our Author does?] (Toldy 1834: 92), or "[h]ogy idegen nyelveket tudunk, az érdem is, haszon is; de hogy tudunk azt más úton kell irásainkban éreztetni" [[t]hat we know foreign languages, is a merit and a benefit; but this fact should be put into relief in our writings in another way] (Toldy 1834: 93)), Toldy attacked the weakest point of Eötvös's literary achievement, his insufficient linguistic proficiency:

[Á]ltal megy Rec. a' *nyelvre*, mellyről kénytelen megjegyezni, hogy az gondatlanabb már nem igen lehetne, úgy hogy minden nyomon hibára akadunk. Hibás hajtogatás [ragozás], az articulusok' [névelők] helytelen alkalmazása vagy kihagyása, az igehatárzók [igekötők] elnyomása ott, hol fölötte szükségesek [...]; szavak' hibás használása [...] 's tb. mind csekélység a' szószerkeztetés' [szintaxis] hibáihoz képest, mellyektől pezsg az egész, p. o. [...] rendez vous*hoz* menni [zum Rendesvous gehen], [...] dolg*on* részt vesz [an etw. teilnehmen] [...]; de vannak egész, illy rosszul alkotott periodusok [összetett mondatok] [...] „Nem hiszi senki, nehéz most egy leánynak établismant találni, mintha a' férfiak az asszonyokat nem is szeretnék többé" [Niemand glaubt, es sei jetzt einem Mädchen schwierig, ein Etablissement zu finden, als ob die Männer die Frauen nicht mehr lieben würden] [...]. Nyelv, vagy inkább beszéd-e ez? – Mikor fogják fiataljaink eléggé érezni azt, hogy mielőtt irnánk, *tanulnunk* kell egyebeken kívül azt a' nyelvet is mellyen írunk
[The reviewer turns his attention to the *language*, about which he is obliged to note that it cannot be more careless; so we stumble upon a fault at every step. Faulty conjugation, wrong usage or omission of articles, the suppression of verbal prefixes there, where they are absolute necessary [...]; mistaken use of words [...] and so on – they are all bagatelle with relation to the faults of the syntax, with which the whole text is riddled, for example [...] rendez vous*hoz* menni [in German mirror translation: *zum Rendesvous gehen*], [...] dolg*on* részt vesz [in German mirror translation: *an etw. teilnehmen*]. Moreover, there are whole compound sentences, which are mistakenly composed [...]: Nobody believes that it is difficult now for a young girl to find an establishment, as if men would not love women anymore. ["Nem hiszi senki, nehéz most egy leánynak établismant találni, mintha a' férfiak az asszonyokat nem is szeretnék többé"] [In German mirror translation: *Niemand glaubt, es sei jetzt einem Mädchen schwierig, ein Etablissement zu finden, als ob die Männer*

die Frauen nicht mehr lieben würden]" [...]. Is this a language, or, to put it better, a [live] speech? When will our youth feel sufficiently that, before writing, they should among other things, *learn* the language in which they write?] (Toldy 1834: 93–94)

This was his final argument at the end of the thoroughly disapproving review. Toldy was the only fellow literary man who publicly stated that the king was naked, that the young Eötvös's linguistic competence was not good enough for creative work in the Hungarian language. However, this review could not breach or hinder Eötvös's career. In response, Eötvös's revenge, or at least non-cooperation and non-relenting dissatisfaction with Toldy, pursued his adversary in various administrative hierarchical connections throughout their lives. This interlinking of their careers began when Eötvös was elected member of the Hungarian Scholarly Society, of which Toldy was the secretary.

4.3 Eötvös's membership of the Hungarian Scholarly Society and the Palocsay project

In 1835, Eötvös became a member of the Hungarian Scholarly Society, the principal raison d'être of which was the promotion of the cause of the Hungarian language. It was a further challenge to overcome – his reports and reviews to the academy had to be grammatically faultless. They were faultless indeed, but they contained words that Eötvös would have never used; in this respect, they indicate that someone apparently must have helped Eötvös to submit these reviews.

One of Eötvös's first projects as a member of the academy was the translation and edition of the poems of his late friend, Tivadar Palocsay, into Hungarian as a fulfilment of Palocsay's personal wish: "Palocsay német költeményeit fordítgatom fáradhatatlanúl; utolsó kivánsága volt 's telyesítem menyiben rajtam ál." [I keep translating Palocsay's German poems indefatigably; this was his last wish and I fulfill it so far as I can] (Eötvös to Szalay, January 1836. MTA KIK Kt. Ms 1186/6. Eötvös 1976: 93). The project also had a collective-national aspect: to give a Hungarian poet to the nation, even if posthumously. As Eötvös wrote to Kölcsey from Vienna in early February 1836: "[Palocsay] kért fordítanám német verseit Magyarra, mert kinos ha arra gondol hogy valaha hazája költöi közé nem számitathatik. [...] A' hon örülni fog költöjének mely csak halála után lett övé" [Palocsay asked me to translate his German poems into Hungarian, because it is painful if he thinks that he won't be counted in the ranks of the poets of his fatherland. [...] The fatherland will be delighted by its poet who became its poet only after his death] (Eötvös to Kölcsey, Vienna, 26

February 1836. Ráday Archives of the Cisdanubian Reformed Protestant Diocese – in the following: Ráday-Arch., Szemere-Tár 1 Pótkötet 111. Eötvös 1976: 95).

The problem with the "naturalization" of the author was that Palocsay wrote his poems in German. Therefore, Eötvös went a step further: he wanted the translations to be presented as originals and made efforts that the academy (would / could) approve – probably not only Palocsay's works in translation as originals, but also the very idea behind the naturalization and nationalization practice of a life's work in a language other than Hungarian. He asked his mentor and friend Kölcsey about this plan:

> Eggyébiránt kivánom hogy fordításaink mint originálok jöjjenek a Magyar közönség elébe talán majd dicsérve említi az Academia, vagy talán megengedi hogy az elhunytnak parentálhassak? [...] Minekutánna a' magyar rész originálként jelenik meg, a szoszerénti forditást szükségesnek nem tartom, csak az értelem maradjon meg.
> [Further, I would like to present our translations as originals to the Hungarian readership. Will it perhaps be approvingly mentioned by the Academy? Or will it allow that I deliver a memorial speech to the deceased? [...] As the Hungarian part will be published as original, I do not think a literal translation necessary; only the meaning should be preserved] (Eötvös to Kölcsey, 13 April 1836. Ráday-Arch. Szemere-Tár 15. kötet 8. Eötvös 1976: 101).

Kölcsey's answer is not known to us. Fact is that Eötvös's idea was not realized: Palocsay's works were published only in their German original (Palochay 1837) and with Eötvös's preface written in German, which was yet another text for Szalay to translate (for an edition that remained unpublished): "Az előszót [ti. Palocsay verseihez] [...] talán csak németül fogom küldeni, ha ugy volna kérlek az Istenért forditsd le máskép szégyenben maradok" [I will send the Preface [to Palocsay's poems] [..] perhaps only in German. Would be this the case, I beg you in the name of God to translate it; otherwise, I will be disgraced] (Eötvös to Szalay, 30 June 1836. MTA KIK Kt. Ms 1186/9. Eötvös 1976: 106).

4.4 Later literary activity

Szalay's friendly assistance is documented in his correspondence with Eötvös until the early 1840s. When Eötvös started with political journalism in the 1840s, this assistance became institutionalized, since Szalay became the editor of the oppositional press organ, *Pesti Hirlap*, in which Eötvös published his political articles. In the case of his two pre-revolution novels, *The Village Notary* (1845) and *Magyarország 1514-ben* [Hungary in 1514] (1847), information about their genesis and publication has survived only in fragments. Accordingly, the extent of their eventual linguistic correction by external assistance cannot be assessed. The stylistic changes made to his first novel, *A Carthausi* [The Chartreuse], are somewhat better documented, as a comparison of the first and second editions show (Eötvös 1842; Gángó 1999b).

Eötvös's linguistic competence did not allow him even at a mature age to publish without linguistic assistance. The surviving manuscript of his fourth and last novel, *A nővérek* [The Sisters] (Eötvös 1857) preserved the extensive linguistic corrections by a hitherto non-identifiable hand. Nonetheless, it seems that his younger protégée, the literary historian Pál Gyulai (1826–1909), was particularly active in proofreading the work of Eötvös's late literary compositions. Gyulai's contribution is evidenced by his correspondence with Eötvös related to the edition of Eötvös's collected aphorisms, entitled *Gondolatok* [Thoughts] (Eötvös 1864). Their correspondence also shows Eötvös's prevailing hesitation in his use of Hungarian lexis and syntax as well as the German roots of his Hungarian prose. As he wrote to Gyulai on 12 September 1863:

> A könyv czime, egyszerüen *Gondolatok*: Az ajánlat Anyám emlékének. A Jelige Ne higy (vagy ne bizzál) oly gondolatnak, melynek szived ellentmond (Anyám leveleiből) a gondolat anyám levelében igy áll (Glaube keinem Gedanken den dein Herz widerspricht) ha tehát jobb forditást tud tegye azt az elöbbinek helyébe.
> [The title of the book is simply Thoughts: dedicated to the memory of my mother. The motto: Do not believe (or do not trust) in a thought which is contradicted by your heart (from the letters of my mother). The thought in my mother's letter is put like this: Glaube keinem Gedanken, den dein Herz widerspricht. Therefore, if you know a better translation, put it in the place of mine] (OSzK Lt. Eötvös 1976: 368–369).

5 Project two: reversing the originals

Eötvös did not risk his life or his political career during the revolution and the following war of independence in 1849. He left his office and the country as early as the end of October 1848. After relocating to Bavaria, he wrote political theory and journalistic articles in German, partly because he addressed himself to an international audience, partly because he lived in Bavaria with his sister's family, far from his linguistic proofreaders in Hungary. His principal linguistic help, Szalay, migrated to Switzerland.

Due to this, Eötvös's linguistic identity became even more complicated by a further aspect. While in his pre-1848 literary works the dissimulation of his non-native competency posed a problem in Hungarian works, after 1850 the fact had to be concealed that the original language of his essays was German. The dilemma of the translation project of Palocsay's poems in 1836 became his own after 1850. In the first case, his poorly written Hungarian works had to be corrected by others. In the second, his good German works not only had to be translated into Hungarian, but these translations also had to be presented as originals. This situation was further complicated by the fact that though his German was much better than his Hungarian, even his German was not good enough to be published alone, without the help of proof-readers. It seems that his "demanding" bilingualism resulted in an overall linguistic imperfection (cf. Aronin and Singleton 2012: 2). His fellow journalist at the "Centralist" circle, at the same time his brother-in-law, Ágoston Trefort (1817–1888) seems to have been destined for this proofreading role. Eötvös wrote to Szalay after his arrival to Munich on 20 October 1848: "Tudod Treffort tökélletesen ír németül, én magam is ha Treff dolgozásaimat átjavítja bátran léphetek fel" [You know, Trefort writes perfectly in German. If Treff corrects my works, I myself can step out too] (MTA KIK Kt. Ms 1186/33. Eötvös 1976: 211).

Among minor contributions to the Augsburg paper *Allgemeine Zeitung*, Eötvös published a path-breaking German study on the nationality problem of the Austrian Empire entitled *Über die Gleichberechtigung der Nationalitäten in Österreich* [On the Equal Rights of the Nationalities in Austria] (Eötvös 1850). These texts remained untranslated in his lifetime as well as the various manuscript preparations for an unwritten *opus magnum* on the history of "Christian" (i.e., European) civilization (Gángó 1999a). The problem of bilingualism resurfaced as he wanted to present the synthesis of his theoretical work written during his stay in Bavaria, published as the two volumes of his *Der Einfluß der herrschenden Ideen des 19. Jahrhunderts auf den Staat* [The Dominant Ideas of the Nineteenth Century and Their Impact on the State] (Eötvös 1854a, 1854b), to the Hungarian public as well.

On the title page of the second 1854 German edition of the first volume (after the first edition in 1851), as well as the 1854 German edition of the second volume, the following can be read: "Vom Verfasser selbst aus dem Ungarischen übersetzt" [From Hungarian translated by the author] (Eötvös 1854a: [iii], 1854b: [iii]). As a matter of fact, they were not translated from Hungarian to German but vice versa and not by the author but others. Both translations can be linked to his "Centralist" collaborators. Only the translator of the second volume can be clearly identified as Antal Csengery (1822–1880), who writes in his recollections about his commission in these terms:

> Eötvös, midőn a forradalom alatt külföldre ment, a külföldön írta [...] most megjelent politikai nagy művét: *A XIX. század uralkodó eszméi* stb. Miután a hazába visszatért, természetes, hogy magyarul is ki akarta azt adni, éspedig azt akarta, hogy a magyar

> legyen az eredeti. De a munkába már belefásulva [...] [e]ngem kért tehát meg az átdolgozásra. Én a télen csináltam meg e munkát bizonyos öszletért
> [Eötvös, as he went abroad during the revolution, wrote his great political work [...] *The Dominant Ideas of the 19th century* etc. there. After he returned to his fatherland, it is obvious that he also wanted to publish it in Hungarian; and he wanted the Hungarian to be the original. As he was tired of this work, [...] he asked me to do the revision. I have done this work in this summer for a certain sum] (quoted in Oltványi 1981: 598).

The translations from German to Hungarian were lexically inconsistent. For many political terms in German, there existed no canonized Hungarian counterpart at that time. For example, the word *Staat (state)* was translated into Hungarian as *státus, álladalom, állodalom,* or *állam,* the latter of which is the present equivalent of the German word (for the differences between the German and Hungarian editions: Nyíri 1980: 52; Oltványi 1981; Jones 1996: 25sqq.; Jones 1998). The very fact that Eötvös did not strive for a coherent terminology in Hungarian and seems not to have checked the translations of others, shows the apparently lower prestige of the Hungarian language in scientific prose for him (Hartig 1987: 300). These inconsistencies made the translator's work indeed "visible" (Venuti 1995: 1–2) and the readers had to look away not to notice it. As to Eötvös's political essays, there was a clear prestige conflict between the Hungarian and the German languages. The German language was not only the language of Austrian bureaucracy established in Hungary after the defeat of the 1849 War of Independence, but also the international language of science. This higher prestige of the German language was impossible even to mention in the early 1850s, let alone to discuss publicly, similar to that of the Hungarian language in the 1830s. In the interest of international scholarly communication, his works had to be published in German but simultaneously with the Hungarian edition, by claiming that the Hungarian text had priority at least in terms of genesis. In the case of his works from his youth, he relegated the form issues to his assistants; in the case of his essays on social science, he did the same with the terminological issues.

As for his political pamphlets in the transitory period from the New Absolutism, *Die Garantien der Macht und Einheit Österreichs* [The Guarantees of the Power and Unity of Austria] was published anonymously in German (Eötvös 1859). As it strongly advocated the interests of the Austrian *Gesamtstaat* after the defeated War of Independence 1849, it was not translated into Hungarian. When the international power relations changed, Eötvös promptly modified his position in another German brochure entitled *Die Sonderstellung Ungarns vom Standpunkte der Einheit Deutschlands* [Hungary's Autonomy from the Point of View of the Unity of Germany] (Eötvös 1860). This latter was published also in

Hungarian, anonymously, from "a Hungarian statesman", in István Toldy's (Ferenc Toldy's son) translation (Eötvös 1861).

6 Eötvös's literary program in context

In Eötvös's personal identification with the national cause and his consequent literary-linguistic program some elements are typical for the period like the partial linguistic assimilation of the Hungarian aristocracy since their contribution to the political struggles of the nation made a certain knowledge of Hungarian necessary. A level of competency, which was sufficient for literary creation was, however, not necessary – this can be regarded as Eötvös's specific objective. It is important to note that at that time literary works displaying an imperfect linguistic competence could indeed be compatible with a particular view of the function and social status of literature. According to this conception, a literary work is a deed for the community rather than an "autonomous" individual achievement. These literary works were created in the interest of the community and the goal was the "enlargement" or "enhancement" of the corpus of national literature. This intention could justify the existence of a literary work and entitle the author to help from those who share this objective and are able to be helpful in attaining this goal.

In contrast to contemporaries like Ferenc Kölcsey, Mihály Vörösmarty, Sándor Petőfi (1823–1849), János Arany (1817–1882), Mór Jókai, or Zsigmond Kemény (1814–1875), Eötvös's works have no linguistic normative authority. His works need assistance also in recent times to survive. As Eötvös's political activity and theoretical oeuvre form an essential part of the collective memory of 19th-century Hungarian nation building, the preservation of his life's work in its entirety seems necessary. Hence, with reference to the intellectual authority of his life's works, including his literary works, literary scholars now accomplish the work that friends or hired help did during Eötvös's lifetime to make sure his works meet the linguistic norms of Hungarian literary classics.

For a proper understanding of the phenomenon of Eötvös's bilingualism, the first ten years of his career from 1830 to 1840 are a crucial period, when he was a poet, playwright, and novelist. His intellectual practices as well as his publicly conveyable artistic and intellectual profile and habitus were formed during these years. Later, Eötvös had only to go on with these practices. Further, it seems worth mentioning that the direct context of Eötvös's works was not that of the greatest – Petőfi, Arany, or Jókai –, who started their careers some fifteen years later, but that of his fellow writers in the 1830s: András Fáy

(1786–1864), József Gaál (1811–1866), Lajos Kuthy (1813–1864), or Miklós Jósika (1794–1865). In these years, the normative aspect of "enlarging" Hungarian literature was generally accepted. The novels of the latter authors did not gain classic status – rather, they became symbols of lacking linguistic problem awareness (like in Péter Esterházy's (1950–2016) quote of Jósika's sentence: "Kinyílt az ajtó" [The door opened] (Birnbaum 1991: 6)). In other words, Eötvös's works in the crucial first ten years appeared in the context of literary achievements, which, although written by native Hungarian speakers, proved unable to survive due to artistic shortcomings of a different nature. Before Petőfi's and Arany's poetic revolution, the linguistic form of a literary work (and, consequently, the linguistic faults committed by a non-native speaker) seemed to be one aspect among many: plot, structure, characterization of the protagonists, collective "message" and so on. Moreover, linguistic form is an aspect that could be corrected more easily than other shortcomings, while respecting Eötvös's authorship regarding the texts as a whole and their conceptual frame. Yet, the more Eötvös advanced in age, the stronger the competition became.

Another comparison with a lexically polyglot Hungarian classic novelist, Mór Jókai, shows that norm building did not primarily regard the level of lexis. There, Jókai succeeded in mirroring the factual multilingualism of 19th-century Hungarian society from juristic Latinity to the wide varieties of linguistic usage of the various ethnic-national groups and social strata staying at different levels of linguistic assimilation (or dissimilation). In contrast to this, Eötvös did not use "foreign" words: his regard to the Hungarian orbit through the prism of the German language was coded into the syntax.

7 Conclusion

Eötvös learned the Hungarian language by writing it. His proficiency improved considerably, but it never reached the level of native competence. He needed assistance even in the 1860s for his literary works. As he did not devote enough time to give his texts – literary, journalistic, or scientific – the ultimate polish, his life's work, in the strict sense of the term, is the outcome of the concentrated efforts made by him and his assistants during his whole life and even beyond.

His grasp of reality was rooted in the sociolinguistic context of the German of the international aristocracy, deprived of the elements of the specific German or Austrian culture, apart from the top of German literature. The whole project of his concealed bilingualism was based on a twofold solidarity: first, the class solidarity of the aristocracy, where Eötvös remained in his primary sociolinguistic environment, and friendship-based solidarity with László Szalay, who knew and kept the secret of his chosen Hungarian artistic identity.

To implement his linguistic-artistic program Eötvös needed external resources. During his early career, in the case of his lyric poems, his friendship with László Szalay provided this resource. He used Szalay's native Hungarian competence in the name of their friendship. Later, this help turned institutional or quasi-institutional as Eötvös's fellow journalist colleagues became his hired assistants.

With his decision to choose Hungarian as a literary language, Eötvös terminated his public loyalty towards the German language in the field of his literary activity. Notwithstanding, German retained an orientational function for him in terms of his appropriation of the world and the articulation of his experience. It provided the basic linguistic framework on the level of syntax and idioms. His linguistic strategy consisted in forcing this framework on the Hungarian language. The start of his career was critical from the point of view of his bilingualism. Once he made himself and his linguistic configuration accepted, he only had to go on with the practice credited by his literary environment. The more his resources and authority increased, the easier this practice became.

This case study hopes to have shown the productivity of the theories of literary multilingualism in 19th-century Hungarian literature, inviting thereby for the extension of the social, chronological, and/or geographical scope of the investigations in order to develop a revised view of the linguistic aspects of (East-Central) European nation building.

8 References

8.1 Primary sources

[Eötvös József]. 1831. B. E. J. *A' kritikus apotheosisa* [The Critic's Apotheosis]. Pest: Trattner és Károly.
[Eötvös, József]. 1833. E. J. *A' házasulók* [Marriageable Youth]. Pest: Hartleben.
Eötvös, József. 1842. *A' Karthausi* [The Chartreuse]. Pest: Hartleben.
Eötvös, József. 1845. *A' falu jegyzője* [The Village Notary] I–III. Pest: Hartleben.
Eötvös, József. 1847. *Magyarország 1514-ben* [Hungary in 1514] I–III. Pest: Ráth.
[Eötvös, József]. 1850. N.N. *Ueber die Gleichberechtigung der Nationalitäten in Oesterreich.* Pest: Hartleben.
Eötvös, József. 1854a. *Der Einfluß der herrschenden Ideen des 19. Jahrhunderts auf den Staat. Erster Theil.* Leipzig: Brockhaus.
Eötvös, József. 1854b. *Der Einfluß der herrschenden Ideen des 19. Jahrhunderts auf den Staat. Zweiter Theil.* Leipzig: Brockhaus.

Eötvös, József. 1859. *Die Garantien der Macht und Einheit Oesterreichs*. Leipzig: Brockhaus.
Eötvös, József. 1860. *Die Sonderstellung Ungarns vom Standpunkte der Einheit Deutschlands*. Leipzig: Brockhaus.
Eötvös, József. 1861. *Magyarország különállása Németország egységének szempontjából* [Hungary's Autonomy from the Point of View of the Unity of Germany]. Budapest: Emich.
Eötvös, József. 1864. *Gondolatok* [Thoghts]. Pest: Ráth.
Eötvös, József. 1976. *Levelek* [Letters]. Ed., transl., and with an introduction and annotations by Ambrus Oltványi. Budapest: Magyar Helikon.
Eötvös, József. 2021. *Költeményeim* [My Poems]. Ed. with a study by Gábor Gángó. Sárospatak: Hernád Kiadó.
Eötvös, József. Ms. *Levelezés 1848-ig* [Correspondence until 1848]. Ed. with an introduction and notes by Orsolya Völgyesi. Manuscript.
Palochay, Theodor Baron von. 1837. *Gedichte*. Pest: Heckenast.
Toldy, Ferenc. 1834. A' házasulók [Marriageable Youth]. *Kritikai Lapok* IV. 57–96.

8.2 Secondary sources

Anokhina, Olga D., Till Dembeck, Dirk Weissmann (eds.). 2019a. *Mapping Multilingualism in 19th Century European Literatures.Le plurilinguisme dans les littératures européennes du XIXe siècle*. Vienna: LIT.
Anokhina, Olga D., Till Dembeck, Dirk Weissmann. 2019b. Close the Gap! Literary Multilingualism Studies and the 19th Century. In Olga D. Anokhina, Till Dembeck, Dirk Weissmann (eds.), *Mapping Multilingualism in 19th Century European Literatures. Le plurilinguisme dans les littératures européennes du XIXe siècle*, 1–5. Vienna: LIT.
Aronin, Larissa & David Singleton. 2012. *Multilingualism*. Amsterdam/Philadelphia: John Benjamins Publishing Company.
Auer, Peter & Li Wei (eds.). 2007. *Handbook of Multilingualism and Multilingual Communication*. Berlin: De Gruyter.
Balogh, András F. & Christoph Leitgeb (eds.). 2012. *Mehrsprachigkeit in Zentraleuropa. Zur Geschichte einer literarischen und kulturellen Chance. Zwei- und Mehrsprachigkeit in der Literatur und Kultur Zentraleuropas; Jahrestagung des Literatur- und kulturwissenschaftlichen Komitees der Österreichischen und der Ungarischen Akademie der Wissenschaften*. Wien: Praesens.
Birnbaum, Marianna D. 1991. *Esterházy-kalauz. Marianna D. Birnbaum beszélget Esterházy Péterrel* [Guide to Esterházy. Marianna D. Birnbaum Talks with Péter Esterházy]. Budapest: Magvető Könyvkiadó.
Blackledge, Adrian & Angela Creese. 2010. *Multilingualism. A Critical Perspective*. London/New York: Continuum.
Bödy, Paul. 1985. *Joseph Eötvös and the Modernization of Hungary 1840–1870*. New York: Columbia University Press.
Czinege, Szilvia. Széchenyi német nyelvhasználata levelei tükrében [Széchenyi's Use of the German Language in Light of His Letters] 2021. *Századok* 155/3, 631–654.
Devescovi, Balázs. 2007. *Eötvös József (1813–1871)*. Pozsony [Bratislava]: Kalligram.
Ferdman, Bernardo M., Rose-Marie Weber, Arnulfo G. Ramirez (eds.). 1994. *Litaracy across Languages and Cultures*. Albany: SUNY Press.

Ferenczi, Zoltán. 1903. *Báró Eötvös József* [Baron József Eötvös], *1813–1871*. Budapest: Magyar Történelmi Társulat.
Gángó, Gábor. 1999a. *Eötvös József az emigrációban* [József Eötvös in Emigration]. Debrecen: Kossuth Egyetemi Kiadó.
Gángó, Gábor. 1999b. Megjegyzések Eötvös József *A karthauzi* című regényének szöveghagyományáról [Comments on the Textual Tradition of the Novel 'The Chartereuse' by József Eötvös]. *Irodalomtörténeti Közlemények* 103/3–4.), 369–375.
Gángó, Gábor. 2010. Joseph Eötvös. In Marcel Cornis-Pope & John Neubauer (eds.). *History of the Literary Cultures of East-Central Europe. Junctures and Disjunctures in the 19th and 20th Centuries*, IV: Types and Stereotypes, 521–526. Amsterdam, John Benjamins Publishing Company.
García, Ofelia, Lesley Bartlett, JoAnne Kleifgen. 2007. From biliteracy to pluriliteracies. In Peter Auer & Li Wei (eds.), *Handbook of Multilingualism and Multilingual Communication*, 207–228. Berlin: De Gruyter.
Hartig, Matthias. 1987. Sprachlegitimation und Sprachloyalität in ihrer Bedeutung für den Dialektwandel. In Els Oksaar (ed.), *Soziokulturelle Perspektiven von Mehrsprachigkeit und Spracherwerb / Sociocultural Perspectives of Multilingualism and Language Acquisition*, 300–315. Tübingen: Narr Verlag.
Jones, D. Mervyn. 1996. Preface. József Eötvös and the Dominant Ideas. In József Eötvös, *The Dominant Ideas of the Nineteenth Century and Their Impact on the State. Vol. 1. Diagnosis*. Transl., ed., and annotated with an introductory essay by D. Mervyn Jones. 13–56. Boulder, CO: Atlantic Research and Publications.
Jones, D. Mervyn. 1998. Note on the German and Hungarian Versions of Volume two. In József Eötvös, *The Dominant Ideas of the Nineteenth Century and Their Impact on the State. Vol 2. Remedy*. Transl., ed., and annotated by D. Mervyn Jones. 573–576. Boulder, CO: Atlantic Research and Publications.
Kühlwein, Wolfgang. 1987. Soziosemiotische Determinanz im kulturübergreifenden sprachlichen Erfassen der Wirklichkeit. In Els Oksaar (ed.), *Soziokulturelle Perspektiven von Mehrsprachigkeit und Spracherwerb / Sociocultural Perspectives of Multilingualism and Language Acquisition*, 1–22. Tübingen: Narr Verlag.
Lanza, Elizabeth. 2007. Multilingualism and the family. In Peter Auer & Li Wei (eds.), *Handbook of Multilingualism and Multilingual Communication*, 45–67. Berlin: De Gruyter.
Mansour, Gerda. 1993. *Multilingualism and Nation Building*. Clevendon/Philadelphia/Adelaide: Multilingual Matters Ltd.
Mende, Jana-Katharina. 2020. *Das Konzept des Messianismus in der polnischen, französischen und deutschen Literatur der Romantik. Eine mehrsprachige Konzeptanalyse*. Heidelberg: Universitätsverlag Winter.
Nyíri, Kristóf. 1980. Forradalom után. Kemény, Eötvös, Madách [After the Revolution. Kemény, Eötvös, Madách]. In *A Monarchia szellemi életéről* [About the Intellectual Life of the Monarchy], 35–65. Budapest: Gondolat.
Oksaar, Els (ed.). 1987a. *Soziokulturelle Perspektiven von Mehrsprachigkeit und Spracherwerb / Sociocultural Perspectives of Multilingualism and Language Acquisition*. Tübingen: Narr Verlag.
Oksaar, Els. 1987b. Vorwort. In Els Oksaar (ed.), *Soziokulturelle Perspektiven von Mehrsprachigkeit und Spracherwerb / Sociocultural Perspectives of Multilingualism and Language Acquisition*, Vii–Xi. Tübingen: Narr Verlag.

Oltványi, Ambrus. 1981. A sajtó alá rendező utószava [The Editor's Epilogue]. In József Eötvös, *A XIX. század uralkodó eszméinek befolyása az államra* [The Dominant Ideas of the Nineteenth Century and Their Impact on the State] I-II. Ed. by Ambrus Oltványi, with an introduction by István Sőtér, II, 595–622. Budapest: Magyar Helikon.

Radaelli, Giulia. 2011. *Literarische Mehrsprachigkeit. Sprachwechsel bei Elias Canetti und Ingeborg Bachmann*. Berlin: Akademie-Verlag.

Szalay, Gábor. 1942. Báró Eötvös József néhány kiadatlan levele. Első közlemény [Some Unpublished Letters of Baron József Eötvös. First Article]. *Irodalomtörténeti Közlemények*. 52. 156–164.

Vardy, Steven Bela. 1987. *Baron Joseph Eötvös (1813–1871)*. Boulder, CO: Atlantic Research and Publications.

Venuti, Lawrence. 1995. *The Translator's Invisibility: A History of Translation*. London/New York: Routledge.

Wandruszka, Mario. 1987. Die Muttersprache als Wegbereiterin zur Mehrsprachigkeit. In Els Oksaar (ed.), *Soziokulturelle Perspektiven von Mehrsprachigkeit und Spracherwerb / Sociocultural Perspectives of Multilingualism and Language Acquisition*, 39–53. Tübingen: Narr Verlag.

Zemanek, Evi & Weertje Willms. 2014. Polyglotte Texte–Einleitung. In Evi Zemanek & Weertje Willms (eds.), *Polyglotte Texte. Formen und Funktionen literarischer Mehrsprachigkeit von der Antike bis zur Gegenwart*, 1–6. Berlin: Ch. A. Bachmann Verlag.

Katrin Gunkel
Multilingualism and Nationality in Theodor Fontane's *Kriegsgefangen. Erlebtes 1870*

Abstract: Theodor Fontane was and is considered a classic German author. And yet: without knowledge of French, English or Latin, parts of his work can hardly be read. How does the portrayal of the "Prussian" author, who dedicates his texts to the Wilhelmine era, fit together with his literary multilingualism? This contrast is relevant in his autobiographical text *Kriegsgefangen. Erlebtes 1870* (1871). His literary strategy is writing multilingually and nationally. The interplay of hidden and manifest multilingualism and nationality in the text, and the peculiarities that multilingual writing possesses in the 19th century German setting will be addressed in the paper. Relevant questions are how the sociopolitical and linguistic attitudes of Fontane's time affect the production and reception of his text. Can *Kriegsgefangen* be understood as a resistance to a forced nationalism or as a type of conformity? Does the reception and French translation of his text suffer the fate of national stereotypes?

Keywords: Theodor Fontane, Nationality, National Literature, Code-switching, Direct Speech, Monolingualism, Translation, Multiperspectivity, Linguistic Purity, Autobiography

1 Introduction

"Effronterien", "Carrièremacher", "Misère" (Fontane 1871: 7, 32, 70): foreign words and multilingual compounds such as these will be very familiar to Theodor Fontane's readers. The philologist, literary critic and publicist Eduard Engel, a contemporary of Fontane's and proficient in several languages himself, commented on this in his *Deutsche Stilkunst* of 1911: "Ihm [Fontane] genügt z. B. nicht 'glänzendes Elend', das doch Goethen genügte; er muß 'splendide Misère' schreiben" [He is not content with "glänzendes Elend", for example, although that was good enough for Goethe; he has to write "splendide Misère"] (Engel 1911: 156). Somewhat further on he writes: "Er fühlte sich nicht wie Chamisso als deutschgebildeten Franzosen, sondern war ein durchaus deutscher Mann [...]

Katrin Gunkel, Humboldt-University Berlin, e-mail: katrin.gunkel@gmx.de

∂ Open Access. © 2023 the author(s), published by De Gruyter. This work is licensed under the Creative Commons Attribution 4.0 International License.
https://doi.org/10.1515/9783110778656-007

Das hat ihn leider nicht gehindert, bei jeder noch so unpassenden Gelegenheit französische Brocken und Fremdwörter aller Art einzustreuen [...]" [Unlike Chamisso, he did not feel himself to be a German-educated Frenchman; he was a German man through and through [...] Unfortunately that did not stop him from sprinkling in chunks of French and foreign words of all kinds at every opportunity, however inappropriate] (Engel 1911: 156). Engel belonged to the *Allgemeiner Deutscher Sprachverein* (ADSV), founded in 1885 with the aim of encouraging all speakers of German to use that language for everything that could be expressed in it. The organization thus conformed to the purist linguistic tendencies of a period in which the term national language was becoming predominant.

The term 'national language' emphasizes the national, political, cultural or even ideological orientation and relevance of language (Sieburg 2017: 69–70). Those views are based on the ideas of Jacob and Wilhelm Grimm, who propagated an equation of language and nation for the purpose of establishing a cultural nation (Sieburg 2017: 70). At the beginning of the 19th century, the monolingualism of writers was already being elevated to the level of dogma, as Weismann explains (2013). During the 1820s and 1830s the "Nexus Muttersprache – Vaterland – Nationalliteratur" [nexus of mother tongue – fatherland – national literature] became established as a binding norm (Weissmann 2013: 323). In the mid-19th century, literary historians such as Georg Gottfried Gervinus presented German literature as a monocultural and monolingual medium for the formation of the German nation (Gervinus 1835–1842, cf. Weissmann 2013: 323). The worsening conflicts between Germany and its neighbours, France and England, reinforced the norm of a monocultural and monolingual national literature.

Fontane did not conform to these norms and imperatives.[1] Erdmann stresses, this seemingly most Prussian among the German-language works is sometimes barely readable without a knowledge of French, English or Latin (2001: 33). Of these, French was predominant in Fontane's life and work, as Burger and Zürrer emphasize (2015: 92). How does Fontane's literary multilingualism fit

---

[1] Fontane was not alone in this attitude. Not all writers internalized the imperative of monocultural and monolingual national literature. In 1889, forty-one well-known authors (including Theodor Fontane, Gustav Freytag and Paul Heyse), Germanists, historians and politicians signed the "Erklärung der 41", which was printed in the March 1889 issue of the *Preußische Jahrbücher*, a periodical edited by Heinrich von Treitschke and Hans Delbrück. Here the basic idea of linguistic purification was accepted, but not the strict demands for linguistic purity. Above all, the signatories refused to have their language usage dictated to them by the ADSV or the state institutions it aspired to create.

with his depiction – common both then and now – as a "Prussian" writer? As an author whose patriotic poems made his name as a "vaterländischer Schriftsteller" [writer of the fatherland] (cf. Wruck 1987), and who dedicated many of his texts, including war books, to the German nation and William I? The hypothesis here is that these two aspects are not mutually exclusive in the case of Theodor Fontane, especially at the beginning of his creative period. His literary strategy was to write both multilingually and nationally. This is particularly striking in his autobiographical German-French text *Kriegsgefangen: Erlebtes 1870* (1871). Here multilingualism can be seen as a stylistic device for a national approach and thus, even if it is visible on the surface of the text, somewhat hidden behind this approach. It becomes even more evident when taking a closer look at the French translation of the text by Téodor de Wyzewa, in which the multilingualism was actively hidden through translation. The analysis of both texts can give us new insights into the writers' intentions, the texts' functions, as well as their reception.

Before I elaborate on these aspects, I would like to propose two main theoretical concepts of multilingualism which help to explain Fontane's texts: Following Guilia Radaelli (2011: 53–66/2014), I differentiate between manifest multilingualism as it appears in different forms of code-switching and code-mixing, and latent multilingualism, expressed by different forms of translation, references to other languages and reflection on languages. I consider the category of hidden multilingualism as a part of latent multilingualism. Manifest multilingualism denotes all forms of multilingualism that are visible to the readers on the surface of a text while latent multilingualism refers to the fact that other languages are not visible on the surface of a text, that they are only implicitly present or even hidden (cf. Gunkel 2020: 36–43). In the first case, the languages are used in the text, in the second case, they are only mentioned or implied (Blum-Barth 2020). Both forms can occur within the same text as we will see in Fontane's *Kriegsgefangen: Erlebtes 1870*.

2 Context and biographical reflections

Theodor Fontane's life was shaped by different languages and cultures. His grandfather, Pierre Barthélemy Fontane, was a Huguenot, and came to Prussia with his family as a religious refugee. In his autobiographical text *Meine Kinderjahre*, published in 1893, Fontane depicted his family as a French family still saturated with "*refugié*" traditions (Fontane 2007: 9). Fontane acquired a good knowledge of French at school and in private lessons from his father and used the language frequently in French-loving Berlin. Though the Huguenots constituted a numerically, economically and culturally significant minority in the city, Höschel points out that they were not the only reason for the Frenchification of Berlin:

> Im 17. und 18. Jahrhundert, der Zeit der französischen Hegemonie in Europa, ist französisch die Sprache grenzüberschreitender Verständigung, die auch an den deutschen Fürstenhöfen gesprochen wird, manchmal sogar ausschließlich. Preußen und besonders das hugenottisch geprägte[...], hofnahe Berlin sind seit Ende des 17. Jahrhunderts einem kontinuierlichen Einfluss des Französischen ausgesetzt, der auch kaum von Sprachpuristen und Sprachgesellschaften gegenteilig beeinflusst wird.
> [In the seventeenth and eighteenth centuries, the time of French hegemony in Europe, French was the language of cross-border communication, and the language spoken – sometimes even exclusively – in German royal courts. From the end of the seventeenth century, Prussia, and particularly Huguenot-influenced Berlin, which had close links to the court, were subject to an ongoing French influence, which was barely affected by linguistic purists and language associations] (Höschel: 2008).

Fontane also worked as a correspondent in London for several years, before returning to Berlin in 1859. There he began to write *Wanderungen durch die Mark Brandenburg*, a work that would continue to occupy him till the end of his life. Even today, the *Wanderungen* are regarded as *Heimatdichtung* [regional literature]. According to Feldt, anyone who studies Fontane will not only encounter the French language but also his veneration for Prussia (2002: 195). Fontane's patriotism was particularly evident at the beginning of his creative period. On 19 August 1856 he wrote the following words about his major project, *Wanderungen durch die Mark Brandenburg*: "Einen Plan gemacht, '*Die Marken*, ihre Männer u. ihre Geschichte. Um Vaterlands- u. künftiger Dichtung willen gesammelt u. herausgegeben von Th. Fontane.' [...] Wenn ich noch dazu komme *das* Buch zu schreiben, so hab' ich nicht umsonst gelebt u. kann meine Gebeine ruhig schlafen legen" [Made a plan, "*Die Marken*, their men and their history. Collected and edited by Th. Fontane, for the sake of patriotic and future literature." If I manage to write *the* book, I won't have lived in vain and can lay down my bones in peace] (Fontane 1994: 161). As early as 1850, in a letter to the publisher and bookseller Alexander Duncker, Fontane mentioned that he was writing "vaterländische[...] Gedichte" [poems of the fatherland] (letter of 26 June 1850, Fontane: 1976: 124). Prussian songs such as "Der Alte Dessauer" or "Der Alte Derfling" appeared in the 1849 anthology *Schöne Neue Lieder zu singen überall im Preußenlande zumal in Heer und Landwehr* [Fine New Songs to Sing Everywhere in the Land of Prussia, Especially in the Army], and made Fontane popular for the first time (Wruck 1987: 649–650). "Der Alte Dessauer" was also published in 1851, along with "Keith" and "Seidlitz", in an anthology by Adolf Müller und Hermann Kletke, entitled *Preußens Ehrenspiegel: Eine Sammlung preußisch-vaterländischer Gedichte von den ältesten Zeiten bis zum Jahre 1840* [Prussia's Mirror of Honour: A Collection of Poems of the Prussian Fatherland from the Oldest Times to 1840]. In 1850 Fontane also published a volume of poetry, *Männer und Helden: Acht Preußen-Lieder* [Men and Heroes: Eight Songs of Prussia] (cf. Wruck 1983). But Fontane's (historical) biographical writing of the 1850s was also characterized by the aspiration to national-Prussian representativity. According to Berbig, he acted as a writer of the fatherland with a focus on biography (2010a: 33–34). On 20 September 1858, Fontane told his paternal friend Wilhelm von Merckel of his growing inclination "vaterländisches Leben künstlerisch zu gestalten" [to give artistic form to the life of the fatherland] (Fontane 1858: 245). As he followed this inclination, the author of patriotic poems became a writer of the fatherland, whose public profile was formed from the Prussian-patriotic orientation of his work (Wruck 1987: 651).

Feldt emphasizes the difficulty of speaking about discourses of nationalism in the German-speaking area in the 19th century (2002: 201),[2] a time in which Germany's national identity was being recoded. According to Feldt, this has partly to do with the fact that there was no German nation as an entity at the beginning of the century: "1806 endete das deutsche Kaiserreich, das bis dahin – als 'Heiliges Römisches Reich Deutscher Nation' – eine nationale Entität zu sein nominal beansprucht hatte, diesen Anspruch indes lange schon nicht mehr realpolitisch verwirklichen konnte" [1806 saw the end of the German Empire, which – as the "Holy Roman Empire of the German Nation" – had nominally claimed to be a national entity up till then, but had long since ceased to be able to realize this claim in practical political terms] (Feldt 2002: 201). Poets and thinkers of the time wanted to achieve this aspiration at least in cultural terms by developing a German national culture. Examples are Johann Gottfried Herder with his folk songs or the Brothers Grimm with their idea of a "German national spirit". According to Feldt, however, Germany as a nation, as an entity with a real political and socio-economic infrastructure, did not develop until unification into the second German Empire in 1871 (2002: 201–202). In the post-Napoleonic period, stresses Feldt, chauvinist discourses of nationalism replace a politics of liberation with a politics of power, developed from the patriotic impulses of the wars of liberation (2002: 202). They found expression in the three wars of 1864, 1866 and 1870/71. Fontane travelled to the theatres of these

---

2 The following remarks on discourses of nationalism in the German-speaking area in the 19th century are based on Michael Feldt's observations (2002).

wars and reported on his travels, initially in the *Berliner Fremdenblatt* and the *Johanniter-Wochenblatt*. Eventually he published his books about the three Prussian wars, imposing volumes in encyclopaedic format, thousands of pages long: *Der Schleswig-Holsteinische Krieg im Jahre 1864* (1866), *Der deutsche Krieg von 1866* (two volumes, 1870/71), and *Der Krieg gegen Frankreich* (two volumes, 1873/76). The titles of his texts, argues Feldt, hint at the shift towards nationalism: "Die kriegerische Auseinandersetzung zwischen Dänemark und dem Deutschen Bund wird noch sachlich benannt; es geht um das Grenzgebiet Schleswig-Holstein. Der Waffengang zwischen Österreich und Preußen (!) hingegen wird schon zum 'Deutschen [sic!] Krieg'. Und dann heißt es nur noch: 'gegen Frankreich'!" [The military conflict between Denmark and the German Confederation is named objectively after the border area of Schleswig-Holstein. The armed conflict between Austria and Prussia (!), in contrast, becomes the "German War". And then it is simply "against France"!] (2002: 202).

Is the shift towards nationalism also reflected in Fontane's account of his own experience, *Kriegsgefangen: Erlebtes 1870*, produced when he was attempting to travel to the theatres of the last war? How did his captivity – and the book – come about? Up till then Fontane had followed the tradition of the travel writer and (war) journalist. But in a letter to his wife on 17 August 1882, he looked back on this book as a turning point: "Ich sehe klar ein, daß ich eigentlich erst beim 70er Kriegsbuche und dann bei dem Schreiben meines Romans [*Vor dem Sturm*] ein Schriftsteller geworden bin, d. h. ein Mann, der sein Metier als eine Kunst betreibt, als eine Kunst, deren Anforderungen er kennt" [I realize clearly that it was only with the war book of 1870 and then while writing my novel [*Vor dem Sturm*] that I became a writer, i.e. a man who pursues his *métier* as an art, and is aware of the requirements of this art] (Fontane 1924: 17).

The Franco-Prussian War began on 19 July 1870. Shortly after, Fontane wrote to his publisher Rudolf Ludwig von Decker, accepting his request to write a third, hopefully final war book (letter of 8 August 1780, Fontane 1988: 156). The author and the publishing house were united in their patriotic Prussian attitude. Rudolf Ludwig von Decker owned the *Verlag der Königlichen Geheimen Ober-Hofbuchdruckerei* [Publishing House of the Royal Privy Upper Court Printing Works]. Publications produced here had an official character, which suited Fontane's aim of gaining recognition as a writer of the fatherland. Fontane thus accepted Decker's commission – in keeping with his own self-image as a national writer propagating Prussia's German destiny, historically and poetically. On 28 September Fontane set out for the theatres of war. The plan was that he would send reports on his journey to France to the *Vossische Zeitung*. But this was not to be. Shortly after his departure, Fontane was arrested in France as a suspected Prussian spy. He was moved across the country from fortress to fortress and subjected to numerous interrogations, then acquitted of spying but nonetheless transported to the Atlantic Island of Oléron as a prisoner of war. Here he was finally released at the end of November.[3] Fontane began to write *Kriegsgefangen* during his captivity, and finished it at the end of December, allowing rapid publication of the text. In March 1871 the book was published by Decker in Berlin. Prior to that it was serialized in the *Vossische Zeitung* from 25 December 1870 to 26 February 1871. *Kriegsgefangen* was an autobiographical offshoot of the planned book about the war in France, which was eventually published as a multi-volume work in 1873/76. In this period of nearly two months in captivity, Fontane spoke, wrote and read a great deal of French, and this is reflected in the resulting book, *Kriegsgefangen*.

3 France – Germany: Linguistic contrast as a contrast between nationalities

Kriegsgefangen begins by explaining why the narrator, who comes from Prussia and bears the name *Theodor Fontane*, has been taken prisoner by the French. It is the character's romantic affinity with the national heroine of France, Joan of Arc, that leads to his arrest: contrary to the warning of his attendants (Radecke and Rauh 2020: 23), the character in the book crosses the German lines to travel to Domrémy-la-Pucelle, the birthplace of Joan of Arc. Instead of following the Prussian troops and the front line – the actual goal is Paris –, the narrator wanders about in pursuit of his literary and historical interests, reads a book about Joan of Arc, and considers how to travel the thirty kilometres from Toul to Domrémy, despite war-related difficulties. The narrator is presented as a traveller on an educational journey, searching enthusiastically for traces of the life of a historical figure. He is guided not so much by the war as by a longing to see the birthplace of Joan of Arc, a name that becomes the epitome of the "alte[s] ro-

---

[3] Numerous people from various circles campaigned for Fontane's release. For example, his friend Moritz Lazarus contacted the French minister of justice, Adolphe Crémieux, and averted the life-threatening charge of espionage. The Prussian bishop Franz Adolf Namszanowski was brought into action by Marie von Wagenheim, a friend of Fontane's in Berlin. When Bismarck became involved, he threatened the French government with reprisals in the territories occupied by German troops (cf. D'Aprile 2018, Radecke and Rauh 2020).

mantische[s] Land[ ]" [old romantic land] – a line from Christoph Martin Wieland's poem "Oberon" (1780). The heading of the first part of *Kriegsgefangen* alludes to this. The narrator presented here possesses an unwarlike, culturally rooted affinity with France (Hettche 1988: 16).[4]

The narrator is not a war tourist or a jingoist, but an observer with an interest in French culture and history. He is represented as such and is also arrested as such. In the middle of a war, as a citizen of the belligerent nation, in an unoccupied village beyond the front, the narrator verifies the authenticity of a statue of the Virgin Mary. While visiting the monument, which is described as a well-intentioned but weak work by the sculptor Eugène Paul (not named in the text), he is seized by *franc-tireurs* and arrested on suspicion of (war) "espionage":

> Ich stutzte [...] und fragte [...] mit Unbefangenheit: aus welchem Material die Statue gemacht sei? Man antwortete ziemlich höflich: "aus Bronce", schnitt aber weitere kunsthistorische Fragen [...] ab. [...] Ich war eben noch im besten Perorieren, als ein junger Bauer [...] die Krücke aus der Stockscheide zog und mit einem "ah, un poignard" die mir zuhörende Gesellschaft überraschte [...]. [Z]ur Initiative greifend, [...] sagte ich mit Ruhe: Naturellement, Messieurs, je suis armé. [...] In eben diesem Augenblick [...] drängte sich durch den dichtesten Haufen ein wüst aussehender Geselle [...] und erklärte mit lallender Zunge: "Je suis le Maire." [...]. Solch trunkener Imbecile, an dem Alles, was Vernunft und Wahrheit ist, nothwendig scheitern mußte, war das Schlimmste, was mir in solchem Momente begegnen konnte.
> [I stopped short [...] and asked [...] impartially: what material was the statue made of? I received a fairly polite reply: "of bronze", but any further queries about art history were cut off. [...] I was still in the midst of my peroration when a young peasant [...] drew the handle out of the shaft of my stick and surprised the group listening to me with an "ah, un poignard" [ah, a dagger] [...]. Seizing the initiative [...] I calmly said: Naturellement, Messieurs, je suis armé [Of course, Messieurs, I am armed]. At that very moment, a wild-looking fellow pushed his way through the densest throng [...] and declared with slurring tongue: "Je suis le Maire." [I am the mayor] [...] Such a drunken imbecile, on whom all reason and truth were certain to founder, was the worst thing I could have encountered at such a moment.] (Fontane 1871: 14–16).

The extract is – in keeping with the multilingual situation presented here– in both German and French, with the French passages set apart visually. The author combines manifest multilingualism and latent multilingualism. A striking

---

[4] This sensibility recalls Fontane himself, as letters to his family at the beginning of the journey show. In early October, before his arrest, he wrote: "Die ganze Reise, wenn es so fort geht, ist im höchsten Maße lehrreich, interessant und geradezu erhebend" [The whole journey, if it continues in this way, is highly instructive, interesting, and positively uplifting] (Fontane 1998: 514).

feature is the French word 'Imbecile' (Ger. 'Dummkopf', Fr. 'imbécile') as a form of code-mixing. Code-mixing denotes the mixing of different languages. It can occur on different levels of the language, from syntax to morphology, phonology to semantics (see Radaelli 2011: 165, Dembeck 2017: 125–126, Gunkel 2020: 52–54). The word 'Imbecile' is used instead of the German term and is capitalized like a German noun, but also adapted to German orthographically and phonetically with the omission of the acute accent. The word as an artistic tool is the result of intense observation and imitation of reality with the function of giving authenticity to the represented.

The French phrases and passages in the form of direct speech can be seen as intersentential code-switching. The term code-switching can be defined by its difference from the term code-mixing. It is the change from one language to another, both languages remain unchanged. Code-switching denotes language change that can occur on different levels of a text: for instance, on the intrasentential level (within a sentence) or on the intersentential level (switching of languages between sentences or longer phrases) (see Radaelli 2011: 165–166, Dembeck 2017: 125–126, Gunkel 2020: 54–56). The code-switchings in Fontane's text have a similar function to the code-mixing. Particularly noticeable is that only the utterances of the other characters are marked as direct speech, not those of the narrator. Multilingualism in direct speech as code-switching is probably the most obvious form of literary multilingualism. However, multilingualism in character speech can also take on much more inconspicuous, hidden forms. This is the case, for example, when one can infer from the text that a conversation is being conducted in a language other than the one in which the text is written (Dembeck 2017: 167–168). Some text parts in Kriegsgefangen are designed like this, using latent multilingualism, as not all the utterances reproduced here are in French. The first phrases of the extract are marked as direct speech, but are in German: for example, the narrator's question about the material of the statue is paraphrased in German, and the response given by a franc-tireur is also rendered in German: "aus Bronce". It can be assumed that the conversation does not take place in German, since it is unlikely that the franc-tireurs would have sufficient knowledge of German for this. The substance of the narrator's question seems to be understood, however, and further enquiries are suppressed. On the other hand, the subsequent exchange, concerned with the dagger and the position of the narrator, takes place in French, or is at least marked as quoted in French. The switch to French can be explained by the increasingly difficult situation. With the threat of capture, the first-person narrator becomes aware of the reality of war. The use of French becomes a necessity in the critical situation presented here. This is no longer just about the character's romantic cultural sensibility, or about a historical overview in support of the unification of the empire; this concerns the constitution of the self. Multilingualism as a stylistic tool takes on an existential dimension. The fateful misunderstanding allows the narrator a different perspective: being in the hands of the military opponent allows him to change perspective to the other side, the French side (Röhnert 2011: 44). It is this special German-French viewpoint that distinguishes *Kriegsgefangen* from other books.

Viewed from a biographical perspective one can assume that Theodor Fontane's imprisonment allowed the author a freer perspective than would have been possible in his war books. Röhnert argues that this is reflected in the narrator: "Seine Kriegs(reise)berichte sind schon deshalb autobiographische Literatur, weil sie, einschließlich seiner ästhetischen und persönlichen Vorbehalte als *freier* Autor Fontane, seine *Differenz* gegenüber der offiziellen preußischen Lesart der Kriegsgeschichte am unverstelltesten enthalten" [His war (travel) reports are autobiographical literature, simply because they – including his aesthetic and personal reservations as the *free* author Fontane – contain in the most undisguised form his *difference* from the official Prussian interpretation of military history] (Röhnert 2011: 44). Fontane did not create the text primarily to serve nationalism, but to further his literary aspirations. It is as if Fontane created a portrayal of himself and others to find traces of himself – or of Prussia.

The main point of comparison is the (national) character of the two peoples. This aspiration is immediately apparent at the beginning of the text: it is argued that France cannot win the war against Prussia because it cannot build a nation. One important point is the way the French population treats the relics of its own national history, an approach supposedly characterized by sheer ignorance. On entering Domrémy, the narrator describes it as gloomy and sinister, despite bright sunshine: "Alles schien auf Verfall und Armuth hinzudeuten. In der Mitte des Dorfes hielten wir vor einem rußigen, anscheinend herabgekommenen Gasthause, das in verwaschenen Buchstaben die Inschrift trug: Café de Jeanne d'Arc" [Everything seemed to indicate decay and poverty. In the middle of the village we stopped in front of a grimy, seemingly derelict hotel, which bore, in faded letters, the inscription: Café de Jeanne d'Arc] (Fontane 1871: 10–11).

Historical amnesia is presented emblematically at the very beginning of the book, when the partisans take the traveller (as a prisoner of war) to a place (the Café Jeanne d'Arc) where the lettering of history is erased (Hebekus 2006: 180). The French are attached to "La France" (Fontane 1871: 94) and the story of their country's glory, but not to their history. Such comparisons are made repeatedly as the text goes on. In order to highlight the differences between the two nationalities, the author uses forms of manifest multilingualism – or deliberately omits them.

After a few weeks as a prisoner of war, in contact with the French population and the military, the narrator feels able to assess the French national character and form a judgement. The positive qualities of the French include the following: they are, individually, "liebenswert" [amiable], "zuvorkommend" [obliging], "gutherzig" [kind-hearted], "neidlos" [free of envy], "rücksichtsvoll" [considerate], educated, and patriotic, but not hostile towards Germany:

> Von nationaler Gereiztheit keine Spur, wiewohl sie alle, ohne Ausnahme, voll lebhaften patriotischen Gefühls waren. Auch ihr Bildungsgrad, um das noch zu bemerken, hatte mindestens, bei sonst gleichen Voraussetzungen, das Niveau des unsrigen, wie ich denn überhaupt glaube, daß wir uns nach dieser Seite hin, allzu selbstgefälligen Vorstellungen hingeben. Wir glauben, eine Art Schul-Monopol zu besitzen.
> [No trace of national irascibility, although they were all, without exception, full of lively patriotic feeling. It may also be noted that their degree of education had at least the same level as ours, under otherwise identical conditions, indeed I believe that we indulge in overly complacent ideas in this respect. We believe we have a kind of monopoly on school] (Fontane 1871: 91–93).

Again, we notice the expanded spacing between letters in certain words. This time it is words like "Bildungsgrad" or "Schul-Monopol", which highlight the main point of comparison between the French and the Prussians. In writing so positively about the education level of the French, and comparing it with that of the Prussians, the author is denouncing the national arrogance of his countrymen. The main targets of this representation will have been those German citizens who set great store by the excellence of the Prussian education system (Tippkötter 1995: 274).

While the French may be amiable individually, the other side of the coin is the image of the French collective, which is characterized by restlessness, irreligiousness, and disrespect for both the state and the law.

> Sie waren so liebenswürdig, gutherzig, neidlos [...]; aber so angenehm der Eindruck war, den sie als Individuen hervorriefen, so traurig war der Eindruck, den jeder einzelne als Theil des Ganzen machte. [...] Ein fester, schöner Glaube existirte an nichts [...] Die Geistlichkeit wurde beständig verhöhnt, der Kaiser war ein Spott, die Marschälle ein Gegenstand der Verachtung [...] Regierung, Kirche, Gesetz, alle drei waren nach ihrer Meinung nur da, um das Volk in Banden zu schlagen.
> [They were so amiable, kind-hearted, free of envy [...]; but however pleasant an impression they made as individuals, the impression that each individual made as part of the whole was woeful. [...] There was no firm, fine faith in anything [...] The clergy was constantly mocked, the emperor was treated with derision, the marshals were an object of

contempt [...] Government, church, law, in their opinion all three were only there to subjugate the people] (Fontane 1871: 93–95).

In the course of the text, the critical remarks made here are substantiated with specific examples and comparisons. It is striking that these passages, in comparison to the description of the positive qualities, are multilingual. For example, the efforts of one of the French commanders to give the narrator good, pleasant accommodation during his captivity are rendered as direct speech in German when in that context the dialogue would have been in French: "Wir traten [...] ein. 'Ich muß nun schon ein Uebriges für Sie thun', sagte der Kommandant, 'wie könnten Sie Ihre Tage besser verbringen, als angesichts des ewigen Meeres!'" [We stepped inside [...]. "I must do you an extra favour", said the commander, "What better way to spend your days than facing the eternal sea!"] (Fontane 1871: 189). In comparison to this latent or hidden multilingualism, another passage illustrating one of the criticisms of the French collective is latent and manifest multilingual. Here the narrator is problematizing the sense of freedom which many French people take pride in, and which (he argues) is prioritized over the good of the state. Describing a French soldier who is a fellow prisoner, the narrator explains:

> Er war wegen Hochfahrenheit zahllose Male bestraft und saß jetzt hier, weil er auf den Zuruf seines Capitains "vous êtes un lâche" geantwortet hatte "pas plus que vous". [...] Auf meine Bemerkung, daß solche Eingaben [...] in Preußen ganz unmöglich seien, antwortete er nur mit superiorem Lächeln: "Je sais, je sais: vous avez encore le régime du bâton; nous sommes plus libres en France."
> [He had been punished countless times for insolence and was now sitting here because, when his captain had cried "vous êtes un lâche" [you are a coward], he had replied "pas plus que vous" [no more than you]. [...] In answer to my remark that such comments [...] were quite impossible in Prussia, he responded with a superior smile: "Je sais, je sais: vous avez encore le régime du bâton; nous sommes plus libres en France" [I know, I know: you are still ruled by the stick; we are freer in France]] (Fontane 1871: 77–78).

It is striking that the soldier's words are given in direct speech in French, and are visually highlighted. The narrator's words are rendered indirectly and in German, although the conversation is in French. This is accompanied by various functions – and effects. One would be to recreate a realistic setting for the situation. Another literary aim would be to use French to evoke different associations, convey different sentiments, and suggest specific sociological and societal connotations. The German and French perspectives are juxtaposed, giving the predominantly German text a different perspective, a German-French angle. In contrast to the previous passages, which are in part latently multilingual because they are rendered in German, manifest multilingualism is needed here to underline the differences and the respective attitudes. Multilingualism is visible when it serves this function. The character expresses himself as a "typical Prussian". "Wie man weiß, hat Hegel, den man in diesem Zusammenhang wohl als preußischen Staatsphilosophen ansehen darf, behauptet, der Einzelne sei nichts, der Staat sei alles" [As we know, Hegel, who can probably be regarded in this context as the Prussian state philosopher, asserted that the individual is nothing, the state is everything] (Sagave 1980: 223).

In France, as described in the book, self-interest is paramount; nowhere is the individual voluntarily guided by the public good, which is embodied in the state and is based on the "nationale Überlieferung" [national tradition], which in turn arises from history (Sagave 1980: 223–224). The French sense of freedom is criticized in a multilingual opposition between "us" (the Germans) and "them" (the French), deploying direct speech and French vocabulary. French and German fulfill a comparative function: The use of the two different languages creates a connection between both sides to highlight the contrast.

Throughout the text multilingual juxtapositions of this kind paint a literary portrait of Prussia, but also of France. The world conveyed here is reflected in the German-French divide. Here we see that: for Fontane, multilingualism as a stylistic tool is a means to an end, that of presenting the problem of nationalities and the political tableau (Erdmann 2001: 43). This serves to depict the differences between a French "revolution" (which the narrator sees as the reason for France's "tiefsten Verfall" [deepest decline] (Fontane 1871: 95)), and a "'preußische[s]' Ordnungswesen" ["Prussian" order system] (Erdmann 2001: 43).

It can be assumed that Fontane's literary description of the French is influenced by the historical experience of the French Revolution. This reflects Fontane's narrator. He is an observer who is well-disposed towards the French people, but also emphasizes how reassuring it is to belong to a nation that respects the prevailing social order (Sagave 1980: 240, esp. chapter "Ein Berliner Kriegskorrespondent in Frankreich: Fontane 1870–71"). It is fear of the French spirit of revolution that resonates here: "glücklich das Land, das diesen Heimsuchungen noch nicht erlegen ist" [happy the land that has not yet succumbed to these afflictions] (Fontane 1871: 95). The narrator goes on to say that while the French are patriotic, they do not think much of law, government – or the church. This last becomes apparent in a passage comparing Prussian with French Protestantism. It describes the visit of "Monsieur le prédicateur Masson, reformierter Geistlicher zu Saint-Pierre auf der Insel Oléron" [Monsieur le prédicateur [preacher] Masson, reformed clergyman at Saint-Pierre on the island of

Oléron] (Fontane 1871: 305), who calls on the narrator on the last Sunday before his release:

> [Monsieur Masson] begann mit gesteigerter Feierlichkeit: "Monsieur, il n'est pas vraisemblable, que nous nous reverrons ici, que nous nous reverrons dans ce monde. Mais nous avons une patrie, grande et éternelle, où n'existe pas de guerre, où la haine, l'animosité ont cessé, où les peuples demeurent en paix par notre Sauveur Jésus Christ, par lui, qui est la lumière, l'amour, et la grâce. Voilà où nous nous reverrons." [...] Bis zu den Worten: "voilà, où nous nous reverrons" war ich ihm ernsthaft und aufmerksam gefolgt, als mir aber plötzlich klar wurde: er predigt, er citirt [...] Niemals hab' ich das Mißliche der pastoralen Redeweise so empfunden wie hier. [...] [W]as unser modernes Empfinden gewiß [...] überwunden hat, das sind solche öden Redensarten. [...] Wir sind wenigstens auf dem Wege dazu; was ich aber in Frankreich vom Protestantismus gesehen habe, machte einen unendlich tristen Eindruck auf mich.
> [[Monsieur Masson] began with heightened solemnity: "Sir, it is not likely that we will see each other again here, that we will see each other again in this world. But we have a fatherland, great and eternal, where there is no war, where hatred and animosity have ceased, where the nations remain in peace thanks to our Saviour Jesus Christ, who is light, love, and grace. That is where we will see each other again." [...] Up until the words "voilà, où nous nous reverrons" [that is where we will see each other again] I had followed him earnestly and attentively, but when I suddenly realized: he is preaching, he is quoting [...] Never have I felt the disagreeable nature of pastoral discourse as I did here. [...] One thing our modern sensibility has certainly overcome is tedious phrases such as these. [...] We are at least on the way there; but what I saw of Protestantism in France made an infinitely dismal impression on me] (Fontane 1871: 308–310).

This is one of the longest passages of French in the text. It owes its length to the fact that Fontane is putting empty French phrases into the character's mouth, thus giving an exaggerated literary presentation of the clergyman and his preaching tone. The narrator uses French Protestantism to take a more distant view of Prussia, to find standards by which he can measure his home country. To do this, once again an opposition between "us" and "them" is constructed. This effect is conditioned and intensified by the linguistic contrast and the use of direct speech marked as quotations to create distance. Multilingualism serves as a literary strategy for national writing. Intention, content and languages chosen are in harmony.

Reflecting on the points described above, one can assume that they are closely connected to Fontane's conservatism;[5] but they can also be linked to his

---

5 An extract from a text of Fontane's written to Ernst Ludwig Kossak in 1864 gives a concise impression of his conservatism: "Daß uns der Conservatismus, den ich im Sinne habe, noth thut, ist meine feste Überzeugung. Speziell unserer guten Stadt Berlin ist die Vorstellung abhanden gekommen, daß Beschränkung, Disciplin [...] auch Tugenden sind [...]" [It is my firm

propensity for the national: "Ich halte es für selbstverständlich, daß jeder, der unter bestimmten Einflüssen seines Landes groß geworden ist, dies Land und seine Nation mehr liebt als andere Nationen" [I consider it self-evident that anyone who has grown up under certain influences of his country will love this country and his nation more than other nations] (Fontane 1892b: 178–179). Erdmann emphasizes, however, that Fontane's preference for the national does not lead to nationalism (2001: 45). This is why the use of multilingualism in the service of the national is not a problem for Fontane: multilingualism appears somewhat hidden under the guise of nationality; it comes in national "packaging".

This effect and function of multilingualism, highlighted by the combination of manifest and latent, not visible multilingualism, becomes very obvious in comparison to the French translation of *Kriegsgefangen*. The translation was carried out by Téodor de Wyzewa, and was published at Perrin et Cie in Paris in 1892. Examining the translation allows to expand the angle of view to include the reception of the text. How was this German-French book received by the reviewers that would probably not expect to find multilingualism in the work of this "Prussian" writer? Fontane deliberately chose not to translate the French passages, though well aware that many readers would not be able to understand them. And he did so at a time when German (war) literature was expected to serve as a monolingual medium of German nation-building, a time when the use of national stereotypes was increasing, and France was being proclaimed as the "Erbfeind", the natural opponent of the Germans. Fontane did not espouse these views. Instead, as Feldt observes, he responded to the "chauvinistische[r] Nationalismus der Kriegsjahre" [chauvinistic nationalism of the war years] with the methods of "narrative[r] und ethische[r] Multiperspektivismus" [narrative and ethical multiperspectivity] (2002: 202). One element of multiperspectivity is strategically placed French elements. Fontane did not write a monolingual, monoperspectival history of the victors, but considered both sides (Feldt 2002: 203). And this made him atypical of his time.

---

conviction that we need the conservatism I have in mind. Our good city of Berlin in particular has lost the notion that restriction, discipline [...] are also virtues [...]] (Fontane 1973: 574).

4 Reception and resonance of *Kriegsgefangen*

Fontane's war books met with a supraregional response in Germany (Radecke and Rauh 2020: 141). According to Necker, however, *Kriegsgefangen* remained more or less unknown to the majority of the population (1892: 176, see also Kittelmann 2015: 109). Though the book enjoyed only a short-term success, it attracted media attention such as Fontane had never known before (Radecke and Rauh 2020: 142 and 146). Fontane also attests to this in his diary on 5 December 1870:

> Meine Gefangenschaft hat mich zu einer Sehenswürdigkeit [...] gemacht; die "Gartenlaube" ist sogar drei Tage lang entschlossen mich, mit Text und Holzschnitt, unter die berühmten Zeitgenossen aufzunehmen, besinnt sich aber schließlich eines Beßren, da sie erfährt, daß alle meine Glieder heil geblieben sind
> [My captivity has made me an object of interest; for three days the "Gartenlaube" was even resolved to include me among the famous contemporaries, with text and woodcut, but then changed its mind when it learned that all my limbs were still intact] (Berbig and Kitzbichler 2010: 1691).

Even before this, the newspapers gave frequent reports on the case of Fontane. It became known that he was working on a book about his war experiences, and other publishers also expressed an interest: For the first time, he did not have to make an effort to find publishing opportunities but could even choose between several offers (Radecke and Rauh 2020: 142). The interested publishers included Wilhelm Hertz and his publishing house, Gartenlaube; this was where the *Wanderungen durch die Mark Brandenburg* had been published since 1862. But Fontane declined the offers and stayed with Rudolf von Decker – this was where the other war books had been published, and Decker was, after all, the catalyst for the journey and the accounts. As with *Wanderungen durch die Mark Brandenburg* and *Jenseits des Tweed* (1860), Fontane intended to pursue a two-pronged publishing strategy: a serial in the (daily) newspaper and a book.

What were the reasons for the book's (short-term) success? One reason may have been interest in and curiosity about Fontane's experiences, as his diary entry suggests. His reputation as a writer of the fatherland is likely to have contributed to this interest (cf. Wruck 1987). Another reason may have been the distinctive perspective: The book presents the neighbouring nation France in a mainly favourable light, defying a nation's expectations. There was also the aspect of writing in a way that was multilingual and compared cultures but was nonetheless national. It can be seen as a replica of the discourses of nationalism, patriotism and monolingualism of the time. All these things gave the book a special status in Germany in 1870/71. The response to it can be divided into two camps (cf. Radecke and Rauh 2020: 146–148). Some reviewers praised it as "das liebenswürdigste aller Kriegsbücher" [the most amiable of all war books] (*Neue Freie Presse*, 18 December 1871). They emphasized the "vorurteilsfreie Darstellung der Franzosen" [unprejudiced portrayal of the French] (Radecke and Rauh 2020: 146) and the "Erzähltalent" [narrative talent] (*Über Land und Meer*, 26 May 1871). But there were also critical voices, complaining that the war report lacked "Feindeshass" [hatred of the enemy] and a Prussian-German sense of superiority towards the French – Fontane was even accused of unpatriotic mildness.[6] The fact that the text showed similarities between the French and the Germans, and even praised the French, was incomprehensible to some readers – just as incomprehensible as the passages in French. The differences between this text and other descriptions of war of the time are very obvious. The absence of a populist, nationalist colouring is evident even from the headings: In Fontane's book the chapters have titles such as "Ins alte romantische Land" [Into the Old Romantic Land] or "Frei" [Free]. In contrast, Berthold Auerbach's text *Wieder unser, Gedenkblätter zur Geschichte dieser Tage* (1871) has headings such as "Kriegskunde" [Military Science] or "Was will der Franzos? Was will der Deutsche?" [What Does the Frenchman Want? What Does the German Want?] (cf. Kipper 2000). In its assessment of France and its multilingual form, the work differs from other contemporary texts which were influential at the time: One other example is Heinrich von Treitschke's well-known article "Was fordern wir von Frankreich?" [What Do We Demand from France?], von Treitschke defined France as the "hereditary enemy" and as an obstacle to national unification (Treitschke 1874: 258–327).

With this in mind, it is understandable that Fontane's war book, with its multiperspectivity and its multilingualism, did not sit well with the nationalist discourses of its time (cf. Feldt 2002). The book does bear detectable traces of the prejudices of Fontane's time, which must be viewed with a critical eye, but these do not change the overall tendency: the effort to be fair towards France.[7]

---

6 See Theodor Fontane's text Aus den Tagen der Occupation: Eine Osterreise durch Nordfrankreich und Elsaß-Lothringen (1871) (Fontane 2007: 872).
7 Fontane endeavoured to be fair towards France, but in his depiction of the French he was well able to distinguish between the individual, amiable Frenchman and the French collective. Tippkötter stresses that Fontane experienced this period of war as a Prussian, who had wanted German unity and still wished to see it achieved, but who did not participate in the systematic demonization of the French, and did not wish to share the national exaltation of many of his fellow countrymen (cf. Tippkötter 1995: 265).

Kriegsgefangen is a text that is multilingual, but nonetheless national; a text that is national, but not hostile towards France.

Taking a biographical approach, Wruck describes Fontane's status as a writer of the fatherland as a role that Fontane made his own, to develop it in original ways for his own purposes, and finally step out of it (Wruck 1987: 663, see also Berbig 2019). He did this with *Kriegsgefangen*. It was here that Fontane, in his own words, became a writer (Fontane 1924: 17). *Kriegsgefangen* is an important and extensive source of experiences, but primarily a literary one, in which Fontane presents not only the events, but also himself. In his report, Fontane arranges the events experienced into a story, which owes its form not only to the writer's memory, but also to his interpretations, views, communicative intentions, and linguistic and artistic ideas. The use of multilingualism comes from a biographical space of resonance: it springs from artistic motives and stylistic and aesthetic considerations but is also linked to the events experienced.

Because the book, in contrast to many other contemporary works on the Franco-Prussian War, was conciliatory rather than embittering in its effect, it was translated into French (cf. Radecke and Rauh 2020: 147). The translation bears the title *Souvenirs d'un prisonnier de guerre allemand en 1870* [Memories of a German Prisoner of War in 1870]. It was a French translator of Polish origin, Téodor de Wyzewa (1863–1917), who made this text available to a French audience. Two chapters were published in advance in the *Revue bleue: Revue politique et littéraire*: these were parts of the chapters "La Citadelle de Besançon" (issue of 12 December 1891: 757–761) and "L'île d'Oléron" (issue of 6 February 1892 170–176). The first of these preprints was accompanied by a text about Theodor Fontane (Fontane 1891: 751–757), which then served as an introduction in the book edition of 1892. In the introduction, Wyzewa explains to the French readership that the book is written with an "étonnante impartialité", an astonishing impartiality (Fontane 1892c: III). This word, Tippkötter argues, characterizes Fontane as a writer who does not take sides (1995: 264). She describes this as surprising, given the topic of war and the general national excitement associated with it, but also in light of the precarious situation of the German author (Tippkötter 1995: 264). Wyzewa goes on to describe the book as "bien écrit" [well written], and praises Fontane's writerly abilities: "[l]e jeunes poètes allemands le tiennent pour un de leurs maîtres" [the young German poets consider him one of their masters] (Fontane 1892c: III). Overall, Wyzewa gives a positive evaluation of Fontane, acknowledging his literary and human strengths. However, the two probably never met. Wyzewa was familiar with Berlin and went there in 1890, but there is no report of any direct contact with Fontane.

Theodor Fontane made no specific comment on Wyzewa's translation – there is no mention of it in either his daily notes or his letters. It can be assumed, however, that a translation into French would have been in his interest. Around 1895, he wrote to his acquaintance Anna St. Cère: "In Frankreich bekannt zu werden, ein Publikum, wenn auch nur ein ganz kleines zu finden, – wer sehnte sich nicht danach?" [To become known in France, to find an audience, even just a very small one, – who would not long for that?] (Fontane 1982: 516). Grimberg and Möller note that Fontane was already perceived as an important contemporary writer in other countries as well during his lifetime, and was also seen as an important contemporary German writer in France, at least among experts (2005: 443, 448). The book was therefore received positively and was regarded as historically important. Despite ongoing tension between Germany and France, even in 1892, French readers were interested to discover how it felt to be a Prussian who had set out for France as a war reporter and ended up as a French prisoner of war – especially as the book showed no signs of "preußisch-deutsche Überheblichkeit" [Prussian-German arrogance], or of "Verachtung den Franzosen gegenüber" [contempt for the French] (Schaefer 2022).

The positive response also had to do with the translation itself. One significant factor was that Téodor de Wyzewa's translation rendered the text monolingual.[8] Wyzewa was actively hiding the manifest multilingualism through the translation. However, the latent multilingualism stayed hidden within the text, still referring to the multilingual situation because the narrator is German. The reader must make more of an effort at "internal translation" when the use of another language is implied but not made explicit. Translations can lead to the loss of characteristics of the source text, but also to new insights.[9] In the case of Wyzewa's translation, both these things happen. Fontane's war report uses the contrast between languages to give a different perspective, a special German-French angle, and to develop a literary, comparative portrait of both Prussia and France. In the French translation this aspect is given less weight,[10] and is

---

8 It would be rewarding to carry out a systematic study of the differences between Fontane's text and Wyzewa's translation – going beyond the topic of the national. As yet no such study exists. In the following discussion only individual aspects can be picked out, and there is no scope to go into greater detail.
9 For further reflections on the topic of multilingualism and translation see Gunkel 2020: chapter IV, 1.2.
10 Also of interest are the differences between the French preprints and the complete edition. In the preprint of "La Citadelle de Besançon" some parts are omitted. For example, in a passage where the narrator describes three people, two Germans and one German-French person, the

replaced by linguistic assimilation. One of the aims of the translation was to give insights about how it felt for a Prussian to be a French prisoner of war. Wyzewa was not interested in highlighting Fontane's German-French viewpoint, which showed a multiperspectivity that went against the nationalist discourses of the time.

The comparison also offers new insights into the source text, revealing the (stylistic) functions of the contrast between the languages. This contrast does not merely reinforce the comparison between nationalities. While the explicit use of French in the German-French text lends character and authenticity, it loses this power in the translation. The translation also dispenses with the visual highlighting of the French language.

> J'eus un mouvement de surprise [...] [et] demandai avec calme en quoi était la statue. "En bronze", me répondit-on assez poliment. J'allais poser d'autres questions de même nature, mais j'en fus tout de suite empêché [...] J'étais dans tout le feu de mes explications, lorsqu'un jeune paysan [...] s'aperçut tout à coup en pressant sur un bouton que c'était une canne à épée, et s'écria: "Ah, un poignard!" Tous les assistants se retournèrent, surpris. [...] Mais je repris tout de suite mon sang-froid, et [...] je répondis tranquillement: "Naturellement, Messieurs, je suis armé." [...] Juste au même moment [...] un individu d'aspect fruste [...] fendit les groups et [...] me dit d'une voix pâteuse en se frappant [...] : "Je suis le maire." [...] Avoir affaire à un sot complètement ivre, près de qui les meilleures raisons et la verité la plus simple ne pouvaient être d'aucun poids, c'était, dans un tel moment, ce qui eût pu m'arriver de plus funeste.
> [I started [...] [and] asked calmly what the statue was made of. "Bronze" was the fairly polite response given. I was going to ask further questions of the same nature, but was immediately prevented from doing so [...] I was in the middle of my explanations when a young peasant [...] suddenly realized, on pushing a button, that it was a sword stick, and cried: "Ah, a dagger!" All those present turned around, surprised. [...] But I immediately recovered my composure, and [...] I replied calmly: "Of course, Messieurs, I am armed." [...] Just at that moment [...] a rough-looking individual [...] forced his way through the groups and [...] told me in a slurred voice while striking his chest [...]: "I am the mayor." [...] To be faced with a completely drunk fool, for whom the best reasons and the truth could have no weight at all, this was, at such a moment, the most disastrous thing that could have happened to me] (Fontane 1892c: 9–12).

The word "Imbecile" is translated into French as "sot" [fool, idiot]. In addition, the direct speech – it is noticeable that the narrator's utterance is now enclosed in quotation marks – is completely translated. These are two examples for the process of actively hiding multilingualism through translation. The bilingual-

---

descriptions of the two Germans are omitted. The French perspective is highlighted – perhaps to increase the French interest in the text.

ism in the source text, which serves partly to express the threat to the narrator's own existence, losses its immediacy. The existential dimension of multilingualism is weakened. The reader must consciously reconstruct what is obvious from reading the original, and what is striking in the original becomes normal and easily overlooked.

The weakening of multiperspectivity by linguistic assimilation is also apparent in the following example, in which the French spirit of freedom is evoked:

> Il avait souvent encouru des punitions pour ses façons trop hautaines vis-à-vis de ses chefs, et il était maintenant en prison parce que, à une apostrophe de son capitaine, qui lui avait dit "Vous êtes un lâche", il avait répondu : "Pas plus que vous." [...] Comme je lui faisais remarquer que de tels mémoires rédigés dans cet esprit seraient considérés en Prusse comme tout à fait inadmissibles, il me répondit avec un sourire de supériorité: "Je sais, je sais: vous avez encore le régime du bâton; nous sommes plus libres en France."
> [He had often undergone punishments for his arrogance towards his seniors, and he was now in prison because, when his captain had said to him "You are a coward", he had replied "No more than you." [...] Since I informed him that such reminiscences, told in this spirit, would be considered utterly inadmissible in Prussia, he replied with a smile of superiority: "I know, I know: you are still ruled by the stick; we are freer in France."] (Fontane 1892: 62–63).

Téodor de Wyzewa's translation reproduces the self-congratulatory element of Prussian culture. Yet it appears in a different light in this monolingual context. It is given a lower weighting. The pluralistic potential of the original is revealed in the contrast with the translation. A comparison between the two versions clearly shows how strategically German-French multilingualism and latent multilingualism were used in Fontane's text. The *how* of the representation is just as important as the *what* – which only takes shape in the *how*.

The final example is the passage about the preacher, "Monsieur le prédicateur Masson". Here too, the monolingualism weakens the functionalization of the linguistic contrast as a contrast between nationalities.

> Monsieur, il n'est pas vraisemblable que nous nous revoyions ici, ni même que nous nous revoyions jamais en ce monde. Mais nous avons une patrie éternelle, où il n'y a plus de guerre, où cesse toute haine et toute animosité, où les peuples demeurent en paix par les mérites de notre Sauveur Jésus-Christ, qui est la lumière, l'amour et la grâce. Voilà où nous nous reverrons.
> [Monsieur, it is not likely that we will see each other again here, nor even that we will ever see each other again in this world. But we have an eternal fatherland, where there is no more war, where all hatred and animosity cease, where the nations remain in peace by the merits of our Saviour Jesus Christ, who is light, love and grace. That is where we will see each other again.] (Fontane 1892c: 247).

The comparison between the translation and the source text heightens the awareness of the poetic qualities of the two versions. It has not been possible to discuss these qualities in detail here. Yet it has been possible to show that the strategic deployment of manifest and latent multilingualism in Fontane's text constitute important elements of the national.

Although the translation was positively received in France, the response was minimal. This was true of the majority of the French translations of Fontane's texts, according to Erdmann. One reason she suggests is the lack of linguistic contrast: "Fontanes Prosa setzt vor allem den Kontrast von Sprachen und Codes, Kulturen und Subkulturen in Szene [...], wobei das Französische eine exponierte Rolle spielt" [The contrast between languages and codes, cultures and subcultures play a key role in Fontane's prose [...], with French taking an especially prominent part] (Erdmann 2001: 33). Thuret makes a similar statement with regard to the editions of Fontane's work published in France: "Die Lektüre Fontanes auf Französisch bereitet dem, der das Original kennt, eine kleine Enttäuschung" [Reading Fontane in French is almost always a small disappointment to anyone familiar with the original]; it almost always lacks the naturalness of the conversational tone, with the different linguistic registers, which are often no longer recognizable in French (Thuret 2000: 119). The same applies to the French translation of *Kriegsgefangen*: here too the (multi)lingual form of the text changes, thus changing the text itself – an effect that may have been intended by Téodor de Wyzewa to give the comparative portrayal of Prussia and France (which is often in favor of Prussia) a different weighting. To end with Fontane's own words, it is a "petite misère" (Fontane 1871: 70). However, one thing has become clear: The analysis of Fontane's text and its comparison to Wyzewa's translation made it particularly evident how relevant multilingualism is for the literary canon of 19th-century European literature, for a critical view of the canon, and for the differentiated relationship between nation, language and multilingualism.

5 References

Auerbach, Berthold. 1871. *Wieder unser, Gedenkblätter zur Geschichte dieser Tage*. Stuttgart: Cotta.

Berbig, Roland. 2010. York, Havelock, Scherenberg und Schulze. Beobachtungen zum Biographen Fontane. In Roland Berbig (ed.), *Fontane als Biograph*, 19–39. Berlin & New York: De Gruyter.

Berbig, Roland & Josefine Kitzbichler. 2010. *Theodor Fontane Chronik*. Volume 3. Berlin: De Gruyter.

Berbig, Roland. 2019. Fontane und … Fontane. Ein Schriftsteller pur et simple. Theodor Fontanes literarische Selbsterfindung 1870/71. *Fontane Blätter* 108. 66–85.

Blum-Barth, Natalia. 2020. '[W]enn man schreibt, muss man […] die anderen Sprachen aussperren' Exkludierte Mehrsprachigkeit in Olga Grjasnowas Roman *Gott ist nicht schüchtern*. In Barbara Siller & Sandra Vlasta (eds.), *Literarische (Mehr)Sprachreflexionen*, 49–67. Vienna: Praesens.

Brinkmann, Richard & Waltraud Wiethholter. 1973. *Theodor Fontane*. Volume 12/1. Dichter über Dichtungen. München: Heimeran.

D'Aprile. Iwan-Michelangelo. 2018. *Fontane. Ein Jahrhundert in Bewegung*. Reinbek: Rowohlt Verlag.

Dembeck, Till. 2017. Sprachwechsel/Sprachmischung. In Till Dembeck & Rolf Parr (eds.): Literatur und Mehrsprachigkeit. Ein Handbuch. 125–166. Tübingen: Narr.

Engel, Eduard. 1911. *Deutsche Stilkunst*. Wien/Leipzig: Tempsky.

Erdmann, Eva. 2001. Der Sprachvergleich im literarischen Text. Am Beispiel Theodor Fontanes. In: Jörn Albrecht & Hans-Martin Gauger (ed.), *Sprachvergleich und Übersetzungsvergleich. Leistungen und Grenzen. Unterschiede und Gemeinsamkeiten*, 30–50. Frankfurt a. Main: Lang.

Feld, Michael 2002. Theodor Fontanes Repliken auf die Nationalismus-, Patriotismus- und Heimat-Diskurse seiner Zeit. Neue Beiträge zur Germanistik. Internationale Ausgabe von „Doitsu Bungaku'. Zeitschrift der japanischen Gesellschaft für Germanistik 110(1). 195–208. https://www.jstage.jst.go.jp/article/nbg/110/0/110_KJ00001023480/_pdf (14.06.2023).

Freytag, Gustav. 1887. *Erinnerungen aus meinem Leben*. Leipzig: Hirzel.

Fontane, Theodor. 1850. *Männer und Helden. Acht Preußen-Lieder*. Berlin: Hayn.

Theodor, Fontane. 1866. *Der Schleswig-Holsteinische Krieg im Jahre 1864*. Berlin: Verlag der Königlichen Geheimen Ober-Hofbuchdruckerei (Rudolf von Decker).

Fontane, Theodor. 1870/1871. *Der deutsche Krieg von 1866*. 2 volumes. Berlin: Verlag der Königlichen Geheimen Ober-Hofbuchdruckerei (Rudolf von Decker).

Fontane, Theodor. 1871. *Kriegsgefangen. Erlebtes 1870*. Berlin: Verlag der Königlichen Geheimen Ober-Hofbuchdruckerei (Rudolf von Decker).

Fontane, Theodor. 1873/1876. *Der Krieg gegen Frankreich*. 2 volumes. Berlin: Verlag der Königlichen Geheimen Ober-Hofbuchdruckerei (Rudolf von Decker).

Theodor, Fontane. 1891. Souvenirs d'un prisonnier de guerre allemand (1870). La Citadelle de Besançon. Traduit de l'allemand de Théodor Fontane. *Revue bleue. Revue politique et littéraire* 28(48), Nr. 24. 757–761 a. 751–757.

Theodor, Fontane. 1892a. Souvenirs d'un prisonnier de guerre allemand (1870): L'île d'Oléron. *Revue bleue. Revue politique et littéraire*, 29(49), Nr. 6. 170–176.

Fontane, Theodor. 1892b. *Wanderungen durch die Mark Brandenburg. Erster Theil. Die Grafschaft Ruppin. Am Ruppiner See*. Berlin: Verlag von Wilhelm Hertz.

Fontane, Theodor. 1892c. *Souvenirs d'un prisonnier de guerre allemand en 1870*. Paris: Perrin.

Fontane, Theodor. 1924. *Briefe an seine Familie*. Volume 2. Karl Fritsch (ed.). Berlin: Fischer.

Fontane, Theodor. 1976. *Werke, Schriften und Briefe*. Walter Keitel & Helmuth Nürnberger (eds.). Abteilung 4. Briefe. Volume 1. 1833–1860. München: Hanser.

Fontane, Theodor. 1968. *Briefe in zwei Bänden*. Gotthard Erler (ed.). Volume 1. Berlin: Aufbau-Verlag.

Fontane, Theodor. 1975. *Werke, Schriften und Briefe*. Walter Keitel & Helmuth Nürnberger. Abteilung 3. Erinnerungen, ausgewählte Schriften und Kritiken. Volume 3. Reiseberichte und Tagebücher. Darmstadt: Wissenschaftliche Buchgesellschaft.

Fontane, Theodor. 1988. *Briefe an den Verleger Rudolf von Decker*. Walter Hettche (ed.). Heidelberg: Rudolf von Decker.

Fontane, Theodor. 1982. *Werke, Schriften und Briefe*. Walter Keitel & Helmuth Nürnberger (eds.). Abteilung IV. Briefe. Volume 4. 1890–1898. München: Hanser.

Fontane, Theodor. 1994. *Tagebücher 1852/1855–1858*. Charlotte Jolles & Rudolf Muhs (eds.). Berlin: Aufbau-Verlag.

Fontane, Theodor. 1998. *Emilie und Theodor Fontane. Der Ehebriefwechsel*. Gotthart Erler (ed.). Berlin: Aufbau-Verlag.

Fontane, Theodor. 2007. *Werke, Schriften und Briefe*. Walter Keitel & Helmuth Nürnberger (eds.). Part 3. Erinnerungen, ausgewählte Schriften und Kritiken. Volume 4. Autobiographisches. 2. Edition. München: Hanser Verlag.

Gervinus, Georg Gottfried. 1835–1842. *Geschichte der poetischen National-Literatur der Deutschen*. 5 volumes. Leipzig: Lang.

Grimberg, Michel & Klaus-Peter Möller. 2005. „Un trop vaste champ à discussion'. Die erste französische Übersetzung von Fontanes „Effi Briest'. *Aus dem Antiquariat* 6. 443–451.

Gunkel, Katrin. 2020. Poesie und Poetik translingualer Vielfalt. Zum Englischen in der deutschen Gegenwartsdichtung. Wien: Praesens Dissertation.

Hebekus. Uwe. 2006. Friktionen der Kriegsmoderne. Theodor Fontanes autobiographische Texte zum deutsch-französischen Krieg von 1870/71. In Stephan Jaeger & Christer Petersen (eds.), *Zeichen des Krieges in Literatur, Film und den Medien*, 167–191. Volume 2. Ideologisierung und Entideologisierung. Kiel: Ludwig.

Höschel, Clarissa. 2008. *Gallizismen in Fontanes Roman „Irrungen, Wirrungen' (1888)*. https://www.xlibris.de/Aufsatz/Autor/Fontane/Gallizismen%20in%20Fontanes%20Roman%20Irrungen%2C%20Wirrungen%20%281888%29 (accessed 8 November 2022).

Kipper, Rainer. 2000. Formen literarischer Erinnerung an den Deutsch-Französischen Krieg von 1870/71. In Helmut Berding, Klaus Heller & Winfried Speitkamp (eds.), *Krieg und Erinnerung. Fallstudien zum 19. und 20. Jahrhundert*, 17–37. Göttingen: Vandenhoeck & Ruprecht.

Kittelmann, Jana. 2015. Theodor Fontane Kriegsgefangen. Erlebtes 1870 (1871). In Hermann Gätje & Sikander Singh (eds.), *Übergänge, Brüche, Annäherungen. Beiträge zur Geschichte der Literatur im Saarland, in Lothringen, im Elsass, in Luxemburg und Belgien*. 103–115. Saarbrücken: universaar.

Müller, Adolf & Hermann Kletke. 1851. Preußens Ehrenspiegel. Eine Sammlung preußisch-vaterländischer Gedichte von den ältesten Zeiten bis zum Jahre 1840. Berlin: Gebauer.

Necker, Moritz. 1892. Neues und Altes von Theodor Fontane. *Die Grenzboten. Zeitschrift für Politik, Literatur und Kunst* 51(1). 175–181.

Radaelli, Giulia. 2011. *Literarische Mehrsprachigkeit: Sprachwechsel bei Elias Canetti und Ingeborg Bachmann*. Berlin: Akademie-Verlag.

Radecke, Gabriele & Robert Rauh. 2020. *Fontanes Kriegsgefangenschaft. Wie der Dichter in Frankreich dem Tod entging*. Berlin: be.bra verlag.

Röhnert, Jan. 2011. Jeanne d'Arc in Domrémy – Fontane auf Oléron. Selbstbehauptung in Fontanes Kriegsgefangen. *Fontane Blätter* 91. 39–61.

Sagave, Pierre-Paul. 1980. *Berlin und Frankreich 1685–1871*. Berlin: Haude und Spener.

Schaefer, Peter. 2022. "Mein besonderes Buch. Souvenirs d'un prisonnier de guerre allemand en 1870" https://www.fontanearchiv.de/bestaende/objekt-des-monats/mein-besonderes-buch (accessed 8 November 2022).
Schöne Neue Lieder zu singen überall im Preußenlande zumal in Heer und Landwehr. 1849. Berlin: Alexander Duncker, königlicher Hofbuchhändler.
Sieburg, Heinz. 2017. Sprachwechsel/Sprachmischung. In Till Dembeck & Rolf Parr (eds.): *Literatur und Mehrsprachigkeit. Ein Handbuch*. 69–76. Tübingen: Narr.
Thuret, Marc. 2000. Fontane in Frankreich. Geistesverwandtschaft und Rezeption. *Fontane Blätter* 70. 108–121.
Tippkötter, Ilse. 1995. Theodor Fontane: Kriegsgefangen. Über die Wahrnehmung des Fremden. *Diskussion Deutsch* 144. 264–276.
Von Treitschke, Heinrich. 1874. *Zehn Jahre Deutscher Kämpfe*. Berlin: Reimer.
Weissmann, Dirk. 2013. Die Erneuerung der deutschen Literatur von ihren sprachlichen Rändern her: Translinguales Schreiben um 1900. *Germanistik in der Schweiz. Zeitschrift der Schweizerischen Akademischen Gesellschaft für Germanistik* 10. 319–328.
Wruck, Peter. 1983. Der Zopf des altes Dessauers. Bemerkungen zum Fontane der Preußenlieder. *Fontane Blätter* 5. 347–360.
Wruck, Peter 1987. Theodor Fontane in der Rolle des vaterländischen Schriftstellers. Bemerkungen zum schriftstellerischen Sozialverhalten. *Fontane Blätter* 44. 644–667.
Zürrer, Peter, Harald Burger. 2015. Plurilinguale Phraseologie bei Theodor Fontane und ihr zeitgeschichtlicher Hintergrund. In Hartmut Lenk & Ulrike Richter-Vapataalo (eds.). *Sie leben nicht vom Verb allein. Beiträge zur historischen Textanalyse, Valenz- und Phraseologieforschung*, 91–117. Berlin: Frank & Timme.
1889. Erklärung der 41. In Heinrich von Treitschke & Hans Delbrück (eds.). *Preußische Jahrbücher*. Volume 63. 312–313.

Orlando Grossegesse
The Hidden Greek Odes in "Um poeta lírico" (1880)
Eça de Queiroz's Self-reflexive Fiction about Migration and Writing

Abstract: Concentrating on the correlation between Eça de Queiroz as a privileged migrant in consular services and his crisis in literary creativity, the present study aims to define the poetological meaning of the hidden multilingualism in the short story "Um poeta lírico" (1880). This interpretation presupposes an approach focused on creative reading and translating as communicating vessels, exemplified by the novel *A Relíquia* (1887), and on the writer's awareness of Portugal's subalternity towards French and English culture. "Um poeta lírico" is about a Greek immigrant in London who in public is confined to the English speech of a waiter, hiding his sublime identity as a poet. This is a parodic mirror of Eça de Queiroz's own dilemma. Living abroad as a consul, he cannot unfold his identity as a Portuguese writer. Significantly, both are enthusiastic readers of Tennyson's Arthurian poems in antiquated English that inspires a rewriting in their own national languages.

Keywords: Multilingualism, Portuguese Literature, Late 19th Century, Alfred Tennyson

1 Introduction

In Portuguese literary history José Maria Eça de Queiroz[1] (1845–1900) appears as the major Realist novelist, akin to Gustave Flaubert and Theodor Fontane in other national literatures. The comparison to these two authors is elucidatory, as both surpassed a literary practice circumscribed by the Realist paradigm.

---

[1] The historic writing of the family name "Eça de Queiroz" is maintained throughout this article, contrary to its modernization in "Eça de Queirós". Bibliographic references are homogenized accordingly. I express my gratitude to Svera Dantas for her critical reading and stylistic revision.

Orlando Grossegesse, Universidade do Minho, e-mail: ogro@elach.uminho.pt

∂ Open Access. © 2023 the author(s), published by De Gruyter. [CC BY] This work is licensed under the Creative Commons Attribution 4.0 International License.
https://doi.org/10.1515/9783110778656-008

This is also the case with Eça de Queiroz.² Rather than limiting the scope to his most praised novels published between 1875 and 1888, it is worth analyzing his minor novels and narratives. In dialogue with essays and letters, they reveal a self-reflexivity that challenges traditional views on the evolution of his *écriture* from its beginnings in 1865 until his premature death at the age of 55. This alternative approach (Grossegesse 1995) transcends the high-valued image of Eça de Queiroz as a novelist in the frame of European Realism and partly Naturalism by concentrating on the correlation between the author's crisis in literary creativity and his life as a privileged migrant in consular services in Newcastle (1874–79) and Bristol, until becoming consul-general in Paris in 1888.

2 Eça de Queiroz as a writer and a translator: communicating vessels

In the more traditional perspective, his absence from Portugal excuses his failure to realize a planned and often announced series of novels called *Cenas da Vida Portuguesa*. This ambitious project inspired by Balzac and Zola was meant to offer a fictionalized panorama of different aspects of Portuguese society. Eça de Queiroz expressed this view of failure in a letter to his friend Ramalho Ortigão (April 8, 1878), in which he bitterly jokes about his inaptitude to execute this project, as it would have been equally impossible for both French writers if living abroad: "Balzac [...] could not have written the *Human Comedy* in Manchester, and Zola could not have produced a line from *Rougon* in Cardiff: I cannot paint Portugal in Newcastle."³ In the same letter, he also complains about a lack of conversation, essential to cultural and literary life and to a writing practice which – in the case of Eça de Queiroz as a typical dandy-writer (Grossegesse 1991: 15–16) – not only is grounded on the observation of social reality but also stems from witty conversation in Lisbon upper class society. He dramatizes his situation in Newcastle as a kind of "exile", being deprived of "all the conditions for intellectual excitement", exclaiming: "It has now been one year since I last

---

2 Without going into detail on the simultaneous reception of French Realism and Naturalism in Portugal.
3 "Balzac [...] não poderia escrever a *Comédia Humana* em Manchester, e Zola não lograria fazer uma linha dos *Rougon* em Cardife: eu não posso pintar Portugal em Newcastle" (Queiroz 2000, IV: 123). All quotations translated into English are mine.

conversed!"[4] Another letter he wrote seven years later in Bristol (May 24, 1885) confirms the experience of alienation, as if watching "life from outside"[5]: "tudo [...] me é desagradável desde a sua estreita maneira de pensar até ao seu indecente modo de cozer os legumes" [Everything about this society is disagreeable to me – from its limited way of thinking to its indecent manner of cooking vegetables] (Queiroz 2000, IV: 291).

During this exact period (1878–85), while Eça de Queiroz was struggling to continue *Cenas da Vida Portuguesa*, with some of its volumes almost finished others roughly sketched out, he produced smaller novels and narratives which have traditionally received less attention since they deviate from the Realist / Naturalist paradigm. They have been understood (1) as a kind of minor filler to satisfy his editor's demands and to stay present in the Portuguese cultural scene or (2) as an increasingly divergent practice that anticipates the so-called *late* or *ultimate* Eça de Queiroz situated in the eclectic *Fin de Siècle*.

Contrary to these views, which are more or less conditioned by the literary canon, this study will go further in the alternative approach by analyzing the short story "Um poeta lírico", published in 1880, as self-reflexive fiction about migration and writing. Linked to an earlier attempt to rewrite Alfred Tennyson's Arthurian poems in Portuguese prose, it has a similar genesis to other shorter narratives created by Eça in the wake of foreign reading experiences, mostly English and French literature. Published in the same year as "Um poeta lirico", the novella *O Mandarim* enacts the thought experiment of killing a Chinese Mandarin which became popular, mainly through Balzac's *Le père Goriot* (1835). As this case has already been analyzed in depth,[6] the genesis and the discursive organization of one of his later novels, *A Relíquia* (1887), deserves a closer look in order to comprehend "Um poeta lírico" within a practice of creative reading and translating as communicative vessels.

In an essay sent from Bristol to the Brazilian *Gazeta de Notícias* (August 24, 1881), Eça de Queiroz ironically comments on Benjamin Disraeli's dubious qualities as a writer and reports mainly on his novel *Tancred; or the New Crusade* (1847). A few years later, the same novel acts as catalyst for inventing a kind of

---

4 "[...] neste degredo faltam-me todas as condições da excitação intelectual. *Há um ano que não converso!*" (author's emphasis; Queiroz 2000, IV: 123).
5 From a letter sent to his friend Bernardo, Conde de Arnoso: "Se vier a *Hyde-Park* ou aos Campos Elíseos, vê só a *Vida por fora*, no seus contornos exteriores" [If you come to Hyde-Park or the Champs Elysees, you only see *Life from the outside*, in its outer contours] (author's emphasis; Queiroz 2000, IV: 291)
6 See Coimbra Martins (1967) who also mentions Auguste Vitu's story *Le mandarin* (1848) and the play *As-tu tué le mandarin?* (1855) by Albert Monnier and Edouard Martin.

mock crusade to Palestine: while young Lord Montacute, who merges dandyism with Jewishness, returns from Jerusalem "to Regent Street as a Messiah and regenerator of societies"[7], the novel *A Relíquia* presents the sly bachelor Teodorico Raposo indulging in debauchery and eager to inherit the fortune of his bigoted aunt by offering her a relic recovered from the Holy Land. His travel companion, the German archaeologist Topsius, shows him how to counterfeit a relic by manipulating scientific and religious "truths". This parodies not only *La Vie de Jésus* (1863) by Ernest Renan but also the problem of dilettantism in European civilization. Without going into further detail, Teodorico – imaging himself being treated as a colleague by Renan (Queiroz 2021: 311) – defends a "shameless heroism of affirmation", which "through universal illusion creates Sciences and Religions".[8] In *Essais de Psychologie Contemporaine* (1883), Paul Bourget identifies Renan's scepticism as one of the causes for the "vacillation de la volonté" (Bourget 1883: 199).[9]

As narrator, Teodorico announces his own story as a "lucid and strong lesson [...] in this century, so consumed by the uncertainties of intelligence"[10] and a necessary rebuttal of what Professor Topsius says about him in the travel report he published in Leipzig with the "fine and profound title *Jerusalém Passeada e Comentada*".[11] All direct quotations from this book appear in Portuguese (Queiroz 2021: 77) and the reader of *A Relíquia* is never informed about Teodorico's multilingual proficiency, nor does s/he get to know in which language(s) the companions speak on their journey to the Holy Land.

---

7 "[...] e tendo partido de London como simples *Lord*, possa regressar a Regent-Street, como Messias e regenerador de sociedades!" (Queiroz 2000, III: 1126). In 1905, this text is included in a volume titled *Cartas de Inglaterra*, reedited until present times.
8 "descarado heroísmo de afirmar que, [...], cria, através da universal ilusão, Ciências e Religiões" (Queiroz 2021: 312).
9 "This is the first negative reference to Renan's dilettantism, which Bourget contrasts with the energy, rigor and serious engagement of the past" (Hibbitt 2006: 91). In a second volume, *Nouveaux essais de psychologie contemporaine* (1885), dilettantism is presented as an effect of the uncertainties of modern existence, leading to pessimism and melancholy, to the so-called *maladie de la volonté*. This is defined by Richard Hibbitt as "Bourget's Revised Conception of Dilettantism" (Hibbitt 2006: 94–99).
10 "uma lição lúcida e forte [...] neste século, tão consumido pelas incertezas da Inteligência" (Queiroz 2021: 75).
11 "[...], com este título fino e profundo – *Jerusalém Passeada e Comentada*" (Queiroz 2021: 77).

Through these brief indications it becomes evident that both the making and the fiction of *A Relíquia* involve switching between languages.[12] Distinguishing the receptive multilingualism from the fictional, the latter is hidden, No reference is made to the translational effort, as if rectifying a (fictive) German travel report through a Portuguese counterstatement were a simple monolingual procedure. As such, not even the original title is mentioned.[13] Nonetheless, Teodorico begs Topsius to publish an amended second edition of his work "to disclose [the truth] to scientific Germany and sentimental Germany as frankly as I have revealed it to my citizens on these pages [...]."[14] A similar tension between hidden and explicit multilingualism can be observed in in the short story "Um poeta lírico", assuming a specific functionality, as we will see. This goes in the direction of Alexander Coleman's groundbreaking study: "Eça used his readings in English literature after 1880 to embark on a new way of thinking about the nature of literature. *The Mandarin* and *The Relic* are a literary *volte face*, [...]" (Coleman 1980: 149),

Coleman's study has not inspired an integrative approach to literary creativity and translation which is, on the whole, disregarded in the historiography of 19th century Portuguese literature. Its "monolingual habitus", to apply Gogolin's term (Gogolin 2021: 300), constructs the irrelevance of multilingualism for national literature. The defence against cultural and linguistic subalternity does not go beyond the discussion that rouse in the late 19th century.

As a student at Coimbra University Eça de Queiroz was familiar with reading contemporary French literature – from Victor Hugo and Gustave Flaubert up to Charles Baudelaire – in the original language. To a lesser extent, this also applies to English literature. Translation became an everyday practice for him at the age of 21 as editor-in-chief of the province newspaper *Districto de Évora* (1866). This refers not only to the incoming press agency news from Paris and London but also to some chapters of Hippolyte Taine's popular *Voyage en Italie* (1864), published in *feuilleton*. At the same time, he sent a translation of Joseph Bouchardy's play *Philidor* to the Lisbon National Theatre D. Maria II, although it

---

12 Teodorico's dream in Palestine of witnessing Jesus Christ is based on *Les Mémoires de Judas* (1867) by Ferdinando Petrucelli della Gattina.
13 The comparison with *Sartor Resartus* (1833–34) by Thomas Carlyle can be elucidatory in contrast: the editor, "a young enthusiastic Englishman," explicitly refers to his partial translation of the work *Die Kleider, ihr Werden und Wirken*, written by Prof. Diogenes Teufelsdrökh and published by the editing house "Stillschweigen & Co." na cidade de "Weißnichtwo". Carlyle's book was a creative reading experience for Eça de Queiroz (see Grossegesse 2000).
14 "[...] divulgue [...] à Alemanha científica e à Alemanha sentimental (...) tão francamente como eu o revelo aos meus cidadãos nestas páginas" (Queiroz 2021: 78).

was never performed on stage (see Bishop-Sanchez 2014). Once again, Alexander Coleman is one of the first and the few to highlight the relevance of "these brilliantly executed translations", not being difficult "to imagine the young translator and future novelist's response to Taine's adept sketches, [...]" (Coleman 1980: 25).

In 1889, after already being recognized as a successful novelist, Eça de Queiroz wrote a slightly reduced and reshaped Portuguese version of Henry Rider Haggard's *King Solomon's Mines* (1885), which first appeared in *Revista de Portugal* and afterwards in book form.[15] Until recently, it remained unclear whether he in fact made the translation since the author himself declared that he revised a previous one. This version was never found, nor was a potential translator among his contacts (França 2000: 9). Probably, Eça de Queiroz himself did not want to appear as a translator. Nonetheless, his continuous translating practice manifests itself in his fiction, essays, and letters.

A cosmopolitan writing style in literary and non-literary texts was quite common among the European aristocracy and urban bourgeoisie throughout the 19th century. In the case of Eça de Queiroz, this is not limited to lexical borrowings mainly from French and English. Purists censured his decadent "afrancesado" Portuguese in morphemes and syntax, which turned out to be the author's signature style. Frequently, Eça de Queiroz ridiculed contemporary Portuguese culture for being imported from France and – badly – translated, applying this to his own practice and work, for instance in a letter (May 10, 1884)[16] to his friend Oliveira Martins, a renowned historian, politician, and social scientist:

> A nossa arte e a nossa literatura vêm-nos feita de França, pelo paquete, e custa-nos caríssimo com os direitos de alfândega. Eu mesmo não mereço ser excetuado da legião melancólica e servil dos imitadores. Os meus romances no fundo são franceses, como eu sou em quase tudo um francês – exceto num certo fundo sincero de tristeza lírica, [...]
> [Our art and our literature come to us from France, by ship and with high customs duties. I myself do not deserve to be excluded from the melancholic and servile legion of imitators. My novels are basically French, as I am in almost everything a Frenchman – except for a certain sincere background of lyrical sadness, [...]] (Queiroz 2000, IV: 235–236).

---

[15] It appeared first in the journal from October 1889 to June 1890; book titled *As Minas de Salomão*, first edition: Livraria Chardron, Casa Editora Lugan & Genelioux, Successores, 1891.
[16] This letter was written in Angers, where the author lived every year for some months in the company of an unknown woman from 1879 to 1884.

Portugal's cultural subalternity reappears as a topic in chapter IV of the novel *Os Maias* (1888) with a similar wording[17] and also in an essay intitled *O Francesismo* [The Frenchism], probably written in 1887 but only posthumously published. It opens retrospectively with

> Há já longos anos que eu lancei esta fórmula: – Portugal é um país traduzido do francês em vernáculo. [...] E de novo a lancei assim aperfeiçoado: Portugal é um país traduzido do francês em calão
> [It has been a long time since I launched this formula: – *Portugal is a country translated from French into vernacular* [...] And again I launched it thus perfected: *Portugal is a country translated from French into slang*] (author's emphasis; Queiroz 2000, III: 2107).

Hence, this subalternity is also determined at the linguistic level within the European context. This consciousness has to be linked to the author's crisis in literary creativity and his migrant, albeit privileged, status in consular services. In the same letter to Oliveira Martins (May 10, 1884), he confesses to suffering from a "crisis of stupidity and intellectual fog" and mutters about limiting his diminished creativity to "children's books and legends of saints".[18] Six years before, he had already considered abandoning Realist writing and indulging instead in "purely fantastic and humorous literature".[19] This thought appears precisely in the letter mentioned at the beginning (April 8, 1878), in which the author complains about a lack of conversation, dramatizing his situation in Newcastle as a kind of "exile" (Queiroz 2000, IV: 123).

---

17 João da Ega's speech within a conversation scene: "Aqui importa-se tudo. Leis, ideias, filosofias, teorias, assuntos, estéticas, ciências, estilo, indústrias, modas, maneiras, pilhérias, tudo nos vem em caixotes pelo paquete. A civilização custa-nos caríssima com os direitos de Alfândega: e é em segunda mão, não foi feita para nós, fica-nos curta nas mangas..." [Everything is imported here. Laws, ideas, philosophies, theories, subjects, aesthetics, science, style, industries, fashions, manners, jokes, everything comes in boxes by the liner. Civilization is extremely expensive for us with customs duties: and it's second-hand, not made for us, it's short on our sleeves...] (Queiroz 2017: 155).
18 Quotations from Queiroz (2000b, IV: 235; 236): "crise de estupidez e névoa intelectual"; "[...] e tenho a ideia de me limitar a escrever contos para crianças e vidas dos grandes Santos."
19 "[...]; ou tenho de me entregar à literatura puramente fantástica e humorística." (Queiroz 2000, IV: 123)

3 Exposed and hidden languages in "Um poeta lírico"

3.1 The waiter / poet Korriscosso

Everything mentioned hitherto helps to contextualize my analysis of the short story "Um poeta lírico" (1880) as self-reflexive fiction about Eça de Queiroz's condition as a migrant, alienated from Portugal, and more precisely about someone who cannot unfold his identity as a notorious writer as he would in his homeland. The reader is invited to project this dilemma on the nameless first-person narrator and character, an experienced traveler. After arriving at his hotel at Charing Cross in London, he becomes curious about one of the restaurant waiters, clearly identified as a Mediterranean immigrant, noting in him "such a clear expression of despondency" and being impressed by his physiognomy of "a long, sad face, very dark, with a Jewish nose and [...] a beard of Christ in romantic print".[20] When the traveler is attended by this skinny, slightly hunched man with long hair, he is reading Tennyson's *Idylls of the King*. It is an opulent edition, displaying rich elements of the Arthurian epic on the cover. It seems that the waiter is interested in the book (197). Later on, informed by a friend, Bracolletti, who identifies this person as an immigrant from Athens named Korriscosso, the narrator is promptly misguided by prejudice, concluding that the waiter's interest must be in the material value (199–200). In the end he discovers that the Greek servant, who steals the book, is not only an enthusiastic reader of Tennyson but also a famous poet in his homeland, exiled for some obscure political reason (202).

Curiously, the analogy between the first-person narrator and the subject of the biographical fiction has been neglected by academic studies. The opposition between poetry and prose is commonly considered the main theme of "Um poeta lírico" – a somehow tautological title. According to this interpretation (see Lepecki 1994; Machado 2002), the prosaic reality of serving meals and drinks causes a silent suffering to the sublime identity and an ongoing psychosomatic decay. Ultimately, this apparently irreversible situation is reinforced by his unrequited love to a blond waitress who does everything to entice a corpulent policeman, described as "a mountain of flesh erected from a forest of beards" in

---

[20] "uma expressão tão evidente de desalento"; "um carão longo e triste, muito moreno, de nariz judaico e [...] uma barba de Cristo em estampa romântica; [...]" (196). All references with this simplified indication refer to "Um poeta lírico" (Queiroz 2009).

contrast to the "body of a sad phthisic".²¹ Significantly, this clear embodiment of the poetry / prose dichotomy becomes relativized by a linguistic argument since the waitress is far from being insensible to "ardent emotions, expressed in melodious language"²²:

> Mas Korriscosso só pode escrever as suas elegias na sua língua materna... E Fanny não compreende grego... E Korriscosso é só um grande homem – em grego...
> [But Korriscosso can only write his elegies in his mother tongue... And Fanny does not understand Greek... And Korriscosso is only a great man – in Greek...] (205).

By drawing this conclusion, the narrator enhances the core theme of literary creativity under migrant conditions²³ which refer to both the traveler and the waiter, albeit determined by different social levels. This becomes clear in the linguistic dimension present in their first encounters: while the Greek waiter announces the breakfast service "num inglês silabado" (196) [in an English pronounced syllable by syllable]²⁴, the (Portuguese) traveler, a regular customer of this hotel at Charing Cross, has the leisure to read English poetry while being attended. Only by stealing the book and retreating to his humble abode the poor servant succeeds in obtaining the same privilege.

One night, when the hotel client gets lost in the corridors, he comes to discover by chance not only the theft but also his error. Spying the Greek at a table strewn with papers writing stanzas of an ode, he senses his intelligence and poetic taste. Korriscosso seems more embarrassed by the revelation of his identity and "de ter no corpo a casaca coçada de criado de restaurante" (201) [having on his body the shabby jacket of a waiter], than by the charge of theft. He remains silent for this is not the moment to communicate in the servile English discourse he is used to at work:

> Mas as páginas do volume que eu abri responderam por ele; a brancura das margens largas desaparecia sob uma rede de comentários a lápis: *Sublime! Grandioso! Divino!* – pa-

---

21 "uma montanha de carne eriçada de uma floresta de barbas" (204); "o corpo de tísico triste" (205).
22 "sentimentos ardentes, expressos em linguagem melodiosa..." (205)
23 There is no doubt about Eça de Queiroz's sensibility concerning migrant working conditions as proven in 1872–74, during his first consular service in Havana: Upon his arrival he found Chinese workers from the Portuguese colony of Macao in a state of severe exploitation. He not only took it upon himself to better their condition, but also wrote a major indictment criticizing the Cuban plantation system (see Coleman 1980: 156).
24 Notably the speech itself appears in Portuguese: " – Já está servido o almoço das sete..." [The seven o'clock breakfast is already served...] (196).

lavras lançadas numa letra convulsiva, um tremor de mão, agitada por uma sensibilidade vibrante...
[But the pages of the volume I opened answered for him; the whiteness of the wide margins disappeared under a network of penciled comments: *Sublime! Grand! Divine!* – words launched in a convulsive handwriting, a tremor of hand, agitated by a vibrant sensibility...] (201)

These comments are reproduced in Portuguese. The same domestication refers to the titles of Greek journals in which Korriscosso published, *Ecos da Ática* and *A Trombeta da Argólida*, as well as to his volume *Suspiros de Trácia* (202). This is the only title of his work mentioned in the condensed biography which the narrator presents based on the conversation he had with the poet, presumably in French as the quoted expression "*là-bas*" (202), pejoratively referring to Greece, insinuates.[25] Nothing is said about the narrator's proficiency to read or to speak Greek. As in the novel *A Relíquia*, the text itself remains almost entirely monolingual, hiding the multilingualism which contributes to the meaning in this specific case of "Um poeta lírico". Only a few expressions and lexical terms appear in English, French, and Italian – but not a single Greek word except the strange proper name Korriscosso and some toponymics. The poet recites the odes, obviously written in his mother tongue, to the (Portuguese) traveler who, without understanding Greek, is enthusiastic about the "ferocidade de linguagem" [ferocity of language] and the "gritos de alma dilacerada" [screams of a torn soul] (204). Does not the same apply to him as to the blond waitress? Despite being sensible to the expressions in melodious language, it is impossible for him to present Korriscosso as a great man, since this would only be possible in Greek.

The hidden multilingualism between Korriscosso and the traveler / narrator precisely indicates an intrinsic companionship. Both are migrants and writers coming from Southern European countries with languages in subaltern positions with respect to English and French. The poet's Christ-like suffering, already present in the first physiognomic portrayal and later asserted in the narrator's comments on his poetry, mirrors the dilemma of literary creativity in a cultural and linguistic "exile" that refers to Eça de Queiroz himself. Reduced to the pragmatic use of gastronomic language, Korriscosso suffers grotesquely from the lack of conversation about which the Portuguese writer complains in his letters from Newcastle and Bristol, where his existence is reduced to diplomatic service. Confined to a repertoire of English sentences in subaltern speech acts, the Greek cannot demonstrate in public his poetic eloquence, which once

---

25 Repeatedly, Korriscosso is observed as a reader of *Journal des Debats* (199; 200).

launched his ephemeral political career in Athens (202). The intended reader easily recognizes contemporary Portugal in the caricature of Greece's governmental instability.[26] Hence, the present occupation as a waiter makes the parody work, establishing an ambivalent dialogical relation to the narrator's position which oscillates between sympathy and superiority.

The nameless traveler is touched by the exiled Greek poet caught in the act of writing odes. Significantly, the narrator seems to forget to tell this important fact, only revealing it after his own confession: "Eu também sou poeta!" [I'm also a poet!]: "Porque não lhes disse?, o que Korriscosso estava escrevendo, numa tira de papel, eram estrofes: era uma ode" [Why didn't I tell you? what Korriscosso was writing, on a strip of paper, were stanzas: it was an ode] (201).

His literary creativity is stirred by commenting enthusiastically on *Idylls of the King*. This mirrors Eça's own attempt, presumably in the years 1876–78, to transcreate Tennyson's poems, composing "Sir Galahad" without ever finishing it (Queiroz 2003). M. H. Piwnik (2003: 53–54) identifies the 1869 republication as the most likely basis containing the parts *The Holy Grail* and *The Passing of Arthur*, without excluding the French version of *Les Idylles de Roi* published in the same year. Unlike Korriscosso's odes, the text is in prose. It is important to consider that Tennyson himself rewrites the ancient Arthurian epic in antiquated English lyrics, expressing thus a kind of exile on the discursive level that is also present as a theme: the situation of the Knights of the Round Table after the disappearance of King Arthur in Avalon. Exactly this is the narrator's stance, chosen by Eça de Queiroz for his text, giving voice to Sir Galahad, who searched for the Holy Grail, and then to Sir Belvedere, now living as a monk, who witnessed King Arthur's end. It seems to be more than a coincidence that Sir Galahad's discourse begins with a Romantic landscape of the soul similar to the one on the first page of "Um poeta lírico":

> Às vezes na noite deserta, por um céu de muita geada, atravesso uma cidade: [...]: os telhados agudos estão carregados de neve: [...] e o meu pensamento vai para os jardins de Camelot, e para o Solar de Artur
> [Sometimes in the deserted night with a sky of heavy frost, I wander through a city: [...]: the pointed roofs are heavily covered with snow: [...] and my thoughts roam to the gardens of Camelot and to King Arthur's Court] (Queiroz 2003: 119).

Curiously, the city mentioned here remains unidentified and does not reappear. In "Um poeta lírico", the unceasing snowfall in London on a Sunday morning in

---

26 The comparison between the two nations as similar cases of decadence in the European panorama is frequent in public Portuguese discourse in the second half of the 19th century.

December becomes linked to the waiter's displacement intuitively perceived by the traveler before learning of his exiled condition: "[...], e toda a sua magreza friorenta se encolhia ao aspecto daqueles telhados cobertos de neve, na sensação daquele silêncio lívido..." [and all his shivering thinness shrunk at the site of those snow-covered roofs, sensing the livid silence...] (196). The similar wording in the two texts suggests not only an analogy between Sir Galahad and Korriscosso but also the idea of the nameless traveler / narrator as the author's figuration. His feeling of displacement in London, akin to Korriscosso's, is already signaled – before the first utterance of speech – by the fact that he stares into the same chimney fire (195), while outside the snow is falling. Throughout the text, the shared condition of Southern Europeans living in the North does not cancel out the distance, established not only by the different social category but also by prejudice towards Greek emigrants to the Levant as "vile plebs, part pirate and part lackey, a cunning and perverse gang of prey".[27] The narrator recognizes the eventual injustice, referring to this pejorative image as having originated in philhellenic disillusion (199).

Nonetheless, his prejudice continues even after the revelation of the waiter's hidden identity and despite the pity felt for "poor Korriscosso" (201). The traveler stretches out both hands, confessing "I am also a poet", as he remembers that "nothing impresses the Levanter more than a gesture of drama and stage".[28] The explicitly histrionic gesture and a sentence that "could seem grotesque and of impudence to a man from the North" are interpreted by the "Levanter" as an "expansion of a twin soul".[29] Hence, the companionship of letters is an illusion intentionally created by the traveller who maintains his superiority.

3.2 The Levanter Bracoletti

This has to be linked to Bracolletti, who reveals the identity of Korriscosso as an immigrant from Athens – but not as a poet. Reluctantly yielding to the narrator's curiosity, he drops some details of their acquaintance already characterized by Korriscosso's migrant condition, working as his secretary in Bulgaria and Montenegro (199). This subalternity does not match with the "solemn, ten-

---

[27] "uma plebe torpe, parte pirata e parte lacaia, bando de rapina astuto e perverso." (200)
[28] "Lembrei-me que nada impressiona o homem do Levante como um gesto de drama e de palco; estendi-lhe ambas as mãos [...], e disse-lhe: — Eu também sou poeta!..." (201)
[29] "Esta frase extraordinária pareceria grotesca e impudente a um homem do Norte; o levantino viu logo nela a expansão de uma alma irmã." (201)

der and sincere shake-hands" observed by the narrator as proof of friendship between both.[30] It also seems incongruent that Bracolletti stirs up prejudice against Korriscosso since the category of Levanter could be applied even more to his own identity, only apparently Italian but in fact born of Greek parents in Smyrna. Probably, Eça de Queiroz was familiar with the two volumes of Francis Hervé's *A residence in Greece and Turkey, with notes of the journey through Bulgaria, Servia, Hungary and the Balkan* (1837). For my analysis of "Um poeta lírico", the attribution of a reduced multilingual proficiency to the Levanter is significant:

> A regular Levanter is supposed to speak several languages badly, and none well. The Greek spoken at Smyrna is execrable. [...]. His answers are generally evasive: he fears to give you a direct one, lest he might in any shape compromise his interests. (Hervé 1837, 1: 326).

This definition, curiously mentioning Smyrna, matches perfectly with Bracolletti, who repeats the exclamation "Eh! mon Dieu!", when asked about Korriscosso. Far from being annoyed, the narrator praises the evasiveness of his friend, comparing this behavior with "the Gods of Attica who retire to their cloud when in trouble on earth".[31] Bracolletti's lack of eloquence does not matter, since he is gifted with "a sweet look, which reminds me of that of a Syrian animal: "[...] in its soft fluid seems to wander the tender religiosity of the races from which stem the Messiahs".[32] The narrator's admiration is superlative describing his smile as "the most complex, the most perfect, the richest of the human expressions".[33]

The praise of non-linguistic expression and of a speech reduced to the exclamation "Eh! mon Dieu!" is in clear contrast to the silent suffering of the eloquent Greek poet, who as a waiter is confined to the English gastronomic discourse, significantly reproduced in Portuguese.[34] Hence, the antagonistic constellation is more meaningful than the traditional interpretation of the fat

---

[30] "foi um *shake-hands* solene, enternecido e sincero" (199). Here the English expression may already hint at hypocrisy.
[31] "[...], como os deuses da Ática que, nos seus embaraços no mundo, se recolhiam à sua nuvem, Bracolletti refugiou-se na sua vaga reticência. — Eh! mon Dieu... Eh! mon Dieu!..." (199)
[32] "Um olhar doce, que me faz lembrar o dos animais da Síria: [...] Parece errar no seu fluido macio a religiosidade meiga das raças que dão os Messias..." (198)
[33] "O sorriso de Bracolletti é a mais complexa, a mais perfeita, a mais rica das expressões humanas; [...]." (198)
[34] An English quotation only refers to the restaurant clients who always add "if you please" when asking the waiter for mustard or cheese (203).

Bracolletti and the thin Korriscosso as an embodiment of the before-mentioned prose / poetry dichotomy. This becomes even more prominent when the narrator's great admiration for the divinely smiling friend seems unaffected by his "debility" of methodically collecting girls between twelve and fourteen years in the slums of London and keeping them "at home like canary birds in a cage".[35] Once again, the discursive aspect is of interest: Bracolletti wants them not only "skinny" and "very blond", but with "the habit of cursing".[36] Aroused by being insulted with the (unquoted) English slang obscenities, he expresses his enthusiasm in the Italian with which he grew up on the Syrian coast: " – Piccolina! Gentilleta!" (199).

This behavior is clearly set in parodistic analogy to Korriscosso's literary creativity motivated by an enthusiasm for Tennyson's verses about the Knights of the Round Table. Bracolletti's reduced multilingualism contrasts with the poet's hidden multilingualism which indicates, according to my interpretation, an intrinsic proximity to the hotel client who also confesses to being a poet but doing so with feigned sincerity. The ambivalence between sympathy and superiority towards the Greek emigrant is maintained until the last sentence of the short story: "Sempre que ele me serve dou-lhe um xelim de gorjeta: e depois, ao sair, aperto-lhe sinceramente a mão" [every time he serves me, I give him a shilling as a tip: and then, on leaving, I sincerely shake his hand] (205).

4 Conclusion: the poetological function of hidden multilingualism

How can the same narrator, understood as the author's figuration, be full of sincere admiration for an immoral person without any capacity of coherent speech in any language? A comparative view on the sly bachelor Teodorico, the protagonist and narrator in *A Relíquia*, may give a concluding idea about the immoral but successful Levanter Bracolletti, who, in contrast with the poor poet Korriscosso, embodies a different attitude towards dilettantism: shameless affirmation instead of vacillation. The first suggests the abandonment of any rhetorical effort – being his smile superlatively valued – while the latter refers to the dilemma of literary creativity and eloquence under migrant conditions. Korriscosso does not invalidate the philhellenic disillusion with the disappear-

---

35 "Instala-as em casa, e ali as tem, como passarinhos na gaiola, [...]" (198).
36 "[...]: gosta delas magrinhas, muito louras, e com o hábito de praguejar" (198).

ance of the "glories of an aesthetical and free race".³⁷ Instead of composing odes inspired by ancient Greek culture, he only takes up writing after enthusiastically reading the *Idylls of the King*.

Hence, the fictional character and the Portuguese writer, both inspired by Tennyson's adaptation of Arthurian epic in antiquated English, and both displaced in the winter of London, accept their own cultural patrimony in a subaltern position. It is reduced – as Eça de Queiroz puts it in "O Francesismo" – to "a certain sincere background of lyrical sadness".³⁸ In conclusion, the commented reading and creative translating of French and English literature can be considered the discursive hiding and eventually vanishing of a Greek / Portuguese writer who disappears as such in London (or Paris) and fears to be forgotten in Athens / Lisbon. If so, Korriscosso has to be seen as Eça's double, with his strange name phonetically similar to Queiroz.³⁹ Contrasting with Bracoletti's divine smile and shamelessly exhibited lack of speech, the hidden Greek odes are the metonymy of a literary dilettantism, demonstrating an incapacity of asserting one's own voice.

5 References

Bishop-Sanchez, Kathryn. 2014. Texto reescrito, texto esquecido: *Philidor*, uma pérola queirosiana [Rewritten text, forgotten text: *Philidor*, a Queirosian pearl]. *Studia Iberystyczne* 13. 29–40.
Bourget, Paul. 1883. *Essais de Psychologie Contemporaine*. Paris: Alphons Lemerre.
Carlyle, Thomas. 1987. *Sartor Resartus*. Oxford: Oxford Univ. Press.
Coimbra Martins, António. 1967. O mandarim assassinado [The murdered mandarin]. In *id.*, *Ensaios Queirosianos*, 11–266. Lisbon: Publicações Europa-América.

---

37 "glórias de uma raça estética e livre" (199). According to the condensed biography presented by the narrator, Korriscosso writes his first elegies when working as a hotel interpreter (202).
38 "[...] eu sou em quase tudo um francês – exceto num certo fundo sincero de tristeza lírica, [...]." (Queiroz 2000: 235–236).
39 A few years after "Um poeta lírico", Eca de Queiroz found another 'mate', this time going beyond a fictional character: he recovered the collective invention of the poet Carlos Fradique Mendes (1865–66) by "posthumously" publishing his letters. This specific editorial fiction was directly inspired by Hippolyte Taine's feigning of the North American industrialist Frédéric-Thomas Graindorge as author of *Notes sur Paris* (1867), written in French. Fradique Mendes, conceived as an upper-class intellectual living in Paris, renounces authorship limiting his creativity to conversation and letters, partly written in French. *Correspondência de Fradique Mendes* (1888) exists as an "original text" only in Portuguese, being some letters — mainly to his beloved Clara — "translated from French" (Queiroz 2014: 289–328).

Coleman, Alexander. 1980. *Eça de Queirós and European Realism*. New York/London: New York University Press.
França, José-Augusto. 2000. Comentário Editorial. In Henry Rider Haggard (ed.), *As Minas do Rei Salomão / As Minas de Salomão* [King Solomon's Mines], 7–23. Lisbon: Livros Horizonte. [parallel edition: translation Ana Carvalho / Eça de Queiroz's version]
Gogolin, Ingrid. 2021. Multilingualism: A threat to public education or a resource in public education? – European histories and realities. *European Educational Research Journal* 20(3). 297-310.
Grossegesse, Orlando. 1991. *Konversation und Roman. Untersuchungen zum Romanwerk von Eça de Queiroz*. Stuttgart: Franz Steiner.
Grossegesse, Orlando. 1995. A propensão dialógica na obra queirosiana [The dialogic propensity in Queiros' work]. In Fátima Brauer-Figueiredo (ed.), *Actas do 4º Congresso da Associação Internacional de Lusitanistas, Hamburgo, 6 a 11 de Setembro de 1993*, 537–543. Lisbon: Lidel.
Grossegesse, Orlando. 2000. O alfaiate filosófico e a morte do dândi. Sobre Carlyle em Eça de Queirós [The philosophical tailor and the death of the dandy. About Carlyle in Eça de Queirós]. *Leituras. Revista da Biblioteca Nacional* 7. 65–76.
Hervé, Francis. 1837. *A residence in Greece and Turkey, with notes of the journey through Bulgaria, Servia, Hungary and the Balkan*. 2 vols. London: Whittaker & Co.
Hibbitt, Richard. 2006. *Dilettantism and its Values. From Weimar Classicism to the fin de siècle*. Oxford: Legenda.
Lepecki, Maria Lúcia. 1994. Num hotel de Charing Cross [At a hotel in Charing Cross]. *Queirosiana* 7/8. 173–189.
Machado, Álvaro. 2002. O retrato do artista no imaginário queirosiano [The Portrait of the Artist in the Queirosian Imaginary]. In Giulia Lanciani (ed.), *Un secolo di Eça*, 57–67. Roma: La Nuova Frontiera.
Petruccelli della Gattina, Ferdinando. 1867. *Les Mémoires de Judas*. Paris: A. Lacroix, Verboeckhoven et C.
Piwnik, Marie-Hélène, 2003. Introdução [Introduction]. In Eça de Queiroz, *Contos II*. 15–60. Critical edn. Marie-Hélène Piwnik. Lisbon: Imprensa Nacional – Casa da Moeda.
Queiroz, Eça de, José Maria. 2009. Um Poeta Lírico [A lyrical poet]. In *id.*, *Contos I*, 37–48. Critical edn. Marie-Hélène Piwnik. Lisbon: Imprensa Nacional – Casa da Moeda.
Queiroz, Eça de, José Maria. 2000. *Obras Completas* [Complete Works]. Rio de Janeiro: Nova Aguilar, vols. III, IV (edn. Beatriz Berrini).
Queiroz, Eça de, José Maria. 2003. Sir Galahad. In *id.*, *Contos II*. 119–134. Critical edn. Marie-Hélène Piwnik (ed.). Lisbon: Imprensa Nacional – Casa da Moeda.
Queiroz, Eça de, José Maria. 2014. *Correspondência de Fradique Mendes (Memórias e Notas)* [Letters of Fradique Mendes (Memoirs and Notes)]. Critical edn. Carlos Reis, Irene Fialho, & Maria João Simões (eds.). Lisbon: Imprensa Nacional – Casa da Moeda.
Queiroz, Eça de, José Maria. 2017. *Os Maias* [The Maias]. Critical edn. Carlos Reis & Maria do Rosário Cunha (eds.). Lisbon: Imprensa Nacional – Casa da Moeda.
Queiroz, Eça de, José Maria. 2021. *A Relíquia* [The Relic]. Lisbon: Critical edn. Carlos Reis, & Maria Eduarda Borges dos Santos. Lisbon: Imprensa Nacional – Casa da Moeda.

Sabira Ståhlberg
Meine lieben fellow-pupils: Edith Södergran's Hidden Multilingualism

Abstract: One of the most famous Swedish-language poets, Edith Södergran (1892–1923), was also one of the most multilingual writers in Northern Europe. She had knowledge of at least seven languages and wrote in five, yet published only in Swedish. Södergran's childhood in multilingual Saint Petersburg, her education in the German-language school St. Petrischule, and travels in Europe, formed a polyglot globetrotter and world citizen, whose linguistic and cultural competences are only beginning to be appreciated in recent years; Södergran's multilingualism has however not been researched in depth. This study discusses the multilingualism in the life of this versatile writer and tries to reconstruct her multilingual biography based on fragmentary archive material. It also provides some examples of how her poetry reflects the multidimensional and multilingual world she lived in, and asks the question if her multilingualism was really hidden or has just been overlooked.

Keywords: Code-Switching, Finland, Language Transfer, Modernist Poetry, Multi-Competence, Multilingual Strategies, Saint Petersburg

1 Introduction

At the beginning of the twentieth century, many writers in Finland were multilingual, yet they would not define themselves as anything but Swedish or Finnish speakers. Several decades before the country became independent from the Russian Empire in 1917, intellectuals and politicians had begun to divide along language lines. A fierce debate raged about the "language question" after independence: which of the two languages should be the official one in the new state? Finally, both were chosen, but the "language conflict", Swedish *språkstriden*, Finnish *kielitaistelu*, left a deep imprint which can still be discerned today in the society (for a historical overview, see McRae 1997). Some writers, well-educated and often with knowledge of more than the two "domestic" languages, tried to create bridges through literature. The editors' efforts of

---

Sabira Ståhlberg, independent scholar, e-mail: sabirien@pm.me

∂ Open Access. © 2023 the author(s), published by De Gruyter. This work is licensed under the Creative Commons Attribution 4.0 International License.
https://doi.org/10.1515/9783110778656-009

the literary and arts journal *Ultra* (1922) had limited results, however, and other similar projects were short-lived. Only in the 2010s, when growing numbers of immigrants drew attention to multilingual issues in Finland, and global awareness of and research about multilingualism were on the increase, a reassessment of multilingual writers began to take place (see for example Grönstrand and Malmio 2011; Domokos et al. 2016; Grönstrand et al. 2020).

One of the authors whose multilingualism is now being acknowledged is the poet Edith Södergran (1892–1923). She was one of the most multilingual writers of her time in Finland, but she published her poetry only in Swedish. Södergran knew seven languages: Swedish, German, French, Russian, English, Finnish, and Italian, and she had possibly some knowledge of Latin. Posthumously she has become a literary superstar and a veritable icon in the Nordic countries. She has been categorized as a modernist, expressionist, symbolist, futurist, and a reformer of the Swedish-language poetic expression. Her poems have been translated into dozens of languages, and her lyrics still inspire readers, musicians, artists, scholars, writers, and many others. Södergran's popularity exceeds by far that of any of her contemporaries, and there are probably more studies about her life and writings than about any other Swedish-language writer in Finland.

Fig. 1: Edith Södergran in the 1910s. SLSA_566_410.

Edith Södergran was born in Saint Petersburg in 1892. Her mother's parents and also her father had migrated there from the Grand Duchy of Finland for work. Finland was the eastern province of Sweden for 600 years before becoming an autonomous part of Russia in 1809. The Södergran family soon moved to a big villa in the nearby village of Raivola (now in Russia, Рощино, Roshchino) in Karelia, where Edith spent most of her early childhood. In 1902, aged ten, she entered the German-language St. Petrischule in Saint Petersburg, where she remained for six years. Her father died from tuberculosis in 1907 and in the following year Edith was diagnosed with the same illness. Between 1911 and 1914 she traveled with her mother Helena in Europe and stayed at a sanatorium in Davos, Switzerland. World War I and the following Civil War in Finland in 1918 put an end to her journeys to the continent and she spent most of her final years in Raivola. Edith Södergran passed away in 1923 at age 31 (see Tideström, 1949; Rahikainen, 2014a and 2014b in Swedish; in English, Schoolfield 1984; Jones and Branch 1992).

Research and writings on Edith Södergran have for the past century focused chiefly on her tragic and short life, ethnicity, womanhood, sexuality, national identity, and literary, feminist, religious, philosophical and psychological topics. Södergran's general biography has been researched by dozens of scholars, but the biographies contain mainly contextual information (family, school, friends, environment, etc.) and discussions about her identity, which seems too elusive to be defined, because it does not fit into one single ethnic and language category. The most extensive and reliable analyses have been published by Agneta Rahikainen (2014a and 2014b). Rahikainen has corrected several persistent myths and recognized multilingualism and multiculturalism as natural aspects of this well-read polyglot writer's everyday life (Rahikainen 2014a: 24).

Södergran's eccentric Swedish language has been much discussed, but her multilingualism has received little attention: Södergran's early German-language poetry has been analyzed by Gisbert Jänicke as a bilingual phenomenon (1984 and 1992); her relations to Russian literature and culture by Göran Lundström (1950), Ljudmila Braude and Nina Belikova (both 1993); and her only preserved Russian-language poem by Per-Arne Bodin (1987), who identified her as trilingual. Södergran's multilingual environments and reading are mentioned and discussed in several works, extensively by Olof Enckell (1961) in relation to her youth poetry, and by one of her first biographers, Gunnar Tideström (1949), however without any deeper analysis.

Although Södergran's multilingualism is now being generally mentioned as something normal (a shift occurred after Rahikainen's works in 2014), there are as yet no studies specifically about the type and character of her multilingualism: was she translingual or multilingual? According to Penelope Gardner-Chloros (2013), there is a difference between *translingual* writers – those who write in another language than their primary or first language (Kellman 2020) – and *multilingual* writers, who have command of several languages since childhood and not only a single first language. With multilingual authors, the question of language choice, for instance, is much more complex than with translingual or even bilingual authors. Both the overall choice of language, and the separate choices – ranging from semantic and syntactic down to word choice, form and construction, as well as audio-visual decisions – depend on numerous factors. Jan Fishman (1972) saw the factors as *domains*, supposing that the choice is not random. There are however other aspects which are far more subtle than the background of the author, language environment, tradition, political context or personal motivation. The language decisions of an author are often the result of a longer process and intricate, interconnected aspects, including circumstances, personal taste, life situation, and also momentary decisions or random choices (Ståhlberg 2023, forthcoming).

In addition to the question if Edith Södergran was translingual or multilingual, it is important to ask if her other languages were active while writing poetry in Swedish, and how this could be assessed. How deep does her supposed monolingualism in Swedish actually go? Is it only on the surface (choice of language), or does it also affect the expressions and linguistic elements? What happened to her other languages when she chose to work in Swedish – did she write just in one language and discard all others? Did her individual language mix influence, interfere and enrich her Swedish writings, and if yes, how? Can we identify multilingual strategies in her Swedish poetry, and how can the influence of those languages remaining behind the scenes be defined and/or measured? Did the degree of knowledge and frequency of use of the languages influence her Swedish writings, and if yes, how?

Creative processes of writers are still vastly unexplored territories, and historical creative processes can be even more difficult to explore because we cannot ask the author, and there are often only a limited number of sources. The sources for Edith Södergran are very scarce and fragmentary. According to her mother Helena Södergran (born Holmroos, 1861–1940), Edith intentionally burned most of her papers before her death. Helena and some friends, especially the writer Hagar Olsson (1893–1978), gathered the remaining documents and notebooks which are now kept in the archives of The Society of Swedish Literature in Finland (Svenska Litteratursällskapet, SLS) in Helsingfors / Helsinki (SLSA 566 Edith Södergran's archive; SLSA 774 Hagar Olsson's archive containing Helena Södergran's memories). Using what the Swedish historian Janken

Myrdal (2012) calls *source pluralism*, even scattered and disparate materials, and even not completely reliable memories like those of Helena Södergran, written in her old age, can be analyzed and brought into play to reveal more information. A cross-scientific approach is also needed for the study of Edith Södergran's multilingualism.

This is the first study of multilingualism in Edith Södergran's poetry. The reception of her poetry will not be discussed here, as it has been analyzed by several scholars and is beyond the scope of this study. In order to understand her multilingualism, it is necessary to map out her language development as well as her multilingual writings and notes, before asking important questions about her multilingual strategies and the hidden multilingualism in her poems, such as: what multilingual influences are there and how can we uncover them? What kind of linguistic and literary strategies did she use when writing in Swedish? Was her poetry so innovative, and does it continue to be considered so refreshing, *because* it contains multiple layers from different languages?

2 Multilingual biography: a reconstruction

When Edith Södergran visited colleagues in Finland, her strange appearance and accent made an impression on her Finland-Swedish and Finnish colleagues. In short: they found her exotic. She was ridiculed not only for her fancy language but also for her dress and behavior. Södergran has been called among others Oriental, Byzantine, fantastic and bizarre (see discussion in Rahikainen 2014a: 151–169). Her strange poetic language has been commented upon and discussed in numerous publications and it continues to fascinate both literary scholars and writers today. An educated guess by a multilingualism scholar would be that this language is based on her multilingualism, but to be able to answer the question if she was multilingual or translingual, an effort to reconstruct her language biography must first be done.

In the following I will discuss four periods of her life: childhood, school, travels, and poet years. The periods are divided according to her language use as reflected in the original sources, the documents and notebooks kept in The Society of Swedish Literature Archives in Finland (Svenska Litteratursällskapets arkiv; SLSA 566 and 774). The aim of this study is not to discuss existing hypotheses or myths about her languages; that would require a separate volume (see Backman and Storå 1996 for a list of the published works about Edith Södergran until 1996; dozens more have appeared since then). The goal here is to analyze the original sources and how her several languages are reflected in her own writings.

2.1 Childhood (1892–1902)

In Helena Södergran's reminiscences (SLSA 774.1), probably written upon request by Hagar Olsson, it is not said explicitly that Edith Södergran spoke and read Swedish in her childhood, but the episodes and exclamations quoted would indicate that Swedish was spoken in her home. An early letter to Helena's mother, dated 17 May 1900 and written in a child's handwriting, and a testimony about the cat Koti being the most beautiful animal, dated 11 October 1902 and written in an adult's handwriting, are both in Swedish (SLSA 566.2.5). Edith's first poem, written at age six or seven, was in Swedish. Her mother remembered a single line but the poem itself is lost. According to Helena Södergran, Edith read Swedish-language authors and commented upon their writings, and in her school notebooks (see below) there are many quotations from Swedish-language literature both from Sweden and Finland.

The childhood environment in Raivola was multilingual: at least Swedish, Finnish, Russian and German were spoken. Helena was multilingual, too. She grew up in Saint Petersburg, studied at the German-language St. Anne school, and spoke and wrote Russian fluently, which quotations in her letters to Hagar Olsson reflect. Much less is known about Edith's father Matts, from Swedish-speaking Ostrobothnia, but he probably had to learn some Russian or other languages in order to work in Saint Petersburg. Edith remained an only child and she especially enjoyed the company of her seniors. An old Estonian who lived on the Södergran premises wrote poetry. She later wrote a poem about him, according to her mother (SLSA 774.1).

Fig. 2: One of Edith Södergran's many cats hiding in the oven in the family house, Raivola, Karelia. Photograph by Södergran, who was very attached to cats and considered them the wisest animals in the world. SLSA_566_53.

A question which should be asked, considering the reactions to Edith Södergran's Swedish-language use, is what kind of Swedish did she actually speak? Finland-Swedish differs somewhat from Swedish in Sweden and there are several dialects of Swedish in Finland, too. Is it possible that her Swedish was a Saint Petersburg-Swedish with variations in vocabulary and pronunciation to "standard" Finland-Swedish, spiced with words, grammar, and expressions from other languages? This variation of Swedish has received very little attention, although Swedish speakers lived in the city from its foundation at the beginning of the eighteenth century, and before that in the Swedish town located in the same place. Saint Petersburg-Swedish does not exist anymore, but there are studies about the Swedish language in nearby Viborg / Viipuri / Vyborg in Karelia (Tandefelt 2002a; 2002b) which show that the multilingual environment strongly influenced the language.

2.2 School years (1902–1908)

Helena Södergran wrote in her reminiscences about Edith (SLSA 774.1) that her daughter was well-prepared for school when she entered the prestigious German-language St. Petrischule in Saint Petersburg. The notebooks and school documents (SLSA 566.2) for each semester between 1902 and 1908 show that Edith was an exceptional student in German language (spoken and written), Russian (spoken and written), French, English, religion, geography and history.

She often received the highest marks, but in natural sciences, calligraphy, drawing and handicrafts she was not that successful.

In English dictation Edith made only a couple of minor mistakes, as shown in two documents from 1906 and 1907 corrected by her teacher. Two tasks in Russian are free from errors, on Tatyana's character in Alexander Pushkin's (1799–1837) *Eugene Onegin* (1833), and a dictation from 9 December 1906 from Sergey Aksakov's (1791–1859) short story Собирание бабочек [Sobranie babochek, Collecting Butterflies] (1859). The first even received the teacher's praise. Russian literature was taught, "but only the oldest ones [writers] were served", Helena Södergran wrote (SLSA 774.1). How Edith related to Russian literature she did not recall, but Pushkin and the romantic author Mikhail Lermontov (1814–1841) were "far away", too distant from her world and interests, and Fyodor Dostoyevsky (1821–1881) was "too heavy". Edith read, so her mother remembered, Victor Hugo's (1802–1885) *Les Misérables* (1862), poems by the English writer A.C. Swinburne (1837–1909) and the "foggy" French-language Belgian author Maurice Maeterlinck (1862–1949). One of her great favorites was Rudyard Kipling's (1865–1936) *Jungle book* (1894), which both Edith and her mother enjoyed very much. Edith also wrote letters in Swedish to family friends during her school years (Södergran 1996: 14–18).

Edith Södergran's earliest literary efforts are preserved in what has become known as *Vaxdukshäftet* (SLSA 566.1.1; Enckell 1961), the "oil-cloth notebook". This surviving school notebook contains 206 poems in German (85%), 27 poems in Swedish (adding four other early poems found later, the total becomes 31 or 13%), one in Russian and four in French, adding up to 242 poems. The topics vary from love declarations and satire about her French teacher, to nature poems, politics, love in general, human existence, friendship and illness. The notebook starts in January 1907 and ends in January 1909 according to dates she provided with some of the poems. The notebook shows that Edith Södergran used fluent, nuanced and for the most part correctly spelled and rich vocabulary in all four languages. The prevalence of German is not surprising, as her school language was German and most of her daily activities, reading, writing and talking in the school environment occurred in German. Södergran also sent some German poems to an illustrated magazine (name and location unknown). At first, the editors found them "deep and beautiful" but a second time they refused her poems (Helena Södergran's memories, SLSA 774.1).

Due to a lack of other writings from the school years, no far-reaching conclusions can be drawn. The dates available point to the fact that Edith Södergran wrote in all her languages during these two years. There are no "language periods" of writing in a certain language for a specific time; one day she apparently wrote in one language and the next in another. Still, the Swedish-language poems are mainly dated from March 1908 to 1909, and the French are dated in 1908. The only Russian poem is from 11 July 1907.

Language mixing occurs in around 9% of the poems: in the Swedish poems, two contain French words or expressions. Among the German poems nine contain French words or expressions, five contain Russian, two English, two English and French, and one Russian and French. One German poem has only a Russian-language title. The French poems and the single Russian poem are not mixed. Most language mixes contain single words or short expressions and very seldom a whole line. A typical example is the undated satirical German-language poem *Die Schule* [The School], in which English is used to emphasize the stupidity of the other pupils:

> In dieser dumpfen Atmosphäre
> von gleichgültiger Ignoranz
> und von Vergnügungssucht und Dummheit
> erstickt mein eig[e]nes Wesen ganz. [...]
> Und meine lieben *fellow-pupils*,
> sie schrei[e]n wie ein Tatarenheer...
> [In this dull atmosphere
> of indifferent ignorance
> and of pleasure addiction and stupidity
> my own being suffocates completely. [...]
> And my dear *fellow-pupils*,
> they scream like a Tatar army]

(Poem 145, *Vaxdukshäftet* [Oil-cloth notebook], SLSA 566.1.1; Södergran 1990: 294; my translation).

Scholars have long been puzzled by the fact that German-language poems cannot be found after September 1908 in Södergran's work; therefore, it is supposed that she stopped writing in German after turning to Swedish. The scarcity and character of the sources (chiefly in Swedish) are the main reasons for this opinion. Most of the letters which have been preserved (published in Södergran 1996) are in Swedish, the recipients being mostly Finland-Swedish friends and writers. Letters from Södergran in other languages have not reached the archives and most of them are probably lost. The question of what the recipients of her letters, especially in Russia, felt it was worth or safe to keep in the turbulent times after 1917 remains open.

An important source reflecting Edith Södergran's multilingual readings is the so called *Franska häftet* [French notebook] (SLSA 566.2.1). This notebook titled *Français,* originally intended for French grammar and exercises, was also used for learning Finnish, English and Russian as well as mathematics and literature. The notebook was apparently filled over several years; the handwriting varies and different pens or pencils have been used. It is impossible to define when an entry was made, as there are no other dates except that Södergran began it in her fifth grade in 1906–1907.

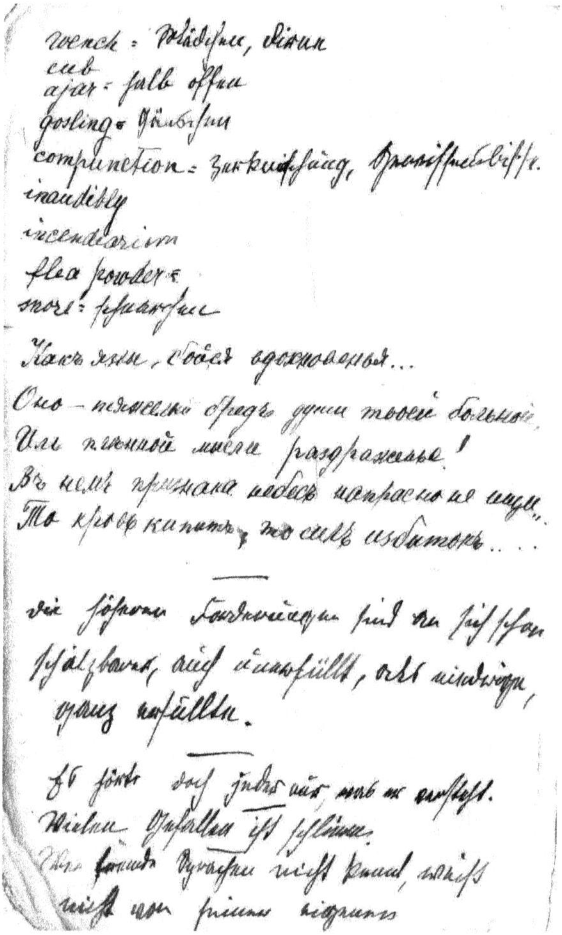

Fig. 3: In her French notebook (1906-), Edith Södergran recorded quotations, words and other useful or interesting information in several languages, often mixed on the same page. This example contains English, German and Russian. SLSA_566:2:1_manuskript 1, page 1.

The entries in the notebook are a mixture between literary quotations, proverbs from the Finnish, Lithuanian, Japanese, etc. traditions, excerpts from folk songs and religious works, a few drawings and one table of the hierarchies of humans, animals, plants and inhabitants of the astral world. Out of more than 300 quotations in the notebook, more than half are in German; there are 50 French entries (17%), 33 Swedish (11%), 19 Russian (6%), 15 Finnish (5%), 11 English (4%), one Italian and one Latin. Seven entries contain mixed language, mostly word explanations or translations of words and expressions: one Russian-German-English, two Finnish-Swedish, one English-German, two French-German and one English-French-German.

The quotations are often from the original language they were written in, but many are in the language Edith Södergran read or found them in. The Latin quotation, for instance, comes from the Swedish statesman Axel Oxenstierna (1583–1654). In Swedish there are excerpts from among others Maeterlinck and the American theologian and author J. Freeman Clarke (1810–1888), poet and philosopher Ralph Waldo Emerson (1803–1882) and priest and writer William Reed Huntington (1838–1909). Swedish authors such as the feminist Ellen Key (1849–1926), poets Gustaf Fröding (1860–1911) and Esaias Tegnér (1782–1846), and the Finland-Swedish writer Arvid Mörne (1876–1946) appear with entries in Swedish. The Russian quotations are mostly from Russian authors such as Mikhail Lermontov, Nikolay Nekrasov (1821–1878), Anton Chekhov (1860–1904), Semyon Nadson (1862–1887) and the fabulist Ivan Krylov (1769–1844), and there is a quotation in Russian from the Prussian chancellor Otto von Bismarck. In French, most of the quotations are from French authors, as in English from English-language writers, but in German William Shakespeare and John Ruskin (1819–1900) stand beside Goethe and Nietzsche. In Finnish, the proverbs, songs, and excerpts are from Finnish-language sources and appear to have been written down during Finnish language lessons.

The French notebook reflects Edith Södergran's vast reading in several languages already during her school years. She read and wrote in the languages or at least copied quotes with very few errors. At the St. Petrischule half of the languages in the notebook, Swedish, Finnish, Italian and Latin, did not figure in the curriculum, so Södergran's knowledge had been gained elsewhere. She apparently learned efficient and systematic study techniques at school, as her meticulous notes reflect, and applied these methods to further language studies. A seemingly irrelevant detail but crucial to understanding her writings is something her mother (SLSA 774.1) mentioned: Edith was very precise and well-organized. This preciseness and attention to detail can be discerned already in her school notebooks and documents, and it is visible in the word choice and imagery of her adult poetry. Edith Södergran was a keen amateur photographer and her pictures further testify to her attention to detail (see Rahikainen 1993).

2.3 Travels in Europe (1911–1914)

Between 1908 and 1911, Edith Södergran was being treated for tuberculosis in Finland. From this period, mainly Swedish-language letters have been preserved, but in one letter a student of hers, Alexey, possibly another patient, wrote a few lines in Polish (Södergran 1996: 25–26). Helena and Edith Södergran decided to travel to Switzerland in 1911 for Edith's treatment, which succeeded *ziemlich gut* [German, fairly well] (Helena Södergran's words; SLSA 774.1). In the multicultural and multilingual surroundings Edith's "small poems" found "resonance with some souls". Mother and daughter also visited Sweden, Germany and Italy, and in the hotels and the sanatoriums they read both Swedish-language and international newspapers. An interest in languages is obvious: Helena's opinion was that Edith loved the South and liked the Italian language which she had learned by "some [new] method". Edith did not like English although she studied it, exchanging German lessons for English with a fellow patient; yet she found the Swiss German dialect "lovely" (Södergran 1996: 38, 40–41, 45, 48; on p. 47 even a song is quoted).

From 1912, there are 26 compositions in English, which are collected in a notebook with the title *English Compositions. Edith Södergran. Davos-Dorf* (SLSA 566.2.2). They describe the doctor in whose care Edith was, landscapes, proverbs, journeys, and various topics gleaned or copied from newspapers, such as the Serbians (the Balkan Wars were in the headlines during 1912–1913), the richest woman in America, women's suffrage, the political parties in Finland, and miscellaneous topics such as ancient England, misfortunes, gardens and earthquakes. Some are original, but several are texts copied from English-language books and plays (compare Rahikainen 2014a: 27). Of these compositions, 15 have glossaries or word lists, five are English-German, three English-Swedish, two English-English, and the remaining five English-German-Swedish. German was used as a reference or intermediate language more frequently than any other languages, which could be a habit Södergran developed at school or because of a lack of dictionaries, or a combination of reasons.

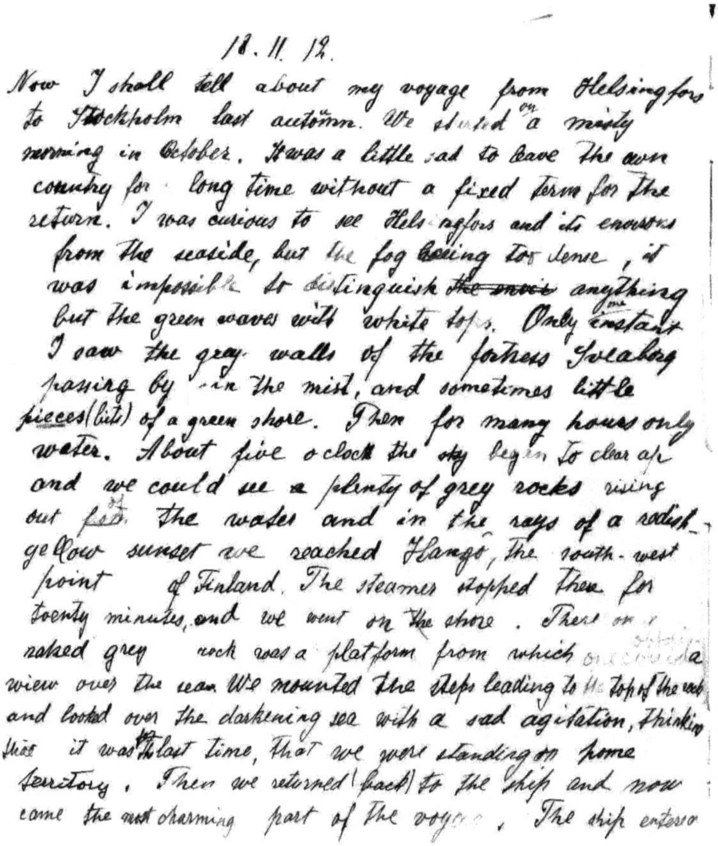

18. II. 12.

Now I shall tell about my voyage from Helsingfors to Stockholm last auttömn. We started on a misty morning in October. It was a little sad to leave this own country for long time without a fixed term for the return. I was curious to see Helsingfors and its environs from the seaside, but the fog being too dense, it was impossible to distinguish the more anything but the green waves with white tops. Only instants I saw the grey walls of the fortress Sveaborg passing by in the mist, and sometimes little pieces (bits) of a green shore. Then for many hours only water. About five o'clock the sky began to clear up and we could see a plenty of grey rocks rising out of the water and in the rays of a reddish-yellow sunset we reached Hangö, the south-west point of Finland. The steamer stopped there for twenty minutes and we went on the shore. There on a naked grey rock was a platform from which one had a view over the sea. We mounted the steps leading to the top of the rock and looked over the darkening sea with a sad agitation, thinking it was the last time, that we were standing on home territory. Then we returned (back) to the ship and now came the most charming part of the voyage. The ship entered

Fig. 4: In the notebook English Compositions (1912), Edith Södergran wrote among others a travel description. SLSA_566:2:2_manuskript 1, page 8.

From the years abroad and later from Raivola, some Finnish-language letters have been preserved, mainly to fellow patients (see Södergran 1996: 55–56; 69). Postcards from Edith Södergran and her mother Helena were sent to their housekeeper, Kirsti Kaikkonen, married Moilanen, between 1912 and 1926 (SLSA 1223). Edith's 22 postcards include descriptions about cats, journeys, landscapes and the weather. In both Edith's and Helena's Finnish language use the interference from other languages is visible, more so in Helena's postcards than in Edith's. In Edith's postcards a Swedish influence can be discerned in vocabulary and grammar, but in her mother's the interference is more mixed and errors frequent. In the postcards, mother and daughter regularly mention news from common friends, neighbors and acquaintances in Raivola and Saint Petersburg. This points to a large and active correspondence with speakers of different languages.

2.4 Poet years (1914–1923)

In 1914, any plans to return to Switzerland were hindered by the outbreak of World War I. The Södergrans remained mostly in Raivola while the political situation changed around them. Traveling became even more difficult after the independence of Finland in December 1917 and the Finnish Civil War in 1918, the turbulence in Russia and the subsequent loss of the family's investments.

Fig. 5: Edith Södergran (right, holding dog) walking with friends and/or fellow patients in Switzerland between 1912 and 1914. Contrary to the prevailing myth of a sick loner, Södergran had a vast international circle of friends and acquaintances. SLSA_566_264.

A persistent myth about Edith Södergran as a poor, lonely, sick and isolated poet dying by inches continues to dominate her public image, although several scholars and foremost Agneta Rahikainen (2014a and 2014b) have deconstructed this myth and brought forward convincing evidence of the opposite. Södergran was never alone despite war and poverty. Friends and acquaintances wrote poems, quotations and aphorisms in half a dozen languages, signed their autographs or painted pictures in a "memory" notebook (SLSA 566.2.3). This notebook dates to the critical period of 1917–1920 when political instability in Karelia, the border region between Finland and Russia, was at its peak. Together with her poems, this notebook shows that she continued to live in a culturally and linguistically colorful world. The first entry is from 1907 but the other entries which contain dates are mainly from 1917, 1918 and 1920. The "friend book" mirrors the available social contacts in Raivola at this period, although some entries have apparently been collected elsewhere.

From a total of 62 entries, 31 are in Swedish (50%), 18 in Russian (29%), six in Finnish (10%), five in German (8%) and one each in French and Italian. German is no longer the forerunner; Swedish has replaced it and Russian comes in second. This reflects partly the fact that Edith Södergran was no longer at the German-language school, and partly the political situation which caused the loss of German-speaking contacts in Saint Petersburg and throughout Europe (Russia was at war with Germany beginning in 1914). The earliest entries from 1907 and again in 1917 were written by school friends in Russian and French, but only one is in German. Some of the entries from 1917 were written in Russian by neighbors or possibly summer guests. Most signatures carry Russian names, but one carries the signature of Nilifer (Nilüfer), a Tatar/Turkic female name. The Russian entries consist of a few pictures and poetry or quotations by famous writers like Ivan Turgenyev (1818–1883), Igor Severyanin (1887–1941), Semyon Nadson (1862–1887), Konstantin Balmont (1867–1942), Ivan Bunin (1870–1953) and Valery Bryusov (1873–1924).

The Swedish entries are mainly written by Södergran's neighbors or gathered from famous Finland-Swedish cultural activists and writers like Hans Ruin (1891–1980) or Runar Schildt (1888–1925), probably during trips to Finland. More than a dozen entries, dated at the end of April 1918, are simply signatures or thanks from Swedish-speaking officers and military who were quartered in the Södergran villa during the Finnish Civil War. The Finnish entries are written mainly by neighbors, but there is a signature by the famous writer Juhani Aho (1861–1921) from February 1917. The German-language entries were written by four women: three of them had German names and one a Swedish name. The Italian quotation from Dante carries a Finnish signature.

Edith Södergran's readings during her last years have been discussed by many of her biographers, but the lack of sources makes it difficult to assess in which languages and what she read except for some mentions in letters to colleagues like Hagar Olsson and the poet Elmer Diktonius (1896–1961). In 1918, she wrote in Swedish to the Finnish poet Eino Leino (1878–1926) that she was reading his (Finnish-language) book in the evenings. She found another of his works too difficult, probably not because of the language, as she planned to buy it during her next visit, but because of the contents. The letter ends with a French goodbye, *au revoir* (Södergran 1996: 81). Russian modernist and Silver Age writers such as Igor Severyanin, Anna Akhmatova (1889–1966), Marina

Tsvetayeva (1892–1941) and several others, and German Else Lasker-Schüler (1869–1945), are supposed to have figured among Edith Södergran's readings in addition to Nietzsche, Rudolf Steiner (1861–1925) and the German poet Heinrich Heine (1797–1856), but if and to what extent cannot be ascertained except for Severyanin. In the original archive materials only one book with Södergran's notes in the margin has survived: *Evangeline and Other Poems* by H. W. Longfellow (SLSA 566.2.6a).

3 The poet: one or more languages?

No existing materials or contextual data point to monolingualism at any period in Edith Södergran's life. The question is therefore: was Edith Södergran multilingual from early childhood, or was she a translingual with a first language (L1, in her case Swedish), who became multilingual during her school years? Considering the sources and circumstances, we can safely assume that Södergran was multilingual. The polyglot environments she lived in during her childhood (compare Rahikainen 2014a: 122), Raivola and Saint Petersburg, would be conducive and supportive to multilingualism. Her mother who also was multilingual certainly encouraged her to learn and read in different languages. When Edith was enrolled in the renowned German-language St. Petrischule at age ten, she must have known German well enough to be able to study in that language and learn additional languages (French, English) through it.

Further, the sources reflect a highly flexible use of languages, extensive reading and notes in several languages and multilingual study practices. Personal interest, curiosity, aesthetic reasons and probably ambition was of crucial significance for Södergran's efforts to improve her English and learn Italian during her stays in Switzerland. She could and did improve her language skills because she knew how to do it; she had already gained experience in language learning and development during her school years, and it would appear that she enjoyed learning. She freely used her previous languages when acquiring new languages, a method which is typical for multilingual persons. Edith Södergran's output and effortless code-switching in poetic form in several languages during her teenage years would also point to an early multilingualism. Agneta Rahikainen (2014a: 24) has expressed her doubts about Södergran even possessing a single mother tongue and the reconstruction of her language biography can confirm this: the writings already during her school years indicate that she was not a translingual who learned and wrote in a second language, but she was from childhood a multilingual who simply added languages to her toolkit.

Helena Södergran did not explicitly mention multilingualism in her reminiscences, probably because the term was unknown to her, and because using several languages was natural in her multicultural Saint Petersburg world. Multilingualism as a modern concept did not yet exist when she wrote about her daughter. In contrast, Finland was locked in a nationalist debate about bilingualism which she certainly knew about. Still today, being multilingual and multicultural often borders on treason in countries with strong nationalist tendencies, but during World War I it was especially important to downplay any German, that is "enemy" connections in Russia and Finland. After 1918, it also became essential to reduce any Russian aspects in Finland, where anti-Russian sentiments ran high. Edith Södergran's friends in Finland became anxious to present her as a Finland-Swedish writer, although she herself both in her letters and poetry proclaimed herself a world citizen (see Rahikainen 2014a: 137–139 for the "de-Russification" of Södergran).

If we accept that Edith Södergran was multilingual, the question of her language skills in each language becomes of less importance than her *use* of the languages. With multilingual writers, the language skills are not constant but fluid, and they are continually being adapted to circumstances, requirements of the environment and personal interest, among others. On the other hand, with disuse a language might retreat into passivity and needs to be reactivated. These fluctuating language skills are extremely difficult to measure, if not impossible, because they depend on dozens of factors and vary according to time, space and topics; any measurement of a multilingual person's language skills could only provide a momentary picture (Ståhlberg 2023, forthcoming).

3.1 Language choice

There has been much speculation about Edith Södergran's decision to write in Swedish. The hypotheses either cite a male authority proposing that she should write in her "real language" or mother tongue Swedish (Enckell 1961: 270), or there is a nationalist and patriotic agenda trying to fit her into a Finland-Swedish mold (Rahikainen 2014a: 141–144). Södergran's first collection, *Dikter* [Poems] was published in 1916. It was followed by *Septemberlyran* [The September Lyre] in 1918, *Rosenaltaret* [The Rose Altar] and *Brokiga iakttagelser* [Varied (Colourful) Observations], a collection of aphorisms in 1919, *Framtidens skugga* [The Shadow of the Future], and *Tankar om naturen* [Thoughts about Nature], again aphorisms in 1920. Edith Södergran passed away in 1923, but in 1925 Hagar Olsson edited and published her remaining poems posthumously in *Landet som icke är* [The Land That is Not] (all collected in Södergran 1990).

Why did this language cosmopolitan, avid multilingual reader and highly literate, cultural and philosophical globetrotter choose Swedish for her literary expression? Influences in her work have been traced back to German, French and Russian literary movements. Why would she choose only one language for channeling thoughts, ideas and emotions, when she had so many languages to choose from? Why not her strongest literary language which she herself said was German (Jänicke 1992: 61; Rahikainen 2011)? Most scholars and biographers have supposed automatically that her other languages besides Swedish were learned and not acquired: Södergran's first language must have been Swedish because her parents were Swedish speakers. Consequently, she wanted to express herself in a language which felt more spontaneous, in contrast to the learned languages at school (German included).

Another line of hypotheses focuses on the language loss: the other languages represented different cultural and social contexts with which she lost touch after the political upheavals in the 1910s (wars and closing of the Finnish-Russian border – the latter actually happened only in the 1920s after her death). After the beginning of World War I, it became difficult or impossible to keep up connections with friends throughout Europe, and from 1918 visits to Saint Petersburg became few and scarce in between. There were less opportunities to use German, Russian, French, English and Italian, all strongly connected with Södergran's life in Saint Petersburg and her friends and acquaintances in Europe. A further assumption is that through Swedish she could explore different topics and write in a different way than before, constructing a new poetic "I" based on symbolic imagery and emotions (for these hypotheses and a critical discussion, see Rahikainen 2014a: 24).

It is difficult to imagine that a person who so intensely used several languages would suddenly stop using other languages, just because she focused on publishing in one language. Södergran had a solid multi-competence both in the input (reading, listening) and output (writing, speech) of the languages she possessed, and she continued reading and using the languages also after supposedly "losing" her contexts and connections. In her letters to Hagar Olsson and others, she often mentioned reading especially in German, but also in other languages. Södergran's translations and short articles in Swedish in the bilingual Finnish-Swedish journal *Ultra* in 1922 supports the hypothesis that she continued to use her many languages; the poems with the Swedish titles *Ouverture* and *Insjöballad* 'Lake Ballad' by the Russian author Igor Severyanin, and an article about his poetry appeared in *Ultra* (No. 2: 20; No. 7–8: 108; and No. 5:

72–73). She also translated the French writer Edmond Fleg's (1874–1963) *Panthéon* (No. 5: 75).

If we accept that she was multilingual, the question about her language choice should be formulated in a different way: was her choice of Swedish a rational or an emotional one? A plausible reason for a rational decision could be publishing. It was easier to publish in Swedish in Finland than to get published in German, for instance. Already during her school years, Edith Södergran had tried to get her German poems published, albeit unsuccessfully (Helena Södergran's notes, SLSA 774.1). World War I made publishing in German even more difficult from her geopolitical position. Competition was much bigger, too: in 1922, Södergran translated Finland-Swedish literature into German, hoping that an acquaintance in Berlin would help her to find a publisher. After a harrowing correspondence with the publisher, she burned the manuscript (several letters starting from Södergran 1996: 217). Her premeditated seeking of contacts among Finland-Swedish writers in the mid-1910s would further point to a rational decision.

An unsolved question remains if Swedish was her emotional language, that is the language she felt was closest to her "own being" and offered her the most possibilities for expression. This question would be relevant if she was monolingual or translingual, but the poetry written during her school years in the oilcloth notebook would suggest that she had several emotional languages, German being the favorite at least since her school years. The emotional language can shift in multilingual writers throughout time, and there can be several at the same time, too (Ståhlberg 2023, forthcoming). Swedish did not *replace* German, but it was there all along in her literary language toolkit, and as a multilingual she could choose on which language to focus.

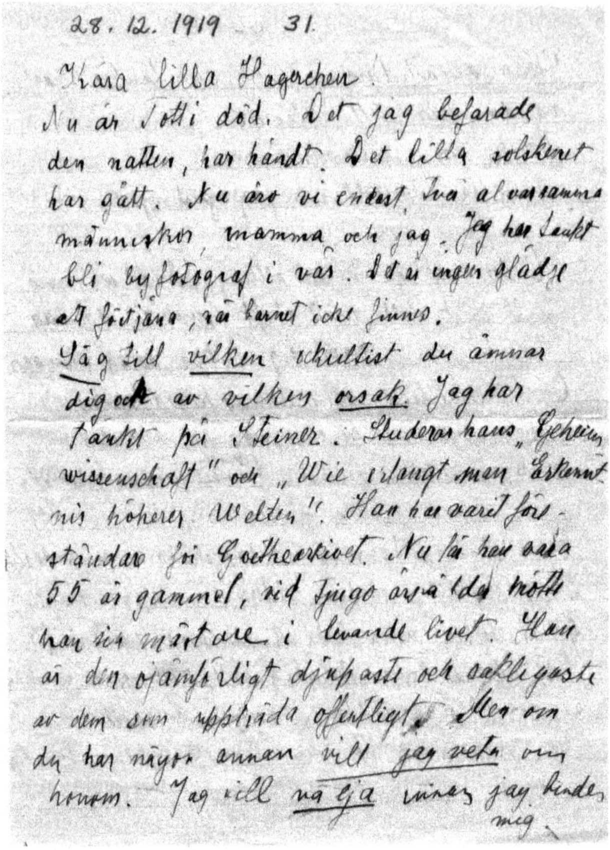

28. 12. 1919 31.

Kära lilla Hagerchen!

Nu är Totti död. Det jag befarade den natten, har händt. Det lilla solskenet har gått. Nu äro vi endast två alvarsamma människor, mamma och jag. Jag har låtit bli byfotograf i vår. Det är ingen glädje att förtjäna, när barnet icke finnes.

Säg till vilken schriftist du ämnar dig och av vilken orsak. Jag har tänkt på Steiner. Studerar hans „Geheimwissenschaft" och „Wie erlangt man Erkenntnis höherer Welten". Han har varit föreståndare för Goethearkivet. Nu är han bara 55 år gammal, vid tjugo års ålder mötte han sin mästare i levande livet. Han är den ojämförligt djupaste och sakligaste av dem som uppträda offentligt. Men om du har någon annan vill jag veta om honom. Jag vill välja vem jag binder mig.

Fig. 6: Swedish-language letter from Edith Södergran to her friend Hagar Olsson, whom she calls in German style Hagerchen. Södergran mentions that she is reading some German-language books by Rudolf Steiner. SLSA_774_brev 31, page 1, 28 December 1919.

3.2 Discovering dimensions

The first step in discovering multilingualism in a text is to acknowledge the presence of many languages; only then can the influence of other languages be discovered in the seemingly, but actually not monolingual text (Dembeck 2017). Edith Södergran's readers however perceived and continue to see her as a Swedish-language writer; anything else would be unthinkable. This attitude is not surprising after a century of upholding the public image that she was a "pure" Finland-Swedish author.

Some of Edith Södergran's Swedish-language poems were published in *Ultra* (No. 3: 47; No. 4: 51; and 7–8: 116) with a portrait and "critical praise" by the Finland-Swedish poet Gunnar Björling (1887–1960) (No. 4: 52–53). Södergran was already being talked about in not very pleasant tones in Finland during her lifetime: her erratic grammar and vocabulary were blamed on her outlandish background and lack of formal, "proper" Swedish-language schooling, and life in the margin of the Swedish-language world. Some decades later, her language was seen as both enriching and avant-garde, a special variation of Swedish which Agneta Rahikainen (2014a: 7) calls "Södergranish", a language only Södergran herself mastered. Several have tried to copy this language, but so far nobody has succeeded in recreating her Swedish variation. It is impossible, because "Södergranish" contains so many languages and multiple language layers that we will probably never be able to fully identify all elements. Edith Södergran tried to tell her critics that she was much more than they could grasp. She was probably thinking of higher things than languages, though, when she wrote in 1918 in the introduction to *Septemberlyran:* "Min självsäkerhet beror på att jag har upptäckt mina dimensioner. Det anstår mig icke att göra mig mindre än jag är" [My self-confidence depends on discovering my dimensions. It does not befit me to make me smaller/lesser than I am] (Södergran 1990: 65; my translation).

One possible method to find out how multilingual authors produce a text is to compare them with monolingual authors, or to compare authors across several languages and cultures and try to find out if multilingualism is language-connected or global. Discovering textual inspirations from other authors in Edith Södergran's poems is relatively easy and it has been done by many scholars, but it is trickier to identify her personal multilingual strategies. Literary analysts have so far found mostly what they identify as German, French, Swedish or Russian inspirations. To discover interference, covert and overt code-switching in her poetry, and the impact of the other languages on her Swedish, is not that simple and requires a deeper linguistic analysis.

Multilingualism and neuroscience have in recent years discovered that all languages are simultaneously active in the multilingual brain. The multilingual brain possesses some specific characteristics, among others higher density of gray matter, faster lexical retrieval, as well as more cognitive control, language-switching and working memory than the monolingual brain. In the process of writing, words, expressions and language norms are interpreted, adapted, created and recreated, engaged and fine-tuned by the multilingual author (see for instance Higby, Kim and Obler 2013; Zanetti et al. 2010). A multilingual brain is still often supposed to be the sum of its parts, but it should be compared to a complex system: when the parts come together, they function as a separate entity; put the same elements together in a slightly different way and you have another entity which functions differently (Ståhlberg 2023, forthcoming). How multilingual author brains actually function is a question which needs cross-disciplinary research, a new set of instruments and more flexible methods.

4 Multilingual strategies: a snail's shell

The complexity of the multilingual brain naturally makes the analysis of a polyglot writer like Edith Södergran very complicated. An important question is: did Edith Södergran consciously hide other languages in her Swedish-language poetry? Was it an unconscious or not completely conscious process to write like she did? Probably both. From her poetry and letters to Hagar Olsson and others, it becomes obvious that she was very much aware of the need to write in correct Swedish, but at the same time her own language sense for Swedish, deeply embedded in her multilingualism, created surprising combinations and un-Swedish words and expressions. A certain curiosity can be discerned in her explorations of the Swedish language, as if she was playing with the language and asking: how far can I push the limitations of this specific language? Playfulness with language and rule-breaking are common features in multilingual persons (see for example Moriarty and Järlehed 2018).

The question as to what kinds of multilingual strategies Edith Södergran used, consciously or subconsciously, and what multilingual layers there are in her poetry, require a deep and broad multi-disciplinary analysis, which would exceed the scope of this study, but will hopefully be done in the future. For this study, it is more important to ask if her multilingualism was really hidden, latent or what Domokos (2018: 87–98) in her gradation of code-switching from zero to five calls *zero code-switching*. In zero code-switching the language does not contain any immediately recognizable foreign elements, nor are they foreign enough to awaken a reaction in the reader. Hidden multilingualism can be found on all levels, from phonetic to semantic, in Edith Södergran's poetry. Most examples I have found can – unsurprisingly – be traced to German. As several scholars have discovered, and as Södergran's notebooks and letters show, there are strong influences from German literature and often direct references to German authors in her writings.

Multilingual elements are found in almost every Södergran poem. The most studied levels are the semantic and semiotic, but in the following I will introduce other linguistic levels and give one or two examples from each category.

All translations of the poems below are mine; it would have been possible to use existing translations but they are all poetic, while here the goal is to highlight the different linguistic elements.

4.1 Homonyms

An example of a possible phonetic interference from German is the use of the homonym *grunden* [the ground], German *Grund*, in an early poem, *Bruden* [The Bride], published posthumously in 1925 in *Landet som icke är* [The Land That is Not]. In Swedish, *grund* means "basis, bottom"; a more common Swedish word in this context would be *marken* [the ground]: "Det ligger något varmt på **grunden** av allt det främmande omkring mig" [There is something warm lying on **the ground** of all that foreign/strange around me] (Södergran 1990: 166, my emphasis).

4.2 Morphemes

Södergran uses some Swedish morphemes, often prefixes or suffixes, which an ordinary Swedish-speaker would not utilize. The words *tigerska* and *talerska* in the following poem *Färgernas längtan* [The Colors' Longing] from *Dikter* [Poems] (1916) are such elements. *Talare* is a commonly used word meaning "speaker"; *tigare* is a less used derivative of the verb *tiga* [to keep silent, quiet]. Södergran tagged the feminine ending *-ska* onto them, showing that the speaker is female, a feature which is very common in German. It is found in older Swedish language use, though, but the two words seem strange anyhow:

> „En **tigerska** skall jag vara i hela min levnad,
> en **talerska** är som den sladdrande bäcken som förråder sig själv"
> [A **quietess** will I be all my life,
> a **speakeress** is like the prattling brook which betrays itself]

(Södergran 1990: 32, my emphasis).

Sometimes what is not there can show that some other language has been at play during the composition of the poem. An older form of Swedish (Södergran read a lot of older Swedish literature) could also influence the use of the word *kring* [around] in *Hemkomst* [Homecoming] from *Landet som icke är* [The Land That is Not] (1925). The word is not incorrect but would more often be in the form *omkring* at the beginning of the twentieth century. In the second line, *mig*

[me] should be between *hälsar* [greet] and *välkommen* [welcome], but stands before it; this is a syntax variation which could be influenced by German:

> Min barndoms träd stå jublande **kring** mig: o människa!
> och gräset **mig** hälsar välkommen ur främmande land.
> [My childhood's trees stand jubilant **around** me: o human!
> and the grass **me** greets welcome from foreign land.]
>
> (Södergran 1990: 183, my emphasis).

4.3 Verb forms

The vocabulary in Södergran's poems is rich and often innovative, but at the same time a common feature is the use of older forms of verbs and nouns, a characteristic which was disappearing from Swedish at the beginning of the twentieth century. In several poems, she used the verb *skola* [shall] instead of the more modern *skall*, nowadays often shortened to *ska*. Her reading in older Swedish poetry might have influenced this usage, or it could be that *skola* felt closer to the German *sollen*.

Sometimes direct grammatical calques appear from German, like *Vad har det blivit av dig*, from *Was ist aus dir geworden* in *Min barndoms träd* [My Childhood Trees] from June 1922, published in *Landet som icke är* [The Land That is Not] (1925). It is grammatically correct Swedish but feels odd. Also, a further line appears to be Swedish, but the use of the verb *bliva* [to become] as the past participle *bliven* does not feel natural; yet if substituted with the German *Du bist Mensch geworden* it makes grammatical sense.

> Min barndoms träd stå höga i gräset
> och skaka sina huvuden: **vad har det blivit av dig**?
> [...] Du är **bliven** människa, främmande förhatlig.
> [My childhood's trees stand tall in the grass
> and shake their heads: **what has become of you**?
> [...] You have **become** a human, strangely hateful.]
> (Södergran 1990: 181, my emphasis).

4.4 Word combinations

Creating word combinations is common in poetry, but with Edith Södergran it is a recurring feature and there are sometimes surprising combinations. Most of her new words in Swedish are combinations of two words, like in the poem *Till en ung kvinna* [To a Young Woman] from *Septemberlyran* [The September Lyre] (1918). They could be translations or calques from German: the word *Strahlenfeuer*, [beam-fire], can be found in three German literary works, one from the seventeenth and two from the nineteenth century, and the word *Eiskammer*, [ice-chamber] 50 times in the historical text corpus of the online *Digitales Wörterbuch der deutschen Sprache* (2022, Digital Dictionary of the German Language): "drag mannens **stråleld** i dina ögons **isgemak**!" [pull the man's **beam-fire [Strahlenfeuer]** into your eyes' **ice-chamber [Eiskammer]**] (Södergran 1990: 75, my emphasis).

4.5 Syntax

The syntax is a further level where non-Swedish language interference is visible. The structure of Södergran's sentences often deviates from the common use of Swedish word order, although the order generally is fairly flexible. This would not cause any feeling of strangeness in a Swedish-language reader, who would see it as a poetic trick for greater effect, like the first line in the poem *Verktygets klagan* [The Lament of the Tool] from *Rosenaltaret* [The Rose Altar] (1919), where "for me" is located where *mich* in German could stand: "Livet sjönk **för mig** tillbaka i blå rök" [Life sank **for me** back in blue smoke] (Södergran 1990: 104–105, my emphasis).

German structures appear sometimes very clearly, especially in the early poems. In *Skymning* [Twilight] from 1916, published in *Septemberlyran* [The September Lyre] in 1918, *Vad kan… mot* is a calque from German *Was kann… gegen*, lacking the verb *göra* [do] in Swedish: "**Vad kan** en drömlik skymning **mot** alla vakna tankar" [**What can** a dreamlike twilight **against** all waking thoughts] (Södergran 1990: 70, my emphasis).

The use of *den* instead of *som* [that, which] occurs often in Södergran's early poetry and less in her later years. In German, *den* [the, which] is a relative pronoun in the accusative. *Den* [the, it, that] has several functions in Swedish and does not disturb the reader; the word is just used in a non-standard way. Sometimes Södergran used both *den* and the usual *som* in the same poem, like in *Jag* [I] in *Dikter* [Poems] (1916). They have however different functions: an analysis of her poetry shows that she preferred to use *den* as a relative pronoun when she would use the accusative in German, and *som* for the nominative case. In Swedish cases have long since disappeared, but, apparently, she felt the need to mark them:

Var jag en sten, **den** man kastat hit på bottnen?

Var jag en frukt, **som** var för tung för sin gren?
[Was I a stone, **that** they threw here to the bottom?
Was I a fruit, **which** was too heavy for its branch?]
(Södergran 1990: 29, my emphasis).

4.6 Semantic level

On the semantic level, the words chosen by Södergran are full of meaning and references. In *Mina konstgjorda blommor* [My Artificial Flowers] from *Rosenaltaret* [The Rose Altar] (1919), personal experiences possibly induced the last lines: in Finland she was seen as something like an Oriental after the publication of her first poetry collection in 1916. The rose altar itself is a reference to a Karelian tradition.

Fig. 7: Rose altars were prepared for birthday celebrations in Karelia. Photograph by Edith Södergran. SLSA_566_29.

Själv sitter jag nere på trappan –
en borttappad **österländsk** pärla
i storstadens brusande hav.
[Myself, I sit below on the stairs –
a lost **Oriental** pearl
in the city's roaring sea.]
(Södergran 1990: 99–100, my emphasis).

4.7 Semiotic level

Edith Södergran's symbolism and expressionism has been discussed in detail by many scholars and is outside the scope of this study. From a multilingual point of view there are many interesting points, but the frequency of geographical locations and names of mythical, historical, or religious personalities should be mentioned. These reflections of her multilingualism and multiculturalism, her extensive readings, travels and personal experiences certainly had a deep significance for Södergran, but conveyed less meaning to her Swedish-speaking readers who were not as well-read and lived in a less multicultural environment. Some symbols, motifs and characters are easy to relate to and interpret, such as Hamlet, God / gods, Aphrodite, the Himalayas, angels and fairies, kings and queens. Others such as Eros and Dionysus were used in the Nietzschean sense and require some reading of this author before they can be understood; the same is true for symbols and images from Steiner, Goethe and her other favorite authors. The Greek figure Tantalus and the Indian deity Vishnu, as well as the mountain Chimborazo in South America, should be known to an educated reader in her time, but others would have to check in an encyclopedia.

In one instance, Edith Södergran put in an explanation with the poem. Mostly references are lacking and because of the scarcity of sources, much becomes guesswork out of necessity. But in the poem *Mina sagoslott* [My Fairy-tale Castles] from *Rosenaltaret* [The Rose Altar] (1919), she indicated that the house is a shell and the philosopher is the German Georg Christoph Lichtenberg (1742–1799), who wrote in an aphorism: *Die Schnecke baut ihr Haus nicht, sondern es wächst ihr aus dem Leib;* [The snail does not build its house; the house grows out of its body]. The word *Schnecke* [snail] she translated into Swedish as the phonetically closer *snäcka* [(sea)shell]; in Swedish the word for snail is *snigel*:

> Jag såg in i filosofens hus*
> och förstod att han var lycklig...
> *Lichtenbergs **snäcka**
> [I looked into the philosopher's* house
> and understood that he was happy...
> *Lichtenberg's **shell**]
> (Södergran 1990: 103, my emphasis)

4.8 Other elements and other languages

Several poems are clearly inspired by German literature, but others cannot be that easily identified. The traces from other languages are far less obvious, more subtle and therefore difficult to assess. Are for instance alliterations a reflection of Finnish, where they are common in folk songs and poetry? In some poems Edith Södergran apparently used folk songs and folk poetry as an inspiration, repeating lines and words like refrains, while other poems are more like fairy tales.

The scarcity of the sources makes it difficult but not completely impossible to find similarities in Edith Södergran's writings and notes on her readings. Inspiration and references are only part of the analysis, however, when researching a multilingual author. A linguistic analysis must be combined with literary research, historical, biographical and contextual data, and artificial intelligence could be employed for processing the texts. The existing research methods and instruments available for an academic analysis must be developed in order to clarify several aspects of the multilingual creative process and its complexity, and how it is related to the writer's reading, writing, thinking processes, communication and a wide range of other factors (Ståhlberg 2023, forthcoming).

5 Conclusions: Hidden or in plain sight?

Why has Edith Södergran's multilingualism been hidden for over a century? Has it really been invisible or is it simply overlooked, not understood or ignored? Her biographers all mention the fact that she knew several languages, but few have ventured further or asked questions about the reasons, implications and consequences. Her multilingualism can therefore be seen as hidden from view, but in fact it has been there all along in plain sight, and it has been felt intuitively but not been uncovered. To discover it, multilingualism research and methods had to develop; just a few decades ago, the understanding about multilingualism and about multilingual authors' writings and life were much more limited.

Researchers agree that Edith Södergran's language was innovative and modernist and several have supposed that she constructed it consciously. Her "exotic" language positively enriched Swedish-language poetry, and it did so by transforming motifs, expressions and visions from many languages into a unique synthesis. Her multilingualism enabled her to stretch and bend Swedish grammar, vocabulary and other language features to suit her goals. Her multilingualism was present all her life, increasing and developing with every fragment she read and every discussion she had in any language. It was never shut off or put out but flowed freely into her Swedish-language poetry. Edith Södergran consciously and unconsciously challenged the language norms by productively using other languages' models and patterns while creating her own poetic language. A multilingual author can choose to write in one single language, but the other languages join in the concert anyway. Multilingual writers are similar to composers who both consciously and intuitively employ different instruments in an orchestra and combine their characteristic voices into an intricate tapestry of music. Multilingual writers, like composers, can shut out the orchestra for a violin solo when they want to, but the orchestra is still present.

A multilingual writer could be viewed like Lichtenberg's snail: the house, the poetry grows from the writer's body, from the writer's life itself. Until now the construction process of language knowledge and skills has been the focus of research about multilingual writers, but more aspects must be considered. Several questions should be reformulated, among them if Edith Södergran hid her multilingualism on purpose within Swedish, or if it happened "naturally" because she was multilingual, because a multilingual author always does both. Like with the snail, any literary production of a multilingual author grows out of the multilingual everyday life, and the multilingual writing always oscillates between conscious and sub/unconscious (Ståhlberg 2023, forthcoming).

Fig. 8: Multilingual authors live and write in multiple realities or worlds simultaneously. Edith Södergran, self-portrait in a mirror, 1910s. SLSA_566_304.

And yet, despite looking in all corners for traces, we might never find out exactly how a snail trailed from a German philosopher into a poem by Edith Södergran. Even if there were many more sources and we knew precisely at what moment of her life Södergran read about Lichtenberg's snail, there is no knowing how she processed it, turned it around in her mind, or how she fed it with new imagery, or the picture of the snail fed her with fresh ideas. These processes happen sometimes consciously and immediately but more often over a longer period of time. A multilingual writer receives, as Edith Södergran's school notebooks show, so many impulses every day from different languages that it is not always possible to remember in which language the writer has read something, or where the image, thought or idea came from, and how it was processed. The challenge for researcher is therefore to discover patterns, interconnections, feedback loops, sensitivity to inner and outer influences and so forth, and the phase transitions from chaos to spontaneous order; in other words, the researcher has to take a similar quantum leap as the writer has done.

The multilingual quantum leaps were shocking and terrifying to several of Edith Södergran's contemporaries, and they are still little understood and seldom recognized. Södergran was clearly conscious about inventing a new poetic language and about her multilingual input into Swedish poetry when she declared in the introduction to *Septemberlyran* [The September Lyre] (1918) that she possessed the full power of words and images only when she was completely free: *Mina dikter äro att taga som vårdslösa handteckningar* [My poems should be taken as careless hand drawings] (Södergran 1990: 65). This comment reflects an important characteristic of the multilingual writer: the freedom to play and create with language is the most essential element in the creation process.

Thanks
The author is grateful to The Swedish Literature Society in Finland for providing the archive materials for this article, and to Marianna Deganutti and Jana-Katharina Mende for suggesting theoretical references.

6 References

6.1 Photos by Edith Södergran

Svenska Litteratursällskapet / The Swedish Literature Society in Finland
Licence: CC BY 4.0

6.2 Archives

Edith Södergran's archive, SLSA 566, Svenska Litteratursällskapet, Helsingfors
Hagar Olsson's archive, SLSA 774, Svenska Litteratursällskapet, Helsingfors

6.3 Literature

Backman, Carita & Siv Storå (eds.). 1996. *Åttio år Edith Södergran. Verk och reception 1916–1995. En bibliografi* [Eighty years of Edith Södergran. Works and reception 1916–1995. A bibliography]. Helsingfors: SLS

Belikova, Nina. 1993. Edith Södergran i S:t Petersburg. *SFV Kalendern 1993.* 78–83.

Bodin, Per-Arne. 1987. Några kommentarer till Edith Södergrans ryska dikt [Some comments on Edith Södergran's Russian poem]. *Historiska och litteraturhistoriska studier* 62: 257–266.

Braude, Ljudmila. 1993. Edith Södergran och Ryssland [Edith Södergran and Russia]. *SFV Kalendern 1993.* 74–77.

Dembeck, Till. 2017. There Is No Such Thing as a Monolingual Text! New Tools for Literary Scholarship. *Polyphonie* 1. https://orbilu.uni.lu/handle/10993/31641 (accessed 30 August 2022).

Digitales Wörterbuch der deutschen Sprache. 2022. https://www.dwds.de/d/korpora/dtaxl (accessed 30 August 2022).

Domokos, Johanna. 2018. *Endangered Literature: Essays on Translingualism, Interculturality, and Vulnerability.* Budapest: Károli Books/L'Harmattan.

Domokos, Johanna; Sanna Grund, Heidi Grönstrand, Hanna-Leena Nissilä, Sabira Ståhlberg & Gruppe Bie. 2016. *Maailma kotona: kohtaamisen opas* [The world at home: a guide to encounters]. Varna: Lecti Book Studio.

Enckell, Olof. 1961. *Vaxdukshäftet. En studie i Edith Södergrans ungdomsdiktning* [The Oilcloth notebook. A study of Edith Södergran's youth poetry]. Helsingfors: Söderström & Co.

Fishman, Jan. 1972. Domains and the relationship between micro- and macro-sociolinguistics. In J. J. Gumperz & D. Hymes (eds.), *Directions in Sociolinguistics: The Ethnography of Communication*, 435–453. New York: Rinehart & Winston.

Gardner-Chloros, Penelope. 2013. On the impact of sociolinguistic change in literature: the last trilingual writers in Alsace. *The Modern Language Review* 108: 4. 1086–1102.

Grönstrand, Heidi; Markus Huss & Ralf Kauranen. 2020. *The aesthetics and politics of linguistic borders: multilingualism in Northern European literature.* New York: Routledge.

Grönstrand, Heidi & Kristina Malmio (eds.), 2011. *Både och, sekä että : om flerspråkighet = monikielisyydestä* [Both and: about multilingualism]. Helsingfors: Schildts.

Higby, Eve; Jungna Kim & Loraine K. Obler. 2013. Multilingualism and the brain. *Annual Review of Applied Linguistics*, 33: 68–101.

Jänicke, Gisbert. 1992. The bilingual identity of Edith Södergran. In W. Glyn Jones & M. A. Branch (eds.), *Edith Södergran. Nine essays on her life and work.* London: School of Slavonic and East European Studies. 59–66.

Jänicke, Gisbert. 1984. *Edith Södergran, diktare på två språk* [Edith Södergran, a poet in two languages]. Helsingfors: Svenska Litteratursällskapet.

Jones, W. Glyn & M. A. Branch (eds.), 1992. *Edith Södergran. Nine essays on her life and work*. London: School of Slavonic and East European Studies.
Kellman, Steven. 2020. *Nimble Tongues. Studies in Literary Translingualism*. West Lafayette: Purdue University Press.
McRae, Kenneth D. 1997. *Conflict and compromise in multilingual societies. Vol. 3, Finland*. Waterloo (Ont.): Wilfrid Laurier University Press cop.
Myrdal, Janken. 2012. Source pluralism as a method of historical research. In Susanna Fellman & Marjatta Rahikainen (eds.), *Historical knowledge. In quest of theory, method and evidence*, 155–189. Cambridge: Cambridge Scholars Publishing.
Lundström, Göran. 1950. Edith Södergrans förhållande till rysk lyrik. [Edith Södergran's relationship with Russian poetry]. *Poesi*, årgång III, häfte 3. 43–53.
Moriarty, Máiréad & Johan Järlehed. 2019. Multilingual creativity and play in the semiotic landscape: an introduction. *International Journal of Multilingualism*, Vol. 16, issue 1: 1–6.
Rahikainen, Agneta. 2014a. *Poeten och hennes apostlar* [The poet and her apostles]. Helsingfors: Helsingfors University dissertation.
Rahikainen, Agneta. 2014b. *Kampen om Edith. Biografi och myt om Edith Södergran* [The battle about Edith. Biography and myth of Edith Södergran]. Helsingfors: Schildts & Söderströms.
Rahikainen, Agneta. 2011. 'Tyskan är mitt bästa språk'. Om Edith Södergrans språkliga verklighet. ['German is my best language'. On the linguistic reality of Edith Södergran]. In Heidi Grönstrand & Kristina Malmio (eds.), *Både och, sekä että. Om flerspråkighet. Monikielisyydestä*. 61–78. Helsingfors: Schildts.
Rahikainen, Agneta, Jukka Kukkonen & Peter Sandberg. 1993. *Som en eld över askan. Edith Södergrans fotografier* [Like a fire over ashes. Edith Södergran's photographs]. Helsingfors: Svenska Litteratursällskapet.
Schoolfield, George C. 1984. *Edith Södergran: modernist poet in Finland*. London: Greenwood.
Ståhlberg, Sabira. 2023. Textus tkano tukıma. On multilingual writer language weaving strategies. Helsinki: Colorit rf (forthcoming)
Södergran, Edith 1996. *Brev. Edith Södergrans samlade skrifter 2* [Letters. Edith Södergran's collected writings 2]. Agneta Rahikainen (ed.). Helsingfors: Svenska Litteratursällskapet.
Södergran, Edith. 1990. *Dikter och aforismer. Edith Södergrans samlade skrifter 1* [Poems and aphorisms. Edith Södergran's collected writings 1]. Agneta Rahikainen (ed.). Helsingfors: Svenska Litteratursällskapet.
Tandefelt, Marika. 2002a. *Viborgs fyra språk under sju sekel* [Viborg's four languages during seven centuries]. Helsingfors: Schildts.
Tandefelt, Marika. 2002b. Viborg som språkmiljö. [Viborg as a linguistic environment]. *Språkbruk*: Svenska språkbyrån: 2. 5–7.
Tideström, Gunnar. 1949. *Edith Södergran*. Stockholm: Wahlström & Widstrand.
Ultra. 1922. Literary journal in Swedish and Finnish.
Zanetti, Dario, Livia Tonelli & Maria Rita Piras. 2010. Neurolinguistik und Mehrsprachigkeit. In Michaela Bürger-Koftis; Hannes Schweiger & Sandra Vlasta (eds.): *Polyphonie. Mehrsprachigkeit und literarische Kreativität*. Wien: Praesens. 165–180.

Part 3: **Hidden Multilingualism: Typologies and Theoretical Approaches**

Sandra Vlasta
Multilingualism in 19th-Century Travel Writing

A First Typology

Abstract: Travel writing was one of the most popular genres in the 19th century. As it often deals with journeys across linguistic boundaries and reports on experiences with other people, other countries, and other cultures, it is a genre that seems bound to be multilingual. Still, the multilingualism of travelogues has hitherto hardly been studied. The present chapter attempts to fill this gap and proposes a fist typology of the use of multilingualism in 19th-century travel writing in Europe. It discusses translingual travel writers, examines forms of manifest and hidden (latent) multilingualism, and analyzes multilingual intertextuality. In addition, the article considers the various functions of multilingualism in these texts: it may be used to create atmosphere or to confirm authenticity, it may serve to stage the author's self, it may be used to create difference, or the authors might use it to illustrate their linguistic interest.

Keywords: Travel Writing, Europe, 19th Century, Typology, Manifest Multilingualism, Latent Multilingualism, Multilingual Intertextuality, Metamultilingualism

1 Introduction

In the long 19th century, travel writing was an extremely popular genre across Europe.[1] Both factual as well as fictional travel accounts were popular, both original works and translations of travelogues.[2] These texts give accounts of very different kinds of journeys: from travels to faraway lands, perhaps exotic or made-up places – such as Ida Pfeiffer's travelogues or Jules Verne's novels that often include journeys – to journeys within one's own land, such as Heinrich

---

[1] See for instance Korte (2016: 173) and Martin (2008) who both corroborate the popularity of travel writing at the time.
[2] For translations of travelogues see Scheitler (1999) and Willenberg (2012).

Sandra Vlasta, Università degli Studi di Genova, e-mail: sandra.vlasta@unige.it

∂ Open Access. © 2023 the author(s), published by De Gruyter. This work is licensed under the Creative Commons Attribution 4.0 International License.
https://doi.org/10.1515/9783110778656-010

Heine's *Die Harzreise* [1826; *The Harz Journey*], and even within one's room, such as Xavier de Maistre's *Voyage autour de ma chambre* [1795; *Voyage Around My Room*]. Whatever kind of journey the texts talk about, they most likely include an encounter between the narrator/traveler[3] and the outer world. Accordingly, Carl Thompson defines traveling as: "the negotiation between self and other that is brought about by movement in space" (2011: 9). But how does this negotiation take place? Most likely, it includes some kind of language, or even languages. Travel writing, the written documentation of an encounter between self and other, reflects this linguistic aspect of traveling. Therefore, we may assume that travel writing, in particular if it talks about journeys across national borders, is a genre that is predisposed to multilingualism. On the other hand, we find many travelogues that include very little linguistic material in languages other than the main one, even though they may report on journeys to very distant places. By analyzing the different kinds of multilingualism in travel writing we can find out how and for what purpose travel authors in the 19th century use different languages in their texts. Furthermore, why do others decide not to mark other languages in their texts and why do they opt for a form of *hidden multilingualism*?

In what follows, I propose a first typology of the forms and functions of multilingualism in travel writing of the 19th century. In order to do so, I will refer both to findings from the field of travel writing studies as well as from the field of literary multilingualism studies. I aim to identify various types of multilingualism in the texts in question and will draw on examples from a variety of travelogues written by European authors from the 19th century. I concentrate on texts that talk about journeys that have actually taken place and that authors undertook themselves. The suggested classification of multilingualism is, of course, not exhaustive. Rather, it is intended to spark further research on an aspect that has hardly been studied to date.

In travel writing studies, translation – a process which may be defined as involving forms of multilingualism – has been addressed and has in fact been called "another form of journey" (Johnston 2016: 2).[4] However, as Michel Cronin (2000) observes, many of the studies in question pay little attention to the actu-

---

[3] Scholars of travel writing have pointed out the difference between the author (who is external to the text), the narrator (who might also be understood as the implied author, constructed by the readers) and the traveling persona (i.e., the self-fashioning of the traveling protagonist in the text). See Drace-Francis (2019).
[4] For studies on translation and travel writing, see Bassnett (2019) and Cronin (2000). For a recent overview, see Aedín Ní Loingsigh (2019) and Pickford (2020).

al linguistic processes of translation. Rather, they use translation in a metaphorical way and concentrate on aspects such as cultural translation (i.e., mediation), not least the one that the writers attempt for their readers. Rarely have scholars analyzed concrete situations of translation in travel writing or referred to translation studies as a basis for their work.[5] Other scholars are more interested in the dissemination of travelogues in translation and in the translator's role in this process.[6] Still, the multilingualism of these texts has yet to be studied in detail, even though multilingualism – be it manifest, latent or hidden (forms I will explain in more detail below) – is a typical phenomenon that can be found in this genre.

Literary multilingual studies to date have concentrated on contemporary literature and authors, while research on historical context is still scarce – a gap this volume intends to close.[7] Although travel writing has not yet been a major focus in this field, Mary Besemers (2022) rightly points out that many language memoirs, that is life writing about experiences that include language change, learning a new language or encounters with different languages, are classified as travel writing by critics and booksellers. Examples would be Alice Kaplan's *French Lessons: A Memoir* (1993), Tim Park's books on his life in Italy, as well as Vladimir Nabokov's *Speak, Memory* (1966 [1951]). However, in literary multilingualism studies these texts have not been studied as travel writing, nor have more conventional travelogues been analyzed. The genre's particularities, therefore, have not been taken into consideration yet.

An analysis of literary multilingualism used in travel writing can give us new insights into these texts: it will tell us more about the writers' intentions, the texts' functions, and their reception. This is particularly relevant because of the genre's popularity referred to above. There are a number of reasons for this popularity. One of them is that, due to improved infrastructure and increased opportunities to travel, there was an increased general interest in journeys. In the 19th century, traveling was not restricted to the highest social classes anymore but began to be affordable and attractive also to other walks of life. First forms of (mass) tourism arose in the form of organized excursions, for instance those arranged by Thomas Cook in the United Kingdom. Reading travel writing

---

5 See Cronin (2000: 102–103) and Ní Loingsigh (2019: 269) who both state this lack.
6 See Agorni (2002) and Pickford (2020) who both focus on translations and translators of travel writing.
7 For exceptions see the three articles in the section on ancient translingualism in the recently published *Handbook of Literary Translingualism*: (Bozia and Mullan 2022; Mahmoud 2022; Patel 2022) as well as Anokhina, Dembeck and Weissmann (2019).

was often a way to prepare for one's travels. For those who still could not afford to travel, the increased number of travelogues offered a way of traveling at least in one's mind (also referred to as armchair travel).

Additionally, the act of traveling was part of the project of Enlightenment: by reading travelogues, one could find out about different places, whether faraway and exotic or more familiar to the reader.[8] Travelogues satisfied people's curiosity about other countries and continents but also included information on numerous other aspects of life, such as climate, landscape, architecture, art, education, food, clothing, traditions, routines and the like. One could find out about current socio-political events, such as the French Revolution, through travel writing.[9] At the same time, in the period of imperialism, travel writing was a source of information on new parts of one's own Empire. Travel writing in colonial contexts – such as the expeditions of Henry Morton Stanley – thus furthered the – actual and symbolic – appropriation of these regions. It enabled the readers to identify with the colonized territories and with the project of colonialism itself.[10] At the same time, 19th-century travel writing furthered and fed into identity discourses in general. This is true both for the construction of collective as well as of individual identities.[11] Whereas the former was part of the development of national states and national cultures, the latter can be attributed to the growth of the middle classes that had been going on since the late 18th century. In travelogues, we can often find both discourses: people are described and presented as representatives of a nation, the narrator/traveler themself at times explicitly identifies with a nation, and/or readers are addressed as belonging to a particular nation. At the same time, the traveler/narrator in a travelogue is an exemplary individual that on the one hand can be a model for the individual's position in society and the new national collective. On the other hand, they can probe what it means to be an individual subject by exploring a distinct identity as a singular member of society. As we will see, multilingualism in travel writing partly also serves to depict, perform, and negotiate identities. Language is constitutive of individual and collective identity; that is, language

---

8 For the importance of travel writing in the Enlightenment see Jäger (1989; 1992) and Brenner (2015).

9 For travelers to France at the time of the Revolution, see Boehnke and Zimmermann (1988), Emma Macleod (2007; 2013).

10 This also led to the perception (and criticism) that travel writing was a rather conservative genre and resulted in a more concentrated focus (of postcolonial scholars) on colonial contexts in travel writing studies. See Korte (1996: 122–127), Lindsay (2016: 173) and Thompson (2001: 137–153).

11 See Vlasta (2021) for a more detailed discussion of this aspect of travelogues.

is used to construct these identities. In so doing, it not only serves as a vehicle for conveying ideas but also speaks for itself and, in literary texts in particular, gestures beyond itself. This is even more the case with multilingual elements in literary texts. In fact, the use of different languages in travel writing can either resist nationalist developments or reinforce the idea of cultural identity and/or difference.

In this chapter, I propose three main forms of multilingualism in travel writing: forms of manifest multilingualism expressed by different forms of code-switching, multilingual intertextuality, and forms of latent multilingualism, in which I will include the category of hidden multilingualism. Before I go into detail on these different forms, I would like to refer to a form of multilingualism that we find on the authorial level rather than on the level of text, namely that of the multilingual or translingual travel writer.[12] For instance, Johann Caspar Goethe, Johann Wolfgang von Goethe's father, wrote his travelogue on Italy, *Viaggio per l'Italia* (1740–1741/1932), in Italian. This travelogue, which was based on a journey undertaken between 1740 and 1741 and was intended for private use only, was published for the first time in 1932. Goethe presumably chose to write it in Italian simply because he knew the language and was able to do so. Another example of a multilingual travel writer is Alexander von Humboldt, who wrote his travelogues in French and later translated them into German.[13] There are different reasons for his choice of language: first, he participated in French expeditions and therefore also needed to publish his findings in this language; second, he was a member of the Parisian *Académie des sciences* and it was important for him to continue to gain visibility as a scholar also in the French scientific world. Finally, as a German polymath, it was important to Humboldt to be read also by a wider German-speaking audience and he thus translated his own writings into the language.[14] A final example is Georg Forster (and his father Johann Reinhold Forster), who wrote and published the account of his *Voyage round the World* (1777) with Captain James Cook first in English and then translated it himself into his native German.[15] The first edition was published in English was due to the fact that Johann Reinhold Forster had been commissioned to write the official report about the journey. However, when he

---

12 I use the term *translingual* as defined by Steven Kellman (2000), i.e., to refer to authors who write in a language or even more languages) hat are not their first one (although they might continue to write in their first language at the same time).
13 See Humboldt (1810) and (1805–1834).
14 Johannes Görbert (2014) has shown that Humboldt not only translated but also adapted his texts for the German audience.
15 The first German edition was published in 1778–1780.

submitted the first draft, the text was rejected by the admiralty. The ensuing dispute led to a complete withdrawal of his commission to compose the official travelogue; furthermore, Forster was denied permission to use the images by the painter William Hodges for his text. Still, as father and son urgently needed money, they decided to write their own version of the travelogue – based on the father's records but written by Georg, whose English was much better than his father's. He wrote the report as quickly as possible in order to publish it before James Cook's book came out. In this case, the choice of language was based on the target audience: the Forsters hoped to sell the travelogue to readers in Great Britain. Nevertheless, Georg Forster had already started working on the German version parallel to the English one, well aware of his father's high profile in Germany and the importance of a German edition. The difference in reception is also underscored by the titles of the travelogues: in the English title, the fact that the expedition was commissioned by the Crown and undertaken by James Cook is stressed (*A Voyage round the World in His Britannic Majesty's Sloop Resolution, Commanded by Capt. James Cook*). The German title, on the other hand, puts Johann Reinhold Forster center stage (*Johann Reinhold Forster's* [...] *Reise um die Welt* [...] [Johann Reinhold Forster's [...] voyage round the world]).

These three cases of multilingual travel writers – Johann Caspar Goethe, Alexander von Humboldt and Georg Forster – led to translingual texts, i.e., to texts that were written in languages that were not the authors' first languages. Even in these texts we furthermore find instances of multilingualism, for example in the form of expressions in native languages Forster records and discusses in his travelogue. The following sections are dedicated to this kind of multilingualism in the texts.

2 Forms of manifest multilingualism in travel writing

In 2011, Giulia Radaelli suggested differentiating between manifest and latent forms of multilingualism in literary texts. Manifest multilingualism denotes all forms of multilingualism that are visible to the readers on the surface of a text. It includes forms of code-switching and code-mixing, that is both language change and the mixing of different languages in order to create at a new idiom.[16] Latent multilingualism describes a situation in which other languages are not

---

16 See Dembeck (2017) who distinguishes between these forms of language change.

visible on a text's surface, when they are only implicitly present or perhaps even hidden. Translation, references to other languages and reflections on language are possible examples of latent multilingualism – they are at the center of the next section. It is important to note that a text is not usually characterized by *either* manifest *or* latent multilingualism. Rather, both forms may occur in one and the same text and to different degrees. In fact, Radelli argues that manifest and latent multilingualism should not be isolated but thought of in a parallel manner: "Bei der Analyse eines literarischen Textes sollen vielmehr die zwei Kriterien der Wahrnehmbarkeit und der Diskursivierung miteinander verknüpft werden, um zu beschreiben, wie wahrnehmbar die jeweiligen diskursiven Figuren der Mehrsprachigkeit sind." (Radaelli 2014: 165) [Rather, when analyzing a literary text, the two criteria of perceptibility and discursivization should be linked in order to describe how perceptible the respective discursive figures of multilingualism are. (my translation)]. Accordingly, although in what follows I analyze manifest and latent multilingualism in travel writing in two different sections, I view them as different forms (that have a variety of manifestations) that may occur within the same texts.

Travel writing seems to be predestined for manifest multilingualism, in particular if it deals with travels abroad. And still, in many of the texts in question we find relatively little manifest multilingualism. This is even more surprising as many of the authors of travelogues were multilingual: Johann Wolfgang von Goethe, for instance, knew Italian which he was taught by his father.[17] Similarly, Mary Shelley, who had lived in Italy for some time as a young woman, read and spoke Italian, and so did Charles Dickens. George Sand understood Spanish when she traveled to Majorca in 1838/39, and Karl Philipp Moritz knew English and Italian when he journeyed to England and Italy, respectively.

A common form of manifest multilingualism is code-switching. Code-switching denotes language change, which can occur on different levels of a text: for instance, on the intrasentential level, i.e., within a sentence, when one or more words in (a) language(s) different to the main one are introduced in a text. Intersentential code-switching, on the other hand, signifies the switching of languages between sentences or, at least, between longer phrases. We can find both forms of code-switching in Charles Dickens' *Pictures from Italy* (1846).[18] This travelogue narrates Dickens' stay in Italy from 1844 to 1845. The writer had traveled there with his family after first visiting places in France,

---

17 On Goethe's language biography see Bär (in this volume).
18 For a more detailed analysis of the use of multilingualism in Charles Dickens' travelogue see Vlasta (2022). Here, I rely on this earlier research.

such as Paris, Lyons and Avignon. In Italy, they rented a place in Genoa, from where Dickens, either on his own or with his wife, traveled to various places: he visited a number of north Italian cities, such as Verona, Mantua, Milan and Venice, and eventually traveled to Rome and Naples.

Dickens uses single words or a small number of words in Italian and French in his otherwise English text, mainly to refer to realities and facts: for place names, buildings, objects, or local customs, he uses the original names. For instance, Genua's famous "Strada Nuova" (Dickens 1998 [1846]: 39, now: Via Garibaldi) and "Strada Balbi" (Dickens 1998 [1846]: 39), "the church of the Annunciata" (Dickens 1998 [1846]: 48), the "Monte Faccio" (Dickens 1998 [1846]: 55), and the "Acqua Sola" (Dickens 1998 [1846]: 55, a public promenade in Genova) are mentioned with their Italian names. The woman who guides the Dickens family through the former rooms of the Inquisition in the Palace of the Popes refers to her profession as a "Government Officer", and her original job title is given in parentheses: "How she told us, on the way, that she was a Government officer (*concierge du palais apostolique*), and had been, for I don't know how many years" (Dickens 1998 [1846]: 21). Also, references to food are given in the original: Dickens mentions "real Genoese dishes, such as Tagliarini" and "Ravioli" (Dickens 1998 [1846]: 38) and he watches "sellers of maccaroni and polenta" (Dickens 1998 [1846]: 42–43). In all these cases of code-switching, the matrix-language of the text is English while Italian and French are the imbedded languages.

The author uses these instances of multilingualism to render the text more authentic – the place names as well as the job title are verifiable and confirm the validity of Dickens' report and of his authority. Small errors, such as Monte Faccio, which is most likely Monte Fasce, would probably not have been detected by his readers. Furthermore, examples such as the ones referring to food create atmosphere, something the contemporary readers of such a travelogue would expect. These Italian words are not translated, and they are not even italicized, thus suggesting that the author expects his readers to be familiar with the Italian terms. They might have gained this familiarity from the many travel texts that at the time had already been written – a fact Dickens himself refers to in the preface, entitled "The Reader's Passport", of his own travelogue, where he mentions the "the many books [that] have been written upon Italy" (Dickens 1998 [1846]: 5). Dickens relies on these precursor texts when he does not translate certain Italian words. And he further builds on them, when he takes multilingualism a step further and even advises his readers on pronunciation. In fact, to a number of Italian words he adds accents that serve to indicate stress, for instance "Vetturíno" (Dickens 1998 [1846]: 60), "Avvocáto" (Dickens 1998

[1846]: 62), "Piazza di Spágna" (Dickens 1998 [1846]: 130), and "bambíno" (Dickens 1998 [1846]: 132). Here, Dickens assumes an almost didactic role and becomes a guide or even teacher to his audience, thus confirming the authority he has expressed right at the beginning of his text by issuing a passport to his readers. The multilingual insertions in his text present the author as an educated traveler who is familiar with the places he visits and acts as a cultural mediator for his readership – language skills are part of this expertise. It is interesting to note that despite his knowledge of Italian the traveler Dickens is never depicted as using Italian or French himself. This confirms his role as a distant yet attentive observer who is never too much involved himself and thus remains in control. In this manner, he has the potential to relate an objective as well as original view of Italy.

George Sand, too, in her travelogue *Un hiver à Majorque* (1842, *Winter in Majorca*) uses multilingualism in the form of one or more word interferences. In autumn 1838, Sand traveled, together with her two children and her lover Frederic Chopin, to Majorca, where they stayed until February 1939. In her notoriously negative travelogue, Sand uses the stylistic devices of irony and hyperbole to mock the locals and their customs. The travelers were particularly annoyed by the lack of hospitality and, at times, open hostility with which they were confronted on the island. The bad weather made their stay even worse – they hadn't expected the winter to be so fierce on a Mediterranean island. To narrate their experiences, Sand every now and then uses insertions in different languages: Catalan (the local language of Majorca, also referred to by Sand as *patois*), Spanish, English, Italian, and Latin. She does so to refer to local particularities, for instance to refer to the name of a house – "La Maison du Vent (*Son-Vent* en patois) […]" [The House of Wind (*Son-Vent* in patois) […] (my translation)] (Sand no year: 81) – or to a linear measure whose Spanish name she cites: "Le *palmo* espagnol est le *pan* de nos provinces méridionales." ["The Spanish *palmo* corresponds to the *pan* in our Southern provinces." (my translation)] (Sand no year: 101, footnote).[19] When she speaks about housing, Sand uses English, Italian, and Latin:

> Mais que dire et que penser des moeurs et des idées d'une famille dont le *home* est vide et immobile, sans avoir l'excuse ou le prétexte de la propreté? (Sand no year: 95) [But what of a family that cannot offer cleanliness as either an excuse or a pretext for an empty and static home (Sand 1956: 53]

---

[19] In an English translation of Sand's travelogue, the footnote is rendered as "Five palms make a metre." (Sand 1956: 56)

[...] comme le *cortile* des palais de Venise, [...] (Sand no year: 91) [[...] resembling the *cortile* of a Venetian palace (Sand 1956: 52)]
Ce sont de véritables préaux, peut-être un souvenir de l'atrium des Romains. Le puits du milieu y tient évidemment la place de l'impluvium. (Sand no year: 91) [They [...] are genuine inner courts, perhaps harking back to the Roman *atrium*. The central well obviously derives from the *impluvium*. (Sand 1956: 52)]

Sand uses these instances of multilingualism in a similar manner as Dickens, i.e., for realities and for local denominations, in rare instances she uses intersentential code-switching and cites a complete phrase in Spanish in order to reproduce a part of a dialogue. In this way, Sand's use of multilingualism has a similar effect as Dickens': it creates atmosphere, it stresses the report's claim to authenticity, it has anthropological qualities, and it emphasizes the author's position as an observer.

Although Goethe, once he entered Italy was glad to be able to speak Italian, there are only few instances of respective code-switching in his travelogue. In a manner similar to Dickens, he sometimes cites Latin inscriptions he reads on buildings or statues.[20] Other instances include a letter Goethe receives from home that is written (and rendered) in French and a diploma in Italian Goethe was given when accepted into the society of the *Arcadia*.[21] The latter, too, is reproduced in Italian and the author himself comments on his decision not to translate it, as otherwise it would lose its idiosyncrasy.[22] However, as a speaker of Italian, Goethe seems to want to demonstrate to his readers that he uses the Italian language frequently at the very beginning of his text. An example of this can be found just after he enters Italophone territory, south of Trent. It is a case of intersentential code-switching and deals with a rather intimate issue – the search for a toilet: "[...] drittens fehlt eine höchst nötige Bequemlichkeit, so daß man dem Naturzustand hier ziemlich nahe kömmt. Als ich den Hausknecht nach einer gewissen Gelegenheit fragte, deutete er in den Hof hinunter, 'qui abasso puo servirsi!' ich fragte: 'dove?' – 'da per tutto, dove vuol!' antwortete er freundlich." (Goethe 1992 [1813–1817]: 29) ["Finally, a highly necessary convenience is lacking, so that one is almost reduced to a state of nature. When I asked the servant for a certain place, he pointed down into the courtyard: '*Qui, abasso puo servirsi!*' – '*Dove?*' I asked. '*Da per tutto, dove vuol!*' was his friendly answer." (Goethe 1970: 42) 'Here, down there you can help yourself!' – 'Where?' I

---

20 For example, the inscriptions on the gable ends of the Villa Rotonda (designed by Palladio) in Vicenza and on a bust of cardinal Bembo in Padova (Goethe 1992 [1813–1817]: 65, 69).
21 See (Goethe 1992 [1813–1817]: 527, 570–571).
22 See (Goethe 1992 [1813–1817]: 570).

asked. 'Anywhere, wherever you like!' was his friendly answer (My translation of the final sentence)].

Thus, on the one hand, in the case of Goethe we seem to find a similar position as in Dickens' and Sand's: Goethe presents his traveling persona as the informed traveler who knows Italian. The multilingualism in this scene adds atmosphere and authenticity to the text. On the other hand, just before the quoted scene, he shares with readers his positive feelings about the Italian language – a language which he was already taught by his father, to whom he directly and indirectly refers in his travelogue. Also, we see him actively using the language; thus, he is not depicted as a distant observer, but as someone who is involved.

3 Travelogues as multilingual intertexts

Apart from these forms of code-switching, some travel writers use a particular form of multilingualism in their texts, which I propose calling multilingual intertextuality. Recent studies in travel writing have shown that travelogues are a highly intertextual genre, that is to say that the texts in question are full of implicit and explicit references to other texts.[23] For instance, Goethe mentions a book by Johann Hermann von Riedesel he carries with him when travelling in Sicily.[24] Furthermore, to finish his travelogue, Goethe cites verses by Ovid who describes his melancholic thoughts of Rome in his exile in order to express his own nostalgia for the eternal city when he had to leave to return to Weimar.[25] On the first pages of her account, George Sand names several books about Majorca that inspired her and served as sources for her own travelogue.[26] Intertextuality is thus a widespread practice in travel writing; accordingly, in current hand-

---

[23] Here, I refer to Julia Kristeva's concept and the idea that every text needs to be read in the context of other texts, in its references to other texts and its demarcation from others. See Kristeva (1972).
[24] See Goethe (1992 [1813–1817]: 344).
[25] See Goethe (1992 [1813–1817]: 654).
[26] More than a century before, Daniel Defoe, on the other hand, did not explicitly name his sources, even though he wrote some of his travelogues without ever having travelled to the place in question but relying exclusively on other travelogues (for instance, *Madagascar or Robert Drury's Journal* (1729). See Pfister (1993: 112–113).

books on the genre, chapters are dedicated to the intertextuality of travel writing.[27]

In 1993, Manfred Pfister presented a first typology of intertextuality in travelogues that comprises forms such as suppressed intertextuality, compiling intertextuality, intertextual references that pay homage to someone, and dialogical intertextuality. The category of multilingual intertextuality can be added to this typology. A number of 19th-century travel writers use intertextual references in different languages in their texts. The practice of using epigraphs, also in foreign languages, at the beginning of chapters or parts was popular with British and French Romantics.[28] In travel writing, these insertions of quotes in other languages, which, linguistically speaking, is a form of intersentential code-switching, had various functions. Like the instances of code-switching discussed above, it serves to underscore the author's authority as a mediator for the language and culture he is writing about and is thus part of a writer's "self-fashioning", as Stephen Greenblatt (1980) called the process of constructing one's identity and public persona. It may also be seen as an even deeper examination of a foreign land that is not restricted to superficial description but allows readers to immerse themselves fully in the language at least for the moment of the foreign quote. Finally, quotes in other languages may serve the authors to reinforce the general aim of their travelogue.

Mary Shelley's travelogue *Rambles in Germany and Italy in 1840, 1842, and 1843* (1844) is based on two journeys to Italy (and through Germany) which the author undertook together with her son, Percy Florence. Shelley's travelogue has a political aspect: in its preface, she expresses her sympathy with the Italian people and their difficult fight for independence (a process that did not conclude until 1870, when Italy was finally unified and gained independence). Shelley also discusses the role that other European states played in this political situation, in particular Britain, given the number of English travelers to Italy and the many members of the Italian resistance who were in exile in the United Kingdom. Furthermore, she states that a political point of view has not yet been expressed in other travelogues on Italy. In contrast, she is particularly interested in the people. This becomes obvious right from the beginning of the text, when she writes (or cites, respectively): "But to speak of the state of Italy and the Italians – / Non è poleggio da picciola barca / Quel, che fendendo va l'ardita prora, / Nè da nocchier, ch'a se medesmo parca." (Shelley 1844: vol. 1, ix) [this is no crossing for a little bark–the sea that my audacious prow now cleaves–nor

---

27 As examples for such contributions see Beilein & Schaff (2020) and Hagglund (2019).
28 For an analysis of mottoes in the Romantic era see Grutman (2010).

for a helmsman who would spare himself. (Dante 1980–1984 [1321/1472]: Canto 23, Verses 67–69)] Shelley does not provide any translation for these lines. However, the quote will have been recognized by the educated readers that were familiar with Italian literature: these lines are from "Paradise", the final part of Dante's *Divina Commedia*, the *Divine Comedy*. On the level of content, they refer to what Shelly discusses in her work, of course – one could argue that with these lines she stresses how difficult it is to speak about the 'state' of Italy (perhaps also to be understood as the 'nation' of Italy) and the Italian people, a huge task that she does not aim to undertake. At the same time, with this insertion of Dante's text in the original (further quotes can be found throughout the travelogue) Shelley underlines her political stance and takes a clear position: she lets the Italians themselves speak through the words of their most important national poet, through their culture and literature, and, above all, she does so in Italian. She thus clearly takes a stand for the Italian people and in this way uses the political potential of the genre. This is even more remarkable for a woman, as politics was a field that was usually dominated by men. However, the genre of the travelogue and its heterogeneous style that, for instance, allowed for this kind of multilingual intertextuality, enabled female writers to comment on socio-political events.[29]

The intertextual multilingualism in Shelley's text – which is not restricted to Dante, but includes quotes of Giovanni Battista Niccolini and Catullus (in Latin) – is furthermore a marker that distinguishes her account from the many other travelogues on Italy. As Hagglund reminds us, the multiplicity of voices created through intertextual and, in Shelley's case, multilingual references underscore the extent to which the travelogue's uniqueness lies in "the combination, the meeting, the encounter" (Hagglund 2019: 134). Finally, by quoting Dante in Italian, Shelley invites her readers to engage and actively interact (perhaps by consulting a dictionary or a translation of the *Commedia*) with the language and culture on which she is reporting, thus reminding her readers that travelling essentially involves interaction and confrontation with something new.

In Karl Philipp Moritz' travelogue *Reisen eines Deutschen in England im Jahre 1782* (1783) [*Journeys of a German in England. A Walking Tour of England in 1782*], the use of multilingual intertextuality has quite a different function.[30]

---

29 See Butler (2021) for a detailed analysis of female British travel writers in Italy and their political roles.
30 I am aware that Moritz's travelogue strictly speaking was published at the end of the 18th rather than in the 19th century. Still, its publication year falls into what has been called the "long 19th century". Furthermore, the text is an example of the modern, more subjective and

Moritz' Dante is John Milton whose *Paradise Lost* (1667) he takes with him on the journey. German readers were familiar with Milton's book, which had been translated into German by Johann Jakob Bodmer.[31] Still, his detailed reading of the text as well as the many quotes in the English original reinforce Moritz' image as an expert on English literature. Furthermore, they are part of the newness of his travelogue, which distinguishes itself from other German travelogues about England for different reasons. First, because Moritz often travelled by foot and wrote about this experience in his travelogue. Second, because of its itinerary: while most travelers would travel to and report on London, "the university cities of Oxford and Cambridge, spa towns such as Bath and also the new industrial centres, for example Manchester and Birmingham" (Maurer 2010: 19), Moritz chose to travel further North and visit Peak cavern in the Peak District. Third, his travelogue is part of a new tradition of travel writing that concentrates on the travelling subject and the impressions the journey makes on them. His reading of Milton, depicted and reflected in the travelogue, is part of this experience. For instance, Moritz frames his visit to the Peak cavern with lengthy quotes in English from *Paradise Lost* that at one point seem the perfect description of the landscape he sees when approaching the cave: "– – delicious Paradise, / Now nearer crowns with her Enclosure green. / As with a rural Mound, the Champain [Champion] Head / Of a steep Wilderness, Whose hairy sides / With Thicket overgrown, grottesque and wild. / Access denied. – –" (Moritz 2000 [1783]: 132–133). Like Shelley, he refrains from translating the quotes but rather delegates this work to his readers.

This non-translation – in Moritz' case just like in Shelley's – can be read as having an elitist ring to it, addressed to a particular group of readers, namely those whose education allows them not only to recognize but also to understand Milton (or Dante) in the original, within the very broad audience to which travel writing appealed. Still, Moritz was also a teacher of English and in fact a year later published an English textbook for a German readership.[32] His quote in the original, just like the remarks he makes in the course of his travelogue about pronunciation and use of words and phrases may have been part of his linguistic interest and pedagogical endeavor and not intended as snobbish at all.

---

aesthetically interested travelogue that is concentrated on the traveling subject rather than on the encyclopaedic collection of scientific facts that started to develop around 1800.

31 I take this information on the translations of Milton from Kofler (2007: 1726–1727) and Maurer (2010: 22).

32 For the textbook see Moritz (1784) as well as Schmidt (1993) for more information on Moritz as a language teacher and linguist.

4 Forms of latent multilingualism and other forms of hidden multilingualism in travel writing

Radaelli calls latent instances of multilingualism "wenn andere Sprachen nur unterschwellig vorhanden und nicht unmittelbar wahrnehmbar sind; er weist also auf den ersten Blick eine einsprachige Oberfläche auf" [if other languages are present only implicitly and are not directly perceptible; the text therefore, at first sight, features a monolingual surface (my translation)] (Radaelli 2001: 61). Typical examples of this kind of multilingualism are dialogs that take place in a different language than in the one in which they are expressed (because it is made clear that the protagonists speak in a different language) or documents that are cited in the text's main/matrix-language but were written in a different one (e.g. letters). Radaelli furthermore cites translations, references to other languages and reflections on language as examples of latent multilingualism.

Natalia Blum-Barth (2020) uses the term "exkludierte Mehrsprachigkeit" [excluded multilingualism] to refer to a similar phenomenon, namely to denote "wenn im Text eine andere Sprache erwähnt oder thematisiert wird, ohne dass sie die Basissprache des Textes beeinflusst" [if another language is mentioned or thematized in the text without influencing the basic language of the text (my translation)] (Blum-Barth 2020: 61). According to Blum-Barth, excluded multilingualism talks about multilingualism without putting it into practice in the actual language of the text. She cites "inquit formula" (Blum-Barth 2020: 61) (e.g. he said in English/in French etc.) and references to other languages as its two main forms.

Rather than an exclusion of multilingualism, I would prefer to see latent multilingualism as a form of hidden multilingualism and agree with Johanna Domokos and Marianna Deganutti (2022) who have coined another term for this phenomenon, namely zero-degree code-switching, which they define thus: "[...] scenes where the story de facto happens in another language, but the cinematic or literary narrator does not address this phenomenon, and the characters speak the language of the targeted audience." (Domokos 2018: 46) Reading this kind of latent multilingualism as a hidden, implicit, or zero-degree form of code switching, means acknowledging processes of translanguaging within a text, despite their invisibility on the surface or at first glance. In the case of 19th-

century travel writing, it is indeed very useful to read texts for this kind of multilingualism, as this is the most common form we find in them.[33]

At times, latent forms of multilingualism may be so obvious that they go unnoticed by the reader (and thus, again, seem hidden): the multilingual authors I mentioned in the first part of this chapter are examples of this. Forster's travelogue in English, Humboldt's travel writing in French, Goethe's personal travel notes in Italian are at first sight monolingual texts (although they all also include instances of manifest multilingualism). Yet, at the same time they are overtly multilingual/translingual, written in a language that is not their author's first language.

Metamultilingualism, too, is a form of multilingualism that does not appear in the form of code-switching or code-mixing on the surface of a text. It is a term I use to refer to instances, in which multilingualism, language learning or living in different languages is mentioned in a text and reflected upon. Elke Sturm-Trigonakis (2007; 2013) has used the term metalingualism in a similar manner to refer to cases in which a text focuses on language or multilingualism on the level of discourse.

In the *Italienischer Reise*, Goethe's entry into the italophone part of Italy is marked by metamultilingualism, when he happily notes "Nun hatte ich zum erstenmal einen stockwelschen Postillon; der Wirt spricht kein Deutsch, und ich muß nun meine Sprachkünste versuchen. Wie froh bin ich, daß nunmehr die geliebte Sprache lebendig, die Sprache des Gebrauchs wird!" (Goethe 1992 [1813–1817]: 28) [The innkeeper speaks no German and I must put my linguistic talents to the test. How happy I am that, from now on, a language I have always loved will be the living common speech. (Goethe 1970: 41)] Here, Goethe expresses his positive feelings about Italian exclusively in German. At the same time, readers are informed that from this point onwards, the traveler will be using mainly Italian rather than his native German. To stress this, the section is succeeded by the cited scene cited above (the infamous search for the toilet) where the latent, metamultilingualism is followed by manifest multilingualism.

Many accounts about scenes with locals and narrations about conversations travelers have with people from a place are instances of latent multilingualism if they are given in the main/matrix-language of the text. For instance, although Johann Gottfried Seume in his travelogue to Italy, *Spaziergang nach Syrakus im Jahre 1802* (1803) [Walk to Syracuse in 1802], at times recounts dialogs in French, a language that he could assume his readers would understand, he

---

[33] See Domokos and Deganutti (2022) who underscore that zero-degree code-switching is both a literary strategy and an analytic approach to reading texts.

restricts himself to single-word code-switching in the case of Italian and, more often, resorts to latent multilingualism when he describes conversations that took place in Italian using German, the matrix-language of the text.

Apart from such encounters with locals (inevitable and often described with regard to the practical aspects of traveling – border crossing, finding accommodation and food, entering museums and other sights etc.), also confrontations with other travelers may lead to situations of multilingualism. For instance, in Caserta, Goethe spends evenings at the British ambassador, Sir William Hamilton, and his wife's, the famous Lady Hamilton, place.[34] The supposed multilingualism in these scenes is not reproduced in the text at all.

Fanny Lewald dedicates a whole chapter of her Italian travelogue *Italienisches Bilderbuch* (1847) [Italian Picturebook] to other travelers that are present in Rome, mainly English, Germans, and French.[35] She talks about their manners, about the infrastructure for travelers from particular countries, such as libraries and food stores, and about the various foreign artists that live in Rome. Lewald is particularly critical of the English, who visit Italy in high numbers, travel with their whole families and behave like tourists, i.e., they wear comfortable clothes made for traveling and always consult their guidebook, the red *Murray*.[36] Eventually, she even exclaims "Diese Engländer sind eine Plage" [These English are a nuisance; my translation] (Lewald 1992 [1847]: 119). Lewald describes several scenes in which she listens in on conversations between foreigners; one could almost hear the different languages that are implicitly present in these instances. Still, Lewald does not render them on the surface of her text – another form of hidden multilingualism.

5 Conclusion

The 19th century is often perceived as the century of nation-building, in which national languages and literatures were formed and thus monolingualism was the aspired norm. In such an environment, there was presumably little space for multilingualism in printed texts. However, we ought to ask ourselves if this view

---

34 See Goethe (1992 [1813–1817]: 257–258).
35 See Lewald (1992 [1847]: 118–126).
36 See Lewald (1992 [1847]: 118). Perceiving other foreigners as mere tourists whereas the narrators are the real travelers who actually see, experience, and understand a place has been identified as a common motif in travel writing, for instance by Thompson (2011: 122–124). For an analysis of the chapter in Lewald's travelogue see Vlasta (2020).

is the result of a 20th- and 21st-century point of view that is often influenced by what Yasemin Yildiz called the "monolingual paradigm" (Yildiz 2012). When analyzing the highly popular genre of 19th-century travel writing, we see that in fact it is a highly multilingual genre that is full of manifest and latent multilingualism as well as multilingual intertextual references. Especially with regard to the latter, authors obviously presumed that their readers would be able to understand the references; thus, we can also assume a multilingual readership. What is more, the use of different languages is usually not reflected in these texts. This might be part of the authors' self-fashioning: for instance, Dickens as well as Shelley simply present themselves as knowing the other language without having to comment on this knowledge. Their linguistic skills corroborate their authority. But the lack of reflection on multilingualism might also mirror the genre's conventions at the time, the authors' and readers' expectations. Like other literary strategies that were developed and implemented in travel writing from the beginning of the long 19th century onwards, multilingualism came to stay: also today, travelogues are a highly multilingual genre, be it in the form of travel books, travel blogs, travel vlogs or other formats.

The typology presented in this chapter is a first attempt to grasp the different forms of multilingualism in 19th-century travel writing. Its intention is to initiate more research on the subject in order to arrive at a comprehensive overview of the different forms, also in travelogues from different cultural and linguistic realms.

6 References

Agorni, Mirella. 2002. *Translating Italy for the Eighteenth Century: British Women, Translation and Travel Writing (1739–1797)*. Abingdon: Routledge.
Anokhina, Olga, Till Dembeck, Dirk Weissmann (eds.). 2019. *Mapping Multilingualism in 19th Century European Literatures/Le plurilinguisme dans les littératures européennes du XIXe siècle*. Zurich: LIT.
Bassnett, Susan. 2019. Translation and Travel Writing. In Nandini Das & Tim Youngs (eds.), *The Cambridge History of Travel Writing*, 550–564. Cambridge: Cambridge University Press.
Beilein, Julia & Barbara Schaff. 2020. Intertextual Travel Writing. In Barbara Schaff (ed.), *Handbook of British Travel Writing*, 113–223, Berlin/Boston: De Gruyter.
Besemers, Mary. 2022. Translingual Memoir. In Steven Kellman & Natasha Lvovich (eds.), *Routledge Handbook of of Literary Translingualism*, 3–17, New York/Abingdon: Routledge.
Blum-Barth, Natalia. 2020. '[W]enn man schreibt, muss man […] die anderen Sprachen aussperren' Exkludierte Mehrsprachigkeit in Olga Grjasnowas Roman *Gott ist nicht schüchtern*. In Barbara Siller & Sandra Vlasta (eds.), *Literarische (Mehr-)Sprachreflexionen*, 49–67. Vienna: Praesens.

Boehnke, Heiner & Harro Zimmermann (eds.). 1988. *Reiseziel Revolution. Berichte deutscher Reisender aus Paris 1789–1805*. Reinbek: Rowohlt.
Bozia, Eleni & Alex Mullen. 2022. Literary Translingualism in the Greek and Roman Worlds. In Steven Kellman & Natasha Lvovich (eds.), *Routledge Handbook of of Literary Translingualism*, 45–59, New York/Abingdon: Routledge.
Brenner, Peter J. 2015. Reisen. In Heinz Thoma (ed.), *Handbuch Europäische Aufklärung. Begriffe, Konzepte, Wirkung*, 429–438. Heidelberg: J. B. Metzler.
Butler, Rebecca. 2021. *Revisiting Italy: British Women Travel Writers and the Risorgimento (1844–61)*. New York/Abingdon: Routledge.
Cronin, Michael. 2000. *Across the Lines: Travel, Language, Translation*. Cork: Cork University Press.
Dante, Alighieri. 1980–1984 [1321/1472]. *Divine comedy* translated by Allen Mandelbaum available: http://www.worldofdante.org/paradiso1.html (accessed 30 September 2022)
Dembeck, Till. 2017. Sprachwechsel und Sprachmischung. In Till Dembeck & Rolf Parr (eds.), *Literatur und Mehrsprachigkeit. Ein Handbuch*, 125–166. Tübingen: Narr Francke Attempto.
Dickens, Charles. 1998 [1846]. *Pictures from Italy*. London: Penguin Books.
Domokos, Johanna. 2018. Multilingualism in the Contemporary Finnish literature (Suomen kirjallisuus). In Johanna Domokos & Johanna Laakso (eds.), *Multilingualism and Multiculturalism in Finno-Ugric literatures 2*, 39–60. Münster: LIT Verlag.
Domokos, Johanna & Marianna Deganutti. 2022. Zero degree code-switching and the narrative framework. *Polyphonie* 11(1). http://www.polyphonie.at/?op=publicationplatform&sub=viewcontribution&contribution=268 (accessed 30 September 2022).
Drace-Francis, Alex. 2019. Persona. In Charles Forsdick, Zoë Kinsley & Kathryn Walchester (eds), *Keywords for Travel Writing Studies: A Critical Glossary*, 181–183. London: Anthem Press.
Forster, Georg. 1777. *A Voyage round the World in His Britannic Majesty's Sloop Resolution, Commanded by Capt. James Cook, during the Years, 1772, 3, 4, and 5*. London: B. White.
Forster, Georg. 1778 (vol. 1)/1780 (vol. 2). *Johann Reinhold Forster's [...] Reise um die Welt während den Jahren 1772 bis 1775*. Berlin: Haude und Spener.
Görbert, Johannes. 2014. *Die Vertextung der Welt. Forschungsreisen als Literatur bei Georg Forster, Alexander von Humboldt und Adelbert von Chamisso*. Berlin/München/Boston: De Gruyter.
Goethe, Johann Caspar. 2017 [1932]. *Viaggio per l'Italia*. Albert Meier & Heide Hollmer (eds.). Acireale: Bonanno.
Goethe, Johann Wolfgang von. 1992 [1813–1817]. *Italienische Reise*. Munich: Carl Hanser.
Goethe, Johann Wolfgang von. 1970. *Italian Journey*. London: Penguin.
Greenblatt, Stephen. 1980. *Renaissance Self-Fashioning. From More to Shakespeare*. Chicago: University of Chicago Press.
Grutman, Rainier. 2010. How to do things with mottoes: recipes from the Romantic era (with special reference to Stendhal). *Neohelicon* 37. 139–153.
Hagglund, Betty. 2019. Intertextuality. In: Charles Forsdick, Zoë Kinsley & Kathryn Walchester, (eds.), *Keywords for Travel Writing Studies: A Critical Glossary*, 133–135. London: Anthem Press.
Heine, Heinrich. 2016 [1826] *Die Harzreise*. Stuttgart: Reclam.

Humboldt, Alexander von. 1810–1813. *Vues des Cordillères et Monuments des Peuples Indigènes de l'Amérique*. Paris: F. Schoell.
Humboldt, Alexander von. 1805–1834. *Voyage aux régions équinoxiales du Nouveau Continent: fait en 1799, 1800, 1801, 1803 et 1804*. Paris: F. Schoell.
Jäger, Hans-Wolf. 1989. Reisefacetten der Aufklärungszeit. In Peter Brenner (ed.), *Der Reisebericht. Die Entwicklung einer Gattung in der deutschen Literatur*, 261–283. Frankfurt am Main: Suhrkamp.
Jäger, Hans-Wolf (ed.). 1992. *Europäisches Reisen im Zeitalter der Aufklärung*. Heidelberg: Winter.
Johnston, Judith. 2016 [2013]. *Victorian Women and the Economies of Travel, Translation and Culture 1830–1870*. London/New York: Routledge.
Kellman, Steven G. 2000. *The Translingual Imagination*. Lincoln/London: University of Nebraska Press.
Kofler, Peter. 2007. Übersetzung und Modellbildung: Klassizistische und antiklassizistische Paradigmen für die Entwicklung der deutschen Literatur im 18. Jahrhundert. In Harald Kittel, Armin Paul Frank, Norbert Greiner, Theo Hermans, Werner Koller, José Lambert, & Fritz Paul (eds.). *Übersetzung. Translation, Traduction. Ein internationales Handbuch zur Übersetzungsforschung. An International Encyclopedia of Translation Studies. Encyclopédie internationale de le recherche sur la traduction*, 1723–37, vol. 2. Berlin/New York: De Gruyter.
Korte, Barbara. 1996. *Der englische Reisebericht. Von der Pilgerfahrt bis zur Postmoderne*. Darmstadt: Wissenschaftliche Buchgesellschaft.
Korte, Barbara. 2016. Western Travel Writing, 1750–1950. In Carl Thompson (ed.), *The Routledge Companion to Travel Writing*, 173–184. New York/Abingdon: Routledge.
Kristeva, Julia. 1972. Probleme der Textstrukturation. In Heinz Blumensath (ed.), *Strukturalismus in der Literaturwissenschaft*, 243–263, Cologne: Kiepenheuer & Witsch.
Lewald, Fanny. 1992 [1847]. *Italienisches Bilderbuch*. Frankfurt am Main: Ulrike Helmer.
Lindsay, Claire. 2016. Travel Writing and Postcolonial Studies. In Carl Thompson (ed.), *The Routledge Companion to Travel Writing*, 25–34. New York/Abingdon: Routledge.
Loingsigh, Aedín Ní. Translation. In Charles Forsdick, Zoë Kinsley & Kathryn Walchester (eds.), *Keywords for Travel Writing Studies: A Critical Glossary*, 259–261. London: Anthem Press.
Macleod, Emma. 2007. British Attitudes to the French Revolution. *Historical Journal* 50 (3). 689–709.
Macleod, Emma. 2013. British Spectators British Spectators of the French Revolution: The View from Across the Channel. *Groniek* 197. 377–392.
Maistre, Xavier de. 1795. *Voyage autour de ma chambre*. Lausanne: Isaac Hignou.
Martin, Alison E. 2008. *Moving Scenes. The Aesthetic of German Travel Writing on England 1783–1830*. London: Legende.
Mahmoud, Alaaeldin. 2022. Literary Translingual Practices in the Persianate World: Past and Present. In Steven Kellman & Natasha Lvovich (eds.), *The Routledge Handbook of Literary Translingualism*, 60–70. New York/Abingdon: Routledge.
Michael Maurer. 2010. Anglophilie. In *EGO*. http://ieg-ego.eu/en/threads/models-and-stereotypes/anglophilia/michael-maurer-anglophilia?set_language=en&-C= (accessed 30 September 2022).
Moritz, Karl Philipp. 2000 (1783). *Reisen eines Deutschen in England im Jahre 1782*. Frankfurt am Main/Leipzig: Insel.

Moritz, Karl Philipp. 2009. *Journeys of a German in England. A Walking Tour of England in 1782.* London: Eland.

Moritz, Karl Philipp. 1784. *Englische Sprachlehre für die Deutschen.* Berlin: Wever.

Patel, Deven M. 2022. The Curious Case of Sanskrit Literary Translingualism. In Steven Kellman & Natasha Lvovich (eds.), *The Routledge Handbook of Literary Translingualism,* 71–82. New York/Abingdon: Routledge.

Pfister, Manfred. 1993. Intertextuelles Reisen, oder: Der Reisebericht als Intertext. In Herbert Foltinek (ed.), *Tales and „their telling difference. Zur Theorie und Geschichte der Narrativik,* 109–132. Heidelberg: Winter.

Pickford, Susan. 2020. Travel Writing and Translation. In Barbara Schaff (ed.) *Handbook of British Travel Writing,* 79–94. Berlin/Boston: De Gruyter.

Radaelli, Giulia. 2011. *Literarische Mehrsprachigkeit. Sprachwechsel bei Elias Canetti und Ingeborg Bachmann.* Berlin: Akademie Verlag.

Sand, George. No year. *Un hiver à Majorque* (La Bibliothèque électronique du Québec, Volume 49: 1.2. https://beq.ebooksgratuits.com/vents/sand-majorque.pdf (accessed 30 September 2022)

Sand, George. 1956. *Winter in Majorca.* Mallorca: Valldemosa Edition.

Schmidt, Hartmut. 1993. Karl Philipp Moritz, der Linguist. In Heide Hollmer (ed.), *Karl Philipp Moritz,* 100–106. Munich: Edition Text + Kritik.

Seume, Johann Gottfried. 2010 [1803]. *Spaziergang nach Syrakus im Jahre 1802.* Frankfurt am Main/Leipzig: Insel.

Shelley, Mary. 1844. *Rambles in Germany and Italy in 1840, 1842, and 1843.* 2 vol. London: Edward Moxon.

Scheitler, Irmgard. 1999. *Gattung und Geschlecht: Reisebeschreibungen deutscher Frauen 1780–1850.* Tübingen: Max Niemeyer.

Sturm-Trigonakis, Elke. 2007. *Global playing in der Literatur. Ein Versuch über die Neue Weltliteratur.* Würzburg: Königshausen & Neumann.

Sturm-Trigonakis, Elke. 2013. *Comparative Cultural Studies and the New Weltliteratur.* West Lafayette: Purdue University Press.

Thompson, Carl. 2001. *Travel Writing.* Abingdon: Routledge.

Vlasta, Sandra. 2020. Writing the Nation, Writing the Self: Discourses of Identity in Fanny Lewald's *Italienisches Bilderbuch* and George Sand's *Un hiver à Majorque.* In Norbert Bachleitner, Achim Hölter & John A. McCarthy (eds.), *Taking Stock – Twenty-Five Years of Comparative Literary Research,* 270–287. Leiden: Brill | Rodopi.

Vlasta, Sandra. 2021. Narrating the Other, Narrating the Self. Intertextuality and Multilingualism as Literary Strategies of Identity Negotiation in European Travel Writing in the Nineteenth-Century. *CompLit. Journal of European Literature, Arts and Society* 2(2). 21–36.

Vlasta, Sandra. 2022. Imagology and the Analysis of Identity Discourses in Late Eighteenth- and Nineteenth-Century European Travel Writing by Charles Dickens and Karl Philipp Moritz. In Katharina Edtstadler, Sandra Folie & Gianna Zocco (eds.), *New Perspectives on Imagology,* 112–127. Leiden/Boston: Brill | Rodopi.

Willenberg, Jennifer. 2012. ‚Dieses ist das erste weltliche Buch, das ich gelesen …'. Leser deutscher Übersetzungen aus dem Englischen im 18. Jahrhundert. In Norbert Bachleitner & Murray Hall (eds.), ‚*Die Bienen fremder Literaturen': Der literarische Transfer zwischen Großbritannien, Frankreich und dem deutschsprachigen Raum im Zeitalter der Weltliteratur (1770–1850),* 45–58. Wiesbaden: Harrassowitz.

Yildiz, Yasemin. 2012. *Beyond the Mother Tongue: The Postmonolingual Condition*. New York: Fordham University Press.

Marília Jöhnk

Literary Multilingualism and Women's Writing in 19th Century Europe

Translingualism and Gender in Madame de Staël and Leonor de Almeida

Abstract: The following paper analyzes multilingual writing techniques that can be found in the work of Germaine de Staël (1766–1817) and Leonor de Almeida (1750–1839). Despite their central position within French and Portuguese literary history, the translingual dimension of both writer's oeuvre remains hidden. The following analysis concentrates on Madame de Staël's translation from Johann Wolfgang von Goethe's ballad *The Fisherman*. In the case of Leonor de Almeida, I investigate exophone writing techniques and code-switching in her letter exchange with Teresa de Mello Breyner and in a poem written entirely in French. After referring to convergences between contemporary translingual discourse and gendered approaches to writing (Yoko Tawada, Gloria Anzaldúa, Hélène Cixous), the paper analyzes in selected close-readings parallels between multilingual aesthetics in contemporary and 19th century discourse. Apart from a rhetoric of imperfection (Leonor de Almeida), translingual writing is used to augment the importance of female characters (Madame de Staël) and goes along with a praise of translation, adaption, mediacy, and literary reception. Those terms collide with the prevalent 19th century nationalistic discourse, which – in the realm of literature and language – grounds on the idea of a singular true mother tongue and values authenticity and originality.

Keywords: Multilingualism, Madame de Staël, Leonor de Almeida, Women and Literature, Female Authors, Women Translators

1 The gender of multilingualism

The following paper is a historical inquiry into the interdependence between translingualism and women's writing in 19th century Europe. The choice of my two case studies represents the scope of hidden multilingualism in 19th century

---

Marília Jöhnk, Goethe University Frankfurt, kontakt@marilia-joehnk.de

∂ Open Access. © 2023 the author(s), published by De Gruyter. This work is licensed under the Creative Commons Attribution 4.0 International License.
https://doi.org/10.1515/9783110778656-011

Europe: On the one hand, I will analyze a very visible woman writer, Madame de Staël, who is above all known as the author of *De l'Allemagne* and as an opponent to Napoleon, but whose work as a translator has remained hidden thus far. On the other hand, I will work with texts from Leonor de Almeida; within Portuguese literature, her name is frequently mentioned – but as it is often the case, the mention remains just a (biographical) reference, and there are very few studies and critical inquiries into her writing. Her writing also remains hidden due to the marginalized position of Portuguese literature in European literature (and even in the discourse on World Literature in the Global North). Leonor de Almeida, who was called the "Stael portugueza" [Portuguese Madame de Staël] (for instance Herculano 1844: 404; Gouveia Delille 2003: 60) was one of the key figures of the Portuguese Enlightenment, but her work is little known, which might also be due to a persisting prejudice according to which there was, despite the political work of reformers such as the Marquis of Pombal, no Enlightenment movement on the Iberian Peninsula.

Those two examples illustrate different multilingual procedures that were important for (female) authors in 19th century Europe, namely translation, code-switching, and exophone writing. Those forms of translingual writing can be considered as forms of 'hidden multilingualism', as I will explore in each section of my case-study. My thesis is that translingualism (a term I use in the present contribution as a synonym to "multilingualism") is a gendered form of writing, but this does not mean that multilingualism is essentially linked to women's writing. Rather, it provided (and provides) a space and opportunity for women to express themselves creatively – often in hidden forms. In the case of Madame de Staël, the translation served emancipatory purposes (maybe hidden or unintended) and augmented the importance of the female voice. In the multilingual writing of Leonor de Almeida, I detect an apologetic tone, which is part of her rhetoric of imperfection. Her translingual writing goes along with an aesthetic conception that praises the unoriginal, values translation and literary tradition and therefore contrasts with the idea of a true mother tongue as a unique literary language of expression.

The connection between multilingualism and female writing traditions becomes palpable in contemporary theory. Two of the most important advocates of literary multilingualism in the French and Spanish speaking world, Hélène Cixous (*1937) and Gloria Anzaldúa (1942–2004), are at the same time key figures for Feminist criticism. Cixous is famously known as the discursive founder of the *écriture feminine*; this gendered dimension of writing is intrinsically connected to her defense of multilingualism, which she elaborates in the letters exchanged with Cécile Wajsbrot (2016) or in her reflections in *Vivre l'orange*

(1989 [1979]), which are concerned with the Brazilian-Jewish-Ukrainian writer Clarice Lispector and work in and through translation.[1]

Anzaldúa, whose *Borderlands/La Frontera. The New Mestiza* recently celebrated its 35th anniversary, is another example of the convergences of translingual writing and an approach to writing that is sensible towards gender. Both for Anzaldúa as for Cixous, multilingualism serves as the expression of a pluralist belonging and as an aesthetic device that represents a non-binary mode of existence. For Anzaldúa translingualism could be characterized as a queer language, which, such as her queer readings and reflections on female writing, stands for the necessity of a "Tolerance for Ambiguity" (Anzaldúa 2007 [1987]: 101), as she states in one subtitle or in the following quotation: "What we are suffering from is an absolute despot duality that says we are able to be only one or the other." (Anzaldúa 2007: 41) Ambiguity is not only a key concept when describing the scope of belonging in terms of language or nation, but also of gender. Anzaldúa's translingualism, as we can see in *Borderlands/La Frontera*, is characterized by self-translations, code-switching, and concepts and citations from different languages (Chicano-Spanish, English, Nahuatl). Another example for this convergence is the German-Japanese (or Japanese-German) author Yoko Tawada (2018a), born in 1960, who also advocates in favor of non-binary ways of thinking gender and language.[2]

Apart from those contemporary examples, the historical convergences between multilingualism and gender can be considered through the concept of the Latin *lingua materna*, which was, ironically, *translated* into different European languages (Yildiz 2012: 147).[3] This term has been discussed in Yasemin Yildiz' study *Beyond the Mother Tongue. The Postmonolingual Condition* (2012: 9), where the scholar points out that the term *mother* tongue expresses a biological approach to language connecting one's language to "a unique, irreplaceable, unchangeable biological origin that situates the individual automatically in a kinship network and by extension in the nation". One's biological mother is not interchangeable and biologically determines an individual – a metaphor that is

---

[1] See on the translingual dimension of Cixous' writing Zepp (2019: 273–277).
[2] See an interpretation on Tawada's *Sprachmutter* in Yildiz (2012: 109–142).
[3] In this context, Yildiz (2012: 147, 247) refers to a historical inquiry into the dimension of this concept in Germany see Ahlzweig (1994). In Renaissance Europe the concept of *lingua materna* was connected to the vernacular languages and emerged in opposition to Latin, the 'father-language'. The Romans designated the first language as *sermo patrius*, stressing the male genealogy and tradition. For the context and a gendered perspective on multilingualism in the Italian Renaissance see Gramatzki (2005: 200–201).

comparable to the concept of "roots", which was prominently used in (German) Romantic discourse and later criticized by translingual theory and literature.[4]

Yildiz develops her reflections on the metaphor in relation to aesthetical discourse: The concept of mother tongue is connected to "an aesthetics of originality and authenticity" (Yildiz 2012: 9). The 18th century is highlighted in the study, because it is the epoch, in which a shift occurs towards this essentialist way of conceiving languages, associated with philosophers and intellectuals such as Johann Gottfried Herder, Friedrich Schleiermacher, and Wilhelm von Humboldt, that fully develops in the 19th century (Yildiz 2012: 6–7).[5] The mother tongue is, according to Yildiz (2012: 7), "a vital element" of nation-building during the 19th century. In this way, an inquiry into the importance of literary multilingualism in 19th century Europe can be especially fruitful, because, in the light of the described historical developments, it constitutes a counter-discourse. National discourse is gendered: Not only the origins of Western masculinity and nationalism are interwoven, but also the conception of colonialism, imperialism, and hegemonic masculinity (Nagel 1998: 249). Women were primarily considered "supporting actors" in the state's project, epitomized through the figure of the mother (Nagel 1998: 243, 256). Although many feminist movements emerged in opposition to nationalistic motivated violence, women played a significant role in nation building and throughout history spoke out in favor of nationalistic ideas (Thomson 2020: 5). Still, the sociologist Joanne Nagel reflects in her broadly cited paper on nationalism and masculinity: "I wonder whether it might not also be true that a woman has no nation, or that for many women the nation does not 'feel' the same as it does to many men" (1998: 261).

Following this line of thought, the multilingualism of 19th-century women writers constitutes a counter-narrative to the patriarchal and nationalistic urge towards a true 'native' mother tongue. Translingual women's writing – and of course, I am not using the term 'woman' in an essentialist way, which would contradict my argument – in this nationalistic climate is characterized by a 'double-margin', from the point of view of female authorship in a male dominated literary market and from the point of view of their opposition to monolin-

---

[4] George Steiner (1972: 4), for instance, writes: "Nevertheless, there is more than nationalist mystique to the notion of the writer *enraciné.*" Steiner (1972: 5) also characterizes Samuel Beckett and Oscar Wilde as "rootless because so variously at home".See for a critique on the metaphorical use of 'roots' Bettini (2018: 42).

[5] This shift in the 18th century is also reflected in Dembeck (2017a: 20) and Dembeck (2017 b: 134–135)

gualism.[6] Examples such as Madame de Staël and Leonor de Almeida – and many other contributions in the present volume – contradict the national myth of a singular true mother tongue as a sole and unique mode of literary expression and show that multilingual practices persisted in 19th century Europe – often in hidden spaces. This hidden status of multilingual traditions is also referenced in one of the few anthologies on translingualism in 19th century writing, in which the editors Anokhina, Dembeck, and Weissmann resume:

> Some writers born in the 18th century and influenced by Enlightenment traditions embodied a certain spirit of multilingual cosmopolitanism which they perpetuated far into the 19th century. Other writers from the next generations quickly understood the cultural and literary odds of nationalist agendas, reaffirming cosmopolitanism and multilingual positions long before the advent of literary modernism. [...] All over the 19th century, multilingual traditions remain largely present in the European literatures. (2019: 5)

The editors suggest a hidden existence of multilingual practices, which we – researchers and readers – must uncover. The concept of 'hidden multilingualism' will be productive for my inquiry into translingual women's writing in 19th century Europe, because it intersects with the concept of invisibility, marginalization, and forgetting, which remain omnipresent when talking about (early) modern women's writing. Both "hidden", "forgotten", and "marginalized" allude to the lack of visibility, although the adjective "hidden" also suggests that this invisibility is intended or still must be uncovered.

2 Madame de Staël and the interventions of translation

At the intersection of multilingualism and women's writing, translation is a key phenomenon. Translation is a multilingual device that creates an interlingual space between two (or more) languages. An often-cited article from Lori Chamberlain discusses the relationship between gender and translation. Chamberlain (1988: 456) begins her analysis with the famous term *"belles infidèles"*, which designates a certain style of free translation and expresses the "implicit contract

---

[6] The concept of 'double margin' was developed by Suleiman (1988: 153) as a spatial metaphor (she speaks of "trope") to explain the position of female artists within the Surrealist movement. Suleiman (1988: 170) also evokes the 19th century and alludes to the regressive tendencies towards women writers in France.

between translation (as woman) and original (as husband, father, or author)".[7] But Chamberlain (1988: 463), surprisingly, doesn't only ground her essay on historical examples from the 18th century, but also on more recent examples of translation theory by well-known authors such as George Steiner.[8] The theory of translation is "gendered" and metaphors such as the *"belles infidèles"* point out that the association of translation and femaleness often carries a sense of "discursive inferiority" (Simon 1996: 1, 10).

Especially for the 18th century the link between women's writing and translation has been analyzed in insightful case studies – recently, for instance, Sanmann (2021) published a monograph, which interprets translations using a concept of another form of creativity in 18th century France and Germany.[9] The 19th century, on the other hand, represents a forgotten century in studies on literary multilingualism, which is partly due to the fact that it is associated with a strong urge towards monolingualism, nationalism, and essentialist discourse.[10] One of the most important figures of European Romanticism is Madame de Staël, maybe the best-known French *femmes de lettres* in general. Her biography already constitutes a multilingual net:[11] as is commonly known, she had to flee France in order to escape Napoleon. She was married to a Swedish nobleman, lived in Coppet, Switzerland and travelled through Europe, visited Italy and Germany, which resulted in her famous treatise *De l'Allemagne*. Part of her engagement with Germany included intellectual friendships, which tied her to the forefront of German Classicism, such as with Johann Wolfgang von Goethe or with an important voice of Romanticism, August Wilhelm Schlegel. As biographers have noted, her castle in Coppet turned into an intellectual meeting and melting point, where, among others, Madame de Staël wrote some of her most important works (Appel 2006: 231–242). For the group of intellectuals gathered there – amongst them Benjamin Constant, Simonde de Sismondi, and

---

7 See on the concept of *"belles infidèles"* Simon (1996: 10–11). There are, however, other theoretical insights into the intersection of gender and translation, see for instance Spivak (1993).
8 See for another historical inquiry into the relationship between gender and translation Simon (1996). It is worth mentioning that Chamberlain (1988: 458–459) also refers to the intersection of the gendered concept of 'mother tongue' and translation in Friedrich Schleiermacher's theories.
9 Sanmann (2021: 28, footnote 90) also provides a thorough inquiry into the existing research on translation and women's writing.
10 On multilingualism in the 19th century see Anokhina, Dembeck, Weissmann (2019).See for an essay on the importance of translation for women's writing in the 19th century Piper (2006).
11 The metaphor of "multilingual net" can be found in the writings of Tawada (2016b).

the already mentioned August Wilhelm Schlegel – translations played a major role (Simon 1996: 62).

Madame de Staël is known for her work as writer. However, less attention has been paid to her work as a translator from English, Italian, and German into French. In addition to the aforementioned languages, she also spoke a bit of Swedish (Amend-Söchting 2015: 241) and also reflected on a theoretical level on the importance of translation in her essay *De l'esprit des traductions*, which she wrote during her stay in Italy in 1816.[12] In this essay, Madame de Staël defines translation as a servant of literature, who helps to make the 'genius' of literary works conceivable in other languages. This conception of translation is, of course, not as emancipated as contemporary translation theorists might wish. In the vocabulary of the present essay, economical metaphors are very present, which also hints that translation is a part – or maybe – at the heart of the literary commerce Madame de Staël envisions. She describes literary works as "trésors" [treasures] and regards the "circulation des idées" [circulation of ideas] as a "commerce" [business] (Staël 1821a: 387). Although the essay intends to convince Italians to translate, Madame de Staël also refers to conventions of translation in France, Germany, and Great Britain and criticizes the French for their translation style and approach.

Even though translations offered a space for female authors, not all translators were protofeminist and, quite on the contrary, many expressed conservative thoughts through their translations (Sanmann 2021: 29–31). The same ambivalence can be perceived when looking at Madame de Staël. While there are some discrete, ambiguous feminist elements in her writing, it would be more than a projection to define her as a protofeminist.[13] Biographers have stated that she, just to cite one example, didn't demand civil rights for women in her work (Appel 2006: 115). Madame de Staël had a privileged social position and didn't need translations to succeed on the literary market or to make a living. This is a significant difference to most female authors, who translated to support themselves financially (Sanmann 2021: 30). For the purpose of the present article, it is, however, important to stress that the question of female authorship and

---

12 This cited essay of Amend-Söchting constitutes one of the few contributions on Madame de Staël's translation.See for another contribution Wilhelm (2004). Amend-Söchting (2015: 241, 242–244) describes the lack of research on Madame de Staël's translations, with very few exceptions regarding her translation of Johann Wolfgang von Goethe's *Faust* and uses, as myself, the theoretical reflections in *De l'esprit des traductions.*, See on Madame de Staël's relation with the discourse and practice of translation Simon (1996, 61–65).
13 Appel (2006: 116, 150) mentions some ambiguous feminist elements in relation to *Corinna* and *Delphine*.

multilingualism cannot ignore the major role of translation, especially for economic reasons.[14]

Apart from Madame de Staël's (fragmentary) translations of *Faust* in *De l'Allemagne*, she also translated his lesser-known ballad *Der Fischer* into French, which had been written in 1778:

> Der Fischer
> Das Wasser rauscht, das Wasser schwoll,
> Ein Fischer saß daran,
> Sah nach dem Angel ruhevoll,
> Kühl bis ans Herz hinan:
> Und wie er sitzt und wie er lauscht,
> Teilt sich die Flut empor:
> Aus dem bewegten Wasser rauscht
> Ein feuchtes Weib hervor.
>
> Sie sang zu ihm, sie sprach zu ihm:
> Was lockst du meine Brut
> Mit Menschenwitz und Menschenlist
> Hinauf in Todes Glut?
> Ach wüßtest du wie's Fischlein ist
> So wohlig auf dem Grund,
> Du stiegst herunter wie du bist,
> Und würdest erst gesund.
>
> Labt sich die liebe Sonne nicht
> Der Mond sich nicht im Meer?
> Kehrt wellenatmend ihr Gesicht
> Nicht doppelt schöner her?
> Lockt dich der tiefe Himmel nicht,
> Das feucht verklärte Blau?
> Lockt dich dein eigen Angesicht
> Nicht her in ewgen Tau?
>
> Das Wasser rauscht, das Wasser schwoll,
> Netzt ihm den nackten Fuß,
> Sein Herz wuchs ihm so sehnsuchtsvoll

---

14 The tie between writing and economic factors is already stressed in Virginia Woolf's (2015 [1929]: 81) famous essay *A Room of One's Own*: "Intellectual freedom depends upon material things. Poetry depends upon intellectual freedom. And women have always been poor, not for two hundred years merely, but from the beginning of time. Women have had less intellectual freedom that the sons of Athenian slaves. Women, then, have not had a dog's chance of writing poetry."

Wie bei der Liebsten Gruß.
Sie sprach zu ihm sie sang zu ihm;
Da wars um ihn geschehn,
Halb zog sie ihn, halb sank er hin
Und ward nicht mehr gesehn.

(Goethe 1987 [1778]: 42)

The Fisherman

The water rushed, the water rose,
A fisherman by the sea
Observed his line in deep repose,
Cool to his heart was he.
And as he sits and listens well,
The billow breaks and parts,
And from the waters' churning swell
A dripping woman darts.

She sang to him, she spoke to him:
'Why lure my kind away
With human wit and cunningly
To the deadly blaze of day?
If you could know how blithe and free
The fishes thrive below,
You would descend, with us to be,
And prosperous to grow.

'Do not the sun and moon take on
Refreshment in the sea?
Do not their faces billow-drawn
Loom twice as splendidly?
This sky-like depth, it calls you not,
This dank transfigured blue?
Your mirrored form enthralls you not
To seek the endless dew?'

The water rushed, the water rose
And wet his naked feet;
His heart with yearning swells and grows,
As when two lovers meet.
She spoke to him, she sang to him,
And then his fate was plain:
Half drawn by her he glided in
And was not seen again.

(Goethe 1955: 99, 101).

Le Pêcheur,
Traduit de Göthe.

Le fleuve s'enfle, et l'eau profonde
Dans le sable a brisé ses flots.
Un pêcheur, sur les bords de l'onde,
S'assied et contemple en repos
Son hameçon et la ligne légère,
Qui vont chercher le poisson dans les eaux.
Mais l'onde paisible et claire,
A ses regards tout à coup s'entr'ouvrant,
Luis laisse voir la nymphe humide
Qui, sur son lit frais et limpide,
Et se balance et se plaint doucement.

Elle lui parle, elle lui chante:
L'esprit de l'homme est si noble et si fort;
Doit-il user d'une ruse méchante
Pour attirer mes enfans à la mort?
L'air brûlant bientôt les dévore;
Laisse-les respirer encore
Dans la fraîcheur et le repos.
Si tu pouvais jamais comprendre
Quel calme on goûte dans les flots,
Toi-même tu voudrois descendre
Au fond de mes tranquilles eaux.

Le soleil, qui charme le monde,
S'est refraîchi dans mon sein;
Et la lune, au regard serein,
Aime à s'endormir dans l'onde,
Du ciel, répété dans les eaux,
L'azur brillant et limpide
Attire-t-il ton pied timide?
Veux-tu partager mon repos?
Vois-tu l'éternelle rosée
Qui peint et réfléchit les traits?
Viens, quitte la rive embrasée,
Les flots sont si purs et si frais!

Le fleuve s'enfle, et l'eau profonde
A mouillé le pied du pêcheur;
Et son cœur, attiré par l'onde,
Éprouve un trouble séducteur.
Ainsi, de sa douce amie,

Il recevroit le salut enchanteur.
La nymphe et lui parle et le prie;
Bientôt le pêcheur est perdu.
Soit qu'un charme secret l'enivre,
Soit que lui-même il se livre,
On ne l'a jamais revu.

(Madame de Staël 1821b: 439–440).

The ballad inscribes itself in the German tradition of *"Lied"* and was consequently first published in a collection of folk songs (Kemmis 2018: 31, 48, footnote 2). The motif of Goethe's ballad is the ancient relationship between mermaids and humans and the seductive capacities of the aquatic creature. Research has stressed the role of acoustics in Goethe's poem, in which sound and the sense of hearing are especially important (Kemmis 2018).

When in fact Goethe designates the mermaid as "feuchtes Weib" [wet woman] and during the ballad only refers to her through the personal pronoun "sie" [she], Madame de Staël alludes to her twice as "nymphe" [nymph].[15] Following this line of thought, Madame de Staël inserts a vocabulary that envisions the mermaid in a more erotic and seductive way, but also directly links her to Greek and Roman mythology, while the description of the mermaid in Goethe's version suggests a more animalistic existence. The voice of the mermaid refers to the other "Fischlein" [little fishes] and complains about human behavior towards her "Brut" [brood]. Madame de Staël, on the opposite, let her refer to "mes enfans" [my children]. This humanization underlines the most significant change in the cited translation: The mermaid is not only humanized, but represented as a seductive, powerful matriarch and femme fatale.[16]

Goethe simply contrasts the world above the water with the "Grunde" [bottom], whereas Madame de Staël, however, describes the sea as "fond de mes tranquilles eaux" [bottom of my tranquil waters]. The possessive pronoun "mes" suggests that the mermaid has power and is the ruler of this world. The French writer also adds this possessive pronoun when translating another deictic reference: "im Meer" [in the sea] is rewritten as "dans mon sein" [in my bottom], which, again, suggests that the nymph is the center of the sea world and hints at her erotic dimension. The persuasive power is stressed through the

---

15 All translations, if not otherwise marked, are my own. I will not translate the primary sources entirely, but only the quotes I analyze in my reading. In my translations, I will respect neither meter nor rhythm but rather concentrate on the semantic dimension.

16 On the motif of *femme fatale* in Madame de Staël's translation of *Maria Stuart* see Amend-Söchting (2015: 260).

semantic field of the translation, given that the French writer inserts expressions such as "salut enchanteur" [enchanting salute], "charme secret" [secret charme], or the verb "l'enivre" [inebriates him]. All those examples represent significant alterations to Goethe's ballad: Whereas the German poet insists on a repetition when announcing the dialogue of the mermaid ("She sang to him, she spoke to him"), Madame de Staël decides not to repeat this verse, but instead moves away from the rather neutral description and accents the seductive nature of the water creature: "Il recevroit le salut enchanteur" [He received the charming salute]. This dimension is highlighted in Madame de Staël's translation, since the French noun for fisherman, "le pêcheur", is ambiguous, being a homonym of fisherman and sinner, 'le pécheur'.

The French version is significantly longer than the German. In her translation, Madame de Staël adds a whole verse, which underlines the role of the female figure, starting with: "Veux-tu partager mon repos?" [Do you wish to share my rest?] The increased importance of the 'nymphe' in the French version is, literarily, expressed through an augmented space. The cited verse also illustrates that the mermaid seduces through her rhetoric and, thus, through language. Madame de Staël adds a verse that implies that the nymph tries to convince through flattery, a classic *captatio benevolentiae*: "L'esprit de l'homme est si noble et si fort [...]" [The spirit of man is so noble and strong]. Goethe's fisherman is characterized by his ambiguous position, he is above the water, but longs for it. The reader of his *Lied* is left with ambiguity and can't decide who is to blame for the fisherman's fate (Schmitz-Emans 2002: 218): "Halb zog sie ihn, halb sank er hin [.]" [Half she tore him, half he sank away] For the reader of Madame de Staël's translation, on the other, it is more obvious that this powerful 19th century femme fatale must be responsible.

Through translation Madame de Staël creates her own creative space and strengthens the female voice.[17] This creative adaption of Goethe's ballad could be connected to Sanmann's concept of "andere Kreativität" [different creativity], which expresses the way women dealt with the cultural technique of translation and used it for the development of their own voices. Needless to say, Madame de Staël is far away from those invisible translators Sanmann and other scholars in the field investigate. Nevertheless, it is striking that most translations of Madame de Staël remain invisible today – translation is therefore, even

---

[17] Amend-Söchting (2015: 256, 259–261) shows in her contribution to Madame de Staël's translation of Friedrich Schiller's *Maria Stuart* that the female protagonist gains a more active part in the translation. The author also draws attention to further aspects concerning translation and gender.

in the case of such a prominent voice as Germaine de Staël, a form of hidden multilingualism.[18] Not only because the products of this important translingual writing technique remain often unpublished – as in the present example –, but also because even the translations of canonical female authors are rarely discussed in research.

3 Leonor de Almeida and the rhetoric of imperfection

The second case study on the intersection of multilingualism and women's writing in 19th century Europe concerns Leonor de Almeida (1750–1839), who became known under the penname 'Alcipe' and as Marquesa de Alorna. Leonor de Almeida stands between the Romantic period and the Portuguese Enlightenment (Gouveia Delille 2003: 60–61). Her biography is an example of a privileged cosmopolitan existence in 19th century Europe, since the Portuguese poet lived in Austria, France, and England (Anastácio 2018: 134). The early years of the Marquesa de Alorna were, however, shaped by a very confined existence, since she was imprisoned in a convent in Lisbon, Chelas, for many years for a crime she didn't commit: Her grandparents were condemned to death for taking part in a conspiracy and an attempt on king João I's life.[19] Only in her twenties was she released by the new queen, Dona Maria (Feijó 2004: 83).

Yet unlike the narrow confines of Chelas, the inner worlds Leonor de Almeida explored in her letters and poems were limitless: In those years of imprisonment, the future Marquesa de Alorna corresponded intensely with her close friend, Teresa de Mello Breyner, who is today primarily known as the author of two works: a translation from the Belgian author Marie-Caroline Murray

---
18 Departing from the work of the Brazilian translator and writer Haroldo de Campos, I consider translation as a form of reading and writing, which transgresses the borders between those philological practices (see for instance Campos 1997: 56). In their handbook on literature and multilingualism, Dembeck and Parr (2017) include multilingual writing techniques, that are also important for my present inquiry, such as code-switching and exophone writing. The importance of translation is, however, investigated in a different part of the book.
19 See as introduction to multilingualism in Leonor de Almeida's life and work my blog post for Café Lumières: Jöhnk (2020): Multilingualism in the Enlightenment. On the biographical dimension of Leonor de Almeida see one of the many publications from Anastácio (2018: 133–134).

on the French emperor Maria Theresia and a tragedy called *Osmia*.[20] A selection of the correspondence of Teresa de Mello Breyner and Leonor de Almeida between 1771–1777 has been published, but those letters only represent a small part of a much bigger corpora, that is still awaiting its publication in Portuguese archives. The edition of those letters between "Lília" (Leonor de Almeida) and "Tirse" (Teresa de Mello Breyner) gives insight into a female multilingual space. Although I will concentrate of translingual writing, translation was also very important for Leonor de Almeida, who translated many important authors from the 18th and 19th century, but only published translations from Alexander Pope and some rewritings from Biblical psalms during her lifetime (Anastácio 2012: 702).[21]

As mentioned in the introduction, a comparison between Madame de Staël and Leonor de Almeida not only sheds light on the intersection of translingualism and gendered writing traditions, but it also reveals further connections between the two authors: Leonor de Almeida reflected on the writings of Madame de Staël, on *De la littérature* and *De L'Allemagne*, in unpublished annotations, which she wrote in French probably during her exile in London (Gouveia Delille 2003: 53). Both authors allegedly met in person in London (Gouveia Delille 2003: 61–63), but more interesting than their biographical intersections are the different translingual aesthetic procedures in their writing. Acting as a source or catalyst for a multilingual aesthetic and a collective experience, reading plays a major role in these translingual literary procedures.[22] This can be observed when looking at the letters exchanged between Leonor de Almeida and Teresa de Mello Breyner, in which both women make sense of their world through their readings: Leonor de Almeida, for instance, compares her situation to Samuel Richardson's *Clarissa*: "Não sei se tu conheces a *clarisse* de Richardson. Esta casa onde te escrevo parece-me a prisão em que ela esteve…" [I am not sure if you know Richardson's *Clarissa*. The house, where I write, resembles to me the prison she was in…] (Almeida 2007: 149). The process of reading is not only a collective enterprise, as has already been shown by research on female reading practices in 18th century Europe (see for instance Williams 2020). It is above all very important for translingual literature: in fact, the library of Leonor de Almeida primarily contained French books, which shows that she lived in a

---

20 See on Teresa de Mello Breyner Bello Vázquez (2004) and Bello & Torres (2018).
21 On the translations of Leonor de Almeida see as well Gouveia Delille (2003: 61, 72).
22 This is another interesting link to multilingual writing in the 20th century: Anzaldúa (2009: 168–170), for instance, repeatedly alluded to the importance of reading for her writing.

translingual literary web, in which languages interacted and were tightly interwoven (Anastácio 2021: 145).

Writing letters in 18th century Europe, was often connected to the model of Madame de Sévigné (Kittelmann 2020: 826), to whom Leonor de Almeida and Teresa de Mello Breyner also directly referred. The work of such as authors as Madame de Sévigné or other literary figures such as Pietro Metastasio were so widely read and thus often memorized that both writers had to be evoked in their original wording, as the following example of code-switching indicates: "Desta vez posso dizer como a Sévigné *si mes pensés ne sont ici pas tout à fait noires, ells sont du moins gris brun.*" [This time I can say like the Sévigné, *si mes pensés ne sont ici pas tout à fait noires, ells sont du moins gris brun*] (Mello Breyner 2007b: 12). It might be worth noting that Teresa de Mello Breyner is not quoting Madame de Sévigné correctly – maybe another hint for the hypothesis that the words of the French *épistolière* were so present that they were known by heart and therefore especially prone to errors. Code-switching is a form of multilingualism that appears often in contemporary literature, in the present case it goes along with the process of citation and appropriation (on the importance of quotations for multilingual writing see Dembeck 2017c: 193–194). Teresa de Mello Breyner appropriates the words of Madame de Sévigné, who – as a look into the original quotation indicates – appropriates the words of La Rochefoucauld: "Quand on se couche, on a des pensées qui ne sont que gris-brun, comme dit M. de La Rochefoucauld, et la nuit, elles deviennent tout à fait noires: je sais qu'en dire." [Going to bed one's thoughts are only gray-brown, as says Monsieur de La Rochefoucauld, but at night, they become completely dark: I know what I am talking about] (1972: 272). The male genealogy of the cited words is – on purpose or unintentionally – hidden in Teresa de Mello's quote. This is especially interesting in light of the periphrases that can be found in the letter exchange: "La Rochefoucault", although spelled differently, is a codeword for Teresa de Mello Breyner's husband (Anastácio 2007: 171).

Writing in a foreign tongue often goes along with imperfection. This becomes evident throughout the exchange; the present letter Teresa de Mello Breyner sent to Leonor de Almeida is not, from an orthographic point of view, correct.[23] Instead of "pensées", Teresa de Mello Breyner writes "pensés". I am not mentioning this for pedantic reasons, but because imperfection is a central element in translingual theory and literature and throughout the cited letter exchange citations and passages in French are frequently misspelled. It also

---

[23] Those orthographic incorrections have also been noted by Gouveaia Delille (2003: 59) in her reflections on Leonor de Almeida's annotations concerning Madame de Staël.

constitutes an element that unites translingualism in 19th century and contemporary literature: One of the laureates of the Leipzig Bookfair of 2022, Tomer Gardi, writes in his best-known novel *broken german* (2016) in imperfect German. The German-Japanese author Yoko Tawada (2016a: 23), who through praise of accents, for instance, accounts for imperfection, even invites us to reconsider linguistic deviations – such as an accent, a sociolect, or a speech impediment – and to look at them as "Chance für die Poesie" [opportunity for poetry]. Errors consequently contain creative potential, a thought I would like to apply to the translingual writing of Leonor de Almeida and Teresa de Mello Breyner. Scholars working on multilingualism have elaborated this dimension, such as Rebecca L. Walkowitz (2020), who stresses the importance of 'not-knowing' for multilingual writers. Those writers look at language differently, they seek to not possess language and instead stress the importance of "linguistic hospitality"[24] (Walkowitz 2020: 324). Walkowitz (2020: 325) consequently states that a translingual literary history has to lay emphasis on the importance of "multilingual adoption, imitation, and collaboration." This leads me back to the quotation, I departed from, in which the act of appropriation, citation, and translingual (collaborative) writing coincidence.

Aside from this example of code-switching, I would like to analyze another form of literary multilingualism: exophone writing (see also Arndt, Naguschewski & Stockhammer 2007). An example of this exophone writing is a French poem Leonor de Almeida never published and which remains hidden until today, given that is has – as far as my research shows – neither been commented nor analyzed before. The heritage of the 19th century national canonization of literature could reinforce the lack of visibility, especially since the text was written in French by a Portuguese writer. The hidden dimension of translingual writing of women in 19th century Europe seems to be connected to a lack of visibility due to editorial and critical gaps.

> **Epître à une dame qui voulait se livrer à l'étude**
> **de l'histoire et qui trouve mauvais que je**
> **fasse des vers français, dissant fran-**
> **chement que je ne reussirai**
> **jamais, ça peut bien être**
> Thémire, c'est en vain que ton esprit me blâme,
> J'ignore l'art des vers, mais Apollon m'enflamme,
> Le méchanisme exact d'un vers sec et limé

---

[24] Many translingual writers criticize the idea of language as possession, see for instance Tawada (2018b: 110)

Veut une âme servile, un cœur inanimé.
La nature me guide, au gré de son génie,
J'invoque en bégayant le Dieu de l'harmonie;
Je m'égare en courant, dans le sacré vallon,
Mais sans désesperer de gravir l'Hélicon.
Peut-être malgré l'art ma Muse trop pressée
Oublie une syllabe en trouvant la pensée.

(Marquesa de Alorna 1960 [1941]: 193. v.1–10)

[**Epistle to a lady who wanted to dedicate herself to the study of history and who disapproves of my French verses, saying candidly that I will never succeed, which is quite possible**
Thémire, your spirit blames me vainly,
I ignore the art of verse, but Apollon enflames me,
The exact mechanism of a dry and polished verse
Demands a servile soul, a lifeless heart
Nature guides me, just as her genius desires,
The God of harmony I invoke, stuttering;
While being in flow, I get lost in the holy valley,
But without desperation to climb Helicon.
Maybe, despite art, my far too urged Muse
Forgets a syllable when finding the thought.]

The present text – from which I am only citing the first stanza – is an epistle, a mixture of poem and letter, and is consequently addressed to someone, specifically to an anonymous woman interested in historiography. This dimension already comprises one of the core topics of the present poem, which deals with the dispute between poetry and historiography, and, not much of a surprise, sides with poetry. The poem is situated between France and Arcadia; neoclassical elements are very present and the reader can encounter references to the antique landscapes of Italy and Greece and to the "Rhôme" (Marquesa de Alorna 1960 [1941]: 193, v. 14), which might be a confusion with the better-known "Rhône". In the edited volume of this unpublished poem, there is neither mention of a date nor a period in which it could have been written.

The tone of the poem is highly self-referential, apologetic, and addresses the poetic capacities of the (female) poetic voice. The title already suggests that the choice of French is criticized for not being the first language of the poetical voice (and, on a biographical level, of Leonor de Almeida). Apart from that, the textual subject depicts a self-defense and alludes to the double-standard of literary criticism towards male and female writers: "Je suis femme; je sais que la lyre en nos mains / Rencontre trop souvent des censeurs inhumains." [I am woman; I know that the lyre in our hands / Too often finds inhuman censors.]

(Marquesa de Alorna 1960 [1941]: 193, v. 19–20). But not only the gender of the lyrical voice and translingualism of the poem seem to be targets for attack, but also the imperfect rhymes. The exophone character of the poem is therefore connected to a rhetoric of imperfection that works on multiple layers: "Thémire, c'est en vain que ton esprit me blâme, / J'ignore l'art des vers, mais Apollon m'enflamme." [Thémire, your spirit blains me vainly. I ignore the art of verse, but Apollon enflames me.] The poetic voice describes her passion for poetry, despite its imperfectness. This rhetoric of imperfection is also mirrored in the following verse: "J'invoque en bégayant le Dieu de l'harmonie". [I invoke stuttering the God of harmony] The imperfectness of the rhyme goes along with the imperfect use of French and with a speech impediment, both are referenced through the verb "bégayer" [to stutter]. Like our contemporary, Yoko Tawada, Leonor de Almeida doesn't seem to consider this deviation as negative, but, in the words of the Japanese-German author, as an opportunity for poetry.

The present epistle also constitutes a reflection on the importance of reading, which, again, stresses the superiority of literature in relation to historiography: "On lit pour s'amuser, pour devenir meilleur." [We read to enjoy ourselves, to get better] (Marquesa de Alorna 1941: 195, v. 14).The poetic voice takes refuge into the neoclassicistic forests of reading to escape the sufferings of the world. In those forests, it encounters mythological (female) figures such as Dido, Juno, or Aphrodite. As the bucolic setting suggests, Virgil is an important reference, whom the poetical voice encounters through Jacques Delille: "Loin des yeux du vulgaire et seule avec Virgile, / Je prends de ses leçons ce qu'il dicte à Delille." [Far away from the eyes of the common man and alone with Virgil / I take from his lessons what he dictated to Delille] (Marquesa de Alorna 1941: 194, v. 11–12). Jacques Delille (1738–1813) was a contemporary of Leonor de Almeida who translated Virgil's *Georgics*. The poetical voice is interested in Virgil's knowledge, which is transmitted to Delille, his translator. She is not primarily interested in Virgil's original text, but in its translation and reception in 18th and 19th century France. "Vulgaire" seems to connect to a "common person" in the present context, but evidently the adjective also evokes a linguistic context, the *"langues vulgaires"*, the vernacular languages such as French or Portuguese. It is not the "original" that catches the attention of the poetic voice, but a contemporary translator and interpreter.

4 Translingual aesthetics and/in 19th Century women's writing

Germaine de Staël and Leonor de Almeida are two representatives of multilingual writing in 19th century Europe and were appreciated women writers. They both had a privileged social position and expressed themselves in and through several languages. Even if these two women authors are known within the scope of national literature, precisely the translingual dimension of their work remains hidden. But even in their own time they were unpublished and, thus, remained invisible and hidden from the public. My article has shed light upon different translingual writing techniques, namely translation, code-switching, and exophone writing. In my analysis, I could detect a connection between gender and those translingual forms of writing, which can also be observed in contemporary discourse, in the work of translingual and feminist authors such as Yoko Tawada, Gloria Anzaldúa, or Hélène Cixous. In conclusion, contemporary translingual theory and literature can – while being aware of the historical gap – inspire new readings on multilingual writing in 19th century Europe.

My analysis has shown that gender and translingual writing techniques are linked, even if both work differently in the case of the present examples: In the translation of Madame de Staël, we can observe significant interventions that result from her own reading of Goethe. Goethe's mermaid is transformed into a 19th century femme fatale, who has a more important role and gains, through her seductive capacities, power (and space). The German song – rooted within folklore traditions, which were often nationalistically instrumentalized – is transformed into a 19th century tale of seduction in French. Translingual writing techniques therefore corroborate, on different levels, national discourse and represent a counter-discursive practice that contrasts with nationalistic movements.

My reading of Leonor de Almeida's and Teresa de Mellos Breyner's letters has shed light upon the importance of multilingual citation and appropriation. As in contemporary theory, imperfection is a constitutive element of exophone writing and code-switching, which is not only due to linguistic imperfection but part of an apologetic rhetoric. The translingual writing of Leonor de Almeida and Germaine de Staël represents an aesthetic that is not interested in the "original", the "mother tongue", or "immediacy", but in translation, literary reception, and imperfect second languages. Translingual women writing remains hidden, given the persisting gender bias in literary criticism. It represents a counter-discourse and subverts patriarchal and nationalistic tendencies in 19th century literature, but still lacks visibility, due to an editorial and critical gap. Beneath the surface of the 19th century and the idea of a one true mother tongue, lies the hidden agenda of translingual women writers.

5 References

Ahlzweig, Claus. 1994. *Muttersprache – Vaterland: Die deutsche Nation und ihre Sprache.* Wiesbaden: Westdeutscher Verlag.
Almeida, Leonor de, Teresa de Mello Breyner. 2007. *Cartas de Lília e Tirse: 1771–1777.* Edited by Vanda Anastácio. Lisbon: Colibri.
Marquesa de Alorna. 1960. *Poesias.* Edited by Hernâni Cidade. Lisbon: Livraria Sá da Costa.
Amend-Söchting, Anne. 2015. 'Ella a rendu l'impression plus fidèlement que l'expression' – zu Madame de Staëls Übersetzung von Schillers *Maria Stuart.* In Anja Ernst & Paul Geyer (eds.), *Deutschlandbilder aus Coppet: Zweihundert Jahre De l'Allemagne von Madame de Staël. Des images d'Allemagne venues de Coppet. De l'Allemagne de Madame de Staël fête son bicentenaire*, 240–263. Hildesheim, Zurich & New York: Olms.
Anastácio, Vanda. 2007 (ed.). *Cartas de Lília a Tirse (1771–1777).* Lisbon: Colibri.
Anastácio, Vanda. 2012. Escrever para o futuro: tempo e duração nas estratégias autoriais da Marquesa de Alorna (1750–1839). In Carlos Reis, José Augusto Cardoso Bernardes & Maria Helena Santana (eds.), *Uma coisa na ordem das coisas: Estudos para Ofélia Paiva Monteiro*, 695–704. Coimbra: Imprensa da Universidade de Coimbra.
Anastácio, Vanda. 2018. Women Writers in an International Context: Was the Marchioness of Alorna (1750–1839) Cosmopolitan? In Francisco Bethencourt (ed.), *Cosmopolitanism of the Portuguese-speaking World*, 132–143. Leiden: BRILL 2018.
Anastácio, Vanda. 2021. Gendering Libraries and Reading (a Glimpse at Three Generations of Portuguese Readers). In Francisco Bethencourt (ed.), *Gendering the Portuguese-Speaking World: From the Middle Ages to the Present*, 137–155. Leiden, Boston: BRILL.
Anokhina, Olga, Till Dembeck & Dirk Weissmann. 2019. Close the Gap! Literary Multilingualism Studies and the 19th Century. In Olga Anokhina, Till Dembeck & Dirk Weissmann (eds.), *Mapping Multilingualism in 19th Century European Literatures. Le plurilinguisme dans les littératures européennes du XIXe siècle*, 1–12. Vienna: LIT.
Anzaldúa, Gloria. 2007 [1987]. *Borderlands/La Frontera: The New Mestiza.* San Francisco: Aunt Lute Books.
Anzaldúa, Gloria. 2009. To(o) Queer the Writer – Loca, escritora y chicana. In AnaLouise Keating (ed.), *The Gloria Anzaldúa Reader*, 163–175. Durham & London: Duke University Press.
Appel, Sabine. 2006. *Madame de Staël: Biografie einer großen Europäerin.* Düsseldorf: Artemis & Winkler.
Arndt, Susan, Dirk Naguschewski & Robert Stockhammer. 2007. Einleitung: Die Unselbstverständlichkeit der Sprache. In Susan Arndt, Dirk Naguschewski & Robert Stockhammer (eds.), *Exophonie: Anders-Sprachigkeit (in) der Literatur*, 7–27. Berlin: Kadmos.
Bello, Raquel & Elias Torres. 2018. Teresa de Mello Breyner, Countess of Vimieiro (1739–1798?). In Ulrich L. Lehner (ed.), *Women, Enlightenment, and Catholicism: A Transnational Biographical History*, 87–97 London & New York: Routledge.

Bello Vázquez, Raquel. 2004. Lisbon and Vienna: The Correspondence of the Countess of Vimieiro and her Circle. *Portuguese Studies* 20(1). 89–107.

Bettini, Maurizio. 2018. *Wurzeln: Die trügerischen Mythen der Identität*, translated by Rita Seuß. München: Antje Kunstmann.

Campos, Haroldo de. 1997. Problemas de tradução no *Fausto* de Goethe. In *O arco-íris branco: Ensaios de literatura e cultura*, 51–59. Rio de Janeiro: Imago.

Chamberlain, Lori. 1988. Gender and the Metaphorics of Translation. *Signs* 13 (3). 454–472.

Cixous, Hélène. 1989 [1979]. *L'heure de Clarice Lispector. Précédé de Vivre l'Orange*. Paris: Des femmes.

Cixous, Hélène & Cécile Wajsbrot. 2016. *Une Autobiographie allemande*. Paris: Christian Bourgois éditeur.

Delille, Maria Manuela Gouveia. 2003. Zu den Anfängen der Staël-Rezeption in der portugiesischen Literatur. In Udo Schöning & Frank Seemann (eds.), *Madame de Staël und die Internationalität der europäischen Romantik: Fallstudien zur interkulturellen Vernetzung*, 51–73. Göttingen: Wallstein.

Dembeck, Till. 2017a. I. Kulturelle und soziale Rahmenbedingungen literarischer Mehrsprachigkeit. 1. Sprache und Kultur. In Till Dembeck & Rolf Parr (eds.), *Literatur und Mehrsprachigkeit: ein Handbuch*, 17–25. Tübingen: Narr Francke Attempto.

Dembeck, Till. 2017b. III. Basisverfahren literarischer Mehrsprachigkeit. III.1 Sprachwechsel/Sprachmischung. In Till Dembeck & Rolf Parr (eds.), *Literatur und Mehrsprachigkeit: Ein Handbuch*, 123–233. Tübingen: Narr Francke Attempto.

Dembeck, Till. 2017c. III. Basisverfahren literarischer Mehrsprachigkeit. III. 3. Zitat und Anderssprachigkeit. In Till Dembeck & Rolf Parr (eds.), *Literatur und Mehrsprachigkeit: Ein Handbuch*, 193–219. Tübingen: Narr Francke Attempto.

Dembeck, Till & Rolf Parr (eds) 2017. *Literatur und Mehrsprachigkeit: ein Handbuch*. Tübingen: Narr Francke Attempto.

Gardi, Tomer. 2016. *broken german*. Graz: Droschl.

Goethe, Johann Wolfgang. 1955. *Goethe, the Lyrist. 100 Poems in New Translations Facing the Originals with a Biographical Introduction*. Translated by Edwin H. Zeydel. Chapel Hill: University of North Carolina Press.

Goethe, Johann Wolfgang von. 1987 [1778]. Der Fischer. In Hartmut Reinhardt (ed.), *Sämtliche Werke nach Epochen seines Schaffens. Erstes Weimarer Jahrzehnt 1775–1786*, vol. 2,1 München: Hanser. 42.

Gramatzki, Susanne. 2002. Die andere Stimme – Frauen und das Mehrsprachigkeitsideal der Renaissance. In Christiane Maaß, Annett Volmer (eds.), *Mehrsprachigkeit in der Renaissance*, 199–213. Heidelberg: Winter.

Herculano, Alexandre. 1844. D. Leonor de Almeida, Marqueza de Alorna. *O Panorama* 106(156). 403–404.

Jöhnk, Marília. 2020. Multilingualism in the Enlightenment. In *Café Lumières*. https://cafelumieres.voltaire.ox.ac.uk/multilingualism-in-the-enlightenment/ (last modified 2020) (accessed 15 June 2023).

Kittelmann, Jana. 2020. Madame de Sévigné und ihre Erb*innen. In Jochen Strobel, Marie Isabel Matthews-Schlinzig, Jörg Schuster & Gesa Steinbrink (eds.), *Handbuch Brief: Von der Frühen Neuzeit bis zur Gegenwart*, 826–833. Berlin/Boston: De Gruyter.

Kemmis, Deva. 2018. Becoming the Listener: Goethe's 'Der Fischer'. *Goethe Yearbook* 25(1). 31–54.

Nagel, Joane. 1998. Masculinity and Nationalism: Gender and Sexuality in the Making of Nations. *Ethnic and Racial Studies* 21(2). 242–269.

Piper, Andrew. 2006. The Making of Transnational Textual Communities: German Women Translators, 1800–1850. *Women in German Yearbook* 22(1). 119–144.

Sanmann, Angela. 2021. *Die andere Kreativität: Übersetzerinnen im 18. Jahrhundert und die Problematik weiblicher Autorschaft*. Heidelberg: Winter.

Schmitz-Emans, Monika. 2002. *Seetiefen und Seelentiefen: Literarische Spiegelungen innerer und äußerer Fremde*. Würzburg: Königshausen & Neumann.

Madame de Sévigné. 1972. *Correspondance*, vol. 1 (mars 1646–juillet 1675). Edited by Roger Duchêne. Paris: Gallimard.

Simon, Sherry. 1996. *Gender in Translation: Cultural Identity and the Politics of Transmission*. London & New York: Routledge.

Spivak, Gayatri Chakravorty. 1993. The Politics of Translation. In *Outside in the Teaching Machine*, 179–200. New York, London: Routledge.

Staël-Holstein, Germaine de. 1821a. De l'esprit des traductions. In *Œuvres Complètes de Mme La Baronne De Staël, publiées par sons fils, Mélanges*, vol. 17, 387–399. Paris: Treuttel et Würtz.

Staël-Holstein, Germaine de. 1821b. Le Pêcheur. Traduit de Göthe. In *Œuvres Complètes de Mme La Baronne De Staël, publiées par sons fils, Mélanges*, vol. 17, 439–440. Paris: Treuttel et Würtz.

Steiner, George. 1972. Extraterritorial. In *Extraterritorial: Papers on Literature and the Language Revolution*, 3–11. London: Faber and Faber.

Suleiman, Susan Rubin. 1988. A Double Margin: Reflections on Women Writers and the Avant-Garde in France. *Yale French Studies* 75. 148–172.

Tawada, Yōko. 2016a. Akzent. In *akzentfrei*, 22–28. Tübingen: konkursbuch Verlag Claudia Gehrke.

Tawada, Yōko. 2016b. Schreiben im Netz der Sprachen. In *akzentfrei*, 29–40. Tübingen: konkursbuch Verlag Claudia Gehrke.

Tawada, Yōko. 2018a. Eine leere Flasche. In *Überseezungen*, 53–57. Tübingen: konkursbuch Verlag Claudia Gehrke.

Tawada, Yōko. 2018b. Die Ohrenzeugin. In *Überseezungen*, 95–114. Tübingen: konkursbuch Verlag Claudia Gehrke.

Thomson, Jennifer. 2020. Gender and Nationalism. *Nationalities Papers* 48(1). 3–11.

Torres, Elias J. Feijó. 2004. 'Ad maiorem gloriam … feminae': Enlightened Women and the Introduction of Models in Portugal During the Second Half of the Eighteenth Century. *Portuguese Studies* 20(1). 73–88.

Walkowitz, Rebecca L. 2020. On Not Knowing: Lahiri, Tawada, Ishiguro. *New Literary History* 51(2). 323–346.

Wilhelm, Jane Elisabeth. 2004. La traduction, principe de perfectibilité, chez Mme de Staël. *Meta* 49(3). 692–705.

Williams, Abigail. 2020. Häusliche Lektüre: Geselliges und einsames Lesen in der englischen Mittelschicht des 18. Jahrhunderts. In Luisa Banki & Kathrin Wittler (eds.), *Lektüre und Geschlecht im 18. Jahrhundert. Zur Situativität des Lesens zwischen Einsamkeit und Geselligkeit*, translated by Julia Landmann. 29–49. Göttingen: Wallstein.

Woolf, Virginia, 2015 [1929]. *A Room of One's Own*. Edited by Anna Snaith. Oxford: Oxford University Press.

Yildiz, Yasemin. 2012. *Beyond the Mother Tongue: The Postmonolingual Condition*. New York: Fordham University Press.
Zepp, Susanne. 2019. Geschichte in Sprachen: Über Französisch und Deutsch im Schreiben von Georges-Arthur Goldschmidt und Hélène Cixous. In Marion Acker, Anne Fleig, & Matthias Lüthjohann (eds.), *Affektivität und Mehrsprachigkeit: Dynamiken der deutschsprachigen Gegenwartsliteratur*, 261–277. Tübingen: Narr Francke Attempto.

Jochen A. Bär

18th and 19th Century Linguistic and Literary Criticism as a Source of Multilingual Research

A Corpus Based Approach

Abstract: The article deals with forms of hidden multilingualism in language and literary criticism of the 18th and 19th centuries. After terminological clarifications and a brief discussion of heuristic methods, different varieties of multilingualism are examined using selected examples, mainly from German discourse, but also from contemporary English discourse. A special focus is given to Goethe as a multilingual and multilingualism-friendly author. The paper concludes with the introduction of a corpus-based approach to multilingualism in 18th and 19th century linguistic and literary criticism, presenting the project of a relational database for systematic research on multilingualism in that period.

Keywords: Language Criticism, Literary Criticism, Hidden Multilingualism, Interlinguality, Goethe, Romanticism

1 Preliminary

The title of this contribution takes two subjects for granted: a) language and literary criticism and b) multilingualism. However, both must briefly be problematized before an attempt can be made to illuminate the former as a source for research into the latter. In determining the time period (18th and 19th centuries), we make a restriction for reasons of manageability. We do not treat two full centuries here, but only one: the period between approximately 1760 and 1840, for which we can draw on a balanced, sufficiently large digital corpus (see below, section 2). Our period under review is therefore the onset of modernity: almost exactly the decades that, in historiography, are often referred to as "die Sattelzeit", to use a term coined by Reinhart Koselleck.

Jochen A. Bär, University of Vechta, e-mail: jochen.baer@uni-vechta.de

2 Language and literary criticism

The first problem to be discussed is itself to some extent a multilingual one: it is not obviously multilingual in and of itself, but a multilingual perspective sheds light on it. If this article were written in German (the author's first language), the title would be "Sprach- und Literaturkritik des 18. und 19. Jahrhunderts als Quelle der Mehrsprachigkeitsforschung". The German equivalent of the word *criticism* is *Kritik*. However, the German word is also used in contexts where English *criticism* is not appropriate – e.g., in the three Kantian *Kritiken*, for which the English language uses the word *critique*: *Critik der reinen Vernunft – Critique of pure Reason*; *Critik der practischen Vernunft – Critique of Practical Reason*; *Critik der Urtheilskraft – Critique of Judgment*. The fact that the semantics of the two English words *criticism* and *critique* coincide in a single German heteronym leads to a different semantic concept of criticism in German than in English: In Germany, language and literary criticism of the late 18th and early 19th centuries is conceived more comprehensively; it encompasses the entire field of critical philosophy, whereas in the contemporary English discourse, the reception of Kant is of no importance (cf. Bär 2015: 109–113).

The broad concept of criticism affects our selection of primary texts. The article is based on the ZBK corpus (Zentralbegriffe der klasssisch-romantischen "Kunstperiode" [Central Concepts of the Classical-Romantic "Artistic Period"]; Bär and von Consbruch 2012: 468–480), a corpus of German-language literary-artistic reflection from the second half of the 18th and the first half of the 19th centuries, which takes into account all relevant text types: Treatises, monographs, essays, reviews, miscellanies, prefaces, collections of fragments, lexicographical and encyclopedic texts, reflections, semi-fiction, narrative prose, poetry and verse, lectures, talks and speeches, dramas, dialogues, libretti, drafts and fragments of treatises, notes, letters, diaries, autobiographical writings, private writings, drafts and fragments of works and sketches (Bär and von Consbruch 2012: 475–476). The corpus has a size of about 100 million tokens. Since comparably large digital full-text corpora of contemporaneous discourses in other European languages are not available, no truly comparative study can be presented here. Our corpus is only supplemented by an English-language corpus of about 10 million tokens, which is available in the Archive "Digitale Bibliothek" (www.zeno.org); see Bär (forthc.).

3 Multilingualism

In linguistic research, multilingualism in the broadest sense is defined either as the knowledge of more than one language by an individual or as the use of more than one language within a linguistic community (state, nation, institution etc). (Franceschini 2009: 29).

Interlinguality, to be distinguished from multilingualism, can be understood as the result of active multilingualism in language communities over longer periods of time. Interlinguality means that "one language interferes with another language, so that, for example, grammatical constructions typical for one language are taken over into the other" (Bär 2021: 39). Since, as mentioned, we are dealing here with language communities, not individuals, interlinguality does concern "not only [...] the single act of speech, as for example in case of bad translation [...] or in mixing up the well-known false friends" but is "incorporated in the language system" (Bär 2021: 39).

Interlinguality is, so to speak, the area in which one language overlaps with another lexically, grammatically, semantically or in pragmatic patterns; or– no longer thought of in terms of this or that individual language – it is the area (as an independent research topic) in which two or even several individual languages participate in one other. For example, the semantic commonalities of different European languages – so-called semantic Europeanisms (cf. Reichmann 1991; 1993; 2001: 54–83; 2014; 2016) – can be considered as a manifestation of interlinguality. The individual languages then appear merely as ideal types, as abstractions of multilingual realities and can only be distinguished from one another as such. This idea coincides with a point of view that has been common in language didactics for some time:

> Einzelsprachen, wie z. B. Deutsch, Türkisch oder Englisch, [sind] als rein soziale Konstruktionen zu verstehen [...]. [...] Das bedeutet, die Sprachen existieren dieser Auffassung nach nicht per se als klar unterscheidbare und damit aufzählbare Einheiten, sondern werden zu solchen gemacht. Erst dadurch also, dass sie über normative Instanzen beschrieben und definiert werden, werden die Einzelsprachen für Menschen greifbar und unterscheidbar[1]

---

[1] Here and thoroughly: my translations, jb. – an English version of the quotations is provided at the publisher's request. I collaborate but reluctantly, because the sense of affirming the dominance of English in, of all things, a contribution to multilingualism research may well be questionable – especially since in a monolingual translation of *multilingual* quotations, multilingualism falls by the wayside...

> [Individual languages, such as German, Turkish or English, are to be understood purely as social constructs. This means, in this view, languages do not exist as clearly distinguishable and thus denumerable units *per se* but are instead made into such units. Only by being described and defined via normative instances do the individual languages become tangible and distinguishable] (Gantefort and Maahs 2020: 1–2)

To put things in linguistic terms: We can distinguish four perspectives on language. Firstly, human language in general, or the ability to speak it, which is referred to, according to Ferdinand de Saussure, by the term *langage*. Secondly, the system of a historical individual language such as German, English or Latin, which, also according to de Saussure, is called *langue*. Thirdly, a pattern of use of a historical individual language, which I call *usage* ([yˈzaːʒə]: general or more specific norms (including exceptional rules such as that in German there is exactly one designation for each day of the week, but two alternative designations for a single one, the sixth: *Samstag* and *Sonnabend*); but also general uses of language that are actually or supposedly contrary to a norm: e.g. German *wegen* together with the dative, the common confusion of *scheinbar* ("seemingly, but probably not the case") and *anscheinend* ("probably the case") or the like. Fourthly and finally, the concrete single speech act, oral or written, which, again according to Ferdinand de Saussure, is called *parole*. (Just to avoid possible misunderstandings: linguists aim to describe *usages*, including deviations from norms, but do not want to postulate or establish linguistic norms, even if they as private individuals might be invested in these norms.)

3.1 Languages and speech acts

The distinction between *langue* and *usage* is related to the fact that using construction rules to form utterances is not the normal case: language is only sometimes grammatical (cf. Bunia 2014: 54). The system postulates, for example, that in German one can derive an adjective from a noun by adding the suffix *-lich*, or that one can negate an adjective by putting in front the prefix *un-*. The *usage* (here: the norm) is that only certain cases work according to this rule, for example, *Tag* ('day') + *-lich* (*-ly*) becomes *täglich* ('daily') and *Feier* ('celebration') + *-lich* becomes *feierlich*. In analogous cases, however, there are other rules. Adjectives like *schläglich* (< *Schlag* 'beat' + *-lich*) or *feuerlich* (*Feuer* 'fire' + *-lich*) might seem possible but are not used. Negations such as *ungesund* 'unwholesome' or *ungut* ('ungood') are standard; negations such as *unkrank* (*krank* 'ill, sick') or *unschlecht* (*schlecht* 'bad, evil'), on the other hand, are not standard; rather, completely different rules apply here, because *krank* and *ungesund* are both antonyms of *gesund*, but since two different meanings of *gesund* ('healthy', 'wholesome') are involved, *krank* is not a synonym of *ungesund*. The same applies to the two antonyms of *gut*, which also are not semantically equivalent.

Usage as well as *langue* always appear as abstractions formed by *parole* in a set of acts (ideally, empirically, based on a valid research corpus). The *langue* consists of several *usages* that can be complementary, but which can also contradict one another. The *langue* can therefore, as shown above, comprise overgeneralised rules that state possibilities, while every *usage* always has a counterpart in the reality of the *parole*. Thus the transition from *usage* to *langue* is fluid, because a *langue*-possibility can at any time pass into the reality of the individual *parole* and also of an individual or group-specific *usage* – just as, conversely, an *usage* can fall into oblivion and then still exist as a possibility.

Langage, langue, *usage* and *parole* can be schematically placed in relation to each other as follows.

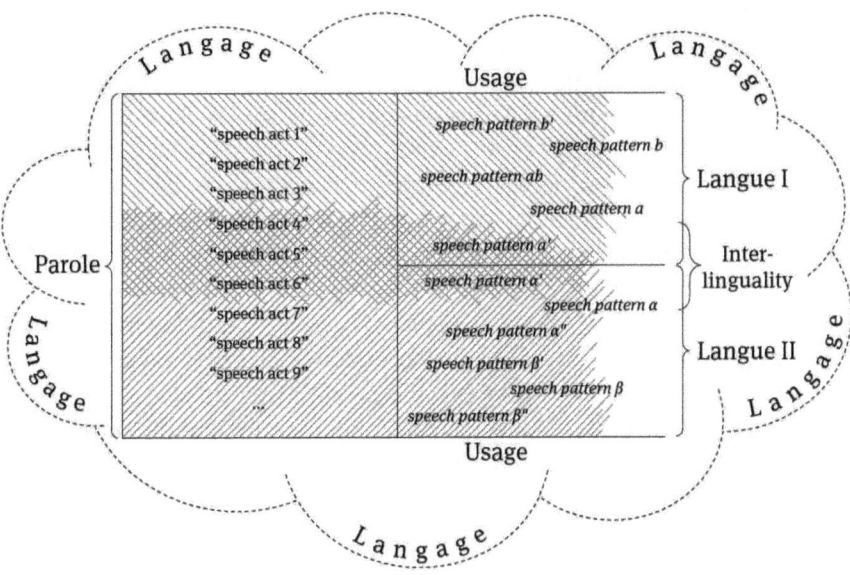

Fig. 1: Multilingual *parole*, *usage*/*langue* and *langage* (considering interlinguality)

Langage is the competence which is the prerequisite for every single speech act and thus for every speech pattern as well. To some extent, it forms the background of the individual speech act. The open transition between *langage* and *langue* perceivable in fig. 1 is intended to symbolize that *langage* does not only mean 'universal language competence' – the early childhood ability to acquire any language as a first language – but also and even mainly the ability to speak a certain language (or several). A multilingual competence can lead to interlingual code-switching, as in Martin Luther's table talks or nowadays in every German schoolyard, but nonetheless also to speech acts that even from a layperson's point of view are clearly specific to one individual language. Based on the French lectures of the Polish poet Adam Mickiewicz, Mende (2020: 33–41) has shown how complex things can be: even more complex due to multiple acts of transcription.

Speech acts are similar to each other and at the same time also different from each other, and the boundary between similarity and difference is completely fluid. The direction of the hatching in Fig. 1 represents the possibility of being assigned to a certain language. What I am hearing or reading: is it German or English, for example? – At first, it is only *parole*; whether it is German or English cannot be said exactly of individual items. Multilingualism and "translanguaging," mutual influence of languages, has always been something completely normal (cf. Kilchmann 2019: 79–80).

The attribution of a speech act to one and only one particular language system is nothing but a cultural-ideological construct, as is the idea that there are clearly delimitable language systems. Language purity as the ideal or even the normal case, lingual interference, especially in vocabulary, as a special and problematic case: this is the ideology in which we have been so deeply rooted since the 17th century that it seems the simple and unquestionable truth (cf. Kilchmann 2019: 79, 82).

Nevertheless, it is of course undeniable that one can find certain speech acts more similar to each other than to others, so that patterns can be discerned. These patterns, if they are closer to the concrete reality of the *parole*, can be called *usage*; if they are further away from it, i.e. more abstract (shown unhatched in fig. 1), they can be called *langue*. The boundary between *usage* and *langue*, as it turns out, is again fluid; there is ideal-typical *usage* and ideal-typical *langue*, but no clear-cut distinction.

Speech acts that deviate from others to such an extent that, even with the greatest possible abstraction from their concrete quality, they cannot reasonably be subsumed together under one system, must be assigned to different systems. Since System I and System II are, as we said, abstractions, i.e. interpretative constructs, they can be clearly distinguished from each other. But it is only an ideal distinction; in the reality of the *parole*, there is always a certain fuzziness, so that the assignment of a speech act to one or another ideal-typical system ultimately appears artificial and questions both systems. In individual cases, one can indeed consider a different classification of a speech act.

3.2 The case of variation

What has been said here about *parole*, *usage* and *langue* applies not only to languages such as English, French or German, but of course also to varieties, be they dialects such as Rhine-Franconian, historiolects such as Middle High German, or even sociolects or functiolects, provided they can be reasonably regarded as linguistic systems of their own. This means that the phenomenon of "multilingualism" has to be conceived even more comprehensively. Even supposedly monolingual persons can thus be regarded as multilingual, if they have only mastered a standard variety in addition to a dialect. And there can be interlingual relations standard language and dialect, just as much as between individual languages.

This linguistic observation is quite consistent with the historical-metalinguistic knowledge of language and variety conceptions in the 18th and 19th centuries (cf. Bär 1999: 372–374). That items such as "German" or "English" are regarded as "languages" (*Sprachen*) is only one possibility. They can also be seen as "varieties" (in the 18th and 19th centuries usually referred to as *Dialekte* or likewise as *Mundarten* without further distinction). In simple words: In relation to a superordinate category, a language appears as a dialect; German, English or Danish, as languages, are at the same time dialects (namely of Germanic). The change of perspective is possible at any time and on all hierarchical levels. Thus, if we want to conduct multilingualism research based on 18th and 19th century primary texts, we have to be aware that it must not only be about the mastery of German, French or Latin, but also about dialect competences.

3.3 Hidden multilingualism

Having said all of the above, it is now evident that the topic of multilingualism is broader than at first sight. However, even if we know what to look for when searching for multilingualism, it is far from guaranteed that it will be found to a significant extent; we would need to know where to look, i.e. we would need an already annotated research-corpus. However, a corpus like this does not exist on the topic of multilingualism in the 18th and 19th centuries; in the best case, we have raw corpora at our disposal that are cleanly described with regard to the metadata on authorship and text history, such as the ZBK corpus and its supplements introduced above. But despite its size, not a single hit for the terms *mehrsprachig*/multilingual** and *zweisprachig*/bilingual** can be found in this supplemented corpus. In other words: If one does not want to leave it at a few anecdotes and chance finds – A.W. Schlegel asks Coleridge to speak English because he cannot understand his German,[2] Thomas Campbell, on the other hand, mocks Schlegel's English[3] – but aims instead at a systematic study of multilingualism, a somewhat more sophisticated heuristic method is required.

In principle, a distinction can be made between two manifestations: thematic and practiced multilingualism.

3.3.1 Multilingualism as a theme/subject

Multilingualism as a topic is prominently encountered, for example, as an explicit thematization of language skills, such as in Notes 3 and 4 or in Boswell's report on Dr. Johnson:

> While Johnson was in France, he was generally very resolute in speaking Latin. It was a maxim with him that a man should not let himself down, by speaking a language which he speaks imperfectly. [...] When Sir Joshua Reynolds [...] presented him to a Frenchman of great distinction, he would not deign to speak French, but talked Latin, though his Excellency did not understand it, owing, perhaps, to Johnson's English pronunciation: yet upon another occasion he was observed to speak French to a Frenchman of high rank, who spoke English; and being asked the reason, with some expression of surprise, – he answered, 'because I think my French is as good as his English.' Though Johnson understood French perfectly, he could not speak it readily [...]. (Boswell 1791: 659–660).

Accounts of foreign language acquisition can also be subsumed under thematic multilingualism. Coleridge (1817: 201) describes how he acquired "a tolerable sufficiency in the German language":

---

2 The anecdote proves Schlegel's multilingualism as well as Coleridge's: "The melody of Coleridge's verse had led me [...] to credit him with the possession of the very soul of song; and yet [...] his pronunciation of any language but his own was barbarous; and his inability to follow the simplest melody quite ludicrous. The German tongue he knew *au fond*. He had learned it grammatically, critically, and scientifically at Göttingen: yet so unintelligible was he when he tried to speak it, that I heard Schlegel say to him one evening, 'Mein lieber Herr would you speak English? I understand it: but your German I cannot follow.' Whether he had ever been before enlightened on his mispronunciation of German, I know not; but he was quite conscious that his pronunciation of French was execrable, for I heard him avow as much. [...] 'I hate,' he would say, 'the [...] flimsiness of the French language: my very organs of speech are so anti-Gallican that they refuse to pronounce intelligibly their insipid tongue.'" (Young 1871: 115)

3 "Schlegel [...] is ludicrously fond of showing off his English to me – accounting for his fluency and exactness in speaking it by his having learnt it at thirteen. This English, at the same time, is, in point of idiom and pronunciation, what a respectable English parrot would be ashamed of." (Beattie 1855: 109)

> To those, who design to acquire the language of a country in the country itself, it may be useful, if I mention the incalculable advantage which I derived from learning all the words, that could possibly be so learnt, with the objects before me, and without the intermediation of the English terms. It was a regular part of my morning studies for the first six weeks of my residence at Ratzeburg, to accompany the good and kind old pastor, with whom I lived, from the cellar to the roof, through gardens, farmyard, &c. and to call every, the minutest, thing by its German name. Advertisements, farces, jest books, and the conversation of children while I was at play with them, contributed their share to a more home-like acquaintance with the language, than I could have acquired from works of polite literature alone, or even from polite society (Coleridge 1817: 201–202).

Implicit multilingualism can also be found, to a certain extent, as a background foil wherever the leading ideology of the 18th and 19th centuries is represented: the program of national unity and demarcation, also and especially in language.[4] Wherever there is polemic against influences from other languages (mostly in the field of vocabulary), multilingualism can be assumed as the basis of such influences – in proportion to the stridency of the polemic. And where a unitary leading variety is propagated, other competing varieties can be assumed. Linguistic historical accounts such as the history of foreign word criticism in Germany (Kirkness 1975) or the illumination of the 'language and nation' concept (Reichmann 1978; Gardt 2000) can thus also be read as histories of multilingualism; compilations of language-critical textual testimonies such as Jones (1995) can be used as collections of primary texts for multilingualism research. In a foreign-word-critical text such as Karl Wilhelm Kolbe's *Über Wortmengerei* [On Mixed-Up Words] (1809), there are explicit statements about the French skills of the author and his contemporaries. Kolbe reports of himself (1809: II–III):

> Ich weis wol, daß man mit den Namen *Pedant, Purist, Silbenstecher* etc. gegen mich nicht kargen wird. Doch kan ich das Gesum an meinem Ohr ziemlich gleichgültig vorbeilassen. [...] Meine Bildung war französisch; ich bin in französischen Schulen zum Jüngling geworden; mein ästhetisches Gefühl hat sich gleichsam in französischer Luft entfaltet; und unter allen Weisen der Erziehung ist wol die französische am wenigsten geeignet, einen Pedanten hervorzurufen.

---

4 "Vor dem Horizont faktisch existierender Mehrsprachigkeit gerade der Gebildeten wird [...] die Idee eines ausschließlichen Schreibens in der Volks- und Muttersprache etabliert, die nicht zuletzt dem aufklärerischen Projekt einer Literarisierung und Bildung breiterer Bevölkerungsgruppen dient." [Against the horizon of factually existing multilingualism, especially among the educated, the idea of writing exclusively in the vernacular and mother tongue is established, which serves not least the Enlightenment project of literarization and education of broader population groups.] (Kilchmann 2019: 81).

[I know very well that people will not be sparing with the names *pedant, purist, quibbler* etc. against me. But I can let the buzzing pass my ear quite indifferently. My education was French; I came of age in French schools; my aesthetic feeling has unfolded, as it were, in the French air; and of all modes of education, the French is probably the least apt to produce a pedant.]

From his contemporaries, we read that their knowledge of French was evidently more strongly influenced by writing than by speaking – at least in regions at a distance from the French border, where, one can assume, there would only have been occasional oral contact (excluding periods of French occupation)[5]:

> Natürlich spricht der Ungeweihte alle jene Wörter so aus wie er sie geschrieben findet. Ich habe sehr gebildete, lateinisch und griechisch gelehrte Männer sogar, gekant, die Mademo-i-selle, To-i-lette lasen. Selbst Dichter trennen hier gewöhnlich die in der Grundsprache einfache Silbe; daß man ungewis ist, ob sie To-i-lette oder Tu-a-lette gemeint haben. Und das ist denn doch wol für ein Wort ein schlechter Empfehl, wenn die Kentnis der Sprache, in der es als ergänzender Teil vorkommt, zur richtigen Ausrede desselben nicht abreicht [...]
> [Of course, the uninitiated pronounces all those words as he finds them written. I have known very educated men, even learned in Latin and Greek, who read Mademo-i-selle, To-i-lette. Even poets usually hyphenate here the syllable which is a single unit in the basic language; thus it remains uncertain whether they meant To-i-lette or Tu-a-lette. It is indeed a bad recommendation for a word if the knowledge of the language of which it is an integral part is not sufficient for its correct pronunciation.] (Kolbe 1809: 83).

The aim of the argument is, as we said, foreign-word purism; statements giving indications of multilingualism and its quality are just a byproduct. Foreign-word purism as such has now been well researched. However, it could be worthwhile to look through the primary texts systematically as a treasure trove of statements about multilingualism. For example, one might find assertions like this: "selbst unter den Gebildeten der höheren Klassen möchten bei weitem

---

[5] For example, Bettine von Arnim reports on Madame de Staël's visit to Goethe's mother in Frankfurt: the former spoke no German and the latter only a little French. After a few introductory phrases, the conversation was continued through interpreting: "Sie [...] sagte [...] mit erhabener Stimme [...]: *Je suis la mère de Goethe: ah, je suis charmèe* sagte die Schriftstellerin [...]. [...] Die Mutter beantwortete ihre Höflichkeiten mit einem französischen Neujahrswunsch, welchen sie mit feierlichen Verbeugungen zwischen den Zähnen murmelte [...]. Bald winkte mich die Mutter herbei, ich mußte den Dolmetscher zwischen beiden machen" [In a solemn voice she said: *I am Goethe's mother: ah, pleased to meet you* said the writer. Mother answered the pleasantries with a French New Year's wish, which she murmured with solemn bows between her teeth. Soon mother waved me over and I had to act as the interpreter between the two.] (Arnim 1835: 316–317). – Regarding the multilingual competences of Madame de Stael, see Jöhnk (in this volume).

mehr als die vollen drei Viertel das Französische entweder gar nicht oder nur kümmerlich verstehn" [Even among the educated of the higher classes, far more than the full three quarters either do not understand French at all or understand it only poorly.] (Kolbe 1809: 108).

3.3.2 Practiced multilingualism

Multilingual proficiency becomes apparent when an author uses different languages, be it in different texts or within one text. Regardless of the (self-)attested language skills of an author like A. W. Schlegel, he could write in more than one language (or indeed speak in more than one language – which, however, before the introduction of sound recordings cannot be directly witnessed but is accessible only as thematic multilingualism). For Schlegel, French and Latin are publication languages in addition to German, and English is a further language of correspondence.

Obvious practised multilingualism occurs when we find more or less extensive heterolingual passages untranslated. Bettine von Arnim, née Brentano, from an upper-class family in Frankfurt, reports that as a teenager she made friends with a Jewish girl and that they together swept a Jewish ghetto alley early in the morning. Later on, her aunt gave her a lengthy French moral sermon:

> Das junge Mädchen was uns sticken lehrt ist eine Jüdin, sie heißt *Veilchen*, es ist ein recht liebkosender Name und ich fand lezt das erste Sträußchen ihrer Namensvettern zusammen, da ging ich ganz früh zu ihr um sie damit zu überraschen, ich fand sie auf der Treppe mit dem Besen in der Hand, sie war beschämt, ich aber gleich nahm ihr den aus der Hand und sagte, ach lassen Sie mich auch ein bischen kehren. Da kam so früh schon denn es war noch nicht sieben Uhr der Hofmeister vom Eduard Bethmann vorbei, der mußte es der Tante gesagt haben daß er mich vor der Hausthür eines Juden auf offner Straße kehrend fand – [...] ich will Dir die derbsten Ausdrücke von der Tante ihrer Mercuriale ersparen, sie meinte nur ich sei [...] für ein besseres Dasein verloren, ich habe mich gänzlich weggeworfen! *Vous n'avez point de pudeur, point de respect humain, on vous trouve balayer la rue main en main avec une juive!* [...] *cachez vous devant le monde, qu'on ne lise point sur votre front les deshonorants signes de votre effronterie*
> [The young girl who teaches us embroidery is a Jewess, her name is Violet, it is quite a lovely name and I recently found the first bunch of her namesakes, so I went to her very early to surprise her, I found her on the stairs with a broom in her hand, she was ashamed, but I immediately took it out of her hand and said, oh, let me sweep a little too. Even that early, for it was not yet seven o'clock, the majordomo of Eduard Bethmann came by, he must have told the aunt that he found me in the open street sweeping in front of a Jew's house – I will spare you the crudest expressions of aunt's reprimands: she said that I was lost for a better existence, I had completely thrown myself away! *You have no modesty, no*

> human respect, you are found sweeping the street hand in hand with a Jewess! Hide yourself from the world, so that no one may read on your forehead the shameful signs of your insolence.] (Arnim 1844: 12–14).

Multilingualism is also practiced when Coleridge, in his *Biographia Literaria*, seeks an etymological explanation of fanaticism and in this context makes mention of the literal sense of the German word *Schwärmerei*:

> A debility and dimness of the imaginative power, and a consequent necessity of reliance on the immediate impressions of the senses, do, we well know, render the mind liable to superstition and fanaticism. Having a deficient portion of internal and proper warmth, minds of this class seek in the crowd *circum fana* for a warmth in common, which they do not possess singly. Cold and plegmatic in their own nature, like damp hay, they heat and inflame by co-acervation; or like bees they become restless and irritable through the increased temperature of collected multitudes. Hence the German word for fanaticism (such at least was its original import) is derived from the swarming of bees, namely, Schwärmen, Schwärmerey. (Coleridge 1817: 29–30)

Instead of a single author, a collection of texts can also be regarded; the *Children's and Household Tales* by the Grimm Brothers (2 volumes, 1812; 1815) e.g. are trilingual, since in addition to the standard New High German (164 tales) German dialects – Low German (11 tales) and Alemannic (1 tale) – are also used (cf. Bär 2015: 139–140).

Multilingualism can be found in texts to varying degrees. Due to the spelling, it may not be obvious at first glance that several French words (*ennuyant, douce, air, honnête homme, intrigue, filoutérie*, each in a Germanized form) are hidden in the following German example:

> Mehl will ich haben, enujanter Kleiefresser, ihr gebt euch ein so douses Air, und wollt immer die Miene eines honnete homme annehmen, und dahinter steckt nichts als Intrigue und Filouterie.
> [I want flour, you tiresome bran-eater, you give yourself such a sweet air, and always want to assume a gentleman's mien, and there is nothing behind it but deceit and trickery] (Brentano 1983 [1810/12], 290).

The superimposition of monolingualism can go even further: any lexical loan-meaning can be understood as a relic of an attempt at monolingualization. A well-known example is the scandal caused by Goethe's wife Christiane and Bettine von Arnim in 1811 when they visited the Weimar art exhibition. Frau von Goethe was apparently most annoyed by Frau von Arnim's exalted affection for Goethe; she took a few pointed comments on the work of Johann Heinrich Meyer, whom Goethe appreciated, as an opportunity to physically attack Bettine von Arnim, knocking her glasses to the ground. The latter then named her "wahnsinnige Blutwurst" [Insane blood sausage] (Wolff and Ludwig 1832: 34). A reliable testimony for the gossip story cannot be identified (cf. the compilation in Kratzsch 2009: 127–130); all the reports are at least second-hand. The exact wording is also uncertain; as alternatives to *wahnsinnige Blutwurst*, the synonyms *wildgewordene Blutwurst* and *tollgewordene Blutwurst* are given; the expression may not even have been used in the dispute itself and indeed may have been coined afterwards (cf. Fröschle 2002: 371). In any case, there are some explicit attempts at motivation – *Blutwurst* allegedly alluded to Christiane's corpulence and red face (Lewes 1875: 580) – which suggests that the term was perceived as unusual. However, the supposed extraordinary linguistic wit[6] could well itself prove to be a 'stereotypical, long-used swearword', considering the possibility that it could be traced to Bettine von Arnim's Frankfurt-Offenbach dialect. There, as well as in other Rhine-Franconian dialects, it is common to use the words *Blutwurst* and the largely synonymous *Blunz(e)* ('blood sausage without or with little greaves') also for a plump person, especially a woman (Friebertshäuser 1990: 37); the expression *dumm(e) Blunz(e)* is a common insult. At whatever point the de-dialectalisation took place, whether in Weimar gossip or already with Bettine von Arnim herself (i.e. whether the word *Blunz* or the also common language word *Blutwurst* was originally used), cannot be clarified. At any rate, dialectal semantics can be assumed and the episode could be seen as an example of hidden bilingualism 'common German – Rhine-Franconian'.

There is a comparable case in the context of Bettine von Arnim's German-French multilingualism referred to above. Following the quoted passage, in which she reports on her aunt's French sermon, she regrets that she will no longer be allowed to visit her friend: "jezt wirds [...] die Tante nicht erlauben, [...] weil ich die Gass gekehrt hab" [Now aunt will not allow it, because I swept the alley.] (Arnim 1844: 15). The e-apocopes in the forms *Gass* and *hab*, the verb *kehren*, and the use of the perfect instead of the past tense are dialect markers;

---

6 "Es ist immer gefährlich Leute anzugreifen, die Meister des Worts sind. Sie haben Waffen zur Verfügung vor denen der Bürger mit seinen stereotypen, längst verbrauchten Schimpfworten wehrlos ist. Die bleiben an niemandem hängen, weil sie für alle gelten. Aber Bettinas ‚wildgewordene Blutwurst' blieb an der armen Christiane für alle Zeiten kleben und nur an ihr. Selbst für Frankreich blieb sie 'le boudin enragé.'" [It is always dangerous to attack people who are masters of the word. They have weapons at their disposal against which the bourgeois with their stereotypical, long-used swearwords are defenseless. They don't stick to anyone because they apply to everyone. But Bettina's 'wild blood sausage' stuck to poor Christiane forever and only to her. Even for France, she remained 'le boudin enragé'] (Faber du Faur: 223).

standard language would be *weil ich die Gasse gefegt habe* (cf. Bär 2015: 141–142).

4 On methodology: how to 'find' multilingualism?

If it is plausible that multilingualism 'hides' in text corpora, it follows that the methods to find it must be considered. And if one accepts that there are forms of multilingualism which are not immediately evident (that is, that recognizing them requires a greater interpretive effort), then it is also clear that there is no sharp boundary between *Finden* (finding) and *Erfinden* (inventing). This does not mean that indirect references to multilingualism have to be excluded; taking them into account, however, requires a significantly greater amount of justification. It is also particularly true here that intuitions without concepts are blind; for this reason, it depends on the expertise of the researcher whether they are able to see multilingualism in a text (or to see multilingualism 'into it,' so to speak).

The "lucky find" in Max Weber's sense (1919: 590–591), i.e., the collection of material based on prior knowledge and unsystematic research, is by no means to be despised. This contingency, which can never be completely eliminated, can of course be reduced by consulting and including available research results (e.g. Balogh and Leitgeb 2012; Dembeck and Mein 2014; Dembeck and Parr 2017; Glaser, Prinz, and Ptashnyk 2021; Havinga and Langer 2015; Hüning 2012 ; Joachimsthaler 2011; Mende 2021; Ptashnyk forthc.).

The lucky find can be supported in two ways by systematic corpus queries. Thematic multilingualism can be found using search terms such as
lingu*, langu* ...
German, French, English, Latin ...
translat*, interpret* ...
...

and of course heteronymous expressions, i.e. equivalents in other languages. Both thematic and practized multilingualism can also be found to some extent using certain search formats. This is due to the fact that foreign-language expressions in texts from the 18th and 19th centuries are often (but of course not always) specifically emphasized: in Roman typesetting usually by italics, in Gothic print frequently by Roman types, sometimes also by italics. Since Gothic types are usually converted to Roman during digitization, there is a possibility of finding heterolingual expressions by searching for italics. This requires, however, that the corpus texts are available in a file format that allows searching for formatting.

It goes without saying that such searches will always find a large number of text passages that have nothing to do with multilingualism. Therefore, each document has to be examined auto-optically, and given the sheer number of references, the expenditure of time is considerable. However, usually one can see in half a second whether it is relevant evidence or not; and the quality of the finds definitely justifies the effort.

A selected individual case is examined in the following. A complete presentation of the evidence, however, is not intended.[7]

5 Multilingualism in Johann Wolfgang Goethe's works

It is unclear how many languages Goethe mastered, especially since the precise meaning of 'mastered' is not clear. Self-statements concerning a lack of language skills should be understood to some extent as a modesty topos or even sometimes as irony; at the same time, the difference between active and passive mastery as well as its degree is often difficult or impossible to verify and undoubtedly also changed during the course of Goethe's life. As a child or adolescent, he received private lessons in the scholarly languages Latin and Greek as well as in English and Hebrew. He wrote Latin reasonably fluently (Goethe 1811: 57–58), and in Ancient Greek he gradually got so far "daß ich fast den Homer ohne Uebersetzung lese" [that I can almost read Homer without a translation] (Goethe WA IV.1: 258). The knowledge is at least sufficient for educated jokes; for instance, Goethe (WA IV.4: 281) invents a pseudo-Greek equivalent for the name of the Thuringian mountain *Kickelhahn* (literally: 'cock-a-rooster'): "Alecktrüogallonax".

Italian, Goethe learns casually, so to speak, by listening to his sister's Italian lessons (Goethe 1811: 58). His father had a good command of French, but his mother hardly any; the son acquired it more or less on his own, mediated via Latin and Italian (Goethe 1811: 202–206). In later years, he occasionally mistrusted his French skills and thought "daß ich es in dieser Sprache hätte weiter bringen sollen" ['that I should have made more progress in this language] (Goethe WA IV.22: 186).

---

[7] For further details see also Schreiner (1992) and Weissmann (2021).

Coming to reading a text in the "wunderliche Sprache" ("curious language") Dutch, he was confident by contrast that he could somehow find his way through (Goethe WA.IV.6, 357). In connection with his work on the *West-östlicher Divan*, he considered learning Arabic (Goethe WA IV.25: 165). In 1821, at the age of 72, he took up Bohemian history and language (Goethe WA IV.35: 68). Serbian poetry, Serbian poetry, he only could read in German translation, so he asked his correspondent Vuk Stefanović Karadžić to translate some poems verbatim (Goethe WA IV.37: 289). Spanish, he read with difficulty; on the *Floresta de Rimas Antiguas Castellanas* by Johann Nikolaus Böhl von Faber, one of the mediators of Romanticism to Spain, which has a very brief German-language appendix, he commented:

> Der Spanische Lustgarten hat mich aufgeregt, dieser herrlichen Sprache und Literatur wieder einige Stunden zu widmen; hätte der treffliche Sammler [...] nur das Doppelte oder Dreyfache an die *Fingerzeige für deutsche Leser* gewendet, so hätte er mich und alle, die ohngefähr in demselben Verhältniß gegen das Spanische sich finden, sehr gefördert und würde uns ohne Mühe viel Mühe erspart haben
> [The Spanish Pleasure Garden inspired me to devote once more a few hours to this wonderful language and literature; if the excellent collector had only spent twice or three times as much on the clues for German readers, he would have helped me and all those who find themselves in roughly the same relationship to the Spanish language and would have without a lot of work saved us much work] (Goethe WA IV.34: 232).

He seems to have had a special, almost emotional relationship to Italian. He signed a letter to the German-Italian Maria Antonia von Branconi in 1780:

> di Vossignoria ††††issima
> il servo ††††issimo
> Goethe
> Ich überlasse Ihrer grösseren Kenntniss der italienischen Sprache, statt der Kreuze die schicklichsten Epithets einzusezzen, es passt eine ganze Litaney hinein
> [Your most †††† ladyship's most †††† servant Goethe. I leave it to your greater knowledge of the Italian language, to use the most suitable epithets instead of the crosses: a whole litany fits in] (Goethe WA IV.4: 276)

However, Goethe (WA IV.5: 267) reports unironically on his "wenigen Kenntniß der italiänischen Sprache" [little knowledge of the Italian language] and even complains: "Hätt ich die Italienische Sprache in meiner Gewalt wie die unglückliche Teutsche" [Had I only the Italian language in my mastery like the unfortunate German!] (Goethe WA IV.7: 217). During his trip to Italy in 1786–88 he then learned Italian fluently; crossing the language border, he notes: "Der Wirth spricht kein deutsch und ich muß nun meine Künste versuchen. Wie froh bin ich daß die Geliebte Sprache nun die Sprache des Gebrauchs wird." [The landlord does not speak German and I must now try my skills. How glad I am that the beloved language is now becoming the language of use.] (Goethe WA III.1, 180–181). In later years, cut off from practical use, he no longer seemed to be quite sure of his mastery of this language: In translating, he asked for assistance of a bilingual Italian (Goethe WA IV.16: 107).

He provided own translations from French and Italian; translations of his works into English (Goethe WA.IV.15: 212) and Latin poems by contemporaries (Goethe WA.IV.25: 140) he was able to judge, in the case of English with the restriction "soweit man eine fremde Sprache beurtheilen kann" [as far as one can judge a foreign language] (Goethe WA III.12: 190). He had one of his essays translated into French for his literary contacts in Milan, since they did not speak German but were nevertheless multilingual. The fact that he did not do the translation himself and directly into Italian was probably due to other obligations and a momentary lack of an Italian-speaking assistant; he at least corrected the French text. To his friend Carl Friedrich Zelter, he wrote:

> Dieß ist ein ganz eigener Spiegel wenn man sich in einer fremden Sprache wieder erblickt. [...] Will ich meine deutsche, eigentlich nur sinnlich hingeschriebene Darstellung im Französischen wieder finden; so muß ich hie und da nachhelfen, welches nicht schwer wird, da dem Übersetzer gelungen ist die logische Gelenkheit seiner Sprache zu bethätigen, ohne dem sinnlichen Eindruck Schaden zu thun.
> [It is a very special mirror to behold oneself in a foreign language. If I want to find in French my German, actually only sensuously written description, I have to help it along here and there, which is not difficult, since the translator has succeeded in using his logically flexible language without interfering with the sensual impression] (Goethe WA IV.29: 91).

Against the monolingual tendencies of the 19th century, which thought and acted towards a national state, Goethe explicitly argued for multilingualism. In December 1813, Achim von Arnim had spoken out in the journal *Preußischer Correspondent* (No. 154: 4) in favour of retaining the juridical achievements of the French era. Goethe comments approvingly on this in a letter to Arnim in February 1814:

> Etwas Ähnliches möchte ich wohl über das neue Bestreben vernehmen, durch welches die aus einer Knechtschaft kaum entronnenen Deutschen sich schnell wieder in die Fesseln ihrer eigenen Sprache zu schmieden gedenken
> [I should like to hear something similar about the new endeavor by which the Germans, who have scarcely escaped from servitude, intend to quickly forge themselves back into the chains of their own language] (Goethe WA IV.24: 177).

For Goethe, dealing with other languages and actively mastering them has the deeper sense of mutual language formation and expansion. He compares German with French, for instance, and suggests introducing a loan meaning for the German verb *stängeln*:

> Eine fremde Sprache ist hauptsächlich dann zu beneiden, wenn sie mit Einem Worte auszudrucken kann, was die andere umschreiben muß, und hierin steht jede Sprache im Vortheil und Nachtheil gegen die andere, wie man alsobald sehen kann, wenn man die gegenseitigen Wörterbücher durchläuft. Mir aber kömmt vor, man könne gar manches Wort auf diesem Wege gewinnen, wenn man nachsieht, woher es in jener Sprache stammt, und alsdann versucht, ob man aus denselben etümologischen Gründen durch ähnliche Ableitung zu demselben Worte gelangen könnte.
> So haben zum Beyspiel, die Franzosen das Wort perche, *Stange*, davon das Verbum percher. Sie bezeugen dadurch, daß die Hühner, die Vögel sich auf eine Stange, einen Zweig setzen. Im Deutschen haben wir das Wort *stängeln*. Man sagt: *ich stängle die Bohnen*, das heißt, ich gebe den Bohnen Stangen, eben so gut kann man sagen: *die Bohnen stängeln*, sie winden sich an den Stangen hinauf, und warum sollten wir uns nicht des Ausdrucks bedienen: *die Hühner stängeln*, sie setzen sich auf den Stangen
> [A foreign language is mainly to be envied when it can express in one word what the other must circumscribe, and in this each language stands at an advantage and disadvantage to the other, as one can see at once by going through both the dictionaries. It seems to me, however, that many a word could be obtained in this way if one were to see where it comes from in that language and then try to see whether one could come to the same word for the same etymological reason by a similar derivation. For example, the French have the word perche, *perch*, from which the verb percher is derived. By this they mean that chickens and birds perch on a pole or branch. In German we have the word *stängeln*. We say: *ich stängle die Bohnen*, that is, I give sticks to the beans; just as well one might say: *die Bohnen stängeln*, the beans wind themselves up the sticks, and why should we not use the expression: *die Hühner stängeln*, the chickens perch on the poles] (Goethe WA IV.23: 375).

Also with regard to the language of science, Goethe pleads for multilingualism. In *Nonnos von Panopolis der Dichter* by the Russian Count Sergei Semionovich Uvarov, published in German and dedicated to Goethe, the latter could read:

> Die Wiedergeburt der Alterthums-Wissenschaft gehört den Deutschen an. Es mögen andere Völker wichtige Vorarbeiten dazu geliefert haben; sollte aber die höhere Philologie sich einst zu einem vollendeten Ganzen ausbilden, so könnte eine solche Palingenesie wohl nur in Deutschland Statt finden. Aus diesem Grunde lassen sich auch gewisse neue Ansichten kaum in einer andern neuern Sprache ausdrücken; und deswegen habe ich deutsch geschrieben. Man ist hoffentlich nunmehr von der verkehrten Idee des politischen Vorranges dieser oder jener Sprache in der Wissenschaft zurückgekommen. Es ist Zeit, dass ein Jeder, unbekümmert um das Werkzeug, immer die Sprache wähle, die am nächsten dem Ideenkreise liegt, den er zu betreten im Begriff ist

[The revival of classical studies belongs to the Germans. Other peoples may have provided important preliminary work on it; but if higher philology should one day develop into a complete whole, such palingenesis could probably only take place in Germany. For this reason, certain new views can hardly be expressed in any other modern language; and that is why I have written in German. Hopefully, we have now come back from the mistaken idea of the political primacy of this or that language in science. It is time that everyone, regardless of the tool, always chose the language that is closest to the circle of ideas he is about to enter] (Uvarov 1817: III–IV).

Goethe (WA IV.28: 41), in a letter to Uvarov, comments on this:

Ich eile meinen [...] Dank herzlich auszudrücken [...]. Denn gerade zu der jetzigen Zeit kommen diese Worte als erwünschtes Evangelium, dem Deutschen zu sagen: daß er, anstatt sich in sich selbst zu beschränken, die Welt in sich aufnehmen muß, um auf die Welt zu wirken. Ihr Beyspiel ist unschätzbar
[I hurry to express my heartfelt thanks. For precisely at this time these words come as a desired gospel to tell the German: that instead of limiting himself within himself, he must absorb the world in order to have an effect on the world. Your example is inestimable!]

He then takes up the idea in a brief discussion of Uvarov's study in *Kunst und Alterthum* [*Art and Antiquity*] and develops it further:

Hier hört man nun doch einmal einen fähigen, talentvollen, geistreich gewandten Mann, der, über die kümmerliche Beschränkung eines erkältenden Sprach-Patriotismus weit erhoben, gleich einem Meister der Tonkunst jedesmal *die* Register seiner wohlausgestatteten Orgel zieht welche Sinn und Gefühl des Augenblicks ausdrücken. Möchten doch alle gebildete Deutsche diese zugleich ehrenvollen und belehrenden Worte sich dankbar einprägen, und geistreiche Jünglinge dadurch angefeuert werden sich mehrerer Sprachen, als beliebiger Lebens-Werkzeuge, zu bemächtigen
[Here, after all, one hears an able, talented, witty man who, raised far above the meagre limitations of a cold language patriotism, like a master of music, always draws the registers of his well-equipped organ, which express the sense and feeling of the moment. If only all educated Germans would gratefully memorise these words, which are both honourable and instructive, and witty young people would be inspired by them to master several languages as discretionary tools of life] (Goethe 1817: 64–65).

His concept of translation can be found most succinctly in an 1827 letter to Thomas Carlyle:

Eine wahrhaft allgemeine Duldung wird am sichersten erreicht, wenn man das Besondere der einzelnen Menschen und Völkerschaften auf sich beruhen läßt, bey der Überzeugung jedoch festhält, daß das wahrhaft Verdienstliche sich dadurch auszeichnet, daß es der ganzen Menschheit angehört. Zu einer solchen Vermittlung und wechselseitigen Anerkennung tragen die Deutschen seit langer Zeit schon bey.
Wer die deutsche Sprache versteht und studirt befindet sich auf dem Markte wo alle Nationen ihre Waren anbieten, er spielt den Dolmetscher indem er sich selbst bereichert.

Und so ist jeder Übersetzer anzusehen, daß er sich als Vermittler dieses allgemein geistigen Handels bemüht, und den Wechseltausch zu befördern sich zum Geschäft macht. Denn, was man auch von der Unzulänglichkeit des Übersetzens sagen mag, so ist und bleibt es doch eins der wichtigsten und würdigsten Geschäfte in dem allgemeinen Weltwesen

[A truly general acceptance is most surely achieved if one leaves the particulars of individual people and nations to themselves, while remaining convinced that what is truly meritorious is distinguished by the fact that it belongs to the whole of humanity. The Germans have been contributing to such mediation and mutual appreciation for a long time. Whoever understands and studies the German language finds himself on the market where all nations offer their wares, he plays the interpreter by enriching himself. And so every translator is to be regarded as a mediator of this general intellectual trade, and as making it his business to promote the exchange. For whatever may be said of the inadequacy of translation, it is and remains one of the most important and worthiest businesses in the general nature of the world] (Goethe WA IV.42: 270).

With such statements, one has to take into account that the late 18th and early 19th centuries often had a rather liberal understanding of translation. To translate a text completely and exactly, without additions or rearrangements of passages, was not necessarily expected. Goethe himself reacted quite patiently to very extensive translational modifications of his works. In 1805, he himself had submitted a translation of an unpublished text from the literary estate of the French Enlightenment philosopher Denis Diderot, to which he added some remarks on persons of French intellectual history as an appendix (*Anmerkungen über Personen und Gegenstände, deren in dem Dialog* Rameau's Neffe *erwähnt wird* [*Notes on persons and objects mentioned in the dialogue* Rameau's nephew]; Goethe 1805: 383–480). Diderot's original manuscript was missing (it was not rediscovered until 1890 and published for the first time one year later) and the copy given to Goethe by his friend Klinger through Schiller's mediation could also no longer be found after the publication of the translation – Goethe (1823b: 159) claims to have returned it. Thus, the first French edition appeared in 1821 as a "humoristische Schelmerey einer Zurückübersetzung" [a humorous joke of a back translation]. (Goethe 1823b: 160), which the authors declared as the original for a time (Goethe 1824: 145). But Goethe's translation was also a rather idiosyncratic mixture of an extremely 'faithful' translation in parts and a relatively free rendering (cf. Albrecht and Plack 2018: 407). Two years later, the retranslators, who partly strayed far from their German original (Albrecht and Plack 2018: 408–409), presented a 'translation' of Goethe's *Anmerkungen über Personen und Gegenstände* as an independent publication, which was in fact a complete reworking and expansion (Saur and Saint-Geniès 1823). Goethe (1823a: 377), however, by no means reveals this text as an impudent plagiarism, but merely hints delicately that it has no counterpart in his oeuvre. Only a letter to Zelter shows that he is nevertheless annoyed:

> Die Franzosen [...] behandeln alle unsre Kunstproducte als rohen Stoff den sie sich erst bearbeiten müssen. Wie jämmerlich haben sie meine Noten zum Rameau durch einander entstellt und gemischt; da ist auch gar nichts an seinem Fleck stehen geblieben
> [The French treat all our art products as raw material that they must first work on. How miserably they have distorted and mixed my notes to Rameau; nothing has remained in its place] (Goethe WA IV.39: 182).

All in all, it can be stated that Goethe had a very positive relationship to multilingualism. With his cosmopolitan attitude, he is admittedly not a representative of that line of ideology which became predominant in the 19th and into the middle of the 20th century and which even today cannot be regarded as having been overcome. Nevertheless, he was not an isolated case in his time. Another example is Franz Passow, a philologist who seems to have been completely ignored in the historiography of linguistic criticism. In 1813, in a review of Karl Wilhelm Kolbe's *Über Wortmengerei*, he takes up an idea that is well-known in early German Romanticism: translation, like the comparative study of language, serves to bring together different languages – as different organs and forms of representation of the human mind, which thereby comes closer to itself – and that the German language is more suited than others to adapt and assimilate peculiarities of other languages (cf. Bär 1999: 273–275; on the prehistory of the concept of language enrichment through translation, cf. Albrecht and Plack 2018: 53–56). Passow writes:

> Nun aber soll jede einzelne Sprache sich möglichst der allgemeinen Idee von Sprache annähern, und dazu gehört dann auch die Verpflichtung, in sich allmählig die verschiedenen Weisen des Ausdrucks zu vereinigen, die wir in verschiedenen Sprachen zerstreut sehn. Der Franzose wird dieß läugnen, weil seine Sprache eine ungefuge Masse ist, die eben nichts anderes als französisches ausdrücken kann, weil der Franzose nichts anders zu fassen vermag. Der Deutsche wird es bejahen, weil er für jede Volksthümlichkeit reinen und empfänglichen Sinn genug hat, um sie wieder in seinem Organ darzustellen, und weil deutsche Musterwerke aller Art glänzendes Zeugniß dafür sind: es genügt hier, an die Uebersetzungen von *Schleiermacher, Wolf, Voß* und *A. W. Schlegel* zu erinnern
> [But now, each individual language should, as far as possible, approach the general idea of language, and this also includes the obligation to gradually unite in itself the various modes of expression which we see scattered in different languages. The Frenchman will deny this because his language is an unstructured mass that cannot express anything but French, because the Frenchman is not able to comprehend anything else. The German will affirm it, because he has pure and receptive sense enough for every folk idiom to represent it again in his organ, and because German model works of all kinds are bright testimony to this: it will be sufficient here to recall the translations of *Schleiermacher, Wolf, Voß* and *A. W. Schlegel*] (Passow 1813: 375).

Consequently, this would mean that some language communities have more talent for multilingualism than others because they work more with it and thus achieve a higher degree of interlingualism for their own language. It could be a quite interesting task for multilingualism research to investigate this curious idea more closely. The first step would be to proceed in terms of the history of ideology: The exponents of this view would have to be identified and their arguments and motives, which are quite various, would have to be compiled. Then, however (following the guiding idea of this contribution, that historical language reflection is related to contemporaneous linguistic realities and can thus possibly serve as an indicator of these), it could be examined whether the ideology has any counterpart in different languages of the 18th and 19th centuries. For example, do German authors master significantly more languages than French? Are there more interlingualisms in German with French than vice versa? – In fact, translations that were not made directly from one language to another but were mediated via a version in a third language, were often not mediated via German at all, but rather via French (cf. Albrecht and Plack 2018: 387–388). It should therefore not go unconsidered that the (wishful) notion of German as a particularly suitable translator's language may also have been merely a reaction to the actual predominance of French in this context.

6 Outlook: an approach to multilingualism in works on linguistic and literary criticism

The main concern of this article is to raise awareness of the fact that multilingualism in linguistic and literary criticism of the 18th and 19th centuries was by no means an exception, but rather the norm. We agree unreservedly with Kilchmann's plea (219: 83–84) that analytic categories must be sought that can take account of transnational and multilingual historical realities. If we do not assume a monolingual consciousness, but instead take multilingualism as the standard, it will be then be obvious not to interpret the 18th and 19th centuries' translation theory and practice in the current way as a transfer from one language to another, but rather as an entry into a sphere of interlinguality, as Schmitz-Emans (2019: 266) considers for early German Romanticism and its 'authorship of the reader' theory

A possible research approach for the systematic evaluation of the material exemplarily illuminated above could consist in the creation of a relational database on the ZBK corpus as well as other corpora in other languages; in this case, unlike in case of a discourse lexicographic project (cf. Bär forthc.), the size of the corpus is not initially of great importance, since it does not have to be primarily about the comparability of multilingualism in different language communities: each reference is valuable as such. One can therefore work with an open corpus without any problems.

If one annotates each individual reference by means of an input mask, as, for example, shown in Figs. 2–5 (although other/further query criteria are of course conceivable and the drop-down menus can be supplemented at any time), there will be in a reasonable amount of time an ordered set of data with the help of which valid findings of concrete multilingualisms can be obtained.

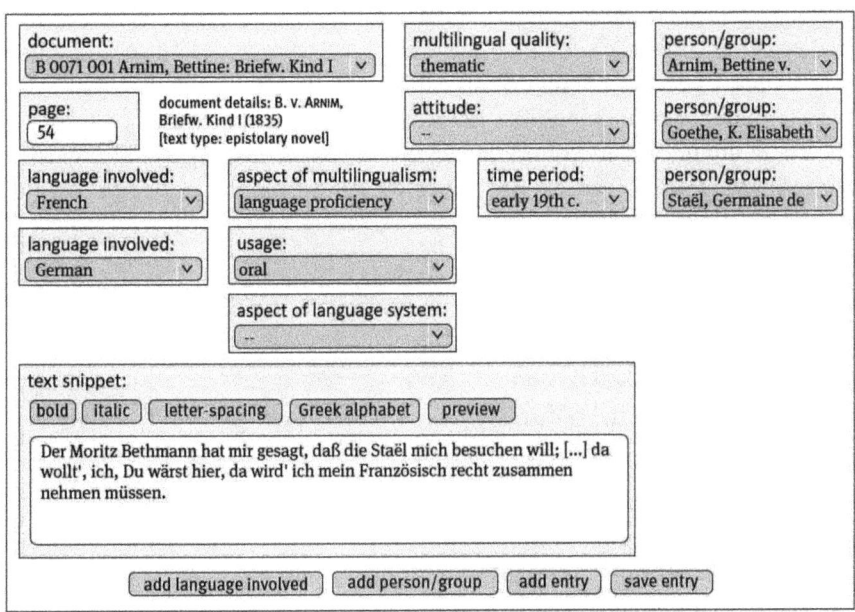

Fig. 2: Multilingualism-related excerpt (Arnim 1835: 54) as entry in the proposed database (view of possible input mask)

In this instance in which French is explicitly mentioned as the language of communication, German is implicitly involved. For instances with additional languages involved, any number of additional input fields can be added via the button 'add language involved' in the footer. The multilingualism-quality is 'thematic' (see above, 3.2.1), an attitude towards multilingualism is not discernible here (cf. however fig. 3 and 4); the multilingualism-aspect in question is language proficiency (it could also be about the aesthetics of languages, for example, as in fig. 4, or about the cognitive value of different languages); it is about oral language use; a particular aspect of the language system such as pronunciation or speech sound (cf. figs. 4 and 5), grammar, lexics or pragmatics is not mentioned; the period in which this multilingualism-evidence falls is not identical with the publication year of the text and must therefore be indicated separately; one learns about the multilingualism of three persons (in Katharina Elisabeth Goethe's case, the French is poor; in the case of Mme de Staël, there is zero evidence). By default, one person or group is provided in the input mask; in need of more than one, further input fields can be added via the corresponding button in the footer. If the names of the persons are well-known, their life data, social background, education level and, if applicable, other relevant information are recorded in the database, which can be retrieved at any time by a special query (also in different combinations). In the case of Fig. 5, only "a German" is mentioned as a multilingual person; since he appears as a member of the circle around Dr. Johnson and Oliver Goldsmith, he may well be apostrophized as 'educated'.

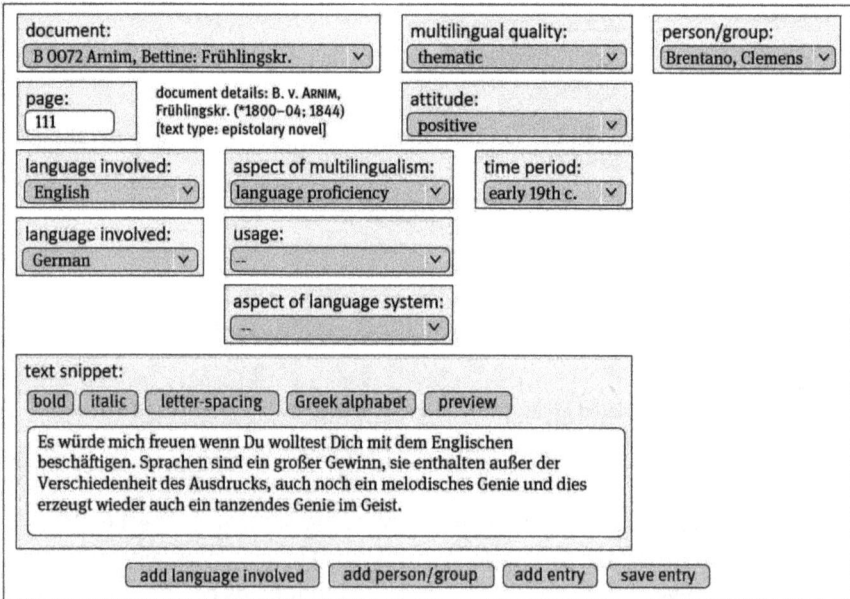

Fig. 3: Multilingualism-related excerpt (Arnim 1844: 111) as entry in the proposed database (view of possible input mask)

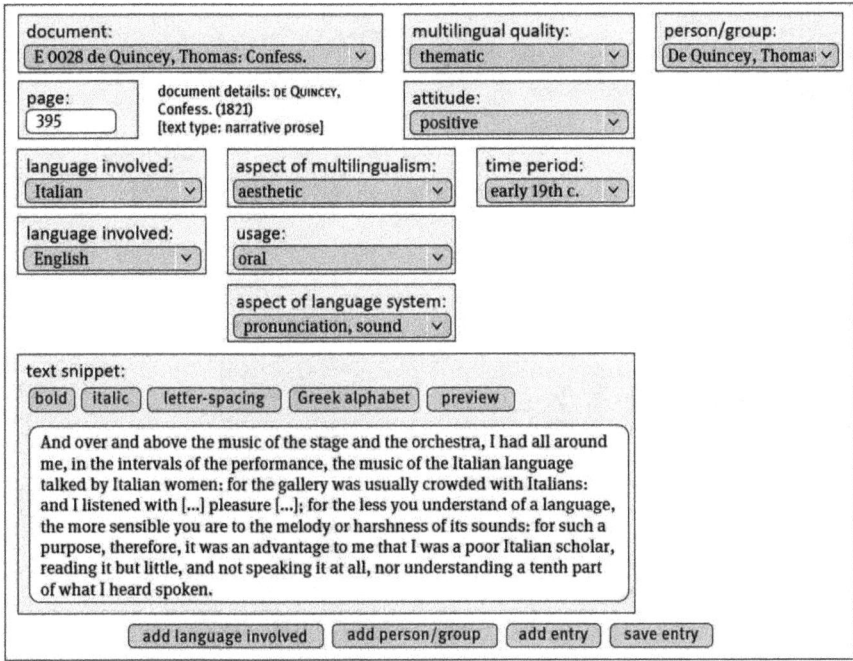

Fig. 4: Multilingualism-related excerpt (de Quincey 1821: 395) as entry in the proposed database (view of possible input mask)

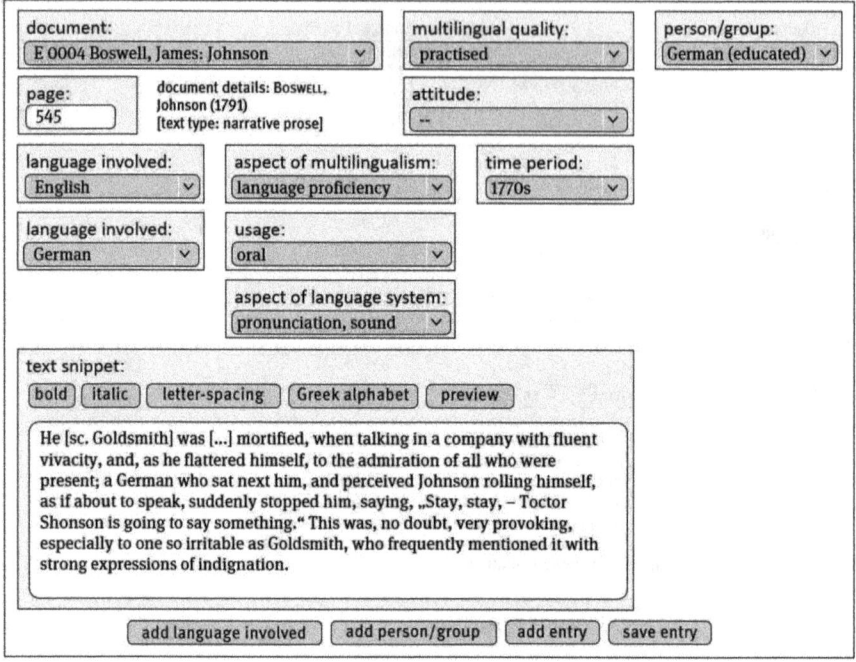

Fig. 5: Multilingualism-related excerpt (Boswell 1791: 545) as entry in the proposed database (view of possible input mask)

Of course, the query categories presented only form a very general grid, and it would be the same with any other or additional category. The interesting details of each instance in their variety and diversity cannot easily be categorized. Therefore, one must still individually take note of the evidence obtained by querying for any criterion or combination of criteria. The database is merely a pre-interpretative tool that does not suspend the actual interpretation. For this, a thorough familiarity with the literary-historical facts and the corpus texts themselves is essential. A database user who cannot make sense of the name of an author or a mentioned person, who cannot comprehend intertextualities or who does not recognize literary perspective and fictionality has not much to gain from a set of references pre-sorted according to certain criteria. The plea for corpus-hermeneutic multilingualism research – which the present article makes – is therefore not a plea for quantitative methods, but for a reasonable combination of distant and close reading (Bär 2016; see also Weitin and Werber 2017).

7 References

Albrecht, Jörn. 2019. Sprachkontakt im Deutschen (eine Bilanz). In Jochen A./Anja Lobenstein-Reichmann/Jörg Riecke (eds.), *Handbuch Sprache in der Geschichte*, 267–311. (Handbücher Sprachwissen 8.) Berlin/Boston: De Gruyter.
Albrecht, Jörn & Iris Plack. 2018. *Europäische Übersetzungsgeschichte*. Tübingen: Narr Francke Attempto.
Arnim, Bettine von. 1835. *Goethes Briefwechsel mit einem Kinde. Seinem Denkmal. Erster Theil*. Berlin: Dümmler.
Arnim, Bettine von. 1844. *Clemens Brentano's Frühlingskranz aus Jugendbriefen ihm geflochten, wie er selbst schriftlich verlangte*. Charlottenburg: Bauer.
Balogh, András F. & Christoph Leitgeb (eds.). 2012. *Mehrsprachigkeit in Zentraleuropa. Zur Geschichte einer literarischen und kulturellen Chance*. Wien: Praesens.
Bär, Jochen A. 1999. *Sprachreflexion der deutschen Frühromantik. Konzepte zwischen Universalpoesie und Grammatischem Kosmopolitismus. Mit lexikographischem Anhang*. Berlin/New York: De Gruyter.
Bär, Jochen A. 2015. Dialect in German Literature, 1760–1930. In Anna Havinga/Nils Langer (eds.), *Invisible Languages in the Nineteenth Century*, 135–148. Oxford et al.: Lang.
Bär, Jochen A. 2016. Langue-Philologie – historische Semantik – hermeneutische Linguistik – wie auch immer. Für eine qualitative Diskurslexikographie. In Anja Lobenstein-Reichmann/Peter O. Müller (eds.), *Historische Lexikographie zwischen Tradition und Innovation*, 101–129. (Studia Linguistica Germanica 129.) Berlin/Boston: De Gruyter.
Bär, Jochen A. Forthcoming. Sprachtransgressionen. Interlingualität und Multimodalität im klassisch-romantischen Diskurskontinuum: ein Blick über das Nebelmeer. *Lexicographica. International Annual for Lexicography/Revue Internationale de Lexicographie/Internationales Jahrbuch für Lexikographie* 38.
Bär, Jochen A. & Benita von Consbruch. 2012. Korpora in der historischen Lexikographie (am Beispiel eines Diskurswörterbuchs zur Goethezeit). In Ekkehard Felder, Marcus Müller & Friedemann Vogel (eds.), *Korpuspragmatik. Thematische Korpora als Basis diskurslinguistischer Analysen*, 451–487. Berlin/Boston: De Gruyter.
Beattie, William (ed.). 1855. *Life and Letters of Thomas Campbell*. Vol. 2, New York: Harper.
Boswell, James. 1791. *Life of Johnson*. Ed. by R. W. Chapman. A new edition corrected by J. D. Fleeman. London: Oxford University Press 1970.
Brentano, Clemens. 1983 [1810/12]. Die Mährchen vom Rhein. In *Clemens Brentano. Sämtliche Werke und Briefe*. Hist.-krit. Ausg. veranstaltet vom Freien Deutschen Hochstift. Bd. 17, 13–331. Stuttgart/Berlin/Köln/Mainz: Kohlhammer.
Bunia, Remigius. 2014. Idiomatik, Rhetorik, Grammatik. Sprache jenseits morphologischer und syntaktischer Regeln. In Till Dembeck/Georg Mein (eds.), *Philologie und Mehrsprachigkeit*, 53–77. Heidelberg: Winter.
Coleridge, Samuel Taylor. 1817. *Biographia Literaria or Biographical Sketches of my Literary Life and Opinions*. Vol. 1. London: Rest Fenner.
Dembeck, Till & Georg Mein (eds.). 2014. *Philologie und Mehrsprachigkeit*. Heidelberg: Winter.
Dembeck, Till & Rolf Parr (eds.). 2017. *Literatur und Mehrsprachigleit. Ein Handbuch*. Tübingen: Narr Francke Attempto.
de Quincey, Thomas. 1821: *Confessions of an English Opium-Eater*. With an introduction and a Life of De Quincey by Malcolm Elwin. London: Macdonald 1956.

Faber du Faur, Curt von. 1960. Goethe und Bettina von Arnim: Ein neuer Fund. *Publications of the Modern Language Association of America* 75(3). 216–230.
Franceschini, Rita. 2009. The Genesis and Development of Research in Multilingualism. Perspectives for Future Research. In Larissa Aronin & Britta Hufeisen (eds.), *The exploration of multilingualism: Development of research on L3, multilingualism and multiple language acquisition*, 27–61. Amsterdam, Philadelphia: John Benjamins Pub. Co.
Friebertshäuser, Hans. 1990. *Kleines hessisches Wörterbuch*. München: Beck.
Fröschle, Hartmut. 2002. *Goethes Verhältnis zur Romantik*. Würzburg: Königshausen & Neumann.
Gantefort, Christoph & Ina-Maria Maahs. 2020. Translanguaging. Mehrsprachige Kompetenzen von Lernenden im Unterricht aktivieren und wertschätzen. https://www.uni-due.de/imperia/md/content/prodaz/gantefort_maahs_translanguaging.pdf (accessed 1 July 2022)
Gardt, Andreas (ed.). *Nation und Sprache. Die Diskussion ihres Verhältnisses in Geschichte und Gegenwart*. Berlin/New York: De Gruyter.
Glaser, Elvira, Michael Prinz & Stefaniya Ptashnyk (eds.). 2021: *Historisches Codeswitching mit Deutsch. Multilinguale Praktiken in der Sprachgeschichte*. Berlin/Boston: De Gruyter.
Goethe, Johann Wolfgang. 1805. *Rameau's Neffe. Ein Dialog von Diderot. Aus dem Manuskript übersetzt und mit Anmerkungen begleitet*. Leipzig: Göschen.
Goethe, Johann Wolfgang. 1811. *Aus meinem Leben. Dichtung und Wahrheit. Erster Theil*. Tübingen: Cotta.
Goethe, Johann Wolfgang. 1817. Urtheilsworte französischer Critiker. *Ueber Kunst und Alterthum in den Rhein- und Mayn-Gegenden. Von Goethe. Drittes Heft*. 56–65. Stuttgart: Cotta.
Goethe, Johann Wolfgang. 1823a. Des Hommes Célèbres de France au dix-huitième siècle, et de l'état de la littérature et des arts à la même époque. Par M. Goëthe: traduit de l'allemand par MM. de Saur et de Saint-Géniès. A Paris MDCCCXXIII. *Journal für Literatur, Kunst, Luxus und Mode* 45. 377–380.
Goethe, Johann Wolfgang. 1823b. Notizen. *Ueber Kunst und Alterthum* 4(1). 159–181. Stuttgart: Cotta.
Goethe, Johann Wolfgang. 1824. Rameau's Neffe. *Ueber Kunst und Alterthum* 4(3). 145–150. Stuttgart: Cotta.
Goethe, Johann Wolfgang. 1887–1919. *WA. Goethes Werke*. Herausgegeben im Auftrage der Großherzogin Sophie von Sachsen. Weimar: Böhlau.
Havinga, Anna & Nils Langer (eds.). 2015. *Invisible Languages in the Nineteenth Century*. Oxford et al.: Lang.
Hüning, Matthias (ed.). 2012. *Standard Languages and Multilingualism in European History*. Amsterdam: Benjamins.
Joachimsthaler, Jürgen. 2011. *Text-Ränder: Die kulturelle Vielfalt in Mitteleuropa als Darstellungsproblem deutscher Literatur*. 3 vols. Heidelberg: Winter.
Jones, Willam Jervis. 1995. *Sprachhelden und Sprachverderber. Dokumente zur Erforschung des Fremdwortpurismus im Deutschen (1478–1750)*. Berlin/New York: De Gruyter.
Kilchmann, Esther. 2019. Mehrsprachige Literatur und Transnationalität. In Doerte Bischoff/Susanne Komfort-Hein (eds.), *Handbuch Literatur & Transnationalität*, 79–89. (Handbücher zur kulturwissenschaftlichen Philologie 7). Berlin/Boston: De Gruyter.
Kirkness, Alan. 1975. *Zur Sprachreinigung im Deutschen 1789–1871. Eine historische Dokumentation*. (Forschungsberichte des Instituts für deutsche Sprache 26). Tübingen: Narr.

Kolbe, Karl Wilhelm. 1809. *Über Wortmengerei. Anhang zu der Schrift: Ueber den Wortreichtum der deutschen und französischen Sprache.* Leipzig: Reclam.

Kratzsch, Konrad. 2009: *Klatschnest Weimar. Ernstes und Heiteres, Menschlich-Allzumenschliches aus dem Alltag der Klassiker. Aus den Quellen dargestellt.* Würzburg: Königshausen & Neumann.

Lewes, George Henry. 1875. *Goethe's Leben und Werke.* Mit Bewilligung des Verfassers übersetzt von Julius Frese. 10th edn. vol. 2. Berlin: Duncker.

Mende, Jana-Katharina. 2020. *Das Konzept des Messianismus in der polnischen, französischen und deutschen Literatur der Romantik. Eine mehrsprachige Konzeptanalyse.* Heidelberg: Winter.

Mende, Jana-Katharina. 2021. Einsprachigkeit, Fremdsprachigkeit, Mehrsprachigkeit und Transsprachigkeit in der sprachhistorischen Forschung zu Text und Diskurs. Eine Reflexion. In Jochen A. Bär (ed.), *Historische Text- und Diskurssemantik,* 48–60. (Jahrbücher für Germanistische Sprachgeschichte 11). Berlin/Boston: De Gruyter.

Passow, Franz. 1813. Sprachkunde. Bruchstücke über Sprachenmischung. *Die Musen* 1. 360–376.

Ptashnyk, Stefaniya. Forthcoming. *Multilinguale Kommunikation und Stadtsprache. Eine historische Untersuchung am Beispiel von Lemberg 1848–1918.*

Reichmann, Oskar. 1978. Deutsche Nationalsprache. Eine kritische Darstellung. *Germanistische Linguistik* 2–5. 389–423.

Reichmann, Oskar. 1991: Gemeinsamkeiten im Bedeutungsspektrum europäischer Sprachen. In Magdolna Bartha/Rita Brdar Szabo (eds.), *Von der Schulgrammatik zur Allgemeinen Sprachwissenschaft. Beiträge zur Gedenktagung für Professor Janos Juhasz,* 75–94. Budapest: ELTE.

Reichmann, Oskar. 1993: Europäismen im Wortschatz von Einzelsprachen. In Baldur Panzer (ed.), *Aufbau, Entwicklung und Struktur des Wortschatzes in den europäischen Sprachen. Motive, Tendenzen, Strömungen und ihre Folgen,* 28–47. Frankfurt a. M. et al.: Lang.

Reichmann, Oskar. 2001: *Das nationale und das europäische Modell in der Sprachgeschichtsschreibung des Deutschen.* Freiburg/CH: Universitätsverlag.

Reichmann, Oskar. 2014: Semantische Europäismen: ein Metapherngeflecht? In: Michel Lefevre (ed.), *Linguistische Aspekte des Vergleichs, der Metapher und der Metonymie,* 45–62. Tübingen: Stauffenburg.

Reichmann, Oskar. 2016: Semantische Gemeinsamkeiten (Europäismen) im Wortschatz europäischer Sprachen und das Projekt ‚Europa'. In Peter Schiffauer/Krzystof Lobos (eds.), *Beiträge zu den Wurzeln der europäischen Integration. Ertrag einer deutsch-polnischen wissenschaftlichen Diskussion ein Jahrzehnt nach der Osterweiterung der Europäischen Union,* 13–36. Berlin: BWV.

Saur, Xavier de & Armand Léonce Varanchan de Saint-Geniès. 1823. *Des hommes célèbres de France au dix-huitième siècle, et de l'état de la littérature et des arts a la même époque; par M. Goëthe: traduit de l'allemand.* Paris: Renouard.

Schmitz-Emans, Monika. 2019. Europäische Romantik als transnationales Netzwerk. In Doerte Bischoff/Susanne Komfort-Hein (eds.), *Handbuch Literatur & Transnationalität,* 259–278. Berlin/Boston: De Gruyter.

Schreiner, Sabine. 1992. *Sprachenlernen in Lebensgeschichten der Goethezeit.* München: Iudicium.

Uvarov, Sergei Semionovich. 1817. *Nonnos von Panopolis der Dichter. Ein Beytrag zur Geschichte der griechischen Poesie.* St. Petersburg: Pluchart.

Weber, Max. 1985 [1919]. Wissenschaft als Beruf. In Johannes Winckelmann (ed.), *Max Weber. Gesammelte Aufsätze zur Wissenschaftslehre*, 582–613. 6th edn. Tübingen: Mohr Siebeck.
Weissmann, Dirk. 2021. *Les langues de Goethe: Essai sur l'imaginaire plurilingue d'un poète national*. Paris: Éditions Kimé.
Weitin, Thomas. 2017. Scalable Reading. *Zeitschrift für Literaturwissenschaft und Linguistik* 47 (1), 1–6.
Wolff, Oscar & Bernhard Ludwig. 1832. *Das Büchlein von Goethe. Andeutungen zum besseren Verständnis seines Lebens und Wirkens*. Penig: Sieghart.
Young, Julian Charles. 1871. *A Memoir of Charles Mayne Young, Tragedian, with Extracts from his Son's Journal*. Vol. 1. London/New York: Macmillan.

Jana-Katharina Mende
Zooming In and Out of Historical Multilingual Literature

Reading 19th-Century Literary Dictionaries on Scale

Abstract: Mixed methods approaches for literary history writing have shown the 'great unread' of 19th-century literature. Here, a mixed methods approach to multilingual literary history attempts to systematically study and model multilingual literature in the 19th century, thus uncovering hitherto unknown or little-known multilingual authors. The analysis is based on data from two historical biographical dictionaries containing biographical and bibliographical data of German authors. Using named entity recognition and visualization tools (Recogito, NodeGoat) biographical information is mined for implicit and explicit references to multilingualism. By mapping places of residence of authors from different multilingual regions, multilingual literary communities become visible. One example, the multilingual literary community of Preßburg (Bratislava), is investigated closely to show societal, cultural, individual, and textual forms of (hidden) multilingualism. The article concludes by critically evaluating the tools and approaches used to explore hidden multilingualism in 19th-century German literature.

Keywords: Distant Reading, Close Reading, Literary History, Mixed Methods, Bratislava

"Lubię mapy, bo kłamią" [I love maps because they lie], Wisława Szymborska

1 Introduction: hidden multilingualism and 19th century literary histories

Multilingualism and multilingual literature are a central phenomenon of a global world and culture, interconnected through migration as well as economic, cultural, and linguistic contact. Multilingual literary history in Europe focus-

---

Jana-Katharina Mende, Martin-Luther-University Halle-Wittenberg, e-mail: jana-katharina.mende@germanistik.uni-halle.de

es on literature in the Middle Ages and Renaissance between Latin and different vernaculars, polyglot Renaissance and Baroque authors as well as modern multilingual texts by George, Rilke, Pound, Joyce, Yvan Goll, or Beckett (Forster 2011 [1968]: 7–9). In any case, knowledge of multilingual authors and literature depends entirely on previous information about their multilingual nature, as most literary histories are written with a monolingual bias. The titles of well-known 19th-century literary historiographies and studies of literary history betray that predisposition: *Geschichte der poetischen National-Literatur der Deutschen* [History of the Poetical National Literature of the Germans] by Georg Gervinus (1844), Wilhelm Scherer's *Geschichte der deutschen Literatur* [History of German Literature] (1883), or Rudolf von Gottschall's *Die deutsche Nationalliteratur in der 1. Hälfte des 19. Jahrhunderts literaturhistorisch und kritisch dargestellt* [The German national literature in the first half of the 19th century presented in a literary-historical and critical way] (1855). From those titles, the national and monolingual focus becomes immediately evident. Indeed, 19th-century literary scholarship as well as later research on multilingual literature has implicitly and explicitly ignored multilingual realities during the time of linguistic and literary nationalization: "In many cases, the multilingual facets of 19th-century literary history have been ignored or actively excluded by the national paradigm" (Anokhina, Dembeck, and Weissmann 2019: 2). The result of this national literary history is aptly described by Casanova: "[...] our literary unconscious is largely national. Our instruments of analysis and evaluation are national. Indeed, the study of literature almost everywhere in the world is organized along national lines" (Casanova 2004: XI). Dembeck describes the paradox of multilingual canonical authors within national literature when he explains how Herder and Goethe both diversified German literature through collections, translations, and demands for other literatures but at the same time contributed to the monolingual paradigm being established via national literature (Dembeck 2017: 3).

Multilingual literary studies are more and more interested in researching multilingual authors who lived and wrote during the time of the nationalization of literature, which coincided with the formation and establishment of modern philologies like German Studies. Nevertheless, the 19th century remains underrepresented in multilingual literary scholarship: one of the few volumes on historical European multilingual literature and a trailblazer in multilingual literary historical research calls the 19th century a "chronological gap", a "dark continent of literary multilingual scholarship" (Anokhina, Dembeck, and Weissmann 2019: 1). However, within the digital humanities it is the opposite. Literary scholarship focuses heavily on 19th-century literature given its accessibility but it has only recently developed methods that include a multilingual approach (Dejaeghere et al.). Tools and software often support only a monolingual corpus and approach.

Multilingual literature also forms part of the "great unread", a description which Moretti borrows from Cohen (Cohen 2009: 59) to refer to the problem of world literature. Of the many books published in the 19th century only a fraction of them are read and belong to the canon (Moretti 2013: 45). Mani uses the term recoding to refer to a new reading of national literature within the paradigm of world literature: "Recoding World Literature asks two intertwined questions: how does our imagination of the world rely on our access to books and libraries? And conversely, how does our access to world literature shape our understanding of books and libraries?" (Mani 2017: 16).

By zooming out of multilingual literary history, much like the bird's-eye view in Google Maps where this metaphor comes from, it is possible to get a first and broad impression of the material. Zooming in enables a close investigation of certain cities, neighborhoods, authors, publications, and texts. However, the metaphor is not a method and the use of scalable reading and mixed methods to analyze multilingual literary history needs further explanation and reflection. How can we recover multilingual literary material when most of the sources provide us with monolingual material and leave out information about existing multilingualism? My approach here is twofold: first, I investigate specific references to multilingualism, which mostly consist of translations and language knowledge in historical biographical and bibliographical dictionaries on German writers.

Second, I combine biographical and bibliographical data with geographical coordinates to establish the places of residence of authors at the time of writing and producing a text. Here, multilingualism is at first hypothetical: writers in multilingual surroundings might or might not be multilingual. However, through zooming in on external linguistic information, language biographies, and texts, it is possible to reconstruct the multilingual lives of lesser-known authors. This leads to two more forms of multilingualism: multilingualism through migration and change of place (as further described in Vlasta (in this volume)) and local multilingualism within multilingual regions.

My hypothesis implies that multilingual surroundings and daily multilingual interactions of the authors influence their writing, causing multilingual interference with and in the texts. Furthermore, the connection between geographical, biographical, and linguistic data reveals networks and neighborhoods of literary and linguistic communities who talk, discuss, and publish together across, along and through different languages. I will provide an example of those neighborhoods in multilingual Bratislava in the 19th century in the second part of this paper.

2 Zooming out: languages and forms of multilingualism in literary dictionaries of the 19th century

2.1 Corpus and data

This study uses historical biographical data on multilingual competences and everyday use of different languages. Biographical data, including information on languages, multilingualism, and places of residence, can be found in historical biographical dictionaries which are useful sources for investigating multilingual authors even if their main aim is to provide information on German literature. These dictionaries are representative of the positivist studies of 19th-century literature scholars. The most extensive collection of biographical data on German authors in the 19th century is Goedeke's *Grundrisz zur Geschichte der deutschen Dichtung aus den Quellen* [Outline of the history of German poetry from its sources] published in 3 volumes between 1859 and 1881. He combined existing biographical and bibliographical data with information gathered through correspondence with authors (Jacob 2003: 163). He advertised in journals asking writers to send in their biographies and even included questionnaires to gather structured data (Jacob 2003: 163) The eight volumes are structured chronologically, beginning in the age of Charlemagne and spanning until the 19th century. (Jacob 2003: 165). The short biographical notes provide information about dates of birth and death, education, profession, and publications with additional private data (Jacob 2003: 166).

Franz Brümmer (1836–1923) began working on his dictionary, *Lexikon der deutschen Dichter und Prosaisten vom Beginn des 19. Jahrhunderts bis zur Gegenwart* [Encyclopaedia of German poets and prose writers from the beginning of the 19th Century until present], after reading a complaint in a journal that it was almost impossible to find reliable information about contemporary writers. Collaborating with publishers, he collected and extracted personal data about writers including those writing under a pseudonym (Jacob 2003: 117). The dictionary was published in installments and later in book format (1876/1877). It contained a list of hitherto unknown authors as well as a plea from the publisher, Brümmer, to send him additional information concerning those authors

(Jacob 2003: 118). The names appear in alphabetical order and the articles contain information on dates of birth (and death), pseudonyms, father's occupation, education, occupation and work, contributions to journals and newspapers as well as bibliographical data on published works. (Jacob 2003: 119).

Sophie Pataky (1860–1915)'s *Lexikon deutscher Frauen der Feder* [Dictionary of German women of the pen] contains biographical and bibliographical information of appr. 5000 female writers. Pataky's dictionary of female writers was not the first of that sort: before her, Georg Christian Lehms (1715), Samuel Baur (1790), Karl Wilhelm Otto August Schindel (1823–25), Abraham Voß (1848), and the first woman, Marianne Nigg, published biographical and bibliographical collections of female writers (Jacob 2003: 135) (Behnke 1999, 1: 5), but Pataky's was the most complete for 19th-century female writers. She was inspired by the International Congress of Women to focus on literature by female writers (Behnke 1999, 1: 53). She herself was born in Podebrad, Bohemia, and lived in a multilingual region herself, just like her husband, Carl Pataky, who came from Arad to Vienna and Berlin (Jacob 2003: 138). The Berlin publisher and Pataky's husband, Carl Pataky, published both volumes of the lexicon in the space of just a few months (Behnke 1999, 1: 52). The subtitle of Pataky's lexicon explains its scope: "Eine Zusammenstellung der seit dem Jahre 1840 erschienenen Werke weiblicher Autoren, nebst Biographieen der lebenden und einem Verzeichnis der Pseudonyme" [A compilation of the works of female authors published since 1840, together with biographies of the living ones and a list of pseudonyms]. Apart from a few exceptions, the dictionary only contains information on living, contemporary writers between 1840 and 1898. It includes all or almost all women writing in German at that time, even if their works do not qualify as literature (such as cookbooks or instruction manuals for knitting, sewing and household keeping). The articles are separated into a biographical and a bibliographical part, the length of the entries differing widely between only the name and full information on name, name changes, pseudonyms, address, places of residence, birth, travels, education, family, marriage, children, language knowledge, and other details. In some cases, all biographical information is missing. (Behnke 1999, 1: 56).

The advantages of Brümmer's and Pataky's dictionaries are their focus on contemporary writers in the 19th century and the structure of the articles. The alphabetical, not chronological, order of the dictionaries makes it easier to extract and re-structure biographical, geographical, and bibliographical metadata semi-automatically.

However, both dictionaries explicitly refer to German and accordingly implicitly to monolingual writers. Information about multilingual authors is occasionally part of the biographical description. Paradoxically, multilingualism plays an important role in the dictionary which – in its title *Deutsche Frauen der Feder* [German Women of the Pen] – emphasizes the fact that the female writers wrote in German. However, a closer analysis reveals the different forms of multilingualism that play an integral role in female authorship, literary production and for female education and serve as a means of economic independence. Pataky reflects on her own invisibility and the invisibility of female authorship in the 19th century. Gender and genre create invisibility for female authors who contribute to publications, translations, journals but remain unnamed or unappreciated which prompted the work of Pataky's dictionary (Pataky 1898a: VI). The dictionary also unmasks pseudonyms to make female authors more visible (Pataky 1898a: XI).

For this analysis, I used Pataky's dictionary to explore quantitative approaches to discovering multilingual authors and added information from Brümmer's dictionary for case studies of multilingual literary regions and their neighborhoods.

Experimentally, I used the smaller data set from Pataky's dictionary as a starting point to test the workflow and mixed methods to research multilingual writers in 19th century German literature. Therefore, the first stage of zooming out does not include male writers, who will be added in the second step of the analysis, the (re-)construction of multilingual literary neighborhoods in Bratislava (Preßburg).

2.2 Forms and functions of multilingualism in Pataky's *Deutsche Frauen der Feder*

Translations are among the most common instances of explicitly named occasions of multilingualism in Pataky's dictionary. Several writers were active translators. As it is visible in Figure 1, texts translated from 26 different languages are included in the bibliographical data and mentioned in the biographies; most of the languages are European; most dominant are translations from French and English into German. These numbers are reflected in the information about language knowledge, reading skills and writing skills that are explicitly mentioned in Pataky. English and French clearly dominate skills of other languages, including old languages like Latin or Greek. The skills mirror the contents of female education and often also resulted from finding employment as a teacher or governess.

However, those languages that are mentioned often differ from the languages of the regions in which the authors grew up, lived, traveled, and wrote.

Fig. 1: Source languages of translations to German from Pataky 1898

Only two entries contain information about a different home language or a different regional language. The Swiss author Marie Bach-Gelpcke grew up bilingual: "Geboren in Bern, am 26. Juni 1836 aber die ersten Jahre am schönen Lemanersee aufgewachsen, erlernte die Kleine die beiden Sprachen französisch und deutsch gleichzeitig" [Born in Bern on June 26, 1836, but having grown up at the beautiful Lake Geneva for the first years, the little girl learned both languages, French and German, at the same time.] (Pataky 1898a: 28). Another Swiss author, Johanna Garbald-Gredig, grew up speaking Romansh and German (Pataky 1898a: 243). The author Julienne van der Chys grew up speaking (and writing) Dutch: "Ihre ersten Verse waren in holländischer Sprache geschrieben [...]. Mit Mühe erlernte sie die deutsche Sprache" [Her first verses were written in Dutch [...]. She had a hard time learning the German language] (Pataky 1898a: 128).

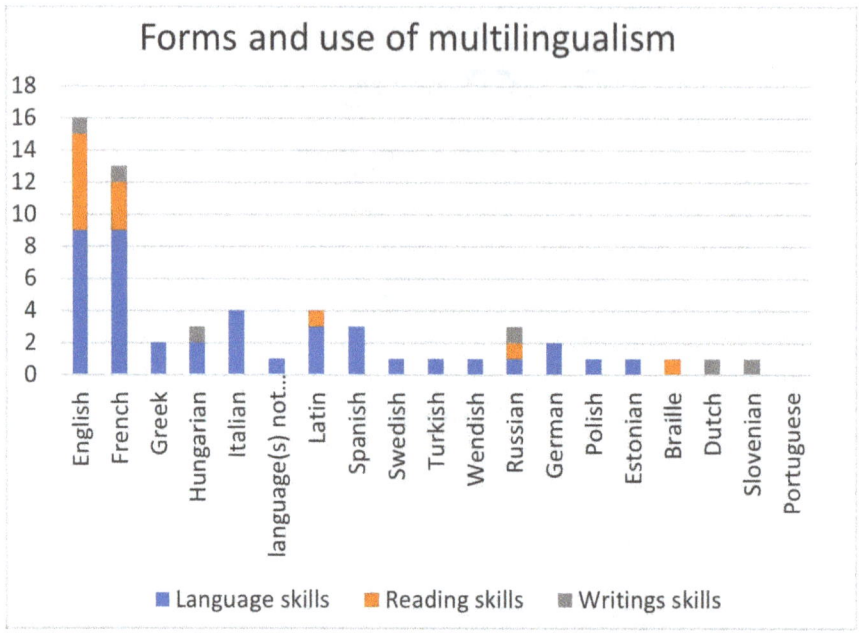

Fig. 2: Language skills mentioned, Pataky 1898

Two examples refer to regional bilingualism in Switzerland, another to a language change occasioned by a change of places where the author, Julienne van der Chys, had to learn German as a foreign language. Both instances include only Western European languages (Germanic and Romance languages).

Fig. 3: Places of residence of female authors, Pataky's Lexikon (map created using Recogito Pelagius)

Geographical data from Pataky's dictionary show the wide range of places of residence of 19th century female writers. Whereas writers congregate within the territory of (today's) Germany, European and international outliers are recognizable as well as a clear regional focus in the East of Europe. However, there are large areas in the world where, according to Pataky, no female German writer lived.

There are three main categories of regions and places in a multilingual context:
– Foreign language surroundings through international migration, often only for one author.
– Historically multilingual literary regions for writers within cultural communities.
– Migrant communities within a foreign language surrounding.

In order to further understand those regions and individual cases, zooming into the now visible, formerly hidden multilingualism completes the picture of the map above.

3 Zooming into hidden multilingualism: networks and neighborhoods of languages, literatures, and writers

Most German writers lived within the (wider) German speaking area, often in Europe, and in individual cases as far as the US, Brazil, Mexico, Melbourne, or Tokyo. Those places of migration can have a strong impact on the language biographies of the authors living there but mostly, linguistic information is missing and cannot be reconstructed due to lack of evidence. To give but a few examples of potentially multilingual authors whose exact language knowledge is unknown: C.W. Emma Brauns (1836–1893) lived in Tokyo with her husband, a university teacher and fellow author. She published a collection of Japanese fairytales and probably learned Japanese during the three years of her stay there (Pataky 1898a: 102). Rosa von Herff-Schacht published poems with Spanish titles while living in Mexico (Pataky 1898a: 341). Maruša Nusko traveled through Egypt and stayed as a teacher in Cairo where she was working on a study on Egypt (Pataky 1898b: 96–97). However, not always did migrant languages and literary production overlap: Hanna Linnekogel, while living in Brazil, translated from French into German (Pataky 1898a: 509) without any mention of her Portuguese surroundings. Nothing more than her name and the information in Pataky's dictionary remain, but it is likely that the author was part of a migrant and colonist community, as German immigrants were the largest group of colonists after the Portuguese in Porto Alegre between 1824 and 1900 where it was also possible to publish in German (Seyferth 1998: 142). The linguistic surroundings were those of a language enclave of German, and she probably translated for a German immigrant community. While it might be difficult to reconstruct individual language biographies, more can be said about multilingual communities in multilingual regions.

Historically multilingual literary regions for writers within cultural communities include large parts of the so-called German speaking area. Linguistic data on multilingualism in the 19th century has similar problems to literary history – a lack of historical data leads to imprecise statements about the actual multilingual situation in those regions. Historical language maps illustrate the problem when they show linguistic borders along national and state borders (see Kiepert 1872). The same holds true for statistical evaluations of multilingualism because language surveys, especially in the 19th century, were also shaped by a monolingual bias (Humbert, Coray, and Duchêne 2018: 6). Historical sociolinguistics and research of linguistic and literary cityscapes have been helpful in reconstructing the multilingual cityscapes of literary centers (Ptashnyk 2013 for Lviv/Lemberg/Lwów). Literary historical analysis of multilingual spaces especially in Central Europe describes literature in Vilnius/Wilno/Vilna, Tartu and Tallinn, Riga, Czernowitz/Cernăuți/Chernovtsy/Chernivtsi/Czerniowce, Danzig/Gdańsk, Bucharest, Budapest, Trieste, and Prague (Cornis-Pope and Neubauer 2006, XX).

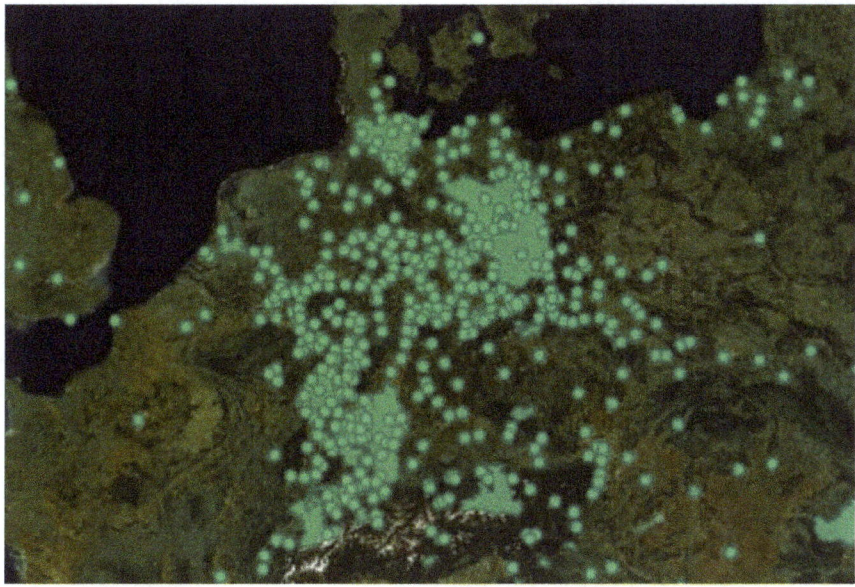

Fig. 4: Places of residence in the German speaking areas, visualisation of Pataky's dictionary (with Recogito)

However, by adopting a systematic and comparative approach, linking sociolinguistic multilingual cityscapes and literary history, the impact of linguistic everyday life on literary production can be discerned. Even contrasting a historical linguistic map which shows relatively clear linguistic boundaries for the 19th century with the places of residence of 'German' authors shows that the German speaking area (red) and the places of residence do not completely overlap (see Kiepert 1872). Multilingualism occurred in those areas in two forms – on the one hand, through German authors who lived in an area where German was not the dominant language (mostly marked in different shades of green on the map for Slavic languages, yellow for Hungarian, as well as blue (French, Italian), orange (Scandinavian), and brown (English)) (Kiepert 1872). On the other hand, there are areas marked as German, but German was only one of several languages spoken, albeit the dominant one. This was the case in Silesia, Bohemia, East Prussia, Galicia, and other zones of language contact.

Cities had double function as multilingual and literary centers within those regions: "Cities have long been the chief locus of language contact, since they are in essence restricted areas dependent on long-term face-to-face interaction" (Mackey 2005: 1304). Cornis-Pope attributes cities in Central Europe the function of "magnetic fields", pulling Eastern and Western literary trends together (Cornis-Pope 2006: 9). Literary and linguistic contact and conflict create fertile ground for new forms of literature and culture: "The literary and artistic production in these areas involved a negotiation of tensions between nationalism and regionalism, metropolitan influences and local patriotism. Regionalism often worked as a corrective, turning potentially chauvinistic projects into intercultural ones" (Cornis-Pope 2006: 5). Places of residence and writing were potential "magnetic fields" and the authors used the linguistic and literary variety to negotiate regional, transregional, and transnational themes and literary forms in their writing.

From the many places of writing, one city will now serve as a case study to investigate whether the claim of a distant-reading, data-driven approach of biographical dictionaries of German writers will indeed succeed in finding multilingual writers.

Less central than during the 18th century, Bratislava, or Preßburg/Pozsony/Prešporok remained a political, administrative, economic, and cultural hub throughout the 19th century. Political distinctions of social and ethnic groups influenced the statistics about the ethnic (and linguistic) affiliation of the population. However, the population was mainly German, with sizable Slovak and Hungarian minorities throughout the 19th century (Meier 2020). While German was the dominant language during the first half of the 19th century, the second half was influenced by Magyarization efforts which produced more bilingual and monolingual Hungarian publications and periodicals. From 1870 onwards, many people were comfortably trilingual with German, Hungarian, and Slovakian (Meier 2020). The city offered a good university, and many authors studied in Preßburg. Similarly, Preßburg was a center of Jewish religion and learning, as it was the place of residence of one of the most famous orthodox rabbis of the 19th century, Moses Sofer (1762–1839) (Meier 2020) and an important yeshiva, a Jewish religious school. Therefore, also Hebrew literature was taught, written, and read in the city.

In Pataky's and Brümmer's dictionaries, Preßburg appears regularly as a place of birth or a place of residence. More than 60 authors lived there at some point in their lives during the time of the analysis. The turn of the 18th century to the 19th century was the most literary active time in Preßburg whereas the city's cultural life became less dynamic towards the end of the century.

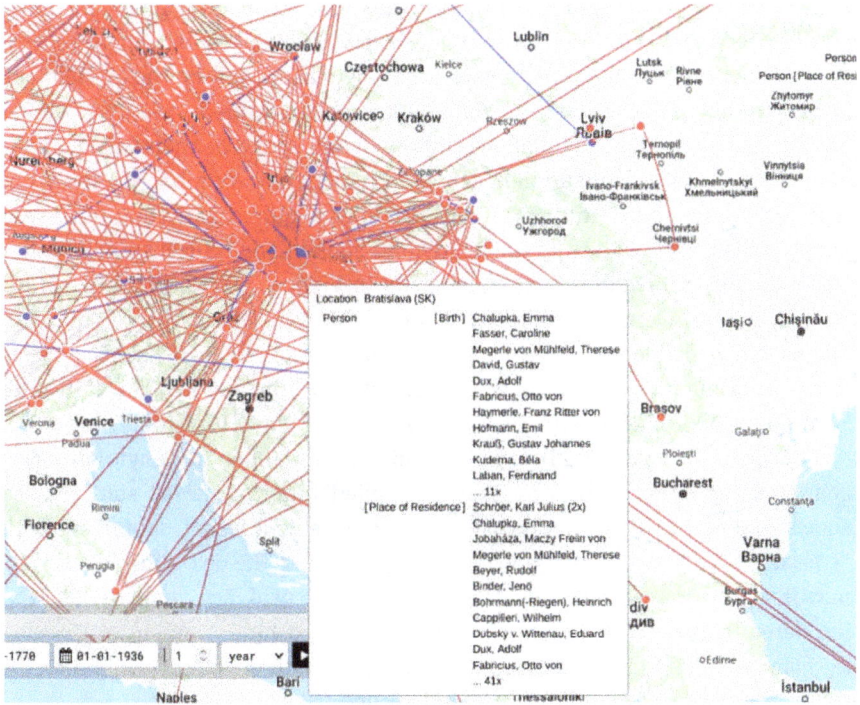

Fig. 5: Places of birth (blue) and residence (red) of authors in Pataky and Brümmer (map created with Nodegoat)

Altogether, there were several main reasons for authors to reside in Preßburg: many of the male authors came to the city to attend schools and the university as part of their studies – like Nikolaus Lenau who studied Hungarian law at Preßburg university in 1821. Jewish authors also came to attend the yeshiva in Preßburg. Some authors were drawn by the Preßburg theater or came through the city as part of a theater company. Several authors were born into families living in Preßburg or moved there during their childhood. Multilingualism was an inevitable part of everyday life for authors growing up in Preßburg where German, Hungarian, Slovakian, Yiddish and Hebrew were spoken in the city. Female authors either moved there with their families or married into a Preßburg family. Not all authors spent enough time in Preßburg to qualify as part of the literary neighborhood in a meaningful way, integrating themselves long enough to take part in the social life of the city.

Regarding multilingualism, authors can be classified according to the languages they knew and the way they used different languages for different purposes. The first group of hidden multilinguals consists of authors who predominantly wrote and published in German despite knowing other languages – a form of passive, receptive or private multilingualism. Among those, Nikolaus Lenau (Nikolaus Franz Niembsch Edler von Strehlenau, 1802–1850), was probably the most well-known. Lenau was bilingual and spoke German and Hungarian. He even studied Hungarian in school in Budapest and probably also used it with his friends there (Ritter 2002: 21). He later acquired Latin and other language skills at school and at university and spoke Latin with his uncle (Ritter 2002: 22). Several lectures at the university in Vienna, where Lenau began his studies in 1818, were given in Latin (Ritter 2002: 40). Traces of the Hungarian language are visible in letters from Lenau to his mother: in 1820, he signed a letter to his mother in Preßburg with the words: "Ihr alle herzlich küßender Édes fiam: Miklós" [(German:) Yours kissing all of you (Hungarian:) My sweet son: Miklós] (Lenau 1989: 23). Code-switching from German to Hungarian seems connected to his mother, who probably called him "my sweet son". It also shows grammatical independence (the reference to himself should make it "édes fiad" [your sweet son]) and relates the phrase to the use within his family, maybe also distancing himself from the German-speaking grandparents who interfered with his literary ambitions and pressured him to pursue a career in German law. His Hungarian skills remained hidden to the public eye during his career as a romantic author from Central Europe.

Hungarian-German bilingualism was a key feature and a coveted ability in the Schröer family (Figure 7), which boasted several writers – the mother, Therese Schröer, née Langwieser (1804–1885), her husband Tobias Gottfried Schröer (1791–1850), and their son Karl Julius Schröer (1825–1900). They all lived in Preßburg and formed a small intellectual circle in the city, nurturing and representing Preßburg literature through various contacts with other authors like Karl von Holtei and joint publications. Therese Schröer came from a family in Preßburg, wrote poems, letter, short stories, as well as books and treatises on education and also composed songs (Glosíková 1995: 130). Research literature paints a picture of her as a patently stereotypical female wo is the soul of the gatherings and who took great care that everybody felt fine in the end – "daß sich letzten Endes alle wohlfühlten." (Pflagner 1974: 186). As a born and raised Preßburger and through the company her husband kept she was surely multilingual enough to navigate those meetings between writers, artists, professors of different (linguistic) background well and amiably.

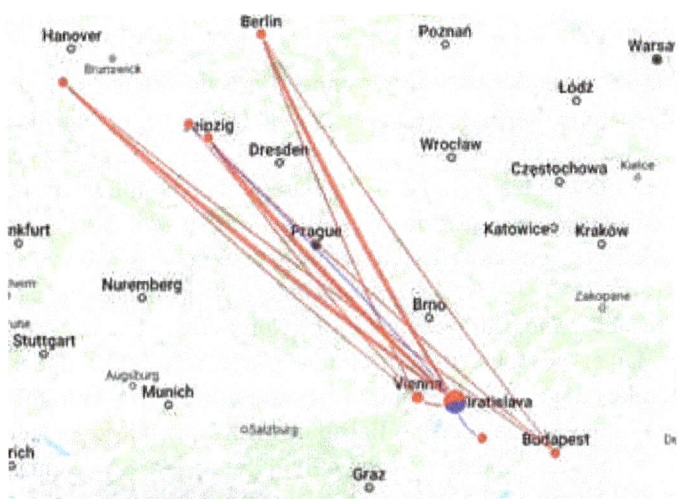

Fig. 6: Movements of the family members - Therese Schröer, Tobias Gottfried Schröer, and Karl Julius Schröer (created with NodeGoat)

Her own works were sparse and appeared only later in her life through the efforts of the author and playwright Karl von Holtei (1798–1880), who became her friend in 1836 and whose correspondence encouraged her to write and later publish her letters and stories. Those texts, while referring to multilingualism and featuring characters who do not speak German or speak German with an accent, are strictly monolingual.

Tobias Gottfried Schröer, her husband, grew up in Preßburg and, after studying in Győr and Halle, taught Latin, German, history, and art in his hometown at the Protestant lyceum (Glosíková 1995: 131). He published literary works as well as studies of history, politics, education, and aesthetics, with a strong focus on Hungarian-German relations. His identity as a German Hungarian, taking sides in the struggle for political independence of Hungary against the Habsburg monarchy made him publish under pseudonyms or anonymously to prevent censorship (Glosíková 1995: 132) The thorough linguistic and cultural education and political orientation also influenced their son, Karl Julius Schröer, who grew up in the intellectual circle around his parents in Preßburg. He studied Latin and Greek at home and at school and started to learn Hungarian at the age of eleven (Horányi 1941: 10). Later, he studied in Leipzig, Halle, and Berlin (Glosíková 1995: 129). He first became a teacher in Preßburg like his father and then a professor for German literature in Budapest and Vienna. His scholarly work focused strongly on literary history and Goethe as well as the role of the German language as a minority language in Hungary (Glosíková 1995: 129).

Karl Julius Schröer's literary publications united German writers and Hungarian German writers from the Preßburg region. He showed a multilingual and multicultural understanding of (German) minorities in Hungary and a sense of national or ethnic identity which includes Hungarian-German multilingualism. His own multilingual competences do not appear in his written work but clearly inform his publication decisions as well as his research subjects.

In a short treaty on *Unsere Deutschen in den nichtdeutschen Kronländern und die Sprachkarte der Monarchie* [Our Germans in the Non-German Crown Lands and the Language Map of the Monarchy], Karl Julius Schröer lays out his understanding of German language minorities and the special role of German in that area. He notes that linguistic maps of the Habsburg monarchy fail to include German language islands and claims that the cultural superiority of German culture, literature, and language will guarantee its continued presence in those regions (Schröer n.d.: 1). He argues that it is also for this reason that Germans can never be fully Magyarized. He describes the multilingual surroundings of an outdoor coffeehouse in Preßburg where men talk in different varieties of German: Austrian, Silesian, Berlin dialect, women in Austrian German, and small children speak Hungarian with their nurses (Schröer n.d.: 3). These differences along the lines of gender (male–female), age (adult–child), and class (members of the city's bourgeoisie and their working-class nurses) manifest linguistically in the use of different language varieties and languages. German varieties are ranked highest as the languages of men whereas the local Austrian dialect is only connected to women. Hungarian is the language of children and nurses and thus has no cultural standing. These multilingual political tensions also appear in the press of that time. Schröer mentions a song, published in the Preßburger Zeitung on February 5, 1860, dealing with the Hungarian-German language question. (Schröer n.d.: 3):

The Song of a Pressburger (*Lied eines Presburgers* [sic]) describes and multilingually imitates the dialect and Hungarian-German language mixing of a German Hungarian in Preßburg and pleads for a continued existence in the city's separate linguistic, cultural, and national groups which nevertheless belong all to the city:

> Ein Unger bin i, des is rein,
> Laßt's mi a deutscher Unger sein:

Sann ja Schlowacken a im Land
Und des is immer no ka Schand.
[...]
Magyar, Schlowack, gebts her die Hand
[I am an Hungarian, that's true,/Let me be a German Hungarian:/There are Schlowacken (Slovakians) in the country/And that's still no shame./[...]/Magyar, Schlowack, give me your hand] (Anonym 1860: 3)

While the German language and identity represent the connection to German and Habsburg power, the multilingual disposition enables Schröer and others to see the rights of other (linguistic) minorities and nationalities. This becomes evident in another publication.

Schröer and his fellow author and neighbor in Preßburg, Rudolf Bayer (or Beyer) published the literary yearbook *Donauhafen* [Port of the Danube] only once, in 1848. It negotiates questions of language, nationality, and belonging in the political frame of the Hungarian revolution of 1848. The volume contains contributions by several multilingual authors from Preßburg. It includes several multilingual contributions, a fact that is not explicitly mentioned. Thus, one can conclude that the internal multilingualism of the texts within a volume published under a German title was nothing worth mentioning - either for monolingual reasons because it would have to sell on the German literary market or because it was simply nothing special. A closer analysis shows that almost 25% of the text contains some form of multilingualism, ranging from minor forms of code-switching to translations. The languages include translations from Persian and Serbian, and code-switching between German as the dominant language and smaller parts in Hungarian, Romanian, French, Latin, and Italian. Apart from regional multilingualism connected to the Hungarian-German surroundings and forms of Habsburg monarchy multilingualism, the volume also contains a few of Georg Friedrich Daumer's *Hafis* translated from Persian (Bayer and Schröer 1848: 76–77).

The Habsburg writers came from different multilingual regions: Ludwig August Frankl (1810–1894) a doctor, journalist, and writer grew up in Prague in a Jewish family, studied in Padua, and lived in Vienna. He published a translation of Serbian national songs in the volume (*Die Gattin des reichen Gavan, Hochzeitlied beim Kolotanz* [The Wife of Gavan the Rich, Wedding song for a Kolo dance]). Leopold Kompert (1822–1886), lived in Bratislava, and studied in Prague and Vienna. Karl Wilm (Karl Wilhelm von Martini, 1821–1885), a journalist and writer, came from the Banat region and lived and worked in Vienna. Many of the authors and poets were multilingual with German as one of their languages, usually as their main language of publication. They came from different parts of the Habsburg Empire. Some of the authors were personally acquainted as well. Josef Rank (1816–1896) was an Austrian author and teacher. He published literary writing in the *Österreichisches Morgenblatt* [Austrian Morning Journal], was in contact with writers of the Vormärz period like Ignaz Franz Castelli and Nikolaus Lenau and had to spend some time in Bratislava in 1844 to escape the notice of the Viennese censors. There, he met Leopold Kompert and Adolf Neustadt (Lengauer 2003).

While the journal gained attention in literary journals and reviews mainly because of contributions by Gottfried Keller and Friedrich Hebbel (Anonym 1848: 796), the regional authors – the editors Karl Julius Schröer and Rudolf Beyer, as well as Josef Rank (1816–1896), Karl Wilm and Leopold Kompert were also mentioned for their description of Hungarian national life (*Ungarisches Nationalleben*). The multilingual character of their works was not revealed; instead, the "foreignness" was attributed to its different national character (Hungarianness), equalizing the multilingualism of the texts with German, Hungarian, Romanian, Italian, French, and Latin with a Hungarian national trait.

Zooming further into the texts of the literary anthology reveals the intricate political and poetical uses of multilingualism, hidden beneath the German title. The fable *Mausöhrlein, Forelle und Dr. Krebs. Ein Mährchen* [Myosotis, trout, and Dr. Crab. A fairytale] by the editor and writer Rudolf Beyer (psd. Rupertus) (Bayer [Beyer] 1848: 1) serves as an example of the ambiguous use of multilingualism. The fable tells the story of the three protagonists, the flower Myosotis and the trout, who fall in love and want to migrate to Hungary. They are joined by Dr. Crab – Dr. Krebs. None of them speaks Hungarian and they know very little about the country. After deciding to go to the fictional place of Cancriháza (a pun playing with the Hungarian word for "house" – ház and the Latin word cancer) myosotis and trout die in the heat of the Hungarian puszta. Dr. Crab bears witness to their demise and afterwards decides to re-migrate to Austria. The political context of the story is the Hungarian Revolution and the war for independence (1848/1849) against the Austrian Empire. While avoiding open political statements, it remains skeptical towards migrating to foreign countries, embodied by Hungary in the text. The foreignness is textually performed via multilingualism and metalinguistic comments on the Hungarian language.

A Hungarian mole who encounters Dr. Crab en route comments doubtfully on his attempt and motivation to stay in Hungary:

> "Lasse ich es auch für den Augenblick ganz außer Betracht, daß Sie als Deutsche sich nie dem Magyarismus accomodiren werden, daß Ihnen unsere Sprache kaum erlernbar sein dürfte, item unsere Gesetze und Lebensweise Ihnen stellenweis etwas unbegreiflich - vom Standpunkt als Deutscher aus - erscheinen dürfte, so verstehe ich namentlich Sie nicht, der Sie als Arzt hierherkamen, wie Sie das, was man im Allgemeinen schon dem

Deutschen versagt, und was der Arzt im höchsten Grade und vorzugsweise besitzen soll, nämlich das Vertrauen, je hier zu finden gedenken"
[Leaving aside for the moment the fact that you, as Germans, will never accommodate yourselves to Magyarism, that our language is hardly something you can learn, that our laws and way of life may in some cases seem somewhat incomprehensible to you - from the point of view of a German - I do not understand you in particular, who came here as a doctor, how you ever intend to find here what is generally already denied to Germans, and what a doctor should preferably possess in the highest degree, namely trust] (Bayer [Beyer] 1848: 14–15).

A German doctor, unable to speak Hungarian, cannot successfully integrate into (monolingual) Hungarian society. Implied in the exchange is the fact that the Hungarian mole converses fluently in German, mirroring the bilingualism of Hungarians with German. The inability to learn the language is presented as a key element against migration.

Linguistically and stylistically, code-switching is used to denote status, belonging, and education of the characters. Dr. Crab uses Latin phrases to sound medical and educated: "'Gewiß, domine illustrissime', unterbrach ihn schnell der Arzt [...]" ['Certainly, domine illustrissime', interrupted the doctor] (Bayer [Beyer] 1848: 25). He also uses French to show his (imagined) worldliness: "'Mais voila' sprach der Krebs [...]" ['Mais voila', said the crab] (Bayer [Beyer] 1848: 25). Given the satirical representation of the crab also the use of Latin and French as markers of education and status as a doctor is ironic. Hungarian words and code-switching with Hungarian are not addressed to the characters, but to the assumed (multilingual) reader. The place where the crab is heading, Cancriháza, contains a plurilingual pun as it is a compound of cancer [Lat. *crab*] and *ház* [Hung. house] which is often used as a suffix for toponyms. Understanding the Hungarian-Latin compound is only possible for multilingual people with at least a rudimentary knowledge of Latin (mostly from those parts like Preßburg where readers understood Hungarian, German, and Latin). Thus, code-switching functions as a shibboleth for multilingual readers, based on region and education, implying class and gender, given that Latin as an old language is typically part of male education. The male educated readership from and around Preßburg could understand the joke of a German crab – Krebs – migrating to Cancriháza – Crabtown.

The analysis of the fable exemplifies the kind of regional, political, and literary multilingualism that is found in several other texts in the volume Donauhafen, next to monolingual German texts and translations. The genre of the anthology hides the fact that several of the texts are multilingual, as it is perceived as a collection of German literature, in which "foreign" elements are labeled as Hungarian national literature (in German).

Apart from the circle around the Schröer family, several other bilingual German-Hungarian authors lived there at the same time. Another typical case of Hungarian-German bilingualism was Therese Megerle von Mühlfeld (1813–1865) who grew up in Preßburg as the daughter of a wealthy Hungarian family. At the age of 16, she married a dentist who used her dowry to change careers and manage the first Preßburger Theater and later a theater in Josephstadt, Vienna, without much financial success. Therese Megerle wrote and published several short stories in German, keeping her multilingual skills hidden (Glosíková 1995: 108). After the death of her husband, Megerle von Mühlfeld became a successful writer and playwright. She translated and adapted plays from French and English into German (Wurzbach 1867: 258). Writing for the stage and translating granted her financial independence. She was multilingual through her upbringing in a Hungarian family and in the multilingual region of Preßburg, where she spoke Hungarian and German. Her publications are exclusively in German. Given the economic hardship and the fact that she wrote for a living, her choice of language must have been motivated by financial reasons. Her multilingual competences included French and English which enabled her to translate and adapt popular works by Victor Hugo or George Sand for an Austrian audience. (Gibbels 2018: 102–103). However, her Hungarian competence equally played a role in her success, as she also translated from Hungarian. The play *Ein entlassener Sträfling* (A released prisoner) was translated and adapted from the Hungarian play *A rab* (The prisoner) by the Hungarian playwright and theatre director Eduard Szigligeti (Megerle von Mühlfeld 1852). Her competence in Hungarian becomes also visible in stage directions and advice about pronunciation (Megerle von Mühlfeld 1849: 14). Thus, Therese Megerle von Mühlfeld qualifies as a multilingual author whose Hungarian and German knowledge was necessitated by her multilingual surroundings in Preßburg and her knowledge of French and English, which formed part of the curriculum of a well-educated woman in the 19th century. She exploited her language skills for her publications, often translating and adapting from different languages, but published and performed for a German language market in Vienna with much success.

The most actively multilingual writer was Adolf Dux, a journalist, translator, and author who grew up in Preßburg, and later lived in Budapest. Dux came from poor Jewish parents in Preßburg where he went to school and studied law and philosophy. He wrote and published in German and Hungarian journals and started working at the journal Pester Lloyd. He is mostly known as the translator of works of Hungarian romantic and realist authors Sándor Petőfi (1823–1849), János Arany (1817–1882), and Mór Jókai (1825–1904). He was also a writer and published his own short stories as well as studies on Hungarian literary history and theater (Glosíková 1995, S. 40).

In his own works, he thematizes linguistic and cultural conflicts as well as general views on nation and nationality. The short story *Mitten im Sturm* (Amidst the storm, 1871) tells of the son of a Hungarian-German family from Preßburg, torn – amidst the storm – between the two nations and nationalities given to him by birth. In ten chapters his story is told as an anonymous we-narrative. The frame of the plot is set in Vienna and begins on the day of the Vienna Uprising on 6th October 1848, when Viennese workers and students protested and fought against the Imperial troops. It ends a little while later with the death of Heinrich at the hand of his father's murderer, the Slovakian rebel Jano. In between, the reader follows the life of Heinrich, his upbringing in a multinational city, Preßburg, and his attempts at poetry. The narrative is set against the background of the Hungarian Revolution and the struggle for independence against Habsburg Austria. Nation is presented as a force of nature, pulling along in one direction. The protagonist of *Mitten im Sturm* (Amidst the Storm) stands between two such forces "wo zwei verschiedene Strömungen miteinander in Berührung und in Widerstreit kommen" [where two currents come into contact and conflict with each other] (Dux 1871, S. 2). The protagonist, Heinrich von Tornai, comes from the city of Pr.[eßburg], not far from the Austrian border between the Danube and green forests and vineyards. The surname of the protagonist (Tornai) also refers to the name of the region. Heinrich's father is a Hungarian noble man, the mother a German (which also includes Austrians). His ancestry and education foreshadow later conflicts, as he is educated exclusively in German by his mother. His nurse, however, is Slovakian. Thus, Heinrich is torn between different national identities which appear in the story as mutually exclusive. The second son, Arpad, is educated in Hungarian and develops a strong Hungarian nationality (Dux 1871, S. 9). The political crisis leads to the murder of Heinrich and Arpad's father by a malcontent Slovakian farmer, Jano, the father of Heinrich's love-interest, Marianka. Whereas Arpad is set on revenge, Heinrich favors a pacifist solution and wants to talk to Jano. Heinrich's pacifist attitude does not go unpunished: wanting to keep the peace, Heinrich refuses to defend himself and after sustaining a bullet wound from a shot fired by Jano, who also kills his daughter as she tries to warn her lover, he dies. In the end, Heinrich's mother and brother survive and tell Heinrich's story as a cautionary tale about belonging, language, and identity to the next generation.

The text contains a few traces of manifest multilingualism, four instances of code-switching between German and Hungarian, and three instances between

German and Latin. The Hungarian words mark the speaker's Hungarian identity: "Éljen a szabadság! (Es lebe die Freiheit!)" [Long live freedom] (Dux 1871: 18) refers to the Hungarian struggle for independence. Code-switching with Latin indicates a speaker's level of education, in this case a group of students (Dux 1871: 67).

Apart from the use of Hungarian and Latin in the text, the characters also think and talk about the meaning and relations of different languages. Heinrich favors equality between different nations and cultures:

> Jeder Volksstamm sollte die größte Freiheit erlangen, sich und seine Sprache zu entwickeln: Alle sollten in dieser Beziehung vollkommen gleichberechtigt sein und in edlem Wettstreit um die Palme der Cultur ringen
> [Each nation should have the greatest freedom to develop itself and its language: All should be completely equal in this respect and compete nobly for the palm of culture] (Dux 1871: 24).

The subjects of nation, nationality, culture, and language are presented along national, monocultural, monolingual lines. This is not a transcultural utopia. The national, monolingual, and monocultural paradigm becomes even more pronounced when the mother tongue is equated with a language of religion: "da doch Jeder zu Gott dem Herrn nur in der Sprache redet, in der ihm seine Wiegenlieder vorgesungen wurden" [Since everyone speaks to God the Lord only in the language in which his lullabies were sung to him] (Dux 1871: 10).

People like Heinrich, between languages, cultures, literatures, nations, find themselves in a perilous situation as the metaphorical title implies. However, the short story does not provide the reader with a definite answer. By creating a polyphonic narrative using the pronoun "we", different voices always put seemingly clear opinions into question. An old neighbor of the murderer of Heinrich's father, Jano, tells how Jano himself suffered greatly from a miscarriage of justice and lost his property and subsequently his life's purpose. Circumstances forced him to make a living by poaching, stealing, and, eventually, killing.

Heinrich is an example of a "krankhaften Kosmopolitismus" [sick cosmopolitism] in the eyes of his brother, Arpad (Dux 1871: 105). Through Heinrich's mother who has the last word, the narrative offers another interpretation: "Die Großmutter aber erzählt ihren Enkeln oft mit Wehmuth und Stolz von ihrem unvergeßlichen Heinrich, dessen liebevolles Herz stets ruhig und milde blieb -- auch mitten im Sturm" [The grandmother, however, often tells her grandchildren with melancholy and pride about her unforgettable Heinrich, whose loving heart always remained calm and mild -- even in the midst of the storm] (Dux 1871, S. 105).

The ambivalent interpretations and polyphonic voices leave the question of nation, language and belonging unresolved. The multilingual language situation is a core element of the narrative, as it provides the background for the action as well as the motive for characters to act. Much as in real life, the linguistic conflicts remain unsolved.

Apart from Hungarian-German multilingualism, which is common among Christian writers, Jewish writers like Max Emanuel Stern or Leopold Kompert (mentioned above) are even more multilingual. Max Emanuel Stern (1811–1873) was born and grew up in Preßburg in a Jewish family. Educated privately by his father and other famous rabbis like M. Schreiber and Moses Sofer, he was trained to become a rabbi himself, studying Hebrew and religious writings. At the age of 14, he replaced his blind father as a teacher in a Jewish religious school where he continued until his father's death. Afterwards, he moved to Vienna to work in the oriental printing press of A. Edler von Schmid as a corrector and writer. After he was supposed to move back to Preßburg to expand the printing business, he terminated his contract and became a Hebrew teacher in Eisenstadt. Later, he moved back to Vienna and worked again as a writer for A. Edler von Schmid, also publishing a journal devoted to enhancing the Hebrew skills of the Jewish community (Heuer 2012: 514–515).

From his publications and writings, it is evident that he spoke and wrote German, Hungarian, and Hebrew. He published religious writings – prayers and homilies – and poetry in German and Hebrew, as well as dictionaries and grammar books (Hebrew-German and a Hebrew grammar book for a Hungarian audience). His works often appear in parallel versions, like in his translation of the book *Rahel* by his acquaintance Ludwig August Frankl (Stern 1845) where one page shows the German original and the other page the translation into Hebrew.

He was also connected with other Jewish writers from Preßburg. He was friends with Leopold Kompert and must have known Ludwig August Frankl. Other connections are a bit looser: in one of his books, he asks the author Moritz Gottlieb Saphir, also from Preßburg, to give back a book he borrowed a year ago. Leopold Kompert and Ludwig August Frankl also appear in the volume *Donauhafen*, published by Karl Julius Schröer and Rudolf Beyer.

Zooming into those social networks, joined anthologies, and texts and their respective multilingual connections shows the width and strength of multilingual neighborhoods and their production in a middle-sized cultural hub like Preßburg in the 19th century.

4 Discussion and conclusion: Adding more data

The networks of writers and publications in Preßburg in the 19th century which were constructed through data from historical literary dictionaries show a limited set of forms and functions of multilingualism, strongly tied to nationality, class, gender, and religion. Christian Hungarian Germans are mostly bilingual as is visible from the works and publications of Karl Julius Schröer, Rudolf Beyer, Adolf Dux, and others. Female authors are equally bilingual but publish mainly in German (Therese Megerle and Therese Schröer). Jewish writers like Leopold Kompert and Max Emanuel Stern are mostly trilingual with German, Hungarian, and Hebrew. Most writers know each other through university, informal meetings, joined publications, or translations. However, the extent of these networks remains unknown due to missing data.

What is surprising is the lack of Slovakian or Czech in the data. This hints at a structural deficit of the data, which seemingly includes German-Hungarian writers but excludes Slavonic writers. Additional sources are needed to verify whether the data is faulty or whether there were no Slovakian writers in Preßburg at that time, which is highly unlikely. To that end, I created a query in the Deutsche Biographie [German Biography] to widen the dataset and search for writers born between 1770 and 1870 who were at some point in their lives in Bratislava.

Through this query, it became clear that Tobias Gottfried Schröer also taught Slovakian students, among them the philologist, and poet Ľudovít Štúr (1815–1856). His works were fundamental in establishing an independent Slovakian literature and language. He studied Hungarian, German, Greek and other languages and literatures, while also publishing in German and Slovakian. As a consequence of the ongoing magyarization in Preßburg, Štúr lost his job as a university teacher in 1843. Therefore, he surely has a place in the multilingual networks of the literary neighborhoods. He is connected to T.G. Schröer and links the Preßburg Slavonic community with other Slavonic writers, e.g., the Polish Silesian author Paweł Stalmach (1824–1891), who was his student in Preßburg. Information on Yiddish literature, writings, and prints are also missing. Here, the *Biographisches Lexikon des Kaiserthums Oesterreich* [Biographical Dictionary of the Austrian Empire] offers supplementary, albeit unstructured data. The Jewish author Adolf Neustadt, an acquaintance of Leopold Kompert, published a collection of Yiddish proverbs (*Maiszim un Schnokes vun e Handelewo*, Leipzig 1845). The printing press where Max Emanual Stern worked also published books in Yiddish. However, Yiddish is not mentioned as a language in any of those biographies due to its status as a dia- or sociolect.

By using data from the Deutsche Biographie as well as other general biographical dictionaries like the *Biographisches Lexikon des Kaiserthums Oesterreich* [Biographical Dictionary of the Austrian Empire] the perceived gaps can be filled. Gaps in the data refer to the heterogenous basis of the study as well as to the instable sources when researching multilingualism within the era of national monolingualism. Or, put differently, the national unconscious (Casanova) of literary history hides the multilingual realities of authors in 19th-century multilingual neighborhoods. Thus, it appears as if multilingualism was an exception rather than the rule. However, almost all authors in Bratislava, even those who were categorized as monolingual German authors like Nikolaus Lenau, were exposed to multilingualism or actively used it in their literary productions. The close neighborhood within the city and the exchange between people in different educational and cultural institutions, seemed to have created bonds beyond national, religious, and linguistic boundaries, visible in publications like the yearbook *Donauhafen*, which included authors from different linguistic, religious, and educational backgrounds.

This systematic and quantitative approach uncovered multilingual authors and explored the functions of different languages in the city of Bratislava – German, Hungarian, Hebrew, Latin and other languages appearing in publications and daily life. The disadvantage of this approach lies in the fact that not all authors were found by mining historical literary dictionaries, data from other dictionaries must be added to create a more complete picture.

Also, this kind of analysis relies heavily on existing (monolingual) research on certain authors, literature, regions, and texts. It serves as a new pair of glasses for looking at existing research and is only possible through exchange with other scholars specializing in those different languages. The advantage of zooming into these networks from a distance lies in the holistic approach which makes connections, transfers, publications, and translations visible that exist because of the multilingual competences of its neighbors. Even if earlier research has already studied those authors and their works within a monolingual framework, the national paradigm excludes aspects that to not belong to one discipline. This un-disciplinary approach helps to visualize hidden multilingualism and broadens the canon of multilingual authors.

5 References

Anokhina, Olga, Till Dembeck & Dirk Weissmann. 2019. Close the Gap! Literary Multilingualism Studies and the 19th Century. In Olga D. Anokhina, Till Dembeck & Dirk Weissmann (eds.),

Mapping Multilingualism in 19th Century European Literatures: Le plurilinguisme dans les littératures européennes du XIXe siècle. 1–5. Vienna: LIT.

Anonym. 1848. Review: Donauhafen. Jahrbuch für Lied und Novelle. Hrsg. v. K. Julius und Rupertus. Pressburg 1848. *Literarische Zeitung*. 796.

Anonym. 1860. Lied eines Presburgers: (Aus einer Sammlung von Gedichten in Pressburger Mundart). *Preßburger Zeitung*. 3.

Bayer, Rudolph & Carl J. Schröer (eds.). 1848. *Donauhafen. Jahrbuch für Lied und Novelle*. Hrsg. von K. Julius (pseud.) und Rupertus (pseud.). Pressburg: Verl. von Carl Friedrich Wigand.

Bayer [Beyer], Rudolph. 1848. Mausöhrlein, Forelle und Dr. Krebs. Ein Mährchen. In Rudolph Bayer & Carl J. Schröer (eds.), *Donauhafen. Jahrbuch für Lied und Novelle*.: Hrsg. von K. Julius (pseud.) und Rupertus (pseud.). 1–30. Pressburg: Verl. von Carl Friedrich Wigand.

Behnke, Dorothea. 1999. *„daß dem weiblichen Geschlechte an Tapfferkeit, Klugheit, Gelehrsamkeit und andern Haupt-Tugenden gar nichts fehle": Lexika zu Schriftstellerinnen aus dem deutschsprachigen Raum; Bestandsaufnahme und Analyse*. Osnabrück: Zeller.

Casanova, Pascale. 2004. *The World Republic of Letters*. Cambridge, Massachusetts/London, England: Harvard University Press.

Cohen, Margaret. 2009. Narratology in the Archive of Literature. *Representations* 108(1). 51–75.

Cornis-Pope, Marcel. 2006. Introduction: Mapping the Literary Interfaces of East-Central Europe. In Marcel Cornis-Pope & John Neubauer (eds.), *History of the Literary Cultures of East-Central Europe: Junctures and disjunctures in the 19th and 20th centuries*), 1-11. Amsterdam: John Benjamins Publishing Company.

Cornis-Pope, Marcel & John Neubauer (eds.). 2006. *History of the Literary Cultures of East-Central Europe: Junctures and disjunctures in the 19th and 20th centuries*; Amsterdam: John Benjamins Publishing Company.

Dejaeghere, Tess, Julie M. Birkholz, Els Lefever & Christophe Verbruggen. Beyond Babylonian Confusion: a case study-based approach for multilingual NLP on historical literature: Abstract [Closing conference of the COST Action Distant Reading for European Literary History].

Dembeck, Till. 2017. Multilingual Philology and National Literature. *Critical Multilingualism Studies* 5, https://cms.arizona.edu/index.php/multilingual/article/view/123 (accessed 20 April 2022).

Deutsches Textarchiv. 2020. *Die DTA-Korpora*.
https://www.deutschestextarchiv.de/doku/textauswahl. (accessed 16 October, 2022.)

Dux, Adolf. 1871. *Deutsch-Ungarisches: Erzählungen*. Wien/Leipzig: Hartleben.

Forster, Leonard. 2011 [1968]. *The Poet's Tongues: Multilingualism in Literature*: The de Carle Lectures at the University of Otago 1968. Cambridge: Cambridge University Press.

Gervinus, Georg G. 1844. *Geschichte der poetischen National-Literatur der Deutschen*. Leipzig: Engelmann.

Gibbels, Elisabeth. 2018. *Lexikon der deutschen Übersetzerinnen 1200–1850*. Berlin: Frank & Timme.

Glosíková, Viera. 1995. *Handbuch der deutschsprachigen Schriftsteller aus dem Gebiet der Slowakei*. Wien: Verlag der Österreichischen Akademie der Wissenschaften.

Gottschall, Rudolf von. 1855. *Die deutsche Nationalliteratur in der 1. Hälfte des 19. Jahrhunderts literarhistorisch und kritisch dargestellt*: Band 1. Breslau: Trewendt & Granier.

Heuer, Renate (ed.). 2012. *Lexikon deutsch-jüdischer Autoren: Band 19 Sand—Stri*. Berlin/Boston: De Gruyter.

Horányi, Károly. 1941. *Schröer Gyula Károly: 1825–1900*. Budapest.
Humbert, Philippe, Renata Coray & Alexandre Duchêne (eds.). 2018. *Compter les langues : histoire, méthodes et politiques des recensements de population: Une revue de la littérature*. Fribourg/Freiburg: Institut de plurilinguisme.
Jacob, Marianne. 2003. *Die Anfänge bibliographischer Darstellung der deutschen Literatur des 19. Jahrhunderts: Untersuchungen zur Vorgeschichte des „Deutschen Schriftsteller-Lexikons 1830-1880"*. Berlin: Humboldt-Universität zu Berlin.
Kiepert, Heinrich. 1872. *Völker[-] und Sprachen-Karte von Deutschland und den Nachbarländern*. D. Reimer.
Lenau, Nikolaus. 1989. *Werke und Briefe: Historisch-kritische Gesamtausgabe*. Wien/Stuttgart: Deuticke/Klett-Cotta.
Lengauer, Hubert. Rank, Josef. In *Neue Deutsche Biographie*, 21, 137–138.
Mackey, William F. 2005. 128. Multilingual Cities/Mehrsprachige Städte. In Ulrich Ammon (ed.), *Sociolinguistics: An International Handbook of the Science of Language and Society = Soziolinguistik: ein internationales Handbuch zur Wissenschaft von Sprache und Gesellschaft*. 1304–1312. Berlin/New York: De Gruyter.
Mani, B. V. 2017. *Recoding World Literature: Libraries, Print Culture, and Germany's Pact with Books*. New York: Fordham University Press.
Megerle von Mühlfeld, Therese. 1849. *Die Gaben der Ahnen: Allegorisches Festspiel*. Pressburg: Schmid.
Megerle von Mühlfeld, Therese. 1852. *Ein entlassener Sträfling*: Volks-Drama in 3 Abtheilungen. Wien: Lell.
Meier, Jörg. 2020. Pressburg/Bratislava: In: *Online-Lexikon zur Kultur und Geschichte der Deutschen im östlichen Europa*. https://ome-lexikon.uni-oldenburg.de/orte/pressburg-bratislava. (accessed 20 April 2022.)
Moretti, Franco. 2013. *Distant Reading*. London, New York: Verso.
Pataky, Sophie. 1898a. *Lexikon deutscher Frauen der Feder: Eine Zusammenstellung der seit dem Jahre 1840 erschienenen Werke weiblicher Autoren, nebst Biographieen [sic!] der lebenden und einem Verzeichnis der Pseudonyme*. Berlin: Carl Pataky.
Pataky, Sophie. 1898b. *Lexikon deutscher Frauen der Feder: Eine Zusammenstellung der seit dem Jahre 1840 erschienenen Werke weiblicher Autoren, nebst Biographieen der lebenden und einem Verzeichnis der Pseudonyme*. Berlin: Carl Pataky.
Pflagner, Margit. 1974. Therese Schröer – Eine Frau als Mittelpunkt literarischen Lebens in Preßburg. *Burgenländische Heimatblätter* 36. 185–192.
Ptashnyk, Stefaniya. 2013. Stadtsprachen historisch betrachtet: Zur Beschreibung der Mehrsprachigkeit in Lemberg 1848–1900. In Christopher Kolbeck, Reinhard Krapp & Paul Rössler (eds.), *Stadtsprache(n) – Variation und Wandel: Beiträge der 30. Tagung des Internationalen Arbeitskreises Historische Stadtsprachenforschung*, 95–110. Heidelberg: Winter.
Ritter, Michael. 2002. *Zeit des Herbstes: Nikolaus Lenau; Biografie*. Wien/Frankfurt,Main/Stuttgart: Deuticke/Klett-Cotta.
Sanmann, Angela, Martine La Hennard Dutheil de Rochère & Valérie Cossy (eds.). 2018. *Fémin|in|visible: Women authors of the enlightenment : übersetzen, schreiben, vermitteln*. Lausanne: Centre de Traduction Littéraire de Lausanne.
Scherer, Wilhelm. 1883. *Geschichte der deutschen Literatur*. Berlin: Weidmann.
Schröer, Carl J. n.d. Unsere Deutschen in den nichtdeutschen Kronländern und die Sprachkarte der Monarchie. In *Heimgarten*, XII. Heft, Leykam-Josefsthal.

Seyferth, Giralda. 1998. German Immigration and the Formation of German-Brazilian Ethnicity. *Anthropological Journal on European Cultures* 7(2). 131–154.

Stern, Max E. 1845. *Rahel: Nach dem deutschen biblisch-romantischen Gedichte Rachel von Ludwig August Frankl.* Wien: Schmid.

Wurzbach, Constantin. 1867. *Biographisches Lexikon des Kaisertums Österreich: Siebzehnter Teil: Maroevic – Meszlenn.* Wien: Druck und Verlag der k. u. k. Hof- und Staatsdruckerei.

Index

adaptation 33
Akhmatova, Anna 199
Aksakov, Sergey 192
Almeida, Leonor de 253, 258f.
Aprilov, Vasil 28
Arany, János 316
Arnim, Achim von 281
Arnim, Bettine von 275ff.
Asachi, Gheorghe 49

Bach-Gelpcke, Marie 303
Bajza, József 131
Bălcescu, Nicolae 52
Balmont, Konstantin 199
Beyer, Rudolf 314, 320
bilingualism 119
biliteracy 127
Bobchev, Stefan 33
Bogorov, Ivan 30
Bonchev, Nesho 29
Botev, Hristo 29
Bouchardy, Joseph 173
Branconi, Maria Antonia von 280
Bryusov, Valery 199
Budai-Deleanu, Ion 49
Bunin, Ivan 199

Călinescu, George 63
Campe, Joachim Heinrich 30
Castelli, Ignaz Franz 314
Chekhov, Anton 195
Chys, Julienne van der 303
Clarke, J. Freeman 195
code-mixing 224
code-switching 151, 205f., 223ff., 230, 242
Coleridge, Samuel Taylor 272, 276
Conscience, Hendrik 75
Constant, Benjamin 246
Cook, Thomas 221
Csengery, Antal 135
cultural transfer 73

D'hulster, Leo 77

Daumer, Georg Friedrich 313
De Foere, Leo 76, 81f., 85, 88
Decker, Rudolf Ludwig von 148
Defoe, Daniel 30
Dessewffy, József 125
dialect 123, 271, 276f.
Dickens, Charles 225
Diktonius, Elmer 199
Disraeli, Benjamin 171
Drinov, Marin 29
Drumev, Vasil 29
Dux, Adolf 316, 320

Eckstein, Baron Ferdinand de 85
Emerson, Ralph Waldo 195
Esterházy, Péter 138

Fáy, András 137
Fleg, Edmond 203
Forster, Georg 223f.
Forster, Johann Reinhold 223
Frankl, Ludwig August 313
Franklin, Benjamin 26, 31
Fröding, Gustaf 195

Gaál, József 138
Garbald-Gredig, Johanna 303
Gaszyński, Konstanty 109
Staël 246
Gervinus, Georg Gottfried 144
Ghica, Ion 52
Goethe, Christiane 276
Goethe, Johann Caspar 223
Goethe, Johann Wolfgang 195, 225, 228f., 246, 248f., 251, 279ff., 284, 298
Golescu, Dinicu 49
Grimm, Jacob and Wilhelm 276
Gruev, Yoakim 30, 33
Gyulai, Pál 134

Haşdeu, B.P. 52
Heine, Heinrich 200, 220
Herder, Johann Gottfried 4, 147, 298
Hertz, Wilhelm 158
Holtei, Karl von 310
Hugo, Victor 192

Humboldt, Alexander von 223
Huntington, William Reed 195

interlingualism 286
interlinguality 267, 286
intertextuality 223, 230

Jókai, Mór 138, 316
Jósika, Miklós 138

Karadžić, Vuk Stefanović 280
Karavelov, Lyuben 29
Kazinczy, Ferenc 125
Key, Ellen 195
Kipling, Rudyard 192
Kogălniceanu, Mihail 52, 54f.
Kolbe, Karl Wilhelm 273
Kompert, Leopold 314, 319f.
Krasiński, Zygmunt 101ff.
Krŭstevich, Gavril 26f., 32, 34, 39
Krylov, Ivan 195
Kuthy, Lajos 138

language choice 53, 56
Lasker-Schüler, Else 200
Lebrocquy, Johan Hendrik 77, 85
Lebrocquy, Pierre 77, 84ff.
Leino, Eino 199
Lenau, Nikolaus 309
Lermontov, Mikhail 195
Lewald, Fanny 235
literary historiography 63

Maeterlinck, Maurice 192, 195
Maistre, Xavier de 220
Manolescu, Nicolae 64
Megerle von Mühlfeld, Therese 316, 320
Mello Breyner, Teresa de 253, 255
Merckel, Wilhelm von 147
metamultilingualism 234
Mickiewicz, Adam 95, 98ff., 115
migration 64
modernism 186
Moke, Henri 75
monolingualism 3f., 63, 72, 102, 119, 144, 161, 188, 276
monolingualization 2f.

Moritz, Karl Philipp 225, 231
Mörne, Arvid 195
mother tongue 243ff.
multilingualism 26, 48, 188
multilingualism, hidden 8, 9, 27, 73, 173, 212, 220, 223, 233, 245, 271
multilingualism, historical 7
multilingualism, latent 8, 122, 145, 223, 224, 233
multilingualism, manifest 145, 224

Nadson, Semyon 195
national culture 147
national language 50, 81f., 119
national literature 44, 54, 144, 298
nationalism 148
nationalization 133
nation-building 157, 244
Naturalism 170
Negri, Costache 52
Negruzzi, Costache 52
Negruzzi, Iacob 52f.
Nekrasov, Nikolay 195
Neustadt, Adolf 314, 320
Nietzsche, Friedrich 195, 200

Odobescu, Alexandru 53
Olsson, Hagar 199

Paisius of Hilandar 37
Palocsay, Tivadar Baron 122, 132
Pann, Anton 50
Petőfi, Sándor 316
Pfeiffer, Ida 219
plurilingualism 7, 48
Poniatowski, Stanisław August 96
Popovich, Rayno 30, 39
Potocki, Jan 96
Pŭrvanov, Nikola 32
Pushkin, Alexander 192

Rădulescu, Ion Heliade 52
Rank, Josef 314
Realism 169f.
reception 30f., 158f., 164
Reeve, Henry 108
Rilski, Neofit 31